ARMAGEDDON 2000

Countdown To Doomsday?

———

Kenneth Rayner Johnson

D1635397

Credits
Armageddon 2000
Kenneth Rayner Johnson
A Creation Book
Copyright © K.R. Johnson 1975, 1995
All world rights reserved
First published as *The Zarkon Principle* by Everest Books, 1975.
This new, revised edition first published 1996 by:
Creation Books
83 Clerkenwell Road
London EC1R 5AR
Design:
Bradley Davis
A Butcherbest Production

The author wishes to thank:
Tim Oliver for assistance
Dedicated to:
My very good friends, Michael and Pauline Astill, their sons and my Godsons, Henry
and Sebastian; also to John Burns, Jim Nittis and Annette, and David Stanlake.

Contents

Prologue

"Love does not consist in gazing at each other, but in looking outward together in the same direction."
Antoine de St. Exupery (1900–1944)

I KNOW nothing, except what I have studied and experienced. I have received no messages, except those already recorded. I hear no voices, except those of other human beings. I have had no revelations, save for those that are there to be experienced and shared by all mankind.

Yet I know this: there are men who have been the instruments of higher forces, who have had access to higher levels of consciousness and higher knowledge. But in every case they have been limited by their own viewpoint in their own historical times. Prophets like the Frenchman, Michel de Nostredame, (Nostradamus, 1503–1566), the American Edgar Cayce – pronounced like Casey – (1877–1945) and many others, appear to have had glimpses, arguably distorted, into the future. But no man or woman, not even avatars such as Mani, Zoroaster, Christ, Muhammad or the Buddha, have been able to grasp the entire picture of this life, this universe and this cosmos.

Perhaps no human being ever will.

But it is possible, with perseverance and effort, to lift, albeit fleetingly, a few veils and to gain some insights. I like to think of my work as a teetering step in that direction.

In *The Zarkon Principle*, I discussed the major possibilities of the way in which all human life might come to an end:

1. By the Earth's collision with a giant comet or meteor, by self-destruction, through irreversible ecological crisis, or by nuclear holocaust.
2. By the expansion of the Sun into a star of the Red Giant class.
3. By the collapse of the entire Universe.

Since writing, of course, further possibilities have arisen: the Earth being swallowed up by a Black Hole; its annihilation by an encounter with a huge concentration of anti-matter.

And this is without taking into consideration what is, to me, only a very remote possibility: the invasion of Earth by hostile extra-terrestrials. (I will enlarge on the reason why I feel this is extremely remote in Chapter 26: The Challenge.)

THE LIFE-EXPECTANCY of the Universe is about 80 billion (in the American and more frequently applied sense of one thousand million) years, according to most leading scientists. Ecologists, meanwhile, say that man may have exhausted all Earth's resources and be forced to extinction in a few decades. Visionary, or millennarianist groups are even more pessimistic and point to the turn of the century – the year 2000 – as the time for the end of the world. And, as we all know, the possibility of a global nuclear holocaust is anyone's guess – tomorrow, next week, next year? Who can predict when someone is bad, mad or just plain daft enough to push the button? Or when some unforeseen malfunction in a so-called failsafe system goes awry and triggers off a conflict accidentally.

Five years, perhaps, to Armageddon. Only 25 years beyond that, maybe, if the fatalism of some ecologists is correct. Or maybe even less...

In any event, we seem to have so little time. So little time left to understand, to take action. So very little time. This book is therefore dedicated, as it only can be, to all mankind, whose last noble quest must be salvation, peace and universal brotherhood.

Foreword

"The most beautiful thing we can witness is the mysterious. He to whom this emotion is a stranger, who can no longer pause to wonder and stand rapt in awe, is as good as dead; his eyes are closed."
Albert Einstein (1879–1955)

"When you hear a strange claim, like black holes exist or acupuncture works, how do you decide whether or not to buy it? We tell people that they really should question such things, they should think, they should evaluate what they hear, and they should realise that if they're told something it's not necessarily because it's true, but it's because somebody has a reason for wanting them to think that."
John Mosley, programme supervisor, Griffith Observatory, Los Angeles, California (1989)

IN ONE FORM or another, man has inhabited this planet Earth for some two million years, probably longer. In fact, in 1983, biologist Dr. Charles Oxnard of the University of Southern California's school of medicine, concluded that human beings diverged from the apes 10 million years ago. His findings were based on the examination of 1,000 fossil teeth found in Miocene Age coalfields of Yunnan Province, in China. The teeth derive from two primates – Sivapithecus, the ancestor of the apes and Ramapithecus, the ancestor of humans – remains of which have also been found in Africa, Europe and India.

Yet even now that he is able to conquer disease, wield vast destructive power and even reach out to his planetary neighbours, man remains divided on the most vital questions:

Is there a God? Is God male or female, or both, or even of some other, unknown, ineffable nature? Who or what is He/She/It? Where is He/She/It? Can He/She/It survive – even in a universe that seems ultimately fated to collapse?

What is human life? What is its purpose? What is its significance, its ultimate destiny? What are humanity's chances of survival... if any?

I have spent much of my adult life trying to delve into and unravel these mind-stretching and often disturbing riddles that confront humanity, before it is too late. Already, to some extent, some of the barriers that have long separated human thinking have either crumbled or broken down: barriers of religion, philosophy and science. And if there can be found any answers to the seemingly endless tangle of questions confronting us, those answers must strive to satisfy all religions, all philosophies, all sciences, all peoples.

I have sought my answers everywhere, rarely judging, merely searching... in the books and scriptures of the religions of Light; in the murky fastnesses of Alchemy, Magic(k) and the Occult; in the strains of many philosophies.

The original Zarkon Principle itself is that life on a cosmic scale will *never* be destroyed, will never end. But the one imponderable – and one that mankind might have a hand in determining – is whether the human race itself is included in the future scheme of things...

I am not a scholar in the strictest sense – I did not truly begin to learn until after I had finished school; in many areas, I am self-taught. And I am far from being a mystic or a prophet.

I simply believe that because human beings have brains capable of examining as much as they can of everything around them, they should do so – *everything*, not simply the areas that appear to fit in with their narrow, conditioned ideas about themselves, their world, their universe. Not simply what they are *told* to study and analyse.

Despite what the academic and business worlds tell us, there is still room for non-specialists in this ever increasingly specialist society; room for people who can step backwards and try to get an overview of the whole canvas of human development, achievement and experience.

It is, incidentally, a known fact that, in nature, overspecialisation can lead to atrophy and, ultimately, extinction.

If this book makes only one person begin to think, it will have served its purpose. If nothing else, I hope it may serve as a springboard for someone more perceptive, more incisive than myself.

Introduction

It is now 20 years since *The Zarkon Principle* appeared in 1975. It was a book that was, on the whole, well-received in the United Kingdom and in the United States and I got, via my publishers, Everest Books in London and New American Library in New York, considerable feedback in the mail, most of which I answered personally.

This year – 1995 – I was informed by a specialist book dealer that good condition copies of the first English edition of my book in hardback (1975), now long out of print, is exchanging hands for up to eight times its original price. And I was advised – even urged – to write an update.

In the 20 years since I wrote *The Zarkon Principle*, I have not ceased to study many of the arcane areas I touched upon in that volume. Indeed, I believe I have learned and understood much more than I attempted to synthesize in the original – and have reformulated many of my ideas and projections.

The present volume is the result of that further 20 years of observation, study and research. It contains that material which appeared in the first volume, wherever it remains valid and relevant. This is for the benefit of those who may not have read the original. I have also added additional material based on findings made since the 1975 publication, plus many projections of my own, based on fresh light shed upon various areas of thought. I hope that, overall, it will satisfy what I have been assured is a need for a "more enlightened" overview since last I wrote.

I must, however, emphasize and paraphrase what I said in the Prologue to the original book:

I know only what I believe I know from my own studies and experiences. I do not have access to any privileged sources of information. I have had no revelations, except those that may be considered to be already apparent and may be shared by all humanity if mankind so chooses.

To this I would add the following. I am frequently approached by people who ask questions like: "You're into the occult, aren't you? Do you believe in it?"

To which I usually reply that, first of all, "occult" simply means "hidden".

"Then what *do* you believe in?"

"Naturally, there are things that are hidden. But I don't *believe* in anything in particular – I try to keep an open mind. I look around and simply wonder..."

Another frequent question I am asked when someone I meet happens to know or discover who I am, is: "Why did you write under the *nom-de-plume*, Zarkon? Why not write under your own name?"

The answer is fairly simple: Because the nature of some of the topics I discussed in the book are, to say the least, unusual, I *knew* that if it aroused any response at all, some of it would undoubtedly come from lunatic and fringe-lunatic sources. As things turned out, I was correct.

For example, someone writing care of my publishers offered me a course in "psychic martial arts", whatever they may be, although I hasten to add that I am aware of the "psychic self-defence" techniques of the occultist Dion Fortune and others; a man in Texas sent his telephone number, assuring me that if I cared to call him, he would explain the workings of a time machine he had invented. (I was tempted to ask him to let me know about it "yesterday".) Yet another person sent me lengthy letters describing his experiences on LSD, relating them to the lyrics of a song by Led Zeppelin. Another letter was datelined Earth, 1976 and began: "Hi, Zarkon, baby! What's happening?" Enough said on that score, I think...

Of course, not all of the mail feedback was of this type. Some readers were quite complimentary and thanked me for pointing them into "new areas of thought".

One letter, which arrived three years after publication, contained a clipping from *The Miami Herald* of July 1, 1978. It carried a UPI news agency story datelined Santa Cruz, California, saying that three University of California scientists, using the 120-inch telescope on Mount Hamilton near San Jose, had found evidence through the observation of quasars, that the Universe is contracting and will collapse in on itself in about 50 billion years.

Attached to the clipping was a business card from a Miami attorney at law. Across it, the sender had written: "Zarkon is right again!"

All very flattering. Although I should point out that the idea of a collapsing – or indeed pulsating – Universe was definitely not my own, original idea.

Since *The Zarkon Principle* appeared, I have come to realise that the situation on this planet has not only grown worse but is probably irreversible. It would seem that during the 1970s, many people were preoccupied with trying to recover from the heady euphoria of the previous decade to the extent that warnings of impending ecological disaster and the dangers of overpopulation were regarded not so much as the ravings of a prophet of doom, but perhaps somewhat premature. The attitude seemed to be: oh, there's always plenty of time.

But quite evidently, there is not!

—*K.R. Johnson, East Sussex, England, 1995*

PART ONE: THIS ISLAND EARTH

Prelude: The Earth In Peril

"We are the playings of universal incoherence; we are tiny stones in a mighty edifice, the completed design of which we shall need more time and more peace to see in its proper perspective."
Antoine de St. Exupery (1900–1944)

"Men are bits of papers, whirled by the cold wind."
T.S. Eliot (1888–1965)

OF ALL the many theories about the formation and state of the Universe – from the idea of a Creation by an all-powerful God in seven days, to the mighty explosion of the Big Bang theory, put forward by 20th century scientists – perhaps the most widely held and most readily acceptable is that of the Pulsating Universe.

This was an elaboration of the Big Bang theory, expounded in 1927 by the Belgian astronomer Georges Edward Lemaitre (1894–1966). He suggested that the stars are the remnants of a mighty nuclear explosion; a chemical reaction in a single, giant, primal atom from which everything in space is made – a "cosmic egg". The component elements of this cosmic egg were unstable and blew apart in what must have been the most colossal explosion of all time. Its fragments became the galaxies, which flew outwards in every direction – and its repercussions can still be seen in the receding galaxies and galactic clusters far out in space.

There have been and still are several physical phenomena in space that point to the possibility of such a beginning. Scientists have studied such stellar occurrences as supernovae; stars whose chemical elements become unstable and suffer uncontrollable surges of radiation until they eventually explode. There also appears to be evidence that the Universe is continually expanding, drifting outward from an original central point in all directions at incredible speeds, like spots on a balloon that is being inflated. And, like the fragments of an explosion, those objects farthest away appear to be moving faster than those near to the projected centre, or seat, of the explosion.

It was one of the scientists who supported Lemaitre's model, the Russian-American astrophysicist George Gamow (1904–1968), who called it the "Big Bang" theory.

The Cosmic Background Explorer (COBE) satellite had, by 1990, precisely measured the blackbody spectrum of the ubiquitous, uniform microwave background radiation, which is a remnant of the original Big Bang explosion. An abundance of light elements such as helium, lithium and deuterium are consistent with the astrophysicists' "hot" Big Bang model.

But what happens, then, when these flying fragments of the Big Bang, of which the Earth, Sun and planets are a part, lose the impetus of the mighty force that drives them apart? Would they not first slow to a standstill and then begin to fall back together again, each exerting its gravitational pull on the others? It certainly seems the most likely prognosis.

In fact, this idea was partially confirmed in January 1993, when four astronomers

---

at a meeting of the American Astronomical Society in Phoenix, Arizona, reported on their findings after using Rosat, the Anglo-German orbiting space observatory. Its X-ray telescope was beamed towards a cloud of gas in the region of three small galaxies. The cloud was estimated to be 50,000 times heavier than the Sun. They suggested that their discovery pointed to the fact that the Universe, rather than continuing its expansion indefinitely, would collapse under its own gravitational influence within about 20,000 million years.

Dr. Richard Mushotsky, of NASA's Goddard Space Flight Center at Greenbelt, Maryland, said: "A cloud of this weight would have dissipated into space long ago, leaving nothing for us to detect, unless it was held together by the gravity of an immense hidden mass. The mass needed to prevent the cloud from dissipating is about 12 to 25 times greater than the mass of the galaxies." The implication is that there is a large amount of dark, heavy matter in the region.

The same process, it was inferred, is probably taking place throughout the Universe, which would eventually retard its expansion. Dr. Jack Burns of New Mexico State University, said: "If these galaxies are typical, then the evidence is that the universe is 'closed'. It is not going to expand forever, because there is more dark matter than we thought."

And when the components of the Universe finally come back together again? Fusion – back into the primal atom which exploded in the first place. Then, more chemical inter-action over the aeons, building up to yet another cosmic explosion – and the entire process begins all over again. New suns and their attendant planets are created; new galaxies of every configuration are re-created. A Universe, then, not without end, but with many endings and many beginnings.

Evidence of this type of probability is demonstrated by the existence in deep space of mysterious Black Holes. These are believed to be the remnants of stars that have exploded, then collapsed in upon themselves under their own immense gravity and become so dense that nothing – not even light – was thought to escape from them, of which, more later. In any case they are, in terms of our own limited senses, invisible. Their presence makes itself known, however, by the aberrational behaviour of other large bodies, such as stars, in their vicinity.

Indeed, although most Black Holes were initially thought to be relatively small, one was detected as recently as late May 1994, estimated to be 10,000 million miles in diameter and 1,000 million million times more massive than the Earth. It was located by the giant, orbiting Hubble Space Telescope – in a galaxy 52 million light years away in the constellation of Virgo, and designated M87. The presence of the Black Hole was indicated by the fact that the heart of galaxy M87, a gaseous conglomeration some 500 light years across, is rotating rapidly around some unseen, supercolossal object.

The gravitational pull of Black Holes is so great that anything – even a star like our Sun – that approached within range of this gravity field, would be sucked in, like a shred of paper into a vacuum cleaner – and torn apart in the process.

The stuff of Black Holes is thought to be anti-matter: a concept that is almost as difficult to grasp as that of infinity. Not simply nothingness, but the opposite of matter.

This is not merely theory. Two years after the English physicist Paul Dirac suggested the notion of anti-particles in 1930, an American, Carl David Anderson, discovered the anti-electron while studying cosmic rays. He called it the positron. Then, in 1956, the anti-proton and the anti-neutron – the opposite of particles that form the nuclei of atoms – were detected.

So the idea of a Black Hole consisting entirely of anti-matter – with exactly the opposite characteristics of all matter that was previously known – became not so incredible as it at first had seemed.

It is also thought that, in keeping with these principles of opposites, time itself runs backwards in Black Holes and at an ever-increasing rate. Eventually, some theorists have proposed, the anti-matter of which the Holes are composed will become so compressed that an explosion will occur – and a small star system will be created. Either that, or the Black Hole will disappear altogether, into another space-time continuum.

It is almost the Pulsating Universe demonstrated in miniature.

All of these scientific projections together put a time limit on our Universe. Each pulsation is thought to occur over a period of 80 billion years.

Our own Sun could begin to grow unstable in a mere eight million years.

The Sun, 864,000 miles in diameter – 109 times larger than the Earth – is in universal terms by no means a big star, nor a particularly small one. Astronomers place it in a category known as Main Sequence Dwarfs. There are giants like A Tauri, which is 36 times the size of the Sun and supergiants like the variable star VV Cephae A, 1,200 times the Sun's diameter.

The Sun is believed to have begun its life, after the explosion of the cosmic egg, as a mass of gas and dust that contracts and heats up through the joint effects of gravity and chemical reactions. Massive nuclear reactions take place in the Sun's core, which contains atoms of helium and hydrogen in a six-to-one ratio.

But when the hydrogen atoms are drastically depleted through these reactions and large amounts of helium are left, the Sun will begin to expand, with the chemical reaction switching to its outer layers. In other words, the Sun will expand into a bloated Red Giant, across about 25 percent of the sky, and swelling out beyond the orbits of Venus and Mars, our closest neighbours. It will be a thousand times brighter and a hundred times greater in diameter. The Earth will be baked at around the melting point of lead (327 degrees C), its oceans evaporated, its surface reduced to a desolate rock. For about 100 million years the Sun will continue burning up its nuclear fuel, until finally, it will contract into what is called a White Dwarf. These objects comprise some 10 percent of our galaxy and are of a density so great that one teaspoonful would weigh a ton. For thousands of millions of years, they gradually lose heat until they are reduced to cinders in space.

The bloated Sun, at the Red Giant stage, will mean the end of all life on our planet.

Even if it is by then possible, say, for man to colonise one of the outer planets such as Neptune or Pluto, using some advanced techniques of planetary engineering to make them habitable, the Sun's usefulness as a life-giving star will be over. Human beings in their present form would have to find a planet with similar life-support conditions to those of Earth – the same size, atmosphere and the same distance roughly, from a similar sun to our own. To reach such a remote planet in a star system many light years away would take centuries, unless some new, dynamic form of propulsion is discovered to allow man to approach the speed of light – 186,000 miles a second. Even then, a trip to our nearest stellar neighbour, Proxima Centauri, would take 4¼ years, travelling at the speed of light itself.

We must for the time being conclude therefore that the time limit of our solar system, so far as humanity is concerned, is eight million years.

But the limitation factor of life on Earth may be much closer than that. In 1959, Dr.

David Price, of the US Public Health Service, wrote a paper entitled: *Is Man Becoming Obsolete?*. In it, he said:

"We live under the haunting fear that something may corrupt the environment to the point where man joins the dinosaurs as an obsolete form of life. And what makes these thoughts all the more disturbing is the knowledge that our fate could perhaps be sealed 20 or more years before the development of symptoms."

Already, 35 years have ticked away since Dr. Price made his pronouncement – and what has been done? In realistic and effective terms, which must mean on a global, co-operative scale, not piecemeal, unilateral action – absolutely nothing. Or at least, very little.

The Earth is like a lunar module adrift in space, in that it has only a limited life-support system that works on the principle of self-renewal. In simple terms, the Earth has its own, built-in system of regeneration.

Basically, it amounts to a band of atmosphere about seven miles deep. This atmosphere, made up largely of oxygen and nitrogen with other elements in lesser quantities, helps to purify the waters of the Earth. These waters nurture animal and plant life and these, in turn, help to renew the Earth and its atmosphere.

But this system can be – and has been – unbalanced and overtaxed. It can even be destroyed. Despite the warnings of scientists and ecologists, we have continued to pollute rivers and lakes with effluent, industrial chemicals and nuclear waste, to over-fish oceans, also similarly polluted, indiscriminately upsetting the balance of marine life, to plunder forests and squander such natural resources as oil, coal and other minerals.

Mankind uncaringly proceeds to pollute the atmosphere with carbon dioxide, DDT, lead, mercury and other harmful substances, along with that other great enemy of natural evolution, radiation.

As recently as September 1993, more warning voices were sounding about our planet's danger of drastic climatic and atmospheric changes, due to those two factors on which so much attention has become focused in the 1980s and early 1990s: rising ocean levels and the hole in the ozone layer.

Over a mere two-week period during that month, scientists made disturbing statements about the changes taking place in the atmosphere.

First, members of the World Meteorological Organisation announced that the Earth's ozone layer had depleted by as much as 35 percent during August, falling to the lowest levels ever recorded that month. Normally, over previous years, truly serious ozone depletion had not started until September.

Ozone is a pale blue, poisonous gas – a danger to human life, even in small proportions. It is naturally caused by electrical discharge of lightning, while high voltage electrical equipment creates it artificially.

Another way it can be formed is through the joint effects of the Sun's interaction with pollution – ozone is one eventual constituent of photochemical smog.

Despite its somewhat negative attributes, ozone has some practical uses: as a bleach agent in the chemical industry and as a germicide sufficiently powerful to sterilize swimming pools and even domestic tap water.

When it is in its natural concentration in the Earth's stratosphere, it serves to protect the planet from the Sun's ultra-violet radiation.

Reporting to the World Meteorological Organisation, Dr. Joe Farman of the British Antarctic Survey predicted record ozone depletion over the United States and Europe during the winter of 1993. This increases the risk of skin cancer among humans and damage to flora. Normally, the stratospheric ozone layer protects against skin cancer by its absorption of the Sun's ultra-violet radiation.

US government scientists have predicted that in the United States alone by the year 2000, the ozone depletion could double, causing some five million further cases of cancer – including around 70,000 deaths.

What causes ozone depletion in the Earth's stratosphere? The ominous truth is that there is not simply one culprit – there are many. And most of them are man-made or generated.

It was a team of scientists with the British Antarctic Survey who, in 1982, originally detected the "hole" in the sky while doing research at Halley Bay, in Antarctica. And the word "hole", incidentally, minimises the issue considerably – it is more like an awesome chasm with an area size of the United States and with a depth equalling Mount Everest's lofty 29,028 feet.

Monitoring instruments revealed that ozone depletion was at its most severe in a segment of the upper atmosphere between about 6.2 miles and 15 miles high. Depletion also occurred on a lesser scale at an altitude of about 25 miles.

What is surprising is that attention had been focused on the ozone question as early as the 1960s, when James McDonald, of the University of Arizona, investigated some of the potential effects of supersonic transport aircraft (SSTs), on behalf of the US National Academy of Sciences.

Even then there were forward-looking fears about entire fleets of SSTs plying the upper atmosphere – and in doing so, damaging the ozone layer with exhaust fumes.

Another potential ozone-depletion contender consists in the launching of the space shuttle – although not the shuttle itself, rather the auxiliary solid fuel rockets used to boost it into orbit. These rockets pump ozone-damaging hydrogen chloride into the stratosphere.

While one or two space shuttle launches a year would do only minimal damage, the shuttle, if used on many flights as a ferry in a space station project – an idea already mooted, as I shall show later – the effects would be considerable. It has been estimated that, say, 60 shuttle launches a year would cause a 0.07 to 0.06 percent ozone layer reduction above the northern hemisphere.

And it is well to remember that the United States is not the only nation with such far-reaching projects in mind. The European Space Agency, for example, is interested in developing a space shuttle and is hoping to build a hypersonic ramjet, which would take off like an orthodox aircraft, suck in air as it rose into the stratosphere – then cut in rocket engines. Although this vehicle would not burn hydrogen chloride-emitting solid fuel, it would still pump out equally harmful nitrous oxide and hydrogen oxide.

(Shortly after writing the above passage, early in November 1993, it was announced that the US and Russia were to enter on a joint project to build a new space station, to be manned by astronauts and cosmonauts, and fully operational by the year 2070. It is not difficult to imagine the increased number of shuttle flights necessary as equipment and their on-site assembly teams are ferried up into orbit.)

The cumulative effects of several such projects would increase the severity of potential ozone layer damage. For example, if a dozen such ventures went ahead, and each caused an ozone reduction of one percent, there would be a 12 percent depletion overall, with no one venture to blame for the whole.

By the mid-1980s, Western observers of the Soviet space programme estimated that the Russians were launching around 100 space shots a year. Among their many aims was to give cosmonauts as much time in zero-gravity conditions as possible,

---

preparatory to a three-year round trip to Mars, possibly in a joint project with the US.

The ozone hole may not stay restricted to the Antarctic, either. A team of researchers at the Max Planck Institute for Nuclear Physics in Heidelberg has concluded that a decrease of only a few degrees in the winter over the Arctic could result in the same effects that have caused the Antarctic ozone hole. Their projections suggest a cooling of the upper polar atmosphere of as much as 6 degrees C, as carbon dioxide and other "infra-red active gases" build up.

Another, rather complex ozone-damaging factor indirectly initiated by mankind was pinpointed by the Dutch-born scientist Paul Crutzen in 1974. He noted that the spreading of nitrate fertilisers on parks, farmland and golf courses, provides food for "denitrifying" bacteria in the soil, which in turn supplements the amount of nitrous oxide in the lower Earth's atmosphere (troposphere) and nitric oxide in the stratosphere beyond. American golf courses, incidentally, account for a sizeable 10 percent of all fertilisers sold in the US.

Most Western governments have agreed that the majority of ozone-destructive chemicals – used mainly in refrigerators and aerosol sprays – will be phased out by 1997. (Work is currently continuing on an "ozone-friendly" refrigerator that uses superconductors, has no moving parts and does not need CFC coolants.) Nonetheless, ozone-depleting chemicals already present in the stratosphere from the late 1960s until the end of the 1980s have already caused considerable damage.

Dr. Farman said: "In the atmosphere, the level of chemicals is beginning to flatten out, but in the stratosphere the build-up is increasing.

"Things will get worse before they get better, both in Antarctica and in northern latitudes, where most people live. I don't expect we will be through the worst until the year 2005."

However, despite Dr. Farman's extremely cautious optimism, other scientists are not so convinced that the problem is reversible. The Sussex, England, based climatologist, astrophysicist and prolific author John Gribbin, has written:

"If the average concentration of ozone declined by one or two percent... there would still be an increase in the average intensity of UV-B [i.e., biologically active ultra-violet radiation] reaching each part of the globe over a long period of time... A change of 3 degrees C from day to day, or from day to night, is common... But a shift of 3 degrees C in the global average temperature would, in one direction, melt the polar ice caps and inundate cities such as New York, London and Leningrad."

The nowadays much-debated and reported, ozone-damaging aerosol sprays are of course another major concern of environmentalists. Aerosols are so-called after their output, a spray of tiny droplets, technically thus termed. It is the actual propellants used to squirt out their contents that are damaging. Until relatively recently, around half aerosol cans used chlorofluorocarbons (CFCs) for this purpose. As their name implies, they consist of a combination of chlorine, fluorine and carbon.

Originally developed in the 1920s, CFCs were first largely used as the active fluid in refrigeration equipment. By the 1970s, they were being used in a whole variety of highly commercial products including underarm deodorants, hair spray, shaving cream canisters, polishes, paints, insecticides and disinfectants. In 1973 nearly three billion aerosol canisters – half the world output – were available in the US alone. And around half of that three billion contained CFCs.

The danger with CFCs is that their various types survive in the atmosphere for variable and considerable periods before they break down. For example, trichlor-fluromethane, known as F11, can hang around for 75 years before it breaks down, while another, dichlorofluromethane (F-12), lingers for up to 110 years. So even if all CFC propellants were withdrawn and their use banned right away, their damaging effects on the atmosphere will still be around at the end of the next century.

It was the climatologist Verrhabadrhan Rmanathan, at the time with the NASA-Langley Research Center, later of the University of Chicago, who first pointed the finger at CFCs as "Greenhouse" gases in 1975. And a report released the following year by the US National Academy of Sciences said that, if the release of CFCs grew at 10 percent a year, before the end of this century, their influence would top that of the carbon dioxide produced by human activities. The report added that the increasing escape of CFCs in the air, even at a growth rate of only a few percent a year, could lead to climatological changes of "drastic proportions".

While most people can tolerate temperature changes of a few degrees Celsius – the relatively mild fluctuations between summer and winter, for example – that is an altogether different issue than the effect of a rise of one or two degrees in overall world temperatures.

For a start, study and computer analysis of warm and cold years in past records show that when the Earth warms up, it is the high latitudes which experience the greater warming, while areas around the Equator warm least. Therefore, an increase in worldwide mean temperatures of only 1 degree C might mean a much greater increase around the poles, at the latitudes of Europe and the United States.

Not only that, changes in temperature also imply changes in weather – such as in wind patterns and the incidence of rainfall. When the Earth warms, some areas of the planet will become drier, while others get wetter. The usual routes of monsoons may change courses – and storms may become more frequent.

And, curiously enough, if the planet warms, some areas may actually experience more severe winters than they are accustomed to. A seemingly negligible average global temperature rise may disguise falls in winter temperatures and rises in summer in some areas.

The problem facing those concerned about stopping CFC emissions is simply that, by the 1970s, as can be seen by the massive manufacturing figures, aerosol sprays had become big business. While environmentalists warned about dangers to our planet, manufacturers were more concerned about protecting their not inconsiderable markets and investments. The scientific community, meanwhile, tended to take a moderate, middle-course view, although some sympathised with the environmentalists.

The latter, naturally, frequently pointed out that most aerosol products are non-essential luxuries, convenient though they may be. And so the various contributory factors to our planet's plight continue to accumulate.

As the debate about damage to the ozone layer raged, Richard Benedick, a US deputy assistant secretary for the environment, lashed out at Britain and France for "being more interested in short-term profits than in the protection of the environment for future generations."

Politicians themselves, meanwhile, were the target of Jim Anderson of Harvard University. In 1987 he admitted he was "shocked at the way the political community has reacted to all this." He criticised politicians for ignoring the warning signs before the ozone hole was confirmed, then going into "complete panic" once it was truly located.

Finally, coming down firmly on the side of the manufacturers, the US Department of Interior Secretary Donald Hodel, in 1987 answered those who feared the ozone-

---

depletion cancer link by suggesting that the government should advise its people to wear "hats, glasses and sunscreen lotion", rather than demand alternatives to CFCs.

Some manufacturers of spray cans point out on the label that the propellants used in them are *not* CFCs. But *caveat emptor* – let the purchaser beware – even some non CFCs are equally damaging. One such example is nitrous oxide – commonly called "laughing gas" – which is used in some spray cans, notably in those which dispense dairy cream.

Within two weeks of the World Meteorological Organisation's report referred to earlier, further scientists reported on that other potentially catastrophic problem mentioned by Dr. Gribbin – the melting of the ice caps.

In general, it was reported that the Antarctic ice cap is melting faster than it can be replaced by snowfall. This creates new fears about the warming of the Earth's climate – the so-called Greenhouse Effect.

Dr. Olav Orheim of Norway, told an international symposium organised by the British Antarctic Survey at Cambridge that 2,500 cubic kilometres of ice was lost in 1992 through melting and iceberg breakaways from the edges of the Antarctic continent. Ice created on the surface by snowfall, on the other hand, amounted to only 2,000 cubic kilometres.

Information collected by watchdog scientists since 1983 suggests that the polar ice cap is actually shrinking at a rate 10 percent faster than it can be replaced.

A week before the Cambridge symposium, British scientists had already announced that a whole ice shelf, known as the Wordie Shelf, had broken up over the previous 10 years, mainly through breakoffs of icebergs.

Meanwhile, back at the symposium, there was further evidence presented by scientists of the breakup of other ice shelves and glaciers, presumed to be caused by climatic warming. It was reported that there is a steady rise of about two millimetres a year of the Earth's sea levels. I summarise the effect of this in a later chapter.

And, it would seem, it is not only polar ice caps that are melting. As recently as October 1993, a news item on BBC Radio 4 reported that the snows of the great Mount Kilimanjaro are melting and could be gone completely within 40 years. Again, climatologists and environmentalists have blamed pollution...

Worst of all, perhaps, little attention has been paid to the trend of overpopulation. It took from the dawn of man to the year 1850 for the Earth's population to climb to one billion. But a look at the figures for succeeding years shows that ever since, man has been eager to overcrowd spaceship Earth.

Within only another 80 years, by 1930, the global population had doubled to two billion. Another 30 years (1960) and we numbered three billion. By 1975, a mere 15 years on, we were quickly heading for four billion.

The time lapses decrease as the billions pile up. Back in 1975, the projections were that a decade on, human population would total five billion and by 1994, six billion, and so on. The projected figure for the turn of the century was seven billion.

Imagine that happening in a space capsule or even a starship if each astronaut represented one billion people. There is absolutely no difference, except that of scale. That is why some scientists write off the future of humanity in dismay.

The nuclear threat – through warfare, or "accidental" cataclysmic upheaval following, for instance, underground tests that disturb the Earth's structural stability, or runaway nuclear "melt-downs", as at Chernobyl, in the USSR, or the potentially disastrous discharge at Three Mile Island, in Pennsylvania – speak ominously for themselves. (A month after the pressure relief valve failure at Three Mile Island in April

1979, Harold Denton, a safety expert with the US Nuclear Regulatory Commission, told the Senate in Washington that similar valve failures had occurred no fewer than 150 times previously at similar reactor installations.)

Those who look to the millennium, a subject to be treated in greater detail in a later chapter, give man a mere five years from now (1995).

So there we have it: the countdown to Doomsday on three major time scales: the end of Mankind, five years on; the End of the Solar System, eight million years hence; the End of the Universe, 80 billion years from now.

There are, in addition, various other ways in which life on Earth might be utterly obliterated.

In 1984 a group of American physicists, headed by Dr. Daniel Whitmore at the University of Southwest Louisiana, suggested that terrestrial life was wiped out every 26 million years by a wandering star they called *Nemesis*, the name of the ancient Greek goddess of retribution. The scientists said Nemesis is a companion star to our own Sun that orbits the solar system in a path which varies from five to 20 trillion kilometres.

At its nearest approach, it collides with the Oort Cloud, a group of comets also in orbit around the Sun. When this occurs some of the comets are smashed and the planets of our system are scattered with debris. Saturn's rings, the physicists theorise, may be the gravitationally captured fragments of one shattered comet.

When the flying debris strikes the Earth, most animal and plant life is annihilated, our planet is plunged into darkness for a million years and new species only re-emerge when light and heat return to Earth. Some scientists believe that the dinosaurs may have been wiped out in this way.

In an article in *New Scientist* (March 15, 1984), one of the scientists, Dr. Muller, of the University of California, Berkeley, said: "These catastrophes give new species an opportunity. It's conceivable that if it had not been for such periodic catastrophes the world might still be dominated by trilobites."

Fossil records and impact craters tend to confirm that the disaster occurs every 26 to 28 million years. On three occasions, 95 percent of life was extinguished 247, 220 and 65 million years ago. On seven others between 20 and 50 percent of life perished – 11, 38, 91, 125, 144, 163 and 194 million years ago.

Another end-of-life scenario comes in the form of further cosmic rubble – clouds of interplanetary boulders that sweep periodically through the solar system. The Earth passes close to one of these, the icy comet Encke – so far, luckily, without mishap – every June 30.

Astronomers have confirmed that debris whirling around in space is plentiful – the Earth itself attracts some 10,000 tons a year. Most of it burns up in the atmosphere, yet a pound of cosmic dust showers every square mile of the Earth every year. Out in space, hundreds of minor wandering planets a mile wide brush past millions of rocks one yard across. Through the study of asteroids and comets, astronomers have identified some 57 objects of a mile wide or more that sweep close to the Earth.

Although rocks a mile wide only strike the Earth about once every 200,000 years, their effect can be devastating. They would cause the equivalent of a 100,000 megaton explosion and gouge out a 12-mile diameter crater. Scanning the night skies, astronomers have determined that the Earth encounters a 100-ton space boulder once a day, a 1,000-ton one every month, a 15,000-tonner annually and a 100,000-ton giant every two decades.

"Space boulders are particularly hazardous," Eugene Shoemaker, of the US

Geological Survey, told fellow-geologists at the spring meeting of the American Geophysical Union in Baltimore, Maryland, that year. "Although we know of the many mile-sized bodies that pass by earth, even modern astronomical cameras and radar cannot find and track the millions of yardsized boulders."

A rock a mere 20 yards in diameter could explode a few miles high and devastate 100 square miles. One measuring 100 yards across could explode on impact with the Earth, gouging out a crater one mile wide. The dust it raised would disrupt our planet's weather for many months.

Professor Shoemaker also expressed the fear that the impacting of a large space boulder could be mistaken for a nuclear explosion. While the major powers' space-monitoring systems should be sophisticated enough to identify a cosmic intruder, nations without such facilities might retaliate, believing it to be a nuclear attack.

The great conundrum that most of the scenarios I have been discussing throw in the face of humanity is this:

They leave no room for any concept of God.

Far too often science swiftly and uncaringly sweeps aside the age-old beliefs of the majority of people on Earth. Not only Christians, Jews, Muslims, Hindus; but every single person who believes in a god – any god – a creator, or even in a pantheon of many gods.

Even the passive, virtually atheistic following of Buddhism, with its beliefs in reincarnation, is not spared. What good is being reborn if mankind has only a few years to go – or even eight million years for that matter? If the Universe dies, where is there to be reborn?

And if, as is believed, the Universe collapses in on itself every 80 billion years, what of God or the gods? How can He/She/It or They survive the cyclic explosions that destroy and recreate the entire cosmos?

This seemingly insoluble dilemma, that sets science and religion at loggerheads, as they have so often been in the past, this time has a more colossal significance than ever. Not even Darwin's theory – that the human race and apes had a common ancestry – coming at the time that it did, could possibly have been so shattering. Whether man is a modified ape or not shrinks to infinitesimal significance beside this relatively new and terrifying concept of the future.

The Pulsating Universe theory leaves no loopholes:

If science is right, then there can be no room for God. If religion is a reality, then science must somewhere be in error.

That, at least, is the way it must appear to many.

Yet humbly, I hope to put forward a proposition that satisfies both sides in the dilemma. I intend to suggest that both the Pulsating Universe and the concept that many people regard as God – in whatever form – can, do and will continue to co-exist throughout all eternity. That despite what seems like a recurring, totally destructive cycle that would, between oblivion and re-creation, render everything non-existent, the all-pervading God-essence can survive.

That concept was what I initially called "The Zarkon Principle".

But before proceeding, it is necessary to do some recapping: to probe back into man's history and what we know of his pre-history; to examine areas of esoteric knowledge and unusual byways of discovery and philosophy.

By its nature, this book may at first appear a tangle of seemingly unrelated facts, theories, speculations and semi-certainties. But hopefully, like a jigsaw puzzle, an overall picture should emerge as the pieces fall into place.

One thing I can promise: it is an exciting adventure with some astounding and fascinating excursions into the unknown.

About three years after the publication of *The Zarkon Principle*, in February 1978, Dr. Robert Jastrow, Director of the Goddard Institute of Space Studies in New York, announced that he was embarking on a long-term programme of research to prove or disprove the existence of God. He modestly conceded that the chances against his success "seemed insurmountable".

Dr. Jastrow maintained that the only rational area of search was the Big Bang of around 18,000 million years ago. He reasoned that, because all physical science is based on the principles of cause and effect, it might be feasible to determine the precise cause of the Big Bang.

What scientists have determined, in their examination of the Universe, however, by implication does suggest some kind of cosmic purpose. This stems from the study of a process known as Stellar Nucleosynthesis.

It has been observed that human beings, animals and indeed planets like our own consist of very much the same mixture and proportion of elements as those found in stars, without the 99 percent of a star's constitution that is made up of hydrogen and helium.

Some 75 percent of a star is helium – the simplest element, whose atom consists of one proton and one electron. Something less than 25 percent is helium, the next simplest element, each of whose nucleus contains two protons and two neutrons with two external electrons. The remaining one percent or so constitutes heavier, more complex elements. And this proportion is a key pointer to the fact that the substances vitally necessarily to life on Earth – carbon and oxygen – were actually "made" inside stars.

In other words, it looks very much as if the Universe were purposefully created for life on Earth – a notion scientifically referred to as the "anthropic Universe".

This apparent coincidence, or suggestion of deliberate purpose, depends upon the strength of what is called the weak interaction, one of the four basic forces of physics. It is the weak force that dictates the process of the rate of radioactive decay. If the weak force had been slightly stronger, all the hydrogen resultant from the Big Bang would have been transformed into helium – and the stars would have burned themselves out too quickly for the formation of planets and the emergence of life.

It was, in fact, the English astronomer/astrophysicist Fred Hoyle (1915—), who, in 1946, suggested that the chemical elements were manufactured inside stars. And, following experiments too complex to enter into here, Hoyle was proved correct. Indeed, his observations led to a precise understanding of how all the other elements are built from hydrogen and helium in the cores of stars. Not only that, the energy levels required for these processes are so critical, that fluctuations in either direction would have negated the results. In other words, as Hoyle himself pointed out, it almost seemed that "the laws of physics have been *deliberately* designed with regard to the consequences they produce inside stars." (My emphasis – author).

When, in 1965, two telephone engineers discovered that quantities of heat were emanating continuously from every part of space, they assumed they had found the fiery remnant traces of the Big Bang. But when one of them looked for more evidence, he came up against what was called "cosmic censorship". It was possible, as it were, to "peer into the past" by probing the furthest reaches of the Universe, but beyond that there was a barrier to any further information. Electrons which, for the first million years, had been supported from the atomic nuclei of the elements, made all matter opaque, impenetrable.

However, in March 1990, winner of the previous year's Nobel Prize for Physics, Professor Hans Dehmelt of Washington University, put forward a theory that, in a sense, looked beyond the "cosmic censorship" encountered by his predecessors.

The big question facing those who delve into Big Bang theory is: what was there before the Big Bang? There simply cannot have been nothing before the creation of something, is the commonsense argument.

Professor Dehmelt's proposal is that there definitely was something before the Big Bang. Although it occupied neither space nor time, he suggested, it was real enough to be unstable – and split into two parts, which he called the cosmon and the anti-cosmon. These, he said, were incredibly small, exceptionally heavy and tightly bonded together.

Since the properties of the cosmon and the anti-cosmon were equal but opposite, said Professor Dehmelt, if their electric charges, masses and spins were added together, they would cancel each other out, producing absolutely nothing. Thus, he concluded, the something of the two emergent particles could have come out of nothingness, which is what they comprised together.

He suggested that every particle now existent in the Universe owes its being to the decay into lighter units of the original cosmon-anti-cosmon unity. And experiments with particle accelerators have managed to trace this process in reverse.

Sub-nuclear physicists have theorised that the hadrons neutrons and protons that comprise the nuclei of atoms – are each made up of three even more minute particles, which have been called quarks. This name was coined by the American physicist Murray Gell-Mann in 1964, inspired by a line from James Joyce's *Finnegan's Wake*: "Three quarks for Musther Mark."

Although no one has so far managed to split a proton – a difficult task because, enigmatically, the farther apart quarks are driven the stronger their attraction toward each other – their existence has been demonstrated indirectly.

Some theoretical physicists believe that quarks are even further divisible – into sub-quarks, sub-quarks of sub-subquarks, and so on. But Professor Dehmelt proposes that this is not an infinite process of sub-division. He suggests that if it were possible to reduce matter in atom smashers to increasingly diminishing sub-sub-subquarks and so on, the particles would diminish in size, but would be greater in mass and more strongly held together.

In due course, he proposes, they would reduce down to the two original particles, the cosmon and the anti-cosmon, out of which everything else had been created. Although parts of Professor Dehmelt's theory are not entirely new, he produced some surprising new evidence to corroborate it. His Nobel Prize was awarded to him for his work in which he had isolated single atoms in powerful magnetic fields so that they could be examined individually. He then proceeded to isolate and trap an electron, which had such distinctively defined properties that he called it Priscilla. These properties have been examined more accurately than those of any electron and can be seen to occupy some space, even if only 100 billion billionth of a centimetre.

It had previously been thought that electrons occupied no space at all. But Professor Dehmelt suggests that, since the radius of Priscilla is more than simply a point, the electron probably has its own internal structure, as does the proton. He further suggests that the electron is not composed of quarks, but of three sub-quarks, which are in turn made of sub-subquarks and on down the scale. So his observation that the electron occupies space fits in neatly with his cosmon/anti-cosmon theory of the Big Bang.

Of course, like Professor Jastrow, Dehmelt has not been able to "isolate" or "identify" God, but it is a start...

1. Climactic Complexities

THE GREENHOUSE Effect is not entirely a new discovery.

Jean-Baptiste Joseph Fourier (1768–1830) was something of a polymath. Born in Auxerre, France, his first calling was as a teacher. By 1794, he had gone to Paris to study and became an assistant lecturer at the Polytechnique. He was selected as a member of Napoleon's exhaustive investigative expedition to Egypt in 1798 and played a part in the preparation of the formidable scientific and cultural report, *Description De l'Egypte*, that followed. For most of the rest of his life, Fourier – created a baron and then a count by Napoleon – devoted his time to scientific research.

It was this indefatigable Frenchman who, as early as 1827, put forward theories suggesting that the Earth is kept at a particular warmth level through what has now come to be known as the Greenhouse Effect. Fournier did not, of course, coin that expression, but he did use the metaphor "hothouse".

But it was not until 1863 that more emphasis was put on the importance of Fourier's first tentative forays into this particular area of study.

In that year, the Irish-born scientist John Tyndall published an article in the *Philosophical Magazine* entitled *On Radiation Through The Earth's Atmosphere*. It dealt with the heat retention effects of water vapour in Earth's atmosphere. In other words, without using the actual term itself, he was saying that water vapour rising from the surface of our planet acted as a Greenhouse gas. Tyndall may have been the first to imply that the various Ice Ages through which the Earth has passed may have happened when, for reasons unknown, the level of carbon dioxide in the air fell, thus making the natural Greenhouse Effect weaker.

It was, incidentally, Tyndall who – among his many scientific findings – was the first man to deduce why the sky appears blue. (Wavelengths at the short end of the observable spectrum, i.e. blue, are more readily scattered by atmospheric particles, reaching human eyes from all directions; longer wavelengths, meanwhile, at the red end of the spectrum, are not so scatter-prone and reach us straight from the Sun.) Tyndall died in 1893.

Three years later, the Swedish chemist Svante August Arrhenius, born in 1859, also submitted an article to the *Philosophical Magazine*. It was entitled *On The Influence Of Carbonic Acid In The Air Upon The Temperature Of The Ground*. Arrhenius based his calculations on the measurements of the American astronomer and pioneer in aviation, Samuel Pierpoint Langley, of infra-red radiation from the full Moon as it passed through different densities of atmosphere at varying angles above the horizon.

Arrhenius' calculations examined the effects of carbon monoxide in the air on worldwide mean temperatures. He was concerned about increased levels of carbon dioxide released into the atmosphere by the burning of coal – "evaporating our coal mines into the air." Langley's measurements had provided the chemist with a means of calculating the amount of infra-red radiation absorbed in the atmosphere. He then went on to work out that, if the concentration of carbon dioxide were to double, it would result in a rise of worldwide mean temperature of about 5 degrees C which would be greatest at high altitudes. He also deduced that a drop in the natural concentration of carbon dioxide by one-third of contemporary levels would result in the Earth cooling by slightly more than 3 degrees C. In formulating these calculations, Arrhenius took account of the fact that global warming causes more oceanic water evaporation, which in turn adds to the Greenhouse Effect.

Arrhenius was awarded the Nobel Prize in chemistry in 1903 for a thesis that only barely won him a Ph.D. 19 years earlier. In it, he had been the first to suggest that ions were charged atoms, as the only way to explain the behaviour of certain solutions that conducted electrical current. It was not until 1890, when the electron was discovered, that Arrhenius' dubiously acknowledged theory was fully vindicated as suddenly making sense.

SINCE THE beginnings of life on our planet, there has always been some carbon dioxide in the atmosphere and it has always served to trap in some sunlight, warming the surface of the Earth. If this were not the case, terrestrial conditions might be similar to those on Mars. It would be extremely cold and unsuitable for sustaining life.

So, in fact, a certain amount of natural Greenhouse Effect, as this process is known, is not undesirable. But the real issue is, how much is acceptable?

The Earth's atmosphere is composed largely of nitrogen and oxygen; normally, there is scarcely more than a trace of carbon dioxide – around 0.035 percent. The concern is if that amount rises to, say 0.055 or 0.06 percent.

Now this may seem an irrelevant leap to make, but it is not. In 1957, Roger Revelle and Hans Suess, scientists at the Scripps Institute of Oceanography in California, published a paper concerning whether the oceans would absorb any extraneous, man-made carbon dioxide. The issue had arisen, on and off, since the 1930s, when the British physicist G.S. Callendar had suggested that growing carbon dioxide levels might be responsible for warmer temperatures in Europe and North America, first noted by meteorologists in the 1880s.

What Revelle and Suess discovered was that the top layers of the oceans absorbed less than half the surplus carbon dioxide that was man-made. Their somewhat scientifically prosaic assertion was that "a rather small change in the amount of free carbon dioxide dissolved in seawater corresponds to a relatively large change in the pressure of carbon dioxide at which the oceans and the atmosphere are at equilibrium."

What they were really demonstrating was that the greater part of carbon dioxide spewed into the atmosphere by countless millions of electrical generating plants, factory chimneys, car exhausts, furnaces, etc., stayed there. This would, of course, cause gradual global warming.

In the journal *Tellus*, Revelle and Suess wrote: "Human beings are now carrying out a large-scale geophysical experiment of a kind that could not have happened in the past, nor be repeated in the future." And the experiment, they added: "...if adequately documented, may yield a far-reaching insight into the processes determining weather and climate."

Following the Revelle and Suess projections, the Scripps Institute took on the scientist Charles Keeling, who set up monitoring stations on the slopes of Mauna Loa, a mountain observatory in Hawaii – 11,500 feet above sea level – and at the South Pole.

The readings he recorded quickly squared with Revelle's and Suess' suggestions that the atmosphere was indeed taking on excess carbon monoxide. The original, 1958, readings on Mauna Loa showed there were around 315 parts per million of carbon dioxide in the air. Succeeding annual figures showed that the amount was on the increase. By 1990, it was galloping along at about 1.5 parts per million each year.

And that rate seems set to increase, as population figures climb, and the need for more energy correspondingly increases by some 2/3 percent annually. (United Nations figures issued in May 1989 suggested that the world population – which has multiplied by more than three times this century – will double, or even triple in the 21st century.)

The greatest increases to meet the growing energy demand may well be in the burning of coal – and coal throws out more carbon dioxide into the air than any other energy source; double that of natural gas, for example.

It is true that, in July 1989, major industrialised democracy leaders announced at their economic summit in Paris that they would "strongly advocate common efforts" to cut down the release of carbon dioxide. But nothing positive was actually done, because to do anything would not be simple. For example, the fitting of some type of filter on power installation chimneys to eliminate carbon dioxide output would seem a logical move. Yet if, say, 80 percent reduction were achieved, the efficiency of the plant would fall by 70 percent.

A changeover to nuclear energy has been mooted in some quarters – as in Britain in April, 1989, when a seminar was held in Downing Street, attended by seven Cabinet ministers and leading scientists and industrialists. Significantly, perhaps, environmentalist representatives were not invited. But, such "we're showing our concern" meetings on the part of governments aside, even if every electrical generating plant were replaced by a nuclear one, the overall output of carbon dioxide through the burning of fossil fuels would only decline by a little less than one quarter.

In addition to coal-burning, deforestation by burning presently annually contributes between 1 and 2.5 billion tons of carbon to our atmosphere. In many instances – as in the case of the Brazilian rainforests – this is often done in the interests of the major burger manufacturers and those who devour their products. But even then, deforestation turned over to pasture for cattle can only remain operable for a few years and quickly reverts to waste, or desert, useless for further cultivation.

2. Oceanswell

IN AN EARLIER chapter, I dealt with scientific concern over the melting and breakaways of large fragments of icecaps – and touched only fleetingly upon the consequences of these phenomena. The result of such geological activity – blamed on the gradual warming of the Earth – is, of course, the rise of ocean levels around the world.

The gradual raising of sea levels, linked with global warming, poses a dire threat during the next 100 years – especially to many densely-populated coastal areas. And roughly half of the world's population lives in coastal areas since they are, after all, often the most aesthetically pleasant and desirable locations on the Earth. However, they will not stay that way for long, if present trends continue.

As I have earlier explained, worldwide temperatures have risen over the past 100 years, largely because of the increased concentrations of carbon dioxide and other trace gases in the air. These gases trap in infra-red radiation that would otherwise disperse into space – and so the Earth is warmed by the Greenhouse Effect.

I pointed out that calculations indicate that the warming of the Earth will probably be more intense at high latitudes. For instance, if the amount of carbon dioxide in the atmosphere is doubled and results in an increase of mean global temperatures between 2 and 4 degrees C, in higher latitudes, the actual increase will probably be more of the order of 6-8 degrees C.

These temperature rises could be with us – or rather, those of you who are left – by around 2050, along with consequent rises in sea levels.

Not only will polar ice sheets melt, but the waters of the oceans themselves will expand, as water does when heated in a pan or kettle. If the entire oceans were raised in temperature by only 1 degree C, levels would rise by as much as 60 centimetres. But by far greater would be the rise from the melting of all the ice caps, bringing sea levels up by 70 metres.

Where icebergs are floating in the seas, of course, their mass displacement already contributes to ocean levels – melting them would make no difference to the levels, in the same way that ice melting in a cocktail does not raise the actual level of liquid in the glass.

It is the ice sheets resting on land which will add to ocean capacities, when they melt. The East Antarctic ice sheet is one of these and, if melted, would cause a 55 metre rise in sea level. The melted West Antarctic ice sheet, meanwhile, which rests on a series of underwater mountains and hills, like columns holding up a temple, would add some six metres to sea levels. And the Greenland ice sheet would top up the oceans to another eight metres.

Now, to show how little rise is needed to bring about drastic change to life ashore, it has been estimated that even an eight-metre rise in ocean levels would make it quite possible for a senator to sail in a small boat from the steps of the Capitol building in Washington, D.C., and row along the coast to the White House south lawn, to see the President of the U.S.

Throughout most of the past 100 years, the actual rate of sea level rise has been little over one millimetre a year. But this figure has been offset to a degree by the intervention of man. Some 6000 cubic kilometres of water has been held from running back into the ocean by being stored in reservoirs. If it were released, this amount of "captive" water would bring sea-levels up by 15 millimetres, effectively setting back the "regular" rise in sea level by 10 to 12 years.

While sea levels gradually creep up year by year, so a large proportion of the Earth's beaches are being eroded. An estimated 70 percent are being worn down by weather and tidally generated waves and scant replacement beaches are being formed.

One metre of sandy beach is eroded for every one centimetre sea-level rise and for each rise of 10 centimetres, the dividing line between salt and fresh water in river estuaries backs up by one kilometre into the narrowing river mouth.

If it were possible to halt the tidal encroachment, in due course, new beaches would be created. But the rate of sea-level rise takes place more quickly than new beaches are able to form. And in many areas, man-made contrivances – harbours, dykes, sea walls, breakwaters, etc. – hinder the movement of sand, pebbles, etc., that might contribute to new beaches by diverting the natural currents that shift them.

So, while these devices do their job, in protecting low-lying or coastal encroachment-prone regions such as Holland, they also effectively hamper potential sites for fresh beaches.

Such constructions are also examples of the costs engendered by man's contribution to climatic changes such as the Greenhouse Effect. The Thames Barrier, for example, which is London's hoped-for protection against flooding, cost £500 million. It was hoped the barrier would afford protection against the kind of flood tides which records show may be expected every 1800 years or so. Yet it is feared that already, the barrier is obsolete.

Thames Water Authority admitted in 1988 that, if it is to be effective against severe tides anticipated around 2050, "we shall have to produce a plan within five to ten years to heighten the barrier."

And it is not only Britain's capital that is under threat. A sea-level rise of around 15 centimetres, doubling the chances of serious North Sea storm surges, would completely inundate such places as the east coast port city of Hull and large areas of East Anglia, both of which already lie below sea level at high tide.

Estimated cost of defending Britain's threatened coastal areas against projected sea level rises over the next 60 years is between £5/8 billion. And, for measures to be effective, says the Institute of Terrestrial Ecology, ideally work should start immediately.

The main question is, of course, what effects would increased ocean levels have on living conditions themselves?

First of all, when trying to calculate the retreat of existing shorelines, various factors, such as flooding and erosion have to be accounted for, and, on a local level, tidal patterns and any changes of these, will also have to be accommodated. So, too, will such features as onshore winds, the flow of rivers in estuaries and even the possibility of hurricanes. All of these factors will, of course, vary considerably depending on geographical locations.

In the developed countries, coastal dwellers are likely to be able to evacuate long before there is any danger to life; and, to a certain degree, areas at risk are already known, along with projections of actual loss of land and the effects on property values.

But in Third World countries, there is cause for greater concern over loss of life, devastation of agricultural land, disruption of food and water supplies, and damage and loss of transport systems and equipment.

Until the period immediately leading up to the mid-1980s, it was possible for scientists to estimate only local risks. But by that period, geographical data in meticulous detail and covering at-risk coastal regions of the whole world had been collected and fed into computer archives.

In June, 1989, Sir Crispin Tickell, British Permanent Representative to the United Nations, and author of *Climatic Change And World Affairs*, addressed the Royal Society in London about global warming. He said that even at a conservative estimate, atmospheric warming would raise ocean levels by an average of one foot over the ensuing 40 years.

When it came to the effects on human life, Sir Crispin said: "If only one percent of a world population of six billion were affected, that would mean some 60 million migrants or environmental refugees; and five percent would produce 300 million."

That would mean a population as large as the British Isles at least, or maybe even larger than the entire European Community, would be homeless within 50 years or so.

Sir Crispin emphasised that he was not being alarmist. The expenditure involved in shoring up the threatened areas of U.S. coastline alone had been estimated at $111 billion.

The Earth's temperature, he said, could rise by 2 degrees F to 4 degrees F by the year 2030 and by at least one further degree by 2050. It would have already risen by as much again in the 200 years to the year 2100 as it did in the 10,000 years since the last Ice Age.

Sir Crispin said one third of the human race lived within 40 miles of the ocean; in the British Isles, no one lives further than 75 miles inland. If ocean levels rose as predicted, many people living in the deltas of the Nile, Ganges, Yangtze and Thames rivers would be made homeless and Bangladesh and much of Egypt would be inundated.

"Such secondary effects as disorder, terrorism, civil war, economic breakdown or even bankruptcy could become endemic," warned Sir Crispin.

It was announced as recently as December 1993 that in a venture jointly financed by British Aerospace and the Australian Space Office, a new £18 million watchdog satellite is to be launched to check on global warming. Known as the Advanced Along-Track Scanning Radiometer (AATSR), it will be carried into orbit aboard the £1 billion Envisat-1 satellite in 1999.

Its sophisticated thermal monitoring equipment will be able to detect temperature changes down to only one-tenth of a degree, covering an area of a few kilometres. In fact, the AATSR will be the third orbital temperature scanner to be sent up. The first, ATSR-1, was taken up aboard the European Space agency satellite ERS-1 in 1991; the second, ATSR-2 is due to be launched aboard ERS-2 in 1994.

Taking advantage of the aforementioned computer archives, Ann Henderson-Sellers and Kendall McGuffie, of the University of Liverpool's Department of Geography, prepared a study in which they tried to assess major worldwide risks, taking a hypothetical rise in sea levels of 10 metres.

In a report in *New Scientist* (June 12, 1986), they explained that the archive they used has a resolution of 50km and shows that more than 10 million square kilometres of land are at risk from a 10-metre sea-level rise.

"To put this in perspective," they wrote, "it would entail flooding a total land area greater than that of either the United States or China. More than 70 percent of the land at risk is in the northern hemisphere."

Their list of high risk areas includes a large portion of America's east coast, an area north of the Caspian Sea, Denmark, the Netherlands, and the Ganges, Amazon and Mekong deltas. An area between the mouths of the Gambia and Senegal rivers is high risk territory in Africa. As for the southern hemisphere, regions that could be inundated include a large part of New Zealand's North Island, and the Spencer Gulf area northwest of Adelaide, Australia.

The researchers also point out that "many of the world's major conurbations, such as Beijing, Seoul, New York and London, lie near sea level and in coastal regions."

Interestingly, they draw attention to a side-effect of the Greenhouse Effect I have failed to note in other sources. This is the fact that, in ordinary, garden-type greenhouses, experiments have shown that plants do not absorb as much water when there is extra carbon dioxide in the air. Which means that, under the global Greenhouse warming, they will allow more water to run off into rivers and soil.

(Plants have control of the movement of water and increase or restrict the loss of water to the atmosphere by opening or closing pores in their leaves. If the volume of water in a plant drops by only 5 percent, its growth slows. If it falls by another 10 percent, photosynthesis – the process in which it converts carbon dioxide and water to carbohydrates, using sunlight – ceases.)

Not only that, the nutrient quality of some plants declines if there is excess carbon dioxide. The soya bean plant, for instance, produces carbon-compound rich and nitrogen-deficient leaves under such conditions. This means that insects which eat the leaves have to eat more to gain sufficient nitrogen – and thus do more damage to the plant. Many weeds, meanwhile, tend to thrive on increased carbon dioxide, more so than food plants.

While on the face of it, this may sound a trivial aside, Henderson-Sellers and McGuffie point out: "The effect could be very large in regions that are relatively dry today, such as the catchment areas of the Nile and the Mississippi. This would create an additional hazard around such major centres of population as Cairo and New Orleans."

They add: "Regions with population densities greater than 200 people per square kilometre that coincide with vulnerable locations include Bangladesh, the Chinese coastal plain, much of Indonesia and many of the island groups of the Indian Ocean."

One plaintive cry for help – so far as I am aware, as yet unheeded – was made to the United Nations General Assembly in October 1987, by Maumoon Abdul Gayoom, president of the Maldive Islands. The Maldives comprise an archipelago of 1,190 tiny islands in the Indian Ocean, some 400 miles to the south-west of Sri Lanka.

Apart from a brief coup by foreign mercenaries that did not survive long after its launching in 1988, the 177,000 Maldivians seem to have led a fairly idyllic existence. Serious criminal offenders, of which there are few, are banished to the outlying islands. The residents thrive on their tropical fare of figs, bread fruit and citron – and the little nation even got over a slump in their export of coir, a flexible fibre woven from the husks of coconuts.

Yet the majority of these people live only about 6.5 ft (2 metres) above sea level.

If the surrounding Indian Ocean rose by only one metre, dangerous storm surges would undoubtedly swamp most of the islands' lowest-lying areas. And double that rise – which *has* been the general forecast of several research studies – and the

Maldives would disappear off the map, except perhaps as a danger to shipping.

President Gayoom, who described his people as "an endangered nation", also pointed out to the UN General Assembly that "we did not contribute to the impending catastrophe, and alone, we cannot save ourselves..."

Rises in ocean levels have occurred in the history of the planet in previous eras. Geologists have ascertained that sea levels were five to six metres higher than they are now some 125,000 years ago, when the West Antarctic ice sheet melted.

Even greater rises have taken place in the relatively recent – geologically speaking – past. And what is alarming is that they appear to have occurred quite quickly – although not, it should be added, over the 40 days-and-nights period of Noah's Deluge. Some 95,000 years ago, over a period of less than 100 years, sea levels rose by between 15 and 20 metres. Researchers believe that this may have been the result of a surge and lifting into the sea of the land-supported East Antarctic ice sheet.

Happily, nothing quite so drastic is forecast for our own times. At the least, however, prognosticians suggest that, as I have already noted, a 100% increase in atmospheric carbon dioxide levels would cause a one-to-two metre rise in sealevels.

Over a period of centuries, though, ocean levels could rise by 10 or more metres, without any single giant ice sheet melting completely. The ice sheets would simply have to become shallower, shedding only a portion of their upper layers.

The big question is, what – if anything – can be done? The political implications of permitting the Greenhouse Effect to get worse are so broad that, in the area of environmentalism, no single nation now has the right to claim that its internal policies are its own, exclusive business.

Every single world nation – including those that are not members of the U.N. – is involved. We are all involved, politics notwithstanding. And each and every single nation should be asked to appoint scientists and political representatives to attend a world symposium on the issue.

Having pointed out, as I have, the financial non-feasibility of a complete switchover to nuclear energy, experts should concentrate on maximum development of such energy conservation areas as wind, wave and geothermal power.

The large-scale destruction of rainforests ought to be stopped immediately and new ones planted on as much of the 20 million acres already left fallow as possible.

It is time to stop playing the haves and have-nots among nations. Richer ones should contribute to the environmental programmes of their poorer cousins.

The eating of meat and the breeding of sheep should be curtailed. (It has been estimated that some 45 million tons of ozone-depleting methane – a product of the decay of organic matter – is released every year through the venting of intestinal gases by cattle and other large animals alone.)

As Frederick Konnanoff, of the U.S. Department of Energy said, in 1986: "The citizens of today's nations have the responsibility for the stewardship of all the Earth, including their actions which may affect climate. Exercising this responsibility requires an understanding of atmospheric CO_2 and its effects. Once understood, stewardship then becomes nurturing rather than unrecognised neglect."

3. Population Proliferation

A BRIEF recap. In my Prelude and in *The Zarkon Principle*, I talked about the limitation factor of life on Earth and quoted from a 1959 paper by Dr. David Price, of the U.S Public Health Service, entitled *Is Man Becoming Obsolete?*. He wrote then (and I make no apology for repeating it here):

"We all live under the haunting fear that something may corrupt the environment to the point where man joins the dinosaurs as an obsolete form of life. And what makes these thoughts all the more disturbing is the knowledge that our fate could perhaps be sealed 20 or more years before the development of symptoms."

My own comment then – as long ago as 1975 – was:

Already, time has ticked away since Dr. Price made his pronouncement – and what has been done? In realistic and effective terms, which must mean on a global, co-operative scale, absolutely nothing.

I likened the Earth to a lunar module travelling through space, in that it has only a limited life-support unit that works on a system of self-renewal.

I then talked about subjects which I have touched upon already – pollution of oceans, rivers and lakes, the overfishing of these, the plundering of forests and squandering of natural resources. In short, the unbalancing, over-taxing and even destruction of Earth's self-renewal system.

As lately as April, 1991, *National Geographic* magazine was to some extent echoing my misgivings of some 16 years earlier, in quoting Te-Tzu Chang, head of the International Rice Research Institute:

"What people call progress – hydro-electric dams, roads, logging, colonization, modern agriculture – is putting us on a food-security tightrope."

In the same issue (Vol. 179, No. 4), Robert E. Rhoades, former senior anthropologist at the International Potato Center, outside Lima, Peru, wrote:

"When farmers began harvesting the first domesticated plants about 8000BC, the earth's population was around four million. Today, that many people are born every ten days. If the trend continues beyond the year 2000, we will have to grow as much food in the first two decades of the new century as was produced over the past 10,000 years."

And the same author wrote: "It is estimated that by the middle of the next century, one quarter of the world's 250,000 plant species may vanish, victims of deforestation, the shift to mono-cultures, overgrazing, water-control projects, and urbanization."

But it is not simply the food factor which makes the conservation of "land race" – as opposed to genetically engineered – crops important. As Rhoades observed:

"AIDS researchers have found a substance in Chinese cucumber roots that may work against the disease. An extract from the rosy periwinkle of Madagascar has proved effective in treating childhood leukaemia. A Mexican yam contributed to the first oral contraceptive. Wild tomatoes, growing in the salty air of the Galapagos Islands, have been used to adapt California varieties to the state's heavily irrigated – and increasingly saline – farmlands. Nature has equipped plants with magical properties that science is only just beginning to discover."

Man uncaringly proceeds, I reiterate, to pollute the atmosphere with carbon dioxide, DDT, lead, mercury, and other harmful substances, along with that other great enemy of natural evolution, radiation.

Again, I pointed out that it took from the dawn of man to the year 1850 for the Earth's human population to climb to one billion. Figures for succeeding years showed that ever since man seems to have been bent on overcrowding this spaceship Earth.

Within only another 80 years – by 1930 – the global population had doubled to two billion. Another 30 years (1960) and we numbered three billion. And in 1975, as I wrote, a mere 15 years on, we were expected to reach four billion.

The time gap decreases as the billions pile up. In only another 10 years, I wrote, if the trend continued, human life would total five billion; by 1994, six billion, and so on.

In fact, as I write today, the figure is actually 5.5 billion. And a projected figure for the turn of the century is a staggering seven billion. By the mid-1980s, the Earth's population was already doubling every 40 years.

It is estimated that there are 333,000 births worldwide every day. And even taking into account some 134,000 deaths every 24 hours, this still makes the net 24-hour birth rate 209,000.

At the time I was writing, 1974, it was already being projected that even if population growth rates decreased, a considerable "built-in" momentum would still continue. There was then, and has been since, talk of a state of Zero Population Growth; that is, only enough births to balance the number of deaths. But even if this state were reached in developed countries by the turn of the century and in emergent nations by 2040, it was forecast – and there was doubt that this could be achieved – Earth's population would still probably increase fourfold, to almost 15,500 million, before it eased off.

The breathless proliferation of the human race is easily discernible on a relatively local scale: the already insanely overcrowded and notoriously unhygienic city of Cairo, in Egypt, for example, adds one million to its population every year.

As long ago as 1952, family planning was made official policy in India. And although full government support for a genuinely national programme did not materialise until the mid-1960s, India could still claim one of the most ambitious birth control programmes of any country in the world. By the mid-1970s, it was spending £32 million of its own budget every year and receiving further millions more assistance from private sources and foreign administrations. Some 20 years ago, this programme included 50,000 clinics and more than 500,000 full-time and part-time workers in the field.

But although India's birth rate was consequently reduced by around 2 million annually, the nation's population was still rising at a net rate of 2.3 percent a year. This was because its death rate had also been considerably reduced, thanks to improved medical facilities. If such trends were allowed to continue, it was mooted, India's population would exceed 1,000 million by the year 2000.

As long ago as 1969, the prophetic science fiction writer Arthur C. Clarke, was peering anxiously over his spectacles and remarking: "I see no reason for more than a few million people on the planet Earth."

The most famous example of the accuracy of his powers as a scientific "prophet" is that, in the 1940s, when Clarke was a young RAF radar officer, he wrote an article for *Wireless World* magazine, in which he suggested that a mere three orbiting communications satellites could beam radio and television programmes to the entire world.

Clarke said each satellite would orbit 22,000 miles about the Earth on a plane coinciding with that of the equator. They would circle the planet – at nearly 7,000 mph – every 24 hours. Because that coincided with the Earth's own rotation period, the satellites would actually appear to hover motionless.

Some 20 years on, Clarke was in the United States to watch a closed-circuit television picture of the Early Bird satellite, weighing 85 lbs, being launched into orbit over the equator – only 300 miles higher than he had predicted. The only money Clarke derived from his original prediction was a small fee for a magazine article he wrote, entitled, *How I Lost A Billion Dollars In My Spare Time*. "It was an absurdly simple idea," Clarke said ruefully later, referring to his original *Wireless World* article, "but the original reaction to it was zero."

Accurate prophet though he has proved himself to be, some of Clarke's projections for the future seem, to me at least, to have a nightmarish quality.

For example, there are those optimists who believe that, to solve Earth's overcrowding problems, mankind can simply travel to other planets, where conditions are conducive to supporting human life, and colonise them. And if Clarke's suggestion of reversing the population explosion is either impractical or ignored, this certainly would initially seem to be the perfect solution.

However, as astrophysicists have pointed out, the nearest star system to our own which might have a planet with conditions similar to those of the Earth, is about 10 light years away. (Light travels at approximately 186,000 miles a second and a light year is the distance that light travels at that speed in one year: around 5,865,696,000 miles, or 9,385,113,600,000km.) To reach such a remote planet in a star system so distant would take centuries, unless some new, dynamic form of propulsion is discovered to allow manned space vehicles to approach the speed of light.

Even then, a trip to our nearest stellar neighbour, Proxima Centauri, would take 4½ years, and to reach a system 10 light years off would take a little more than 10 years.

Two main solutions to centuries-long voyages – one of them Clarke's own – have been suggested. One is massive starships, carrying small colonies of people who would be born, breed and die en route, leaving their succeeding generations of children, grandchildren and perhaps even great-grandchildren to complete the journey and final colonisation. Life aboard these giant vessels would, necessarily, have to be self-supporting. I would also submit that it would necessitate perhaps a new type of human being – certainly in mental attitude, if not physically – to be able to adapt to such a lifestyle, along with the finality of never seeing their home planet ever again and the prospect of dying and perhaps being "buried" in space. There are still misgivings among those who work at such installations as NASA headquarters about the physical and psychological long-term effects of living aboard a vessel in deep space.

Clarke's alternative solution for extremely long journeys is not to launch living humans into space, but to send egg and sperm cells. Computers aboard would be programmed to "mate" these, around 20 years before arrival at the vessel's destination. The embryos would be born along similar lines to today's laboratory processes in artificial and automated conditions. Further, humanoid, or cybernautic computers – robot minders – would then nurse and educate the space-born children and teach them who they are and what their ultimate role, purpose and inheritance may be.

In the 1970s, it was reported – notably by former *Newsweek* correspondent Patrick

M. McGrady Jr., in his book *The Youth Doctors* (Ace Books Inc., New York, 1971) – that Soviet scientists were conducting research in life-prolongation – hopefully to a span of 600-700 years. The main goal of this research was so that future cosmonauts could survive extremely long journeys to distant solar/planetary systems.

McGrady, Moscow correspondent for *Newsweek* claimed that more than 100 scientific research establishments throughout the then-USSR were involved in the quest. He interviewed several of the scientists involved and one of them, Lev Vladimirovich Komarov, head of the entire programme, told him:

"This problem should be resolved with even more resolution than that devoted to the solving of the A-bomb problem a while back, or the current problem of conquering the cosmos.

"Every year's delay means that some of us will lose decades... others perhaps even hundreds of years."

The intensity and implied urgency of the Russians' research has prompted some cosmo-theorists to suggest that perhaps the Soviets know more about what may be out there than any other nation. Such speculations may not be far off the mark – as recently as 1986, the highly esteemed *National Geographic* magazine ran a lengthy, illustrated lead article by science editor Thomas Y. Canby which confirmed that the Soviets were certainly ahead of the U.S.A. in their space programmes and research. Nonetheless, all of these proposed "solutions" seem equally grim and somehow devoid of whatever spark it is that makes the condition of being human unique.

Another uncomfortable question that both these "solutions" somehow fail to address is: what will the possibly hapless voyagers – either the starship dwellers or the artificially-generated, almost Huxleyan space babes – do, if intelligent, extra-terrestrial life is encountered? Certainly, no-one – least of all the robot "minders" – can possibly tell them precisely "who" or "what" to expect.

Some forward-looking optimists have foreseen a time when either manned or unmanned, remote controlled, missions could be sent to other planets or asteroids to mine various valuable resources that have become depleted on Earth. These, it is suggested, could then be freighted back for use on Earth.

But this ambitious proposal simply does not stand up to reality. The cost of mining what is left of our own planet's fast-disappearing resources is, even now, becoming a non-viable proposition. And even if it were possible to discover planets – or even one of the larger asteroids or one of our solar system neighbours' moons – with the resources we require, the costs of such operations would be equally prohibitive.

Once again, even supposing it were financially and technologically viable, and materials could in some way be towed or hauled back to Earth, the problem of getting large and heavy quantities of materials safely back into the atmosphere and to the surface would seem, at least for the foreseeable future, insurmountable.

4. The New Atlanteans?

ONE futuristic proposal for solving the inevitable overcrowding of our planet, due to overpopulation, is to build vast, underwater cities, or smaller, village-style communities.

These, it is projected, would be constructed of moulded concrete resin and secured to the ocean or seabed by a network of steel cables. To allow residents to breathe, artificial "gills" – whatever they might be! – would be installed in the walls of these submarine settlements. Power for light and heating would be provided by "geothermal" generators, with thermostats sensitive to temperature changes of the surrounding water outside.

It is proposed by some advocates of submarine survival that edible seaweeds might be farmed by residents and that deliveries of other necessities might be carried out by submarine freighter vessels, specially designed for the purpose. Access to loading bays would be through airlocks, similar to those used on manned space vehicles.

While all but the more culinarily adventurous might at first turn up their noses at a seaweed diet, in an age in which more conventional food and industrial chemicals are running short, edible varieties are gradually gaining ground as an economically sound alternative.

And in addition to providing food substitutes, seaweed, which has high concentrations of iodine and minerals, also has various medical applications, many of which have been employed down the centuries. In 19th century Britain and France, for example, *carrageen*, extracted from carrageenin, a reddish algae similar in appearance to parsley, was used to treat stomach ulcers. It is still used in rural Ireland today to ease chest ailments. The ancient Greeks and the Chinese used seaweeds for the treatment of goitre and various other cultures have used it to relieve arthritis and rheumatism.

Today, frequenters of health food stores will find various seaweed-based "beauty" preparations, from skin treatments to bath oils, and pills that are claimed to stabilise the nervous system and metabolism.

But even as a food, seaweed is not some New Age discovery. Carageen is used in Ireland in jellies, blancmanges and other desserts, and both there and in Scotland, the common red seaweed dulse is used as a vegetable or salad. In South Wales, meanwhile, laver bread is made from purple laver seaweed rolled in oatmeal cakes and fried.

In the Pacific and throughout Asia, of course, seaweed as a food source easily outstrips its slowly growing popularity in the West. Since ancient times, Hawaiians have regularly consumed more than 20 different types of *limu*, or edible seaweed, to supplement their regular diet of fish and *poi*, a paste prepared from the root of the *taro*, or cocco plant. And a popular snack in Hawaii today is *poki*, which is raw tuna fish, garnished with *ogo*, a form of red algae that tastes rather like celery and is as popular as lettuce in the modern supermarkets of Honolulu.

Thanks to the work of British marine botanist Kathleen Mary Drew in 1949, the Japanese, probably the world's prime consumers of edible seaweeds, were able to multiply production of one type of alga, *nori*, that has long been part of their regular diet. For years previously, Japanese coastal "sea farmers" – now popularly known as "aquaculturalists" – had been cultivating it, first on bamboo poles, then transferring them to nets placed over the shallow offshore seabeds. It was sold in pressed sheets of a purplish hue. By 1947, some 860 million sheets a year were produced. After Dr. Drew's work in 1949, when she identified the tiny spores of *porphyra*, from which *nori* could be seeded, the annual figure rose to 7,000 sheets.

By the 1980s, China was producing *laminaria* or kelp, worth some £200 million annually, making it the world's top producer of edible seaweed.

The advantages of aquaculture over agriculture are varied: the sea itself provides the equivalent of land-based, costly fertilisers; there is no drought or soil erosion, and the areas farmed do not require subdivision.

In the West, species of giant kelp are being carefully studied as possible alternative fuel sources. As part of this research, the US Gas Research Institute of Chicago has sponsored experimental plantations of kelp off the coast of California, where kelp population had become depleted, due to sewage discharge, and the hunting of sea otters, which feed on kelp-grazing creatures such as sea urchins. In addition, in 1983, the giant South Californian kelp beds had been further damaged by the warming of ocean waters, causing great atmospheric and oceanic disturbances known as *El Nino*. *Sargassum*, a floating variety of seaweed and *gracilaria*, from which *ogo* may be obtained, are also among smaller algae types being studied.

Further depletion of wild seaweed growth has been experienced in Hawaii and around the coasts of Japan by inexperienced, amateur collectors who often pluck an entire plant, reducing the kelp's potential for regeneration. In Hawaii, kelp pickers are urged by conservationists to pluck only the top portions, while in California it is illegal for seaweed gatherers to sever plants deeper than four feet down.

In addition, of course, fish would form a great part of the underwater denizens' diet – bred and farmed by the residents themselves.

Perhaps most improbable-sounding of all is that it has been suggested that travel between different sections of an underwater community would be by swimming – along cylindrical, water-filled streets. Presumably, then, elderly and infirm people would either be unwelcome in such settlements, or would be transferred to orthodox accommodation back on the land, if such is by then available. People who cannot swim or those with a fear of water – aquaphobia – would obviously not make ideal contenders for submarine survival.

On the question of hygiene, it has been suggested that specially-designed ultra-violet light "baths" would be provided in all homes and work areas – presumably operating at some "safe" level of radiation output. Another suggestion for protection against infection would be for residents to take daily antiseptic showers.

One man who is more than enthusiastic about the idea of cities under the sea, is Jacques Rougerie, a Frenchman who currently lives on a houseboat on the Seine in Paris. He apparently believes that, after an indeterminate period of time growing acclimatised to underwater living habitats, human beings might develop or evolve attributes more suitable to this particular mode of existence. M. Rougerie and the members of an international organization of which he is a member, foresee a completely new sub-species of humans to whom they refer as "amphibious man."

Nor is all of this exactly some nightmarish notion that belongs in the realms of science fiction. Rougerie and other fellow researchers and enthusiasts have actually constructed and lived in underwater modules for up to one month at a time.

Yet another enthusiast for taking to the depths is Wolf Hilbertz, a German-born architect now living in the United States. Hilbertz discovered through his own researches that it is possible to grow – or "accrete", as he terms it – a type of hardy building material by passing an electric current through wire, although I have yet to learn precisely how his method differs from the one we use in everyday domestic life. However, I have been informed that already, in Galveston Bay, Texas, the first sizeable building is being "accreted" or "grown". Appropriately, it has been christened "Seacrete".

5. Windows On The Future

MORE and more uncertainties seem to have crept into science as our century draws towards its close. Especially in the area of sub-nuclear physics.

In the early part of this century, dissatisfied with the idea of the atom as the basic building block of all things, scientists began probing deeper and deeper into particle physics, discovering smaller and smaller breakdowns of matter. But it began to seem that the further they probed, the more distant their supposed ultimate goal receded.

It was almost as if some Cosmic Joker was deliberately leading them on a merry dance.

In the 1920s and early 1930s, along came the German theoretical physicist Werner Heisenberg (b.1901) who pointed out – in his Uncertainty Principle – that "the objective observation of atomic particles is an impossibility, the very nature of atomic particles being such that the very act of observation was interfering and altering, instead of fixing and preserving the object."

Or, as that other Nobel prizewinner Niels Bohr (1885–1962), expressed it, scientists are all actors as well as spectators as they attempt to delve into the true nature of things.

So, as the scientists tried to focus their attention down to more and more minute levels, things got curiouser and curiouser, just as they did for Alice.

Take, for example, sub-nuclear particles, such as quarks, or tachyons. These entities, observed by physicists in diagrammatic format as they are made to collide in bubble chambers and particle accelerators (cyclotrons), do not actually exist, necessarily. On the other hand, they are not necessarily non-existent, either. Such is one of the ways in which science seems constantly to be shading into areas of thinking resembling metaphysics.

Around the beginning of the century, scientist Richard C. Tolman had put forward the idea that tachyons – particles that are believed to travel *only faster than light* – might someday be used to travel backwards in time. Nor, curiously enough, does the notion of particles travelling faster than light, contradict Einstein's relativity theory in which he proposed that the speed of light – 186,000 miles a second – was the speed limit of the universe.

The somewhat complex notion of using tachyons for backward time travel hinges around the fact that time measurement is, in a sense, based on our perception of light. For example, we calculate the length of a year based on our planet's orbital speed around its own segment of the solar system. Similarly, months are regulated in accordance with the orbit of the Moon. And the length of a day is determined by our observance of the Sun's apparent motion as we orbit it. In other words, all time factors depend on our actual observations – what we perceive from our viewpoint of the solar system.

In a greatly simplified manner, the basic current theories of how tachyons might be employed to "break" the time barrier, may be outlined as follows:

The nearest star to our Sun is Alpha Centauri, the brightest in the constellation of Centaurus. Alpha Centauri is 4.3 light years away – which is equal to 270,000 times the distance between the Earth and the Sun. Now, if it were possible – and there are scientists already thinking along these lines – to implant a message on a tachyon and fire it off to Alpha Centauri, at a speed just in excess of the speed of light, it would take around 4.3 years, or slightly less, to arrive at its destination. If any answer from any intelligent life in the Centaurus system were immediately sent back to us by the same method, we could expect it to arrive around 8.6 years after our original was sent. However, if the same technique were to be used to send a message to a much closer destination – to one of the planets in our own solar system, for example – at such speed, our message would theoretically arrive *before it was sent*. In fact, at such speeds, *we would probably get an answer before we posed the question.*

The notion of time not being constant is experienced, on a more basic level, by everyone. There is more than a grain of truth in the saying that time seems to fly when one is enjoying oneself. When I am doing something or studying something in which I am deeply engrossed, time seems to go by at a much faster rate than it does when I am bored, or performing some boring task.

Consequently, as Jeremy Campbell has pointed out in *Winston Churchill's Afternoon Nap: A Wide-awake Inquiry Into The Human Nature Of Time*, (Paladin, 1989): "...a tedious day, in which nothing specific happens, seems to stretch out interminably, while it is going on, because the mind attends to the passage of time itself, and is in the state of a person waiting for a tea kettle to boil. There is little nontemporal information to distract the attention from focusing on time. Once the day is over, however, and the mind looks back, the time shrinks and shortens, because the number of memorable events that symbolise its length are sparse."

It may be that these kinds of perceptions are in fact involved in actual different rates of the passage of time.

Consider, while on the subject of time, the basic fact that even an observer using only the naked eye is, in effect, when gazing at a distant star, actually seeing back in time. The light image from such a star is, because of the time it takes to reach the Earth, how that star appeared, say, 10 years ago – if the star is at a distance of 10 light years away. Even the light from our own Sun is something around eight minutes old by the time it reaches us.

While most average people continue to think of time as linear – that is, moving in a single direction, from past to present to future – a growing number of modern physicists actively doubt such a seemingly "common sense" viewpoint. Indeed, some theoretical physicists deny the very existence of a "now" concept – the present moment which marks the dividing line between the past and the future and which is common to everyone.

Metaphysicians, particularly Eastern ones, have been saying much the same for centuries, possibly millennia. The term the Eternal Now is a common phrase, for example, in many ancient Hindu and Buddhist texts. But scientists are now talking in more or less the same terms.

The astrophysicist Thomas Gold, of Cornell University, at Ithaca, in upstate New York, has categorically stated that the very idea of "the flow of time has been abolished". And the British physicist Sir Alan Cottrell believes that physicists' denial within their discipline of any place for the notion of time passing "has brought us right up to the edge between the material and mental world – and it does look as if there might be an unbridgeable gap between them."

In his book, *Synchronicity: An Acausal Connecting Principle* (Ark edition, 1987), the great psychoanalyst Carl Gustav Jung wrote:

[The parapsychologist J.B.] "Rhine's experiments show that in relation to the psyche space and time are, so to speak 'elastic' and can apparently be reduced almost to vanishing point, as though they were dependent on psychic conditions and did not exist in themselves but were only 'postulated' by the conscious mind. In man's original view of the world, as we find it among primitives, space and time have a very precarious existence. They became 'fixed' concepts only in the course of his mental development, thanks largely to the introduction of measurement. In themselves, space and time consist of *nothing*. They are hypostatized concepts born of the discriminating activity of the conscious mind, and they form the indispensable coordinates for describing the behaviour of bodies in motion. They are, therefore, psychic in origin..."

The British cosmologist and theoretical physicist Stephen Hawking, author of the best-selling *A Brief History Of Time* (Bantam Press, 1988), has suggested an entirely new manner of looking at time. In a lecture given in Tokyo in July 1991 – reprinted in his second book, *Black Holes And Baby Universes* (Bantam Press 1993) – Professor Hawking examines the extraordinary concept of what he calls "imaginary time", a theme already dealt with in his first, popular above-named book.

It was in 1973 that Hawking embarked on investigating what possible effect Heisenberg's Uncertainty Principle would have on a particle near a Black Hole, where it is thought that the space-time continuum is curved. First of all, to his own and everyone else's surprise, he determined that a Black Hole would not be utterly black.

Although light could not escape from a Black Hole, he calculated, the Uncertainty Principle indicated that some particles and radiation would be able to leak out steadily. This involved invoking the work of American physicist Richard Feynman who, in 1948, was recognised for his work on the quantum theory of light. Feynman formulated a concept known as the sum over histories. Basically, this posited that a system did not have simply a single history in space-time, but all possible histories. In other words, a particle could move along *any* path from a given point, A.

Professor Hawking's simplified analogy of this rather complex concept is that of an inkblot's ability to spread – even if a cut is made in the paper – in all directions from its point of contact.

In approaching the problem of "doing the sum over histories" for the whole of space and time, Hawking introduces the idea of "imaginary time."

This is yet another abstruse concept for the layman to grasp. But basically, it can be thought of as a form of time at right angles to the normal concept of linear, left-to-right, past-to-future "real" time.

The motive for introducing what must at first seem a way-out concept is that, in concert, matter and energy have a tendency to cause space-time to curve inwards upon itself.

In ordinary or "real" time, this effect results in singularities – that is, a point in space-time where the curvature of space-time becomes infinite. Under these conditions, the equations of physics cannot be applied to forecast what will occur, because in effect, singularities are places where space-time terminates.

At these points, it is not possible to calculate what will happen.

But, as Hawking emphasizes, the direction of imaginary time is at right angles to real time, yet acts similarly to the three directions involved in movement through space. Because the matter in the Universe causes the curvature of space-time, the three space directions and that of imaginary time would eventually meet up "around the back", as Hawking expresses it, forming a closed surface analogous to that of the Earth's globe.

The resultant space-time would be "closed in on itself", without boundaries or edges, without any beginning or end, much as the surface of our planet cannot be said to have any single location that could be described as the beginning or end.

Now, referring back to Feynman's sum over histories, Jim Hartle of the University of California, Santa Barbara, suggested that this should not be taken over histories in real time, but over the closed-in-on-themselves histories of imaginary time. Having no beginning or end – singularities – the internal events of these closed-in histories would be subject to the laws of physics and could therefore be worked out. Once the history of the Universe in imaginary time has been determined, it would then be possible to calculate how it performs in real time.

"In this way," Hawking says, "you could hope to get a complete unified theory, one that would predict everything in the universe."

As he points out, because he distrusted quantum mechanics, Einstein failed when he spent his latter years looking for a unified theory.

"He was not prepared to admit that the universe could have many alternative histories, as in the sum over histories," says Hawking. He goes on to admit, though: "We still do not know how to do the sum over histories properly for the universe, but we can be fairly sure that it will involve imaginary time and the idea of space-time closing up on itself."

He then goes on to predict confidently: "I think these concepts will come to seem as natural to the next generation as the idea that the world is round."

In what has come to many to be recognised as a unique blend of humour and boldness, Hawking actually contradicts the great Einstein when he says:

"It therefore seems that Einstein was doubly wrong when he said, 'God does not play dice'. Consideration of particle emission from black holes would seem to suggest that God not only plays dice but also sometimes throws them where they cannot be seen."

While the enigmas of time/space are continuing to be investigated, there are already those who see the future generations of humanity preserved not on some distant planet or in some far distant star system, but in man-made, giant space environments. In the early 1970s, physicist Gerard K. O'Neill of Princeton University began to develop such a plan. Following a series of refinements after various workshops and study groups, by 1980 Professor O'Neill was convinced that the majority of humanity could be living in space colonies within only a few decades.

Although it is a less popular idea among NASA top brass than among America's science student population, O'Neill's plan is, to say the least, visionary, in terms of providing at least a temporary solution to humanity's ultimate survival problems.

The first stage in O'Neill's space-colony plan would be for the NASA Space Shuttle to ferry 2,075 tons of fuel tanks into orbit. There, they would be pulverised to provide a unique fuel for a propulsion system known as a mass driver.

This is analogous to a catapult, except that instead of having rubber bands, it would have a number of tank-like cylinders with built-in coils of superconducting wire. (Superconductivity, which is possible only within a few degrees of absolute zero, is achieved through a superconductor: a material in which an electric current, once initiated, continues almost indefinitely.)

The tanks would hover above an aluminium track, held there by the effect of the current in the coils upon the track's metal. Electrical pulses would accelerate the tanks to high velocities. The pulverised material of the Shuttle's tanks would be hurled backwards and, on a spiral path, some 1,100 tons of pulverised metal would be used as fuel to put a 730-ton payload into lunar orbit. The mass driver would then return to Earth's orbit, ready to repeat the journey.

A mining colony, manned by about 24 personnel would be established on the Moon, to provide materials to build the space colony. This would involve some 100 Shuttle flights putting a further 2,800 tons of payload in orbit around the Earth, to propel the mass driver in transporting further materials – about 1,000 tons – to the Moon.

The lunar mining camp's annual target would be the processing of more than 600,000 tons of Moon rock. Professor O'Neill says that lunar rock contains virtually all the materials needed to build a space colony structure. They contain some 40 percent oxygen, to supply atmosphere; 20 percent silicon to manufacture electricity-generating solar cells, and around 20 percent of various useful metals, including aluminium, iron and magnesium.

Space work crews would live in converted Shuttle tanks, connected by cables, and which would spin in lunar orbit to simulate gravity. Operatives down below, would use the mass driver buckets to propel materials from the surface to the orbiting "building site" of the space colony structure.

With these materials, the massive structure could be built. Several NASA-sponsored studies have drawn up plans of such a colony, which Professor O'Neill has designated Island One. Original plans suggested a ring doughnut-shaped habitat, called a torus. But a later proposal was for a Bernal sphere – so-named in honour of the British visionary scientist J.D. Bernal – slightly less than a mile in circumference and accommodating 10,000 colonists.

Initially, Professor O'Neill envisaged a self-sufficient society aboard, growing food in soil relayed from the Moon by the mass driver. But further studies indicated the viability of the project even if food supplies were shuttled from Earth, a suggestion that would be self-defeating in terms of dwindling terrestrial food sources. The colony structure would rotate at two revolutions per minute to simulate Earthlike gravity for its inhabitants, with zero gravity at its centre.

Solar cell generated electricity, beamed back to Earth as microwave beams would provide Island One's eventual source of funding and income. O'Neill envisages a number of such orbital generators supplying the Earth, pointing out that a solar power station in space would benefit from continuous sunlight, instead of half of that enjoyed by a land-based plant.

Estimated cost of setting up O'Neill's Island One project, taking into account inflation rates, would have been around $60 billion by about 1982. And its potential for returning financial benefits within one year of operation, O'Neill calculated, would amount to around $20 billion, in the form of solar power and other products manufactured *in situ* and relayed to Earth. Some of these products, though, would also be used to build further space Island communities.

In a book on his project, *High Frontier*, O'Neill envisaged the Island One colonists being able to select their own flora and fauna – and, "perhaps, too, we can find less annoying scavengers than the housefly and can take along the useful bees while leaving behind wasps and hornets."

It would be possible for inhabitants to choose their own climate by controlling the

---

amount of sunlight allowed to filter in. And an imitation blue sky could be provided by reflecting sunlight from large mirrors onto tinted windows.

Once several such colonies had been established, travel between them would be cheap and effective – by using the rotation of the Bernal spheres to propel small shuttlecraft from one to another at high speeds. O'Neill estimated that within only 35 years after the initiation of the project, more than seven billion immigrants could be occupying the colonies.

The scientists who are in agreement with O'Neill's visionary project believe that it is humanity's only hope of survival, in the face of depleted resources and growing population on Earth.

PART TWO: EARTH SKYWATCH/ALIEN EARTHWATCH?

1. Wisdom Of The Ancients

"The ancients were as wise as we are; perhaps wiser. Could we have done as much with as little?"
Isaac Asimov (1920–1992)

"People will be cleverer and more penetrating, but not better, not happier, not more energetic."
Goethe (1749–1832)

THE TREND in the proliferation of partially speculative, but documented wherever possible, books such as this – began in earnest, I believe, during the 1950s. Hitherto there had been a popular inclination to regard ancient peoples as, at worst, ignorant savages and pagans; at best, only semi-cultured people. They were seen as groping blindly in a fog of unknowing, inventing myths, rituals, totems and legends to fill gaps in their "real" knowledge.

As I commented at the time, it was perhaps an understandable trait. Especially in view of the very way in which modern thinking had become conditioned – partly through education (indoctrination?), inclining towards an expectation of logical progression in all things: slow but steady development from point Alpha to some indiscernible point Omega in the infinite future. Humankind was looked upon as having developed from apelike creatures who wore skins and lived in caves, through a steady evolution: the discovery of fire, the wheel and metals to the high technology of today and, hopefully, onward to a race of Superhumankind.

But in the past few decades it has become patently obvious that evolution – if that is the correct term – does not work like that. It has now been acceded that there have been great civilisations that looked set to dominate the world... then suddenly regressed into a state of intellectual limbo, decline and utter dissolution. It is still debatable, for example, what caused the sudden demise of such long-lived civilisations as those that flourished in the Tigris-Euphrates valley of Mesopotamia, along the banks of the Nile; those of the Inca, Aztecs and Maya of South America, and so on.

At last, 20th-century humankind, for all its materialistic traits, finally appears to have shaken off the turgid, wasteful and self-satisfied ideals of its Victorian predecessors to learn more, for example, about the Universe in the past few decades than any of its more speculative and often, highly imaginative forbears.

All history is peppered with sudden surges of inspiring achievement, periods of stagnation, or even retrogression. It is almost as if the various cultures that have emerged on our planet have been guided by universal traffic wardens as they approached the complex intersections of knowledge and development.

The Roman polymath Pliny the Elder (23–79AD) wrote of an inventor who produced a shatter-proof, flexible glass, which he demonstrated to the Emperor Tiberius (14–37AD), by dashing a goblet made of it on the marble floor of his palace. It did not break. The inventor picked it up and hammered out the few dents. Supposedly daunted at the invention's potential effect on the value of gold and silver, Tiberius is

---

said to have had the glassmaker executed. What became of the formula is not known.

It was also Pliny, preceded by the Greek poet Aristophanes (c.445–380BC) and the Latin poet Gaius Valerius Catullus (84–c.54BC), who mentioned a plant, *silphion*, effectively used by the Greeks as a contraceptive. In his *Historia Naturalis*, Pliny noted that the price of *silphion* had soared because of its rarity by the 1st century. In Roman times, over-harvesting caused it to become extinct, although one of a similar species, asafoetida which survives today, notably as an aromatic ingredient of Worcester Sauce, was also used by the ancient Greeks and Romans as a contraceptive.

Another was Queen Anne's Lace, then known as wild carrot. And modern research, involving tests of the latter's seeds used on mice, disrupted the fertility cycle and inhibited both the growth of the ovaries and foetus.

Traditionally, the wild carrot seeds were said to be effective as a "morning-after pill", taken after the sexual act. Scientists have managed to isolate chemical compounds from the seeds which halt the production of the hormone progesterone, which readies the uterus for reception and development of the fertilised ovum.

According to a report in the *British Journal Of Archaeology* (47 No.2: 29-35) by a team under Professor John M. Riddle, inhabitants of the Appalachian mountains still use a teaspoonful of the seeds in water as a contraceptive. And women in some regions of India also chew the seeds for the same purpose.

Also used in ancient societies were various plants that promoted abortion. These included pennyroyal, a wild herb containing pulegone, which can terminate pregnancy in both humans and animals; pomegrantes, date palm and willow also contain fertility-inhibiting agents, and acacia gum is a form of spermatocidal.

The report said: "We can be reasonably certain that many women in antiquity knew what only a few women know today. Many historians still assume that these women relied solely on magic: they are wrong. Women in antiquity had significant control over their reproductive lives."

Much scepticism about the abilities of the ancients was rooted in the notion that sophisticated tools and equipment were required to produce high quality work with precision. But Abbott Payson Usher, an American authority on ancient manufacturing techniques, has said that while contemporary furniture and linen may be different, they are no better than those of ancient Egypt; that modern architecture is no better than that of ancient Greece and Rome, and that modern porcelain cannot surpass that of ancient China. Usher said: "Technological improvement involves a substantial intellectual development, but it is not precisely synonymous with progress."

As we shall see in a later chapter, the Egyptians used copper saws to make incisions in stone, then drove in wooden wedges which they doused with water – and thus split the limestone, granite and marble they used to build temples and pyramids. And, like their Mesopotamian predecessors, they moved colossal statues weighing many tons on log rollers, manoeuvring them into position with leverage systems. In mountainous regions, tunnels were bored which met with an error of only inches, using a four-legged stool with hanging weights and a basic level as surveying instruments.

In 1978 Soviet archaeologists announced the discovery of a human skull during the excavation of 5th/6th century burial mounds in the foothills of the Tienshan mountains of Kazakhstan. It bore unmistakable signs of successful cranial surgery. The skull, since displayed in a museum of medical history, shows signs of trepanation – the drilling of a hole through the cranium to relieve pressure on the brain. An anthropologist determined that the operation was carried out using a metal implement and that the patient lived for nearly a year following the surgery. The patient was estimated to have been 40 years old.

Human skulls, with bone-and ivory-carved false teeth and dating back to 700BC, have been unearthed in Etruscan burial sites. And Egyptian mummies have been examined whose teeth showed signs of intricate dental work.

By the age of the Greek philosopher-scientist Aristotle (384–322BC), the civilised world of Greece and Rome buzzed and rang with various devices. In his treatise, *Mechanical Problems*, Aristotle enumerated various technical innovations of his time: the counterweighted lever; the equal-armed balance; the roller, wheel, pulley and composite pulley; the potter's lathe which, in a modified version, could be used for wood-turning; the sling, oar and cord-wheel of bronze or copper, which could rotate in varied directions, and the tongs, axe, wedge and winch. In their wake followed many devices that continued to be used down to our own times: the screw in its many forms, the cylinder, the valve and the piston.

In his major work on architecture, construction and mechanics, *De Architectura*, the 1st century BC Roman Vitruvius appears to put forward a wave-theory of sound.

Sadly, many thousands of valuable works containing the knowledge of ancient thinkers and inventors have been lost. The great Library of Alexandria, for example, contained more than 700,000 texts until Caesar's siege of the city in 47BC, in which more than 40,000 of them were destroyed. These were replaced by 200,000 volumes – a gift from Antony to Cleopatra, a great many of which, due to space shortage, were housed in the Serapeum. This was destroyed around 390AD by a mob of fanatics, led by one of the "Church Fathers", Bishop – later Saint – Cyril (c.376–444). Another act attributed to this "holy" man was the murder of the philosopher Hypatia (c.370–415). A mob of Nitrian monks dragged her from her chariot, stripped her and scraped her to death with oyster shells. Her crime? Teaching mathematics. The Alexandrian Library was finally utterly destroyed in 646AD on the orders of the Caliph Omar when the Arabs overran Egypt.

The Greek-born mathematician Hero of Alexandria, believed to have flourished during the latter half of the first century – he mentioned an eclipse of 62AD – was a prolific experimenter and inventor. He specialised in geometry, mechanics and pneumatics and wrote several treatises, including: *Mechanica*, *Pneumatica* and *Captoprica*. The first contained designs for machines incorporating wheels, screws, levers, pulleys and wedges; the second listed 78 experiments with air and steam pressure. Hero built a steam turbine, which he called an Aeolophile, later known as "Hero's Fountain". It comprised a large, sealed vessel half filled with water, that was placed over a fire. Two hollow tubes protruded from the lid, carrying a central cylinder like an axle. Inside this was a hollow globe with two further tubes projecting at right angles. When the steam in the vessel built up sufficient pressure it was forced up the tubes into the "axle" and globe, making it spin, faster as the pressure increased. The two tubular arms acted as safety valves, turning like the sails on a windmill.

His work *Captoprica* was devoted to the study of light refraction and the properties of mirrors. In another work, *Dioptra*, he described surveying methods. Hero's other inventions included a water-clock, a coin-operated holy water dispenser which worked on precise balances, a geared meter to measure the mileage on large wagons and chariots, and various other automata.

The Roman architect Vitruvius, of the 1st century BC, author of *De Archictectura*, also took an interest in mechanics – and described the twin fire-pump invented by the

Greek scientist Ctesibias, (c.300–230BC). Vitruvius wrote:

"It is made of bronze and has at the bottom a pair of cylinders set a little way apart, and there is a Y-shaped pipe connected with both and joining them to a vessel which is between the cylinders. In this vessel are valves, accurately fitted to the upper vents of the pipes, which stop up the ventholes, and keep what has been forced upward by pressure from coming down again.

"Over the vessel a cowl is adjusted, like an inverted funnel, and fastened by means of a wedge thrust through a staple, to prevent its being lifted off by the pressure of the water. On top of this, a pipe is jointed, which rises vertically. Valves are inserted in the cylinders beneath the lower vents of the pipes and over the openings which are at the bottom of the cylinders.

"Pistons, smoothly turned and rubbed with oil and inserted in the cylinders, work with their rods and levers and as the valves stop up the openings, force and drive [out] the water."

Vitruvius also described the designs of various waterdriven striking clocks and an alarm clock, with various gears and dials, and one on which "small figures are moved, posts turn, pebbles are dropped into a gong, trumpets sound..."

Ctesibias' pupil, Philo of Byzantium, described another of his twin fire-pumps, designed to be worked by hand. A hose was dropped into a well or cistern and water could be raised to a height of about 15 feet by two men pumping on either end of a hinged handle.

In Roman times, fire-fighters used hand-operated fire-extinguishers, *siphonii*, consisting of water bags made of skin with ox-gut fire hoses.

The siphon, which works on the same pressure principle as the pump, was also used in early clocks, one of the oldest on record dating back to about 1500BC. Ancient Egyptian models involved immersing an inverted, cup-shaped vessel, pierced underneath and with a long hollow stem, in water. When the vessel was full, a thumb was placed over the open end of the stem, the device was removed from the water and hung up. Water dripped out slowly and regularly. Such devices were used to time speeches, measure heartbeats and check on cooking times.

A much larger version, again designed by Ctesebias, was described by his pupil Philo. It comprised a tank with a four-foot cylinder rising from it. Water ran into the tank through a "washer", made of gold or some precious stone to cut down on wear and tear. As the cylinder rose, it lifted a float carrying a sculpted figure holding a pointer. This showed the hours on a series of calibrated squares. After a certain distance, a network of rustproof bronze gears in the tank turned the cylinder slightly. After the cylinder had completed one revolution, the "clock" had been running for 365 days. Surplus water in the tank drained automatically, lowering the float and pointing figure, to start another week or month. Seasons were measured by the signs of the zodiac at the top of the cylinder.

The 6th century AD Byzantine historian Procopius, author of *Buildings Of Justinian*, wrote of a highly ornate clock that worked on the same principles and was the public clock of Gaza, in the south-west of Judaea. It was encased in a model temple, the clock's face protected by the portico. Two rows of 12 decorated doors – one each for the day and night hours – were set into the facade below. The water-driven mechanism moved a figure along, pointing in turn to the appropriate door. On the hour, the door opened and inside were miniature representations of the 12 Labours of Hercules. A bronze figure of the mythological Greek hero struck the hours on a gong.

After nightfall, the doors were illuminated from within. Surmounting the entire elaborate device was a head of the Gorgon Medusa with swivelling eyes.

Although many mills were turned by human slaves or by mules, by the 1st century BC, some at least were water-driven. Vitruvius wrote: "Wheels are used in rivers. Around them, boards are attached and these, being struck by the force of the stream, move forward and cause the wheel to turn, and in this fashion they draw up buckets of water to the top without workmen to tread the wheel." An accompanying drawing shows the shaft of the water mill capped by a gear which turns another that drives the axle of the mill stone.

Three centuries later, it was fairly common for water wheels to drive machinery, such as stonecutter saws and flour mills. In 390AD, the Spanish-born poet and composer Aurelius Clemens Prudentius bemoaned a famine that stopped "the motion of Janiculum's mills". The flour mills of Rome were located across the Tiber on Janiculum Hill. Procopius described it as the place "where are all the mills; a large body of water being conveyed by timber structures direct from the top of the hills, and the water falling down the slopes with considerable force".

Some Romans must have clandestinely "tapped" the wooden sluices that carried the water down from the hills, for a 398AD law decreed: "If any man be so audacious as to draw off the water serving the mills used to supply the city with abundant bread, he shall be fined 12 pounds of gold unless he immediately desist."

Another problem that ancient inventors efficiently tackled was that of providing lighting. Most lamps were small, basic wick and oil reservoir types which needed constant re-filling and trimming. Philo, of whom we have already taken note, designed a large, double-wick, self-replenishing lamp, which used the principles of air pressure.

Its wicks were on opposite sides, as were two openings. A bronze tube with a hole at its lower end inside the lamp was inserted through the lid. Around the tube was the large, enclosed oil container. As the lamp burned and the oil depleted, the hole in the tube became exposed to the air. The air fed up the tube to the globular container and its pressure caused more oil to flow down through two spouts into the side openings. Once the oil covered the lower hole in the tube again, the supply was cut off automatically.

A lamp with a self-replenishing wick had also been invented during the first century AD by Hero of Alexandria. The wick was wound around a small axle in the lamp, fitted with cogs and a float so that, as the level of the oil fell, the axle turned and raised the wick.

He also designed and built a highly decorative and mechanical lamp which was a model of the Temple of Bacchus, god of wine. The figure of Bacchus stood in the centre with a goblet in his hand, while a ring of miniature dancing girls encircled the temple. A large circular base housed the mechanism. Light came from two fires on tiny altars within. The release of a trigger caused a large lead weight, suspended by cords on a cylinder filled with mustard seed or millet, to descend. The seeds flowed through a tiny aperture, causing the suspension rope, which was wound over pulleys, to turn axles and cogs. This sent the dancing girls whirling around the temple while the model of the god turned slowly as he poured a drink into his cup.

As early as the 15th century AD, the city of Antioch and the province of Cappadocia, in the mid-eastern part of Asia Minor, were equipped with street lighting – shielded oil lamps slung between poles on either sides of the streets.

In addition to their percussion, wind, brass and stringed instruments, the ancient

Romans also had hand-pumped, water and air-powered organs. By the action of pumping, air was forced into compression chambers which were linked to a central chamber of water, which acted as a stabiliser. The pressing of a key allowed air to flow into the appropriate pipe, causing it to sound.

The Romans also had such mod-cons as sulphur matches, gelatine-makers – and the equivalent of the modern pressure cooker.

The Spanish-born Latin poet Marcus Valerius Martialis – known as Martial – (c.40–104AD), mocked a contemporary Caecilius, whom he considered what would today be called "flash" or ostentatious. "Caecilius," he wrote, "you think you are a real sophisticate [urbanus]. Believe me, you are not. Then what are you? You are just like the peddlar from across the Tiber who swaps pale sulphur matches for broken glass."

It was Philumenos, a Greek physician of the 3rd century AD, who described the making of gelatine in what amounts to a pressure cooker:

"The meat is placed in a pot containing rain-water. This pot is then closed and sealed with grease and placed at night in an oven filled with glowing coals. It is left all night. The steam causes the meat partly to dissolve and produces a thick, gelatinous brew."

To make aspic, which the Romans used lavishly in the decoration of banquet food, Philumenos noted: "Many people also cook calves' feet in the broth all night until they dissolve and then the liquid becomes stiff and gelatinous."

It becomes clear that is utterly wrong, therefore, to assume that because a given race, tribe or nation emerged X thousand years ago, they were unsophisticated. Or that they were necessarily deficient in their perception of the world, or even of the Universe and the general nature of things. One aspect of human culture that may have contributed to this kind of impression is simply that of language – of expression – or lack of it.

In trying to reconstruct the framework of such ancient cultures as the Maya, the Toltecs, the Aztecs, the Aborigines, the Polynesians, the Chaldeans, the Sumerians, the Egyptians, we are often confronted not only by the barrier of time, but by that of communication.

Such peoples presumably knew what they saw and experienced, but frequently, from our own point of view, lacked the utensils – the words – to record the events accurately in terms understandable to later interpreters.

What would, for example, a scribe of the ancient Egyptians actually write down if it were possible to convey to him a rough idea of the modern theory of the formation or creation of the Universe?

The answer is fairly elementary. He not only would, but did say, that the god Khnum made an egg from the mud of the Nile and from it emerged everything. And it is not such a ridiculous analogy when we consider that the Egyptians did not have in their vocabulary words to express "thermo-nuclear reaction," or "primal atom", let alone the capacity to absorb and understand such concepts in our contemporary scientific terms.

In fact, some so-called "myths" bear an uncanny resemblance, in other terminology, to the modern theory of creation from a primal atom, or cosmic egg: the Big Bang theory. Take, for example, the Kojiki, an ancient Japanese chronicle, on a parallel with those of other cultures – the Hindu Mahabharata, the Hebrew Talmud, or the Islamic Koran. The Kojiki tells how everything had its beginning in an egg in which all the ingredients for creation existed in a state of chaos until the egg hatched (exploded?).

Although the Kojiki was not committed to writing until 712AD, its stories and legends had, like the secret Hebrew oral teachings of the Qabalah, been transmitted by word of mouth for centuries.

It was committed to parchment by a Japanese nobleman, Ono-Yasumaro, as an official Record of Ancient Matters, on the dictation of a court official, Hiyeda-No-Are. The text, in curious and fascinating character-symbols (pictographs), extremely ancient in form, goes on to relate how two minor deities, Izanagi and Izanami, on instruction from the Heavenly Divinities, formed land on Earth by stirring its turgid waters with a jewelled spear until it curdled and solidified.

That does not to me, at any rate, sound entirely like a fanciful story invented to cover up ignorance. Allegory, perhaps, but with imagery that is rooted in an inkling, at least, of how the Earth and planets were formed. Who told the Japanese that that was how it all began? Or the Egyptians for that matter?

Perhaps if we follow the egg-allegory further into ancient beliefs, we may get an answer.

In the British Museum is the Papyrus of Ani, believed by many scholars to be one of the finest copies of the Egyptian Book of the Dead, more properly called The Book of the Coming Forth by Day. It is a scroll 78 feet long and 1 foot 3 inches wide and was made for the royal scribe Ani of Thebes around 1320BC. Such scrolls were placed into tombs, supposedly to instruct the spirits of the dead on how to proceed in the after-life. The papyrus contains the following passage:

"O Thou, who art in the Egg, who shinest from Thy disc and risest in Thy horizon and dost shine like gold above the sky, like unto whom there is none among the gods, who sailest over the Pillars of Shu [the atmosphere], who givest blasts of fire from the mouth, who makest the two lands bright with Thy radiance, deliver the faithful worshippers from the Gods whose forms are hidden..."

Before I put any ideas into the reader's mind, I suggest that the passage be read again. Then the reader can ask him or herself what the imagery of the prayer conveys. Many classical scholars have interpreted it as an invocation to Re, or Ra, the Egyptian sun-god. But, having read the passage once more, see if there flashed through your mind similar impressions to the ones I experienced.

First, let us deal with the classical view. For a start, the Sun does not and, as far as is known, never has resembled an egg. Even the most primitive peoples knew what eggs were and looked like and could discern the difference between an ovoid and a sphere.

Secondly, if the ancient Egyptians who composed the "invocation" were addressing it simply to Re, the Sun-god, why should they have said, "like unto whom there is none among the Gods"? Could they, perhaps, have been questioning their ideas about their own "invented" gods, because they had seen something so strange and marvellous that it seemed more important?

What, other than the Sun, would rise "in the horizon" and "shine like gold above the sky", sail above the atmosphere with "blasts of fire from the mouth"?

The Sun certainly apparently rises from the horizon and shines like gold, but from the viewpoint of an early observer looking upward with no optical aids, would it not seem to be a part of the sky, rather than "above" the sky? Nor does the Sun appear to give of "blasts of fire" from anything resembling a "mouth". Its fire – again to a casual, unaided observer – appears to be constant, not emitting blasts, and the only features on the Sun that could be said to resemble a mouth or mouths are sunspots, which the Egyptians, without the aid of protective filters on some kind of optical device, would hardly have been likely to have detected.

If not the Sun, then what? Did you, like me, get a fleeting impression – one that you perhaps dismissed as too fanciful – of a kind of spacecraft, sailing across the clear Egyptian skies, shining like gold and emitting a fiery exhaust? If this is too outrageous an idea to accept at this stage, let us simply file it for the moment, in the pigeon-hole of our minds marked, "perhaps".

To return to the "prayer". If it were not addressed merely to the Sun-god, as I have suggested, why should it then make the distinction "the Gods whose forms are hidden"? Could it be because this something, this new phenomenon, had appeared before them and made them question the validity of the hitherto "unseen Gods" they had been worshipping?

Most religions, at some stage in their development, undergo either modification by some new prophet, thinker, or council of elders – even a general upheaval and reshuffling, like the fragmentation of the Christian faith into Catholic, Protestant and all the other offshoot variations. Wouldn't the appearance of something new and inexplicable, something like a god – flying through the skies and shining like gold – be enough to shake the tenacity of the most faithful?

I believe it would. Therefore, in my hypothetical file marked "perhaps", remains the following resumé:

Subject:
Egyptian invocation, circa 1320BC, believed by classical interpreters to be a prayer to the Sun-god Re, and containing imagery that could be assumed to describe the path of the Sun across the sky. *Alternative Hypothesis:* Could be interpreted as a description of a craft, possibly extra-terrestrial, in the skies of ancient Egypt. No absolute way to resolve either theory. File left open.

The Papyrus of Ani, however, is by no means the only Egyptian reference to an egg-shape in connection with a god. Ptah, god of the city of Memphis, first capital of ancient Egypt, was believed *to have descended to Earth in an egg*. According to the inscription on the Shabaka Stone, also housed in the British Museum, he then "created the gods, made the cities... set the gods in their cult-places, he established their offerings, he founded their shrines".

At the centre of Hermopolis, a creation "myth" prevailed that suggested that the Sun-god who created all things, emerged from an egg deposited on an island by eight beings, represented as serpents or frogs. Indeed, according to an inscription on the tomb of a priest of Hermopolis, around 400BC, pilgrims were still being shown fragments of this "egg". Sadly, what became of these fragments is not recorded.

In the Pyramid Texts – similar in supposed purpose to the Book of the Dead scrolls, except that they were inscribed on the walls of burial chambers at Sakkara, necropolis of Memphis – is yet another intriguing invocation. It has been interpreted by Egyptologists to be an incantation to enable the dead to rejoin the Sun-god, and reads:

"He flieth as a bird, and he settleth as a beetle on an empty seat that is in the *ship* of Re... He roweth in the sky in thy ship, O Re, and he cometh to land in thy ship, O Re."

Surely, this seems more than a literal supplication to a god associated with the Sun? But let us not simply take the word of the ancient Egyptians. Our enigmatical "egg" imagery turns up elsewhere. Examples:

• The amazing Polynesians who, in their 80-foot canoes, managed to populate islands over a vast area of the South Pacific, believed that an *egg* descended from the sky and splashed down into the primeval fluid of the Earth. From it emerged Tangaroa, the creator. Part of Tangaroa's journey through space is described in Polynesian mythology, with an amazing similarity to the work of later science fiction writers:

"Tangaroa sat in his *shell* in darkness from eternity. The shell was like an *egg* revolving in endless space, with no sky, no land, no sea, no moon, no sun, no stars. All was darkness..."

From whence, you might wonder, did this being suspended in his cosmic void, travel to carry out his purpose?

• In Peruvian tradition, it is stated that human beings first came down to Earth in not one, but three different types of egg. Each established a separate level of society: golden eggs for the rulers, silver for the aristocratic hierarchy, and copper for the common people.

• Hawaiian legends say that the islands were formed by rising up out of the sea, after a god had descended and laid an egg.

• In Hindu mythology, it was the Hiranagarbha [golden world-egg] that hatched the god Brahma, who then proceeded to create the rest of the Universe.

• There is a beautiful stone carving that shows, in relief, a god coming out of an egg that, marked with zodiacal signs, represents the Earth. The god is Mithras, worshipped between 1400BC and 400AD by the Indians, Greeks and Persians and taken to Britain by the Romans. It was among fragments found in the Mithraeum (Temple of Mithras), at Houseteads, then in Northumberland, on Hadrian's Wall. It is kept in the Museum of Antiquities of the University of Newcastle-upon-Tyne and the Society of Antiquaries.

• In Greek mythology, the god Zeus, chief of all the Olympian deities, transformed himself into a swan, flew down to Earth and seduced Leda. She conceived and laid two eggs. Out of the first came Castor and Pollux, the twins, and from the second came Clytemnestra and Helen (of Troy). In Orphic literature – centred around the Greek poet-musician hero Orpheus – the god Eros, or Phanes (Apparition), hatches from an egg as a creature with four eyes and horns, golden wings, several animal heads and the organs of both sexes. He then creates men and the gods.

The omnipresent egg even turns up in a subject I have dealt with elsewhere – Alchemy. In this much-maligned mixture of science and philosophy, alchemical reactions were supposed to take place in the "Philosopher's Egg", a sealed, ovoid vessel. Indeed, the egg has become so implanted in man's conscious and subconscious, it has even passed into surviving versions of old folk customs.

For example, Easter is a time when the egg enjoys symbolic, though rarely considered, prominence – at least in the Christian world. The word Easter is derived from *Eostre*, the name of an Anglo-Saxon goddess of spring, the supposed time of the rebirth of nature. What better device than the egg, then, for Christians to adapt or absorb into their symbolic celebrations of the resurrection or rebirth of Christ?

Yet the old paradoxical riddle – which came first, the chicken or the egg? – was one that apparently did not escape the attention of the ancient peoples, either.

Alongside all the egg-legends, associated with creation and the birth or emergence of gods, are bird-legends. In many of the ancient cultures already mentioned, there

---

are other stories of some amphibious creature, more often than not a bird, descending from the heavens and forming dry land by dredging up mud from the bed of the all-enveloping seas.

Traditionalist thought tends to suggest that all the legends of eggs were generated by early man's wonder and amazement at the idea of a living creature emerging from an oddly-shaped, seemingly inanimate object. Because ancient peoples could not think in abstract terms – or so some traditionalists would have had us believe – they chose this astounding phenomenon to symbolise the great birth of everything: their world, their gods, even themselves. And this is where we return to the irritating tendency to underestimate or misinterpret the ways in which earlier cultures reasoned or expressed themselves.

The truth is, though, that while many ancient cultures contained egg-legends, not all of them did. Others, including some pockets of Egyptian tradition, looked to more orthodox imagery, of human-like gods and goddesses procreating the human race.

Why didn't everyone? Could it be that some cultures did not share the same experiences, the same cosmic truths?

The so-called myths with which I am dealing clearly state that eggs came down from the skies, sometimes to form the Universe, other times to carry "gods" to Earth. Are we to believe that early societies such as those that produced the rich cultures of Egypt, India, Peru, Polynesia, Japan, etc., were so stupid as to think that eggs, as well as birds, were capable of flight? Or that they would talk of eggs flying when they meant bird-like objects with wings, or the Sun, when they meant an ovoid, golden object, flying through the skies?

It boils down to a matter of interpretation and to the fact that, by our standards, they were hampered by a less technological language in attempting to describe things that lay outside their experience. They clearly could grasp *something* of the way in which the Universe was formed. Why shouldn't they also be reasonably relied upon when describing strange objects descending from the skies with god-like occupants?

Whether *we* believe in these entities or not, the ancient peoples of many cultures most certainly did.

Is it conceivable that these strange beings were visitors or even colonists from other planets? No one can rule out that possibility. Because the one, underlying fact remains: no one can explain how such different peoples, so widely separated geographically and having no contact whatever in many cases, could have such parallel experiences and arrive at such similar conclusions when trying to assess the Universe. Unless, that is, someone told them. Unless the information were imparted to them, in a way they could understand, by someone else, some extra-terrestrial, or unearthly intelligence, able to make, as it were, a whistle-stop educational tour of the Earth.

And these "myths", remember, are only a tiny fragment of ancient records and beliefs. There are many more parallel areas of thought and philosophy that link the peoples of Earth in the same way, with the same inexplicable consistency.

Before we close the "perhaps" file, we shall have to dig much, much deeper...

2. Dynasties Of Clay

"Clay lies still, but blood's a rover;"
A.E. Housman (1859–1936)

IN ADDITION to the creation allegories I have already mentioned, three of the world's great religions, Judaism, Christianity and Islam, state that man was made from mud or clay. The fact that there are parallels here is, of course, not surprising, since the latter two are greatly derived from the much older religion of the Israelites.

The Old Testament, Genesis 2, verse 7, says: "And the LORD God formed man of the dust of the ground, and breathed into his nostrils the breath of life; and man became a living soul."

In the original Hebrew creation myth, which scholars call the Yahwist tradition – after the God, Yahweh, or Jehovah – God creates man before the animals. Yahweh makes Adam from the ground, or earth: adamah in Hebrew.

The Islamic holy book, The Koran, (Surah VI, verses 1–3) describes man's beginnings like this:

"1. Praise be to Allah, Who hath created the heavens and the earth, and hath appointed darkness and light..."

"2. He it is who hath created you from clay..."

Elsewhere, (Surah XV, verses 26 and 28), The Koran, in which God is often speaking directly to the reader, reaffirms:

"26. Verily, we created man of potter's clay of black mud altered..."

"28....Lo! I am creating a mortal out of potter's clay of black mud altered."

Finally, in Surah XXXII, verse 7:

"Who made all things good which He created, and He began the creation of man from clay."

Curiously enough, the Hebrew word for "formed" was regularly employed when describing a potter making clay.

So, as in the Egyptian story of Khnum and the legends of Sumerian deities, man is said to have been created from clay, or earth.

Most scientific theories about the origins of life on Earth revolve around the "primordial soup" that is believed to have covered the Earth about 3½ billion years ago. The effect of the Sun (solar flares), cosmic rays and electrical storms on this "soup" are thought to have created amino acids and proteins that promoted the original, primitive life forms, from which all living creatures eventually evolved.

In 1953, Stanley Miller, then a student of the Nobel laureate for chemistry, Harold Urey, of the University of Chicago, performed a milestone laboratory experiment. He simulated the type of atmosphere that it was assumed originally existed on Earth, in a flask. It consisted of a mixture of methane, ammonia, hydrogen and water.

Miller then placed electrodes in the flask and subjected the mixture to periodic sparks, emulating solar ultra-violet radiation and lightning. He then heated the flask to boiling point and the water circulated through a series of tubes in a closed loop. After a while, the water turned a pinkish colour, turning to deep red within the space of a few days. On analysis, various organic compounds – including four of the amino acids normally found in protein – were discovered in the water.

Although previous experiments had produced lesser results in the same laboratory conditions, the Urey-Miller experiment was important because it showed that it was clearly possible to obtain large quantities of organic compounds from the starting point of nothing more than air and water. Many variation experiments around the same basic principles have been performed since.

Philip H. Abelson, for example, in work at the Carnegie Institute, Washington, D.C., demonstrated that organic molecules could be generated using various mixtures of gases – so long as oxygen was not the main constituent. In more scientific parlance, the artificially simulated "primeval soup" had to be reducing, rather than "oxidising", that is, combining freely with anything with which it is in contact. A reducing atmosphere contains compounds, like methane and ammonia and hydrogen – themselves reducing agents – but little or no oxygen.

Since the early experiments, various scientists have worked with reducing atmospheres, producing the basic chemicals essential for life, with positive results: in 1963, an electron beam from a particle accelerator was used by Cyril Ponnamperuma and Melvin Calvin at the University of California, Berkeley, as the energy source; ultraviolet light has been substituted by Soviet and German experimenters.

"All these different types of experimentation and simulation of pre-biological conditions have produced many of the building blocks of life, such as amino acids, purines, pyrimidines, carbohydrates, etc.," said Cyril Ponnamperuma.

But in 1974, there came an indication that life may have originated almost exactly as the Bible, the Koran and other religious texts suggested: from clay.

Dr. Graham Cairns-Smith, of the University of Glasgow's Department of Chemistry, was working on such a hypothesis. But before describing Dr. Cairns-Smith's ideas, let us first take a simplified look at the process of genetics – the passing on of characteristics from generation to generation in all forms of life.

The process involves deoxyribonucleic acid (DNA). It consists of long, microscopic threads of molecules found in simple viruses, and in chromosomes, the nuclei of living organisms. The threads take the form of intertwined, double spirals, or helixes. They store all the genetic information or code that determines the characteristics of living things.

But Dr. Cairns-Smith was not satisfied that the DNA material, which is extremely complex, was sufficiently primitive to have been the original pattern for the beginnings of life. He began therefore to look for some alternative that might work under truly basic, primitive conditions and decided that the most likely was a type of crystal that grew spontaneously.

Clay, he found, appeared to have the type of properties required – the ability to retain a pattern or code of information in a stable form and to be able to "print" this pattern, rather like a duplicating machine, when new material is formed.

Clay consists of stacks of thin, interlocking plates containing aluminium and silicon atoms that can be arranged in random patterns.

The patterns can undergo changes as new clays "print" near old layers. This, Dr. Cairns-Smith believed, was a system capable of development by natural selection, by trial and error – the first stage necessary to produce molecules and arrangements of molecules that would eventually form the more complex systems for early life forms.

From these, he said, the biological processes could have taken place that eventually resulted in DNA.

In simple terms, then, clay therefore could well have been the basis of primitive life; the "blueprint" for humankind. At some stage in the spontaneous "experiments" produced by the clay patterns, substances called nucleotides, from which DNA molecules are made, were produced.

As Dr. Cairns-Smith said, the clay process "might have done other things and doubtless did do other things. That all modern organisms use the same genetic material does not mean that this is the only genetic material that is possible, it means simply that it's the only one that's left."

Three years later, in 1977, James Lawless and Nissim Levi, a visiting Israeli scientist, working at the National Aeronautics and Space Administration's Ames Research Center in California, also reported on the efficiency of clay as a catalyst in putting together the building blocks of life. Their research team found that clays, all of which contain metals, attract amino acids. And they discovered that one type in particular, containing nickel, attracted precisely the 20 amino acids found in terrestrial life.

The scientists submitted seven other clays to tests which turned out not to have an attraction quality. Instead, they destroyed the amino acids which were not protein-forming.

Lawless and Levi had therefore shown that clays could work in two ways to produce the macro-molecules of life. While most clays destroyed large numbers of amino acids, one particular kind promoted chains of other amino acids to form.

In one test the scientists carried out, amino acid-clay solutions were dried, then warmed, then wetted, then dried, in a cycle designed to emulate tidal action. As a result, chains of up to eight amino acids were formed, suggesting that, over vast periods of time, even longer and more complex chains would be created.

Similar results emerged in the scientists' tests with nucleotides and clays. One zinc-containing clay concentrated the same nucleotides that go to form DNA. Zinc plays a key part in the enzyme DNA polymerase. It is found in living cells and connects nucleotides to form large DNA molecules.

The whole of the Ames team's work served to emphasize the fact that large, complex molecules can be formed from basic molecules of the type that are thought to have abounded in the early stages of development on Earth.

Over the aeons, as billions upon billions of macromolecules formed, some of which broke down, one somehow must have brought together simpler molecules to replicate itself. Eventually, these copies would outnumber all others, the more efficient copycats ultimately predominating.

As larger and larger combinations of molecules formed, coming together by accident, but sticking together, eventually a configuration of them resembling a living cell took shape. Meanwhile, however, "food" supplies, in the form of other molecules, must have been depleted because of increasing competition. At this stage, the next important evolutionary step must have occurred – the ability to "manufacture" its own food supply by some primitive combination of molecules. This was done by drawing upon solar energy in a primitive form of the process known as photosynthesis, using hydrogen sulphide and emitting sulphate ions.

By now there was probably an entire range of comparatively complex forms of life in existence, and they may have led to those found in living organisms by taking over and using lesser forms, in the same way that giant business conglomerates engulf smaller, independent operations today.

Seven years later – in April 1984 – the Ames researchers produced fresh evidence lending support to Dr. Cairns-Smith's theory.

The team, by then headed by Dr. Lelia Coyne, had been studying the possible origins of life for some 15 years. Their object was to try to provide designers of interplanetary space vehicles with a better understanding of the experiments required in searching for life on other planets.

Dr. Coyne's team demonstrated some of the processes that can take place in clay minerals. They discovered that ordinary clay minerals have two basic properties essential to life – the capability of storing and transferring energy.

Through such energies – radioactive decay from the Earth's interior and solar radiation – early clay could have functioned like chemical laboratories, processing inorganic raw materials into more complex molecules.

Analyses of the clay minerals frequently revealed a kind of flaw in the microstructure of crystals which had occurred naturally, but which could also be duplicated under laboratory conditions. The flaw gave the mineral the characteristic of being able to retain energy, releasing it only under particular conditions.

Experiments demonstrated that clay yielded energy, as ultra-violet light, only when the mineral was reacting with water or other liquids added to it. To fulfil the next step of Dr. Cairns-Smith's hypothesis, the mineral would have to react with compounds containing carbon, which have an affinity for clay, perhaps beginning with carbon dioxide in the atmosphere, thus laying the foundation for organic chemical synthesis.

Now, the question is: who told the ancient Egyptians, the Hebrews, and all the other men-from-clay believers?

Since the beginnings of civilisation, individuals and, indeed, entire races of people, have believed that they were divinely inspired or chosen to represent God or the gods on Earth, or to carry out some particular task or scheme. Practically all religions share the idea that this divine knowledge or wisdom was imparted to their founders, leaders or wise elders, either directly by God himself, or through some intermediary source – messengers, angels, emissaries, oracles, however they may be regarded.

Thus, around 2150BC, Gudea, governor of one of the city states of the Sumerian civilisation in Mesopotamia, claimed that three divine beings had given him plans for a temple.

The great law-giver Hammurabi shared a similar experience. Hammurabi was ruler of Babylon, capital city of Babylonia, about 50 miles south of Baghdad on the River Euphrates. Hammurabi ascended the throne in 1792BC and reigned for 42 years.

The religion of Babylonia involved the worship of many gods and each city-state had its own principal deity and hierarchy of attendant gods: Anu at Erech, Ea at Eridu, Sin at Ur, and Bel (later Marduk), at Babylon itself.

The famous stele, or upright stone, upon which Hammurabi's code of laws is engraved, commemorating him as the first historically documented law-giver, is now in the Louvre, Paris. Above the cuneiform code is a relief carving of the king himself, being instructed to write down the laws by Shamash, a Sun-god. (It is interesting to note that Babylon, first mentioned in a cuneiform tablet dated around 2700BC, is the Greek form of the Hebrew *Babel*, meaning "the gate of God".) Hammurabi's uncompromising laws, with their "eye for an eye, tooth for a tooth" principles, are to some extent echoed in the laws which the Lord gave to Moses, detailed in Exodus.

In a similar way, such Hindu scriptures as the fascinating and beautifully constructed Vedas and Upanishads, are regarded as *sruti* – the revelation of divine truths to elect sages.

Unfortunately, in dealing with beliefs dating back as far as Hammurabi, we have only fragments in which we can examine what is said about these "gods" who appear to have contacted selected individuals. But in the texts of the major religions, there are many more details. The best course, perhaps, is to look at these divine manifestations one by one and try to compare them.

3. Voices In The Sky

"We all know UFOs are real. The question is, where do they come from?"
Capt. Ed Mitchell, US astronaut and sixth man to walk on the Moon (1974)

"The loneliness of personality in the universe weighs heavily upon us. To put it somewhat quaintly, it seems terribly improbable that we should exist."
Austin Farrer: *The Freedom Of The Will* (New York, 1960)

FROM BEFORE 3000BC until the middle of the 14th century BC, Egyptian religion, like that of Babylonia, had flourished as polytheism: the worship of an elaborate system of many gods, major and minor. There was Isis, winged guardian of the dead; Osiris, her husband/brother, master of life and death; Horus, their son; the jackal-headed Anubis; Re-Harakhti, falcon-headed sky-god; the cat goddess Bast, the crocodile-headed god Sebek, and countless others. Then, at some time between 1376 and 1365BC, a most remarkable thing occurred.

Amenophis IV, taking over as pharaoh from his father, suddenly swept away the great pantheon of all the old gods.

He abandoned the royal city of Thebes and ordered a new one built at a place now known as El Armarna, approximately half-way between Thebes and Memphis. The new city, thought to have been built in the incredibly short span of two years, he dedicated to Aten, a new god represented by a disc with long rays extending from it. On the end of each ray was a huge human hand.

He then discarded his name of Amenophis in favour of Akhenaten (or Ikhnaten), meaning "pleasing to the Aten".

Until Akhenaten's reign the pharaoh had always been regarded as one among the many gods, usually associated with Re-Harakhti, or Horus, the falcon-headed sky-god. But in introducing Aten as the one and only supreme deity, Akhenaten brushed aside all the other gods and identified himself as spokesman for the new, all-powerful one.

On a stone at the boundary of his new city, Akhenaten declared that it was the god himself who had told him to locate the city there and, in his famous Hymn to Aten, says: "there is none other that knows thee save thy son, Akhenaten. Thou hast made him wise in thy plans and power."

Classical Egyptologists have referred popularly to Akhenaten's poem as a "Hymn to the Sun", and it does indeed associate the god with the Sun.

But when examined closely, the hypothesis that the god *was* the Sun does not entirely make sense.

Before Akhenaten came along, there was already the Sungod, Re, or Ra. If Akhenaten's idea was simply to establish a totally new god and associate himself with the deity to gain supreme power for himself, why choose a symbol that was already claimed by a long-established god?

How would he go about convincing everyone, especially the powerful hierarchy of priests, many of whom would undoubtedly lose a lot of prestige and influence under a new, monotheistic system? Remember, it took only about four years for Akhenaten to establish his new godhead in a specially-built city.

And if Akhenaten literally thought of Aten as the Sun, why, in his hymn, did he say: "there is *none other* that knows thee save thy son, Akhenaten"? Surely, every other Egyptian with eyes to see was well aware of the solar orb that brought warmth, light and life to the Earth?

It is true that, even after the pharaoh had established his city, called Akhetaten ("Horizon of the Aten"), the old capital, Thebes, was still steeped in its pantheon of ancient gods. It is also true that, after Akhenaten's death, his successor, the boy-king Tutankhamun, reintroduced the old gods and had their names re-inscribed on the monuments from which Akhenaten had ordered their removal.

But there is every indication that Tutankhamun, being a mere youth, was forced to do so by the priestly conspirators who wanted to regain their lost power. It is even thought by some commentators that Akhenaten was assassinated on the orders of these priests. Certainly, it is a fact that Tutankhamun, brought up himself as an Aten worshipper, was forced to change his name from Tutankhaten after the pharaoh's death.

There is no evidence that Akhenaten was a cruel, bullying tyrant; the type, perhaps, who single-handed might be able to impose his will on an entire, reluctant nation. There is no suggestion that he was some kind of political bully with the fanatical drive and charisma of a Hitler. Yet, during his reign, his monotheistic system flourished and he was popular with his people.

In fact, honesty seems to have been a hallmark of the Aten period, certainly so far as the pharaoh and his family were concerned. His wife was Nefertiti, whose face today is known to millions because of the beautiful sculpture of her discovered at El Amarna and now in Berlin's Dahlem Museum. Together, the royal couple, unlike previous monarchs, paraded in public freely, showing off their six daughters proudly, like any happy family.

And the stylisation that had hitherto prevailed in Egyptian art was, during Akhenaten's reign, replaced by a less idealised kind, with a refreshingly honest mode of execution. No longer did the pharaoh appear as a shining member of the divinities, but as a noble-featured, but nonetheless patently human figure with a face that suggests great intelligence, sensitivity and compassion. Definitely not the face of a megalomaniac who would invent a new religion simply to further his own power.

Indeed, Akhenaten was a tall, gangly, somewhat ungainly figure, with a distinctive pot-belly – all of which features are clearly depicted in surviving reliefs and murals of him.

Akhenaten, it would seem, had in some mysterious manner become one of the elect, chosen by the god to transmit a new philosophy to his people. Perhaps the Sun-disc, with its long arms extended in friendship, as depicted in the art of the Aten period, represented not simply the celestial fire, but some extra-terrestrial intelligence that had chosen to impart wisdom to one of Earth's great leaders.

Why I believe so, I will explain later. I will also suggest an explanation of why the influence of this intelligence lasted only a few decades in the case of Akhenaten. Sadly, the enlightened pharaoh – though some have dubbed him a heretic – left no exact impression of how his god made himself known. But it may be significant that Aten's temples were open-air structures.

For it was in the open air that the unearthly intelligence – the same, I suspect, that made itself known to the pharaoh – manifested to other great leaders, like those of the Children of Israel.

The intervention of God in the affairs of the Israelites dates back, if we take the five books of Moses (The Pentateuch) as reference, as far as Adam, Cain, Abel and Noah. As I have already dealt with the so-called "myths" of the Creation, it will perhaps be best in treating the subject of Israel's "election" to begin with Noah.

Traditions of a Great Deluge like that described in Genesis occur among many peoples throughout the world. The Book of Genesis describes how, ten generations after Adam, the Hebrew god Yahweh decides to drown all mankind, which has become corrupt and wicked – except for Noah, an upright, godfearing man. Unlike many other Old Testament stories, Noah's actual contact with God, such as the manner of His manifestation, is not described in any detail. God simply "speaks", declaring his intentions and his reasons for his proposed action, and explaining why Noah and his family will be exempt.

"The LORD saw that the wickedness of man was great in the earth, and that every imagination of the thoughts of his heart was only evil continually. And the LORD was sorry that he had made man on the earth, and it grieved him to his heart."
(Genesis 6:5–6)

And further:

"So the LORD said, 'I will blot out man whom I have created from the face of the ground, man and beast and creeping things and birds of the air, for I am sorry that I have made them.'"
(Genesis 6:7)

The next verse says:

"But Noah found grace in the eyes of the LORD."

Noah was the only man whom God considered "righteous... blameless in his generation," just one man who "walked with God".

God warns Noah of his plans to destroy the world by a great flood and instructs him to build an ark "of gopher wood". He gives precise instructions on the dimensions of the vessel and which creatures, along with members of Noah's family, to take aboard.

The main feature about Noah's story, from the point of view of this book, however, is that *someone*, some great intelligence, warns him of an immense impending disaster – and tells him how to deal with it.

Tantalisingly enough, archaeologists have found evidence of considerable flooding in Mesopotamia. While excavating a Sumerian burial pit at the ancient site of Ur, on the River Euphrates, in 1929, the English researcher (later Sir) Leonard Woolley, found an 8.2-foot stratum of alluvial clay, containing no shards or rubbish. Beneath it, he unearthed relics of an earlier culture. Woolley asserted that a massive deluge had indeed inundated the area some time late in the fourth millennium BC. Other archaeologists following in his footsteps, later discovered similar flood deposits at other sites in Mesopotamia.

However, since some archaeologists have dated these findings a millennium later than Woolley, debate and controversy continues as to whether these were indeed remnants of Noah's deluge. Down the years, there have even been attempts to try to find the remains of Noah's Ark.

A supposed fragment of the Ark now reposes in a museum attached to the cathedral of Echmiadzin, headquarters of the Armenian Church. It was brought there in the fourth century by an expedition to the slopes of Mount Ararat, which lies over the Turkish border and is visible from Echmiadzin. The cathedral, founded in 304AD, three years after Christianity had become the state religion, also has in its museum the tip of a spear, set in gold, which it is claimed was that which pierced the side of Jesus on the cross. (See Chapter 17)

In August 1984, American explorer Marvin Steffins, president of International Expeditions, was detained for several hours at Yesilkoy Airport, Istanbul. A week earlier, he had announced that he had found remnants of the ark on Mount Ararat. Turkish customs officials freed Steffins, his wife Marjorie and daughter Marianne, after several hours' interrogation and after they had handed over four kilograms of their "findings".

At a press conference in Ankara, Steffins showed samples of small, oxidized pieces of flat-shaped rocks and wood. He also had small packages of sand and soil.

"We believe further archaeological investigation and scientific investigation will prove this to be the site of the remains of the Ark of Noah," Steffins said. "The boat shape and the dimensions correspond to the ones given in the book of Genesis."

Mount Ararat – 16,945 feet – lies in a sensitive military area near the borders of Turkey, Iran and the former Soviet Union. At the time of Steffins' visit, the zone was closed to foreigners because the Soviets had complained that previous expeditions had included cover-up intelligence operations.

Since the incident, little further has been heard of the alleged find, but in December 1986, Turkish "officials" were said to have confirmed the claim of another American arkhunter, Ron Wyatt, a 53-year-old anaesthetist from Nashville, Tennessee. Press reports said the officials from the Ministry of the Interior were studying a "boat-shaped formation" on a hill near the Turkey-Iran border.

"They called me and said they had decided it was the remains of Noah's Ark, partly based on my research," Wyatt was quoted as saying. Ms. Mine Uneler, of the Ministry, said: "Our government exactly agrees with Mr. Wyatt."

"Other", unnamed geologists, however, were said to believe the boat-like formation could have been natural – the result of millennia of erosion. Again, there has been little, if any, further news...

However, another, even earlier story of a great flood which to some extent parallels that of Noah, is in the classic Babylonian Epic of Gilgamesh. It originated in ancient Sumer, in what is nowadays Iraq. The earliest form of it is known as the Epic of Zuisudra, which was found on inscribed clay tablets at Nippur in 1890.

The Sumerian/Babylonian epic poem tells how the god Enlil decides to destroy "the seeds of mankind".

Its hero is Utnapishtim of Shuruppak, who is warned while asleep by the god Ea, that Enlil, chief of the later Babylonian gods, plans to send a flood which will wipe out the human race.

As in the Genesis account, Ea gives Utnapishtim instructions to build an ark. The hero does so, taking aboard his family, servants, silver, gold and "the seeds of all living things".

In the Gilgamesh account, the flood-storm "waged war like an army" for seven days and nights – as opposed to the 40 days and nights of the Noah story. On the seventh day, Utnapishtim's vessel comes to rest on Mount Nisir and, to test whether it is safe to disembark, he releases first a dove, then a swallow, and finally a raven. (Noah sent only a raven, then a dove).

"When the seventh day came," says Utnapishtim, "I sent forth a dove. I released it. It went, the dove; it came back, as there was no place, it came back.

"I sent forth a swallow, I released it. It went, the swallow; it came back, as there was no place, it came back.

"I sent forth a raven, I released it; it went, the raven, and beheld the subsidence of the waters.

"It eats, it splashes about, it caws, it comes not back."

Atop the mountain – again like Noah, upon disembarking – Utnapishtim offers up a sacrifice. Enlil accepts the offering and confers immortality upon the hero and his wife. (Noah is said to have lived 600 years).

Now while the details of Noah's actual contact with God are sparse, the Book of Genesis does at least tell us that God not only spoke with Abram, but "appeared to him". (Genesis 12:7) But there is no *description* of this appearance.

However, what is perhaps most interesting about the Genesis story of Abram and his nephew, Lot, is the account of the destruction of the twin cities of Sodom and Gomorrah.

Abram, born in "Ur of the Chaldees", according to Genesis, is promised by God that he will be progenitor of the children of Israel, who will inherit the Land of Canaan. Oddly enough, Ur of the Chaldees, or Chaldeans, is regarded by many scholars as an anachronism, because the city was not inhabited by the Chaldeans, who migrated from the Persian Gulf, until around the 11th century BC. Biblical archaeologists, meanwhile, tend to place the story of Lot somewhat earlier, between the 20th and 16th centuries BC.

Be that as it may, Abram sets up camp at a place between Beth-el and Hai, while Lot goes off to the city of Sodom. At this spot, God asks Abram to prepare him an offering of a heifer, she-goat and a ram, all three years old, along with a turtledove and a pigeon. Abram lays them out on the ground and drives off any carrion. He eventually goes to sleep and "lo, a great horror of darkness fell upon him". (Genesis 15:7)

Then, in verse 17:

"And it came to pass that, when the sun went down, and it was dark, behold, a smoking furnace and a burning lamp that passed between those pieces [of meat]."

There is some suggestion here that, for an unknown reason, God cannot show himself to Abram and, after putting him into some kind of trance, passes stealthily by to pick up the meat.

After God has warned Abram of his intentions toward the twin cities of sin and evil, Lot is next to experience the divine presence. Two "angels" appear to Lot at the gate of Sodom. He persuades them to be guests at his home, but before they retire, the corrupt men of the city surround the house, lusting after the two strangers.

"Where are the men who came to you tonight? Bring them out to us, that we may know them." (Genesis 19:4–5)

"But the men [angels] put forth their hand and pulled Lot into the house to them, and shut to the door. And they smote the men that were at the door with blindness, both small and great: so that they wearied themselves to find the door." (Genesis 19:10–11)

It is at this point that these two beings with unearthly powers – variously described as "men" and "angels" – warn Lot to get himself and his family out because they are going to destroy the city. We have seen that God has not revealed himself properly, but that these two representatives have done so and, as far as Lot is concerned, have the appearance of men.

Supposing that, for technical reasons, God cannot appear – unsuitable life-support conditions, danger of infection or radiation – is it so unreasonable to assume that these men-like emissaries were perhaps cybernauts, or robots? Men would surely find them less daunting, less frightening, perhaps, than the appearance of an extra-terrestrial intelligence itself.

These men-like beings, then, urge Lot and his kin to escape to the mountains – and warn them not to look back.

"Then the LORD rained upon Sodom and upon Gomorrah brimstone and fire from the LORD out of heaven; And he overthrew those cities and all the plain, and all the inhabitants of the cities and that which grow upon the ground. But his [Lot's] wife looked back from behind him and she became a pillar of salt." (Genesis 19:24–26)

The next day, from some distance away at Mamre, Abram is another eye-witness: He "looked toward Sodom and Gomorrah and toward all the land of the plain, and beheld, and, lo, the smoke of the country went up as the smoke of the furnace".

We have even further accounts of the holocaust. The Dead Sea Scrolls, which partly consist of an alternative version of the Old Testament, say:

"A column of smoke and dust rose into the air like a column of smoke issuing from the bowels of the Earth. It rained sulphur and fire on Sodom and Gomorrah, and destroyed the town and the whole plain and every growing plant. And Lot's wife looked back and was turned into a pillar of salt."

And Lot lived at Isoar, but afterwards went to the mountains because he was afraid to remain at Isoar. The people were warned that they must go away from the place... and *not stay in exposed places*; nor should they look... but hide beneath the ground. Those fugitives who looked back were blinded and died.

Before 1945, it was easy to take such descriptive writing as highly imaginative accounts of God hurling down thunderbolts of doom. Then came Hiroshima... and Nagasaki and, later, the hydrogen bomb. We are left to wonder about this God of the Children of Israel.

Some commentators have suggested that what occurred at the twin cities was a violent volcanic eruption. But if this were so, why the advice not to look back? It is quite possible to view such phenomena from a safe distance. And why also the suggestion in the Dead Sea Scrolls that the fugitives take refuge under ground?

Those who have seen film footage of the first atom bomb test in the New Mexican desert will recall how the outside observers had to turn their backs on the initial flash, wore protective goggles and watched from what was considered a "safe" distance.

Nor would molten volcanic lava or ash necessarily turn someone it fell upon into a "pillar of salt". In any case, presumably, Lot and the rest of his family could not have been considerably further away from the blasted cities than Lot's wife.

It may also be significant that even today, visitors to the southern region of the Dead Sea, are struck by the odd configurations of salt deposits in the region.

In Hiroshima, there is a bank building with a strange, permanent shadow on the steps outside; an almost perfect outline of a man. He sat in the early morning sun on the steps of the bank, eating a bowl of rice, his legs stretched out comfortably. Then, at 8.15AM on August 6, 1945, he was blasted – fused – into the stone steps; one of 60,000 who died that day when the atom bomb feel. No one knows his name. All that remains is a grey shadow that fades gradually with the years. Lot's wife, I would submit, may have suffered a similar, terrible fate.

Nor, I think, can it be denied that the references to the devastation of the surrounding plain and the shunning of the territory sounds all too similar to the lingering radiation blight and sickness that followed Hiroshima and Nagasaki.

But, the rationalists may ask: a nuclear explosion all those millennia ago?

The answer is: yes, quite possibly.

In September 1972 the French Academy of Sciences was presented with a report on the subject of the finding of the remnants of a nuclear chain reaction that took place on Earth – in *prehistoric* times. It was handed over by no less a luminary than Dr. Francois Perrin, former chairman of the French High Commission for Atomic Energy.

Dr. Perrin first became curious over a report by workers at the French Uranium Enrichment Centre that uranium ore from a mine at Oklo, in Gabon, West Africa, showed a significant depletion of uranium 235. While all uranium deposits on Earth have 0.715% of this element, its levels in that from the Gabon mine were as little as 0.621%.

The only solution seemed to be that the deficient uranium 235 had been burned up in a nuclear chain reaction.

Dr. Perrin's report ended with the suggestion that the uranium from the Oklo mine had been subject to a *spontaneous* chain reaction, triggered by natural causes.

The uranium deposits were estimated geologically to date back 1.7 billion years and, because that was the time when the element would have been in its purest form, Dr. Perrin ventured that that was when the nuclear reaction took place.

But after publication of Dr. Perrin's report, the former head of the United States Atomic Energy Commission, Glenn T. Seaborg, who in 1941 discovered the element plutonium, raised some doubts about the Frenchman's conclusions. He drew attention to the fact that, for uranium to burn up in a chain reaction, precise conditions are required.

To sustain the reaction, extremely pure water is required as each atom is split, to retard the release of neutrons. A ratio of a few parts per million of any impurity would be sufficient to stop the reaction.

And, Seaborg emphasized, *there is no water anywhere on Earth that occurs naturally in sufficient a state of purity.*

As the generations of Noah, Abram – by now become Abraham, for Qabalistic reasons I will not enter into here – and Lot progress, the elect of the Old Testament appear to grow more adept at the application of strange powers. Jacob was the last of this lineage to gaze in awestruck wonder at the unusual events that accompanied the manifestations of God. Jacob, the younger son of Isaac, appears to stumble upon something that smacks of extra-terrestrial visitation:

"...and behold a ladder set up on the earth, and the top of it reached to heaven; and behold, the angels of God ascending and descending on it."

The experience is recounted as a dream in Genesis 28. But was Jacob really asleep? Or was this the same kind of dark, paralytic trance that Abram experienced when the curious lights appeared near the meat offerings? In any event, the Lord appears at the top of this "ladder" and reaffirms his promise to the Israelites.

The entire incident sounds as if Jacob had (accidentally?) stumbled upon an extra-terrestrial vessel, its occupants going about some undefined task, moving in and out by ladder. He was then immobilised in some strange manner and reassured, told not to worry. God would keep his promise.

4. The Master Of Dreams And The Magus

"Deep into the darkness peering, long I stood there, wondering, fearing,
Doubting, dreaming dreams no mortal ever dared to dream before."
Edgar Allan Poe (1809–1849)

STRANGE AND wondrous though the lives of his predecessors may seem, Moses stands out above all the early Hebrew adepts as the truly elect leader of Israel.

But it was through Joseph, 11th of Jacob's children – by four different women, two wives and two concubines – that the Israelites first came to reside in the land of Egypt. He was the first son of Rachel, Jacob's second wife and the one he really loved.

Joseph was hated by his 11 brothers – there was one stepsister, Dinah – because Jacob "loved him more than all his brothers" and doted upon him. Through the brothers' jealousy and hatred, he was sold into slavery and thrown into prison on false charges. The brothers took Joseph's famed "coat of many colours", splashed with goat's blood, to their father, Jacob, who had made the coat for his favourite son. Naturally, Jacob assumed the youth had been killed by a wild beast.

Exactly what the significance of Joseph's colourful coat was is not certain. *Passim*, the Hebrew word used to describe the coat, was interpreted by the Greek translators of the Pentateuch as "multi-coloured". And this passed into the King James version as "a coat of many colours".

Various scholars have suggested different reasons for the singling out of this garment as worthy of mention: that it was an ornamented ceremonial robe of some kind, or that it was a long robe with sleeves, as opposed to the rough, animal-skin tunics that Joseph's brothers might have worn.

Another factor that angered the brothers against Joseph was his apparent possession of some kind of psychic faculties; his ability to interpret dreams. And the interpretations he gave were scarcely conducive to currying favour, either.

In the first of his dreams, the sons were binding sheaves in the fields. The sheaf that Joseph had bound stood upright, while those of his brothers bowed – "made obeisance" – to it. In the second dream, Joseph said: "Behold, the sun and the moon and the eleven stars made obeisance to me." (Genesis 37:9)

This offended even the doting father, Jacob:

"What is this dream that thou hast dreamed? Shall I and thy mother and thy brethren indeed come to bow down ourselves to thee to the earth?" (Genesis 37:10)

It was after these incidents that the brothers decided to dispose of their favoured brother. The brothers were tending Jacob's flocks to the north of Hebron. At Jacob's bidding, Joseph, in his multi-coloured coat, went to see how they were getting on. But when he got to Shechem, where he had expected them to be, he was told they had gone to Dothan, a town outside Jacob's protective jurisdiction.

As Joseph approached the town, the brothers saw him and said to one another: "Behold, this dreamer cometh." (Genesis 37:19) In fact, the word used in the original Hebrew literally means "master of dreams".

They were conspiring to kill him but Reuben, the eldest brother, intervened and persuaded them to cast Joseph into a pit. Reuben secretly hoped to return later and rescue him, but before he could do so, a camel caravan came by, bearing gum, balm and myrrh, en route from Gilead to Egypt. The brothers promptly sold Joseph into slavery for 20 silver shekels. It was then that Joseph's bloodstained coat was taken and shown to Jacob.

Transported to Egypt, Joseph was sold to Potiphar, a nobleman, captain of the guard and a royal official. His name means "He whom Re has given".

Joseph quickly became popular and favoured in Potiphar's household and from being merely a slave was appointed overseer.

Potiphar's wife, who is not named, led to Joseph's imprisonment. She tried to seduce him and, when he resisted, she tore part of his garment and accused him of trying to rape her.

Instead of having Joseph executed, as he was legally entitled, Potiphar had the youth thrown into prison. There, Joseph quickly gained favour and was made overseer of his fellow inmates. And it was here, once again, that Joseph's talents as an interpreter of dreams was demonstrated.

He correctly forecast the dreams of the Pharaoh's butler and chief baker, both of whom were fellow prisoners. The butler's dream, of squeezing grapes from a three-branched vine into the Pharaoh's cup, he divined as meaning that the man would be back in his master's service within three days. The baker dreamt of three white baskets on his head from the uppermost of which the birds ate "all manner of bakemeats".

"And Joseph answered and said, This is the interpretation thereof: The three baskets are three days.

"Yet within three days shall Pharaoh lift up thy head from off thee, and shall hang thee on a tree; and the birds shall eat thy flesh from off thee." (Genesis 40:18-19).

Both dreams came true. Joseph asked the more fortunate butler to mention him to the Pharaoh, but the butler forgot him until two years had gone by, when his master had two seemingly prophetic dreams and could find no one to interpret them satisfactorily. Joseph was sent for and correctly deciphered them. A dream of seven well-fed cows ("kine") being devoured by seven lean ones which notwithstanding grew no fatter, and of seven healthy heads of grain being devoured by seven blighted ones, he interpreted as forecasting seven years of fruitful harvest, followed by seven years of famine.

Not only did the Pharaoh heed Joseph's warning, and stocked up his granaries in readiness for the famine, but he freed Joseph and appointed him viceroy of all Egypt, in charge of agricultural supplies. He presented him with his royal signet ring and named him Zaphnath-paaneah, "God speaks! He is living!" He gave Jacob a wife: Asenath, the daughter of Potipherah, priest of On (Heliopolis), and they had two sons, Manasseh and Ephraim.

As the famine spread eastwards to Canaan, the ageing Jacob sent 10 of his sons to buy grain from Egypt. On meeting Joseph, the brothers did not recognise him, but bowed to him – thus fulfilling Joseph's earlier dream.

Joseph then set his brothers a series of trials to test their true character. After they had undergone them to his satisfaction – including the emotional blackmail of one of them, Judah, into begging to be substituted for the condemned Benjamin, the youngest, whom he had framed for theft – he made himself known.

"I am Joseph your brother, whom ye sold into Egypt. Now therefore be not grieved, nor angry with yourselves, that ye sold me hither: for God did send me before you to preserve life."

Although archaeologists have been unable to discover any trace of the particular famine experienced in Joseph's time, ancient Egyptian writings have recorded various periods when the Nile, upon which the land's fertility depends, failed to rise to its normal levels to irrigate the rich alluvial plains on either side. And a 2nd century BC inscription, actually records a seven-year period when this occurred – during the 28th century BC. In it, Djoser, earliest of the pyramid-building pharaohs, says:

"I was in distress on the Great Throne and those in the palace were in heart's affliction from a great evil, since the Nile had not come in my time for a space of seven years. Grain was scant, fruits were dried up, and everything which they eat was short. Every man robbed his companion."

"And Joseph died, and all his brethren, and all that generation.

"And the children of Israel were fruitful, and increased abundantly, and multiplied, and waxed exceeding mighty; and the land was filled with them."
(Exodus 1:6–7)

So the Book of Exodus sums up the years of plenty and prosperity of the Israelites in the land of Egypt. But then:

"...there arose up a new king over Egypt which did not know Joseph.

"And he said unto his people, Behold, the people of the children of Israel are more and mightier than we:

"Come on, let us deal wisely with them; lest they multiply, and it come to pass, that, when there falleth out any war, they join also unto our enemies, and fight against us, and so get them up and out of the land." (Exodus 1:8–10)

The Bible does not identify this unsympathetic, what would now be termed racist, pharaoh, but some scholars have suggested he was Seti I, first monarch of the 19th Dynasty (1308–1290BC).

Whoever he may have been, this pharaoh launched several programmes to try to reduce the Israelites' growing numbers. First, he tried enforced hard labour, putting them to task on his extensive building projects of many new cities, hoping that it would slowly wear them down, killing off all the young men. But the Hebrews went on multiplying and flourishing, so they were then put to "all kinds of work" in the fields. This, too, failed to reduce their numbers even though their lives were "bitter with hard bondage". (Exodus 1:14)

Next, he ordered the two Hebrew midwives, Shiphrah and Puah, to kill all sons born to Hebrew women. But, fearful of God, they refused to carry out the pharaoh's orders. Their excuse was that, unlike the Egyptians, Hebrew women were so lively and vigorous that, invariably, they delivered their offspring before the midwives arrived.

The pharaoh's final ploy was to order his people to cast any Hebrew-born male child into the Nile. However, one married couple of the house of Levi hid their baby son for three months. Then the mother, fearful that she could hide him no longer, "took for him an ark of bulrushes, and daubed it with slime and with pitch, and put the child therein; and she laid it in the flags by the river's brink. And his sister stood afar off, to wit what would be done to him". (Exodus 2:3)

The child was discovered by the pharaoh's daughter, who, when the babe cried, took pity on him and said, "This is one of the Hebrews' children". The sister then

---

offered to find a Hebrew woman to nurse the child – and brought the mother. She was actually paid by the pharaoh's daughter for nursing the baby until he was weaned, when he was returned to the pharaoh's daughter. She called him Moses, or Mosheh, a name similar to the ancient Egyptian word meaning "be born" or "child" – present in such names as those of the pharaohs Tutmose or Rameses. In its Hebrew form, though, Moses may be phonetically related to mashah, meaning "drawn out" (from the waters). Indeed, Exodus 2:10, says: "And she called his name Moses: and she said, Because I drew him out of the water."

The Old Testament text tells nothing of Moses' growing up and education, but the Jewish historian, Flavius Josephus (37–c.101AD), in his *Antiquities Of The Jews*, describes his service as a general in the pharaoh's army. And the Graeco-Jewish philosopher Philo (born c.20–10BC), a native of Alexandria, described how Moses absorbed all fields of knowledge and excelled all the teachers that were brought to him from all the civilised world. Later Jewish lore ascribes to Moses the invention of hieroglyphics, inventing machinery for irrigation and teaching philosophy to the Greeks.

Despite being raised as an Egyptian noble, Moses was fully aware of his Hebrew roots – he killed an Egyptian he found "smiting" one of his brethren. The following day, when he caught two Hebrews fighting and intervened, one of them said: "Who made thee a prince and a judge over us? Intendest thou to kill me as thou killest the Egyptian?" (Exodus 2:14)

Realising that his act of murder must be generally known, Moses fled to the Arabian peninsula, where he became a shepherd among a nomadic tribe and married Zipporah, one of the seven daughters of the Midianite priest, Jethro. They had a son, whom he called Gershom – "a stranger here" – "for he said, I have been a stranger in a strange land." (Exodus 2:22)

While still working as a shepherd, tending his father-in-law Jethro's flocks, Moses came to know that he had been singled out by God. Back in Egypt, the old pharaoh died. If Seti I was indeed the pharaoh of Exodus, the monarch who succeeded him was Rameses II (reigned c.1300–1234BC). The suffering of Israelites in bondage worsened and they cried to God for help.

About this time, Moses the shepherd came to the "mountain of God" – Horeb, in Midian, near Sinai. And it was here that Moses received his first "divine revelation", as described in Exodus 3:2:

"And the angel of the Lord appeared unto him in a flame of fire out of the midst of a bush: and he looked, and behold, the bush burned with fire, and the bush was not consumed."

One seemingly rationalist theory for this phenomenon is that the bush was a type of desert plant, *fraxinella*. It contains a highly inflammable oil which can, given the right conditions, be set afire by the Sun. The burning oil is quickly consumed without the plant being damaged. But, since this is a natural phenomenon which would doubtless have been known to nomadic shepherds of the period, it is unlikely that it would have been included in so mysterious a passage as described in Exodus.

Rather, the fact that Moses was warned "draw not nigh hither" (Exodus 3:5), suggests that something particularly unique and momentous took place. Could it not be, perhaps, that what Moses saw was the plume of flame beneath a descending extra-terrestrial vessel, behind some dense vegetation? Such an event would surely make the bushes appear to be on fire and yet not consumed.

Another curious detail during this episode is that described in Exodus 3:5:

"...put off thy shoes from thy feet, for the place whereon thou standest is holy ground."

Later, in Exodus 4, God apparently teaches Moses the magical arts – a few devices designed to convince the pharaoh that he is countering a mighty celestial power and ought to allow the Israelites to go free. He taught Moses how to turn his staff into a serpent by casting it on the ground; to make his hand appear leprous by thrusting it into his bosom, and to turn water into blood.

On several occasions, Moses and Aaron, a Levite, who was instructed by God in the desert and encountered him on Horeb, went before the pharaoh, saying: "Thus saith the LORD God of Israel, Let my people go." (Exodus 5:1) But the pharaoh would not listen and imposed even greater burdens upon the enslaved Israelites. Later Moses and Aaron went before the pharaoh with such impressive, seemingly magical displays described above, but neither the monarch nor his court magicians were impressed or persuaded.

Again on God's instructions, the pair confronted the pharaoh and his court. They turned all the rivers and waters into blood, sent plagues of frogs, lice, flies, murrain that killed all the cattle, and a plague of boils.

All of these phenomena could conceivably be arranged using today's knowledge of bio-engineering. So if these events indeed occurred, it is fair to assume that the entity that taught Moses how to create such havoc among the Egyptians was highly versed in some form of bacteriological warfare and, as already demonstrated by the Flood, perhaps in controlling the elements:

"And Moses stretched forth his rod towards heaven: and the LORD sent thunder and hail, and the fire ran along upon the ground; and the LORD rained hail upon the land of Egypt." (Exodus 9:23)

God, it appears, could also produce – "fire that ran along upon the ground" – something that is the equivalent of napalm. A plague of locusts, a period of darkness then, the mysterious slaughter of all Egypt's firstborn – people and animals. It was the final blow to the stubbornness of the pharaoh. Today, the same effect could be achieved by bombarding the unborn foetus with a lethal dose of radium. Is that what God's "angel of death" did to the Egyptian mothers?

The Israelites were spared by marking their doors with blood, an act that evolved into the institution of the Hebrew Passover. They were also instructed to stay indoors and feast only on *freshly-slaughtered* mutton and unleavened bread. God obviously did not want them to consume meat from the fields that might be contaminated with the blight (radiation?) that affected the cattle.

With that, the children of Israel were out of Egypt, hotly pursued by the understandably enraged Egyptians. But *something*, something utterly other-worldly, was on the Hebrews' side:

"And the LORD went before them by day in a pillar of cloud, to lead them the way; and by night in a pillar of fire, to give them light; to go by day and by night." (Exodus 13:21)

These phenomena, seemingly produced to order – a smokescreen and a giant flare, possibly on some kind of remote-controlled unit – stood between the camps of the Egyptians and the Israelites to keep them apart as they approached the Red Sea. Then, after giving the Israelites precise instructions on where to wait by the shore:

"And Moses stretched out his hand over the sea; and the LORD caused the sea to go back by a strong east wind all that night, and made the sea dry land, and the waters were divided." (Exodus 14:21)

Even if this were some freak of nature that happened at the opportune moment, how could Moses have *known* it was going to happen? Clearly, this God-entity was capable of technological wonders beyond our comprehension – a force-field, perhaps, that held back the waters?

With the towering walls of the divided sea on either side, the Israelites crossed over. Then, as the Egyptians followed, the force-field, or whatever power it may have been, was switched off and the waters crashed in on the pursuers. At last, the Children of Israel were liberated.

Even later, when Moses' people began to bemoan their plight, saying they were better off in Egypt than wandering in the desert, the God-entity provided. Quail and "manna" fell mysteriously from the skies. Manna is described as "a small round thing, as small as the hoar frost on the ground", and "like coriander seed, white; and the taste of it was like wafers made with honey". (Exodus 16:31)

There have been many speculations as to exactly what this "manna" was. Greek monks – Coptics, Gnostics – living in the Holy Land in the first millennium AD thought it was a sweet substance excreted from the burrowings of insects into the bark of the tamarisk tree. Once dried, it apparently solidifies. The nomadic Bedouins apparently still eat it in our own times. But, like the somewhat shaky "explanations" of the destruction of Sodom and Gomorrah, the question must be asked: how come the Children of Israel, long used to desert conditions, did not already recognise this phenomenon for what it was?

Later, (Numbers 20:8–11) Moses – instructed by God – is seen to extract water from a rock by striking it with a rod: "the water came out abundantly and the congregation drank, and their beasts also".

He also affects the outcome of a battle between the Israelites and the Amalekites, by the raising and lowering of his staff (Exodus 17:11–13). What was this rod, or staff? Was it some kind of signal to an extra-terrestrial entity that power was required to perform some task? Or was it some unknown, highly technological device, capable of creating force fields, extracting minerals from the earth and carrying out bacteriological changes? We are merely left to wonder and speculate.

The next important event in Exodus, so far as this survey is concerned, is the strange manifestation/non-manifestation of the entity known throughout as the Lord, God, or Yahweh. First, God tells Moses he will "come down in the sight of all the people upon Mount Sinai". (Exodus 19:11) But he warns Moses not to let the people go up on the mountain, nor to touch the border of it. There is, it seems, still some insurmountable difficulty in effecting an appearance without endangering (or terrifying?) the people. Moses, however, who has already had contact of a limited kind, must be in some way immune; he has either developed, or been endowed with, a resistance to whatever danger there may be. The relevant passages speak for themselves:

"And it came to pass on the third day in the morning, that there were thunders and lightnings, and a thick cloud upon the mount, and the voice of the trumpet exceeding loud; so that all the people that were in the camp trembled,

"And Moses brought forth the people out of the camp to meet with God; and they stood at the nether part of the mount.

"And Mount Sinai was altogether on a smoke, because the LORD descended upon it in fire; and the smoke thereof ascended as the smoke of a furnace, and the whole mount quaked greatly.

"And when the voice of the trumpet sounded long, and waxed louder and louder,

Moses spake, and God answered him by a voice.

"And the LORD came down upon Mount Sinai, on the top of the mount: and the LORD called Moses up to the top of the mount; and Moses went up." (Exodus 19:16–20)

Apart from the idea that the whole account is entirely fabricated, there is no other sane interpretation of these events than that some kind of alien vessel landed on the mountain, belching smoke and flame. The people stood back as they had been warned so that the blast would not harm them. Then, it would seem, some kind of communications/loud-hailer system comes into operation and addresses Moses. The Lord, the extra-terrestrial entity, descends from the vehicle and Moses goes up to meet him.

Moses, Aaron, Nadab, Abihu and 70 of the elders of Israel are allowed to approach the visitor, but *only* Moses is allowed to "come near the LORD". Yet, we are told:

"And they saw the God of Israel: and there was under his feet, as it were a paved work of a sapphire stone, and as it were the body of heaven in his clearness.

"And upon the nobles of the children of Israel he laid not his hand: also they saw God, and did eat and drink." (Exodus 24:10–11)

This rather obscure description is difficult to interpret. But it *could* suggest that what the elders saw was some kind of vehicle, detached from the main body of a space vessel; a device made of some transparent blue material and possibly a clear substance, such as glass, plastic or quartz. How were they to know whether what they saw was the Lord or not?

Moses then goes up into the mount and is engulfed in a cloud, which covers the peak for six days. He is eventually called up even higher and disappears for 40 days and nights. Why this time lapse? We are not told precisely what goes on for that period, perhaps because Moses was unable to describe it in the everyday language of his times. There is, however, a possible explanation.

Whereas earlier experiences of this God were vague, full of awe and somewhat mystical, by Moses' day, contact has developed to a much more sophisticated degree. Where hints of telepathic or remote audio contact are present in earlier accounts, Moses' experience emerges as a much more personal affair; no angel/automaton messengers or intermediaries – he is called into the very presence of the unearthly intelligence itself.

Now one of the first rules of space exploration has already been formulated for astronauts of the future: if any alien life-forms are encountered, there should be *no interference* with that life-form. The immediate dangers are obvious: either the astronauts could contaminate and destroy a living, evolutionary process, or become themselves contaminated and bring alien bacteria back to Earth with possibly disastrous consequences.

The British astronomer Sir Fred Hoyle and his colleague Chandra Wickramasinghe indirectly point up this possibility in their book, *Diseases From Space* (J.M. Dent, 1980). Their thesis was that micrometeorites – minute dust particles from space – because of their size, descend gently to sea level without damage to their organic contents. Then, like astronauts from their modules, the biologically active contents emerge and take effect.

So perhaps the 40-day period that Moses spends upon the mountain in part constitutes some kind of conditioning, some inoculation process that will eliminate the dangers of such close contact on either side. The rest of his sojourn is spent receiving the Commandments and Laws and, most interesting of all from our viewpoint,

---

directions for building the mysterious Ark of the Covenant.

To many theologians, the Ark was merely symbolic of the pact that God made with the children of Israel. A stylised, ornate, portable container in which the Laws will be kept. But, once having made such interpretations, scholars generally rarely go back to re-examine the possible alternatives in the light of modern technology. While re-reading the Old Testament in this light, I was amazed at the information its books contained; details that, in the pre-nuclear, pre-space age, seemed perhaps insignificant. *Here, staring us in the face, was an eyewitness account of visits from extra-terrestrial beings, the equipment they used, and an apparent vested interest in the affairs of Earth's inhabitants.*

This Ark, for all its apparent simplistic form in the Biblical description, emerges as something more than a reliquary for the Laws of God. It sounds for all the world like some kind of receiver. We have seen how difficult, through reasons unknown, contact can be made between the God-power and men. Why shouldn't that be made easier through a piece of equipment similar to a transmitter/receiver? Here is how the Ark is described:

"And they shall make an ark of shittim wood: two cubits and a half shall be the length thereof [about 45 inches]; and a cubit and a half the breadth thereof [27 inches], and a cubit and a half the height thereof.

"And thou shalt overlay it with pure gold within and without shalt thou overlay it, and shalt make upon it a crown of gold round about.

"And thou shalt cast four rings of gold for it, and put them in the four corners thereof; and two rings shall be in the one side of it, and two rings in the other side of it.

"And thou shalt make staves of shittim wood and overlay them with gold.

"And thou shalt put the staves into the rings by the sides of the ark, that the ark may be borne with them.

"The staves shall be in the rings of the ark: they shall not be taken from it." (Exodus 25:10–15)

Could these "rings" perhaps be some form of electrical coils, or even circular aerials, rather than simply part of the transportation fitments? The admonition not to remove the staves and the reference to the Ark being "borne" could just as easily refer to it as bearing messages.

For after giving instructions to place God's testimony in the Ark and for the construction of a "mercy seat" with two "cherubims" of beaten gold at each end, to go on top of the structure, there follows this intriguing information:

"And there I will meet with thee, and I will commune with thee from above the mercy seat from between the two cherubims which are upon the ark of the testimony, of all things which I will give thee in commandment unto the children of Israel." (Exodus 25:22)

It is possible that the Israelites did not construct the Ark properly to meet the specifications of a communications system, and used it merely to house the Covenant. But there was definitely some form of power source built into the device. In a later book of the Old Testament, it actually kills a man who touches it:

"And when they came to Nachon's threshing floor, Uzzah put forth his hand to the ark of God, and took hold of it; for the oxen shook it.

"And the anger of the Lord was kindled against Uzzah; and God smote him there for his error; and there he died by the ark of God." (Samuel 6:6–7)

Did Uzzah accidentally touch some electrically-charged component in his concern for the ark, which was apparently rocking about on the cart drawn by oxen?

Impossible so long ago? In the Iraqi State Museum, Baghdad, there are ancient fragments of clay vessels containing copper cylinders and iron strips that have been classified as the components of a crude type of galvanic dry battery. They date as long ago as 250BC and were found around 1939 by German archaeologist Wilhelm Konig during excavations of a hill at Khojout Rabu'a, southwest of Baghdad.

Konig, who was then working for the Iraqi Museum, shortly afterwards heard that four similar objects had turned up in the hut of a reputed magician at Seleucia, some miles down the Euphrates. Later, on a visit to Berlin, he found in the city's museum ten more "batteries" similar to those from his original dig. But these were components that had not been assembled.

Konig published his discovery in a book in German, *The Lost Paradise*, which was eventually read by the German-born, American astronomer and rocket scientist, Willy Ley. Ley wrote about the find in various American magazines and the information came to the attention of Willard F.M. Gray, of the General Electric High Voltage Laboratory, in Pittsfield, Massachusetts.

Provided with details of the components, dimensions and diagrams by Ley, Gray built a replica of the battery. It worked perfectly, with an output of about two volts per cell and was still in the Berkshire Museum in Pittsfield in the late 1950s.

Because the electrolyte used by the original makers was not known, Gray used copper sulphate, although it was surmised that citric or acetic acid – both known to the people of the period, the Parthians – would have worked. The cell was a sheet-copper cylinder about five inches long and one-and-a-half inches in diameter. Its edges were soldered with a 60-40 lead-tin alloy. A concave copper disc was fitted into the base of the cylinder and above this was a layer of pitch to insulate it from the electrode. The electrode was an iron rod inserted into an asphalt stopper and pushed into the top of the cylinder.

It is thought by some researchers that the Parthians may have used the batteries for electro-plating and that, being nomadic warriors, rather than craftsmen, they may have learned the skill from the earlier Babylonians or Sumerians.

Despite the relatively weak charge of the batteries, it is possible that a considerable number of them, connected, could conceivably produce an electric shock sufficient to give a human being a sizeable jolt.

It is perhaps very easy to imagine a primitive human coming to the same fate as Uzzah, if he were given a plugged-in television set to play with.

The continuing aura of mystery shrouding the Ark of the Covenant which remains to this day is: what became of it? After five years of field research in Israel, Egypt and Ethiopia, the British journalist Graham Hancock believes he knows.

In his book *The Sign And The Seal* (Heinemann, 1992), he claims to have traced the Ark to a private sanctuary of the Church of St Mary of Zion, at Axum, what was in the third century the capital of Ethiopia, to the south-west of the Red Sea. Hancock says that the Ark was rescued from its original home in Jerusalem around 650BC, to save it from destruction by Manasseh, a pagan king who overran the city.

It was guarded for 1,000 years by Jewish priests at various locations in Egypt and Ethiopia. One was on the Nile island of Elephantine-as-Aswan, where a second Jewish temple had been built in 650BC. Papyrii unearthed on the island in the early 1900s record that sacrificial rites were practised there which, according to custom, would have necessitated the Ark's presence.

Tradition says that the Ark was next kept on a small island in Lake Tana (Lake of Smoke), after the Elephantine Jews fled south east into Ethiopia. Again, on this island, Hancock found ancient sacrificial altars.

When Ethiopia was converted to Christianity in the 4th century AD, the Ark was moved to Axum. It is said to have stayed there for some six centuries until the black Jewish (Falasha) queen Judith destroyed the first church of St. Mary of Zion. The ark was again rescued and secreted on an island in Lake Zwai, 400 miles to the south of Axum.

Once Christian rule had been re-established, 70 years later, the Ark was returned to Axum. In medieval times, it is believed, the Ark went on public view four times a year and in the 13th century, Abu Salih, an Armenian geographer, saw it being carried in procession.

The second church built to house the Ark was destroyed in 1535 by Ahmed the Left-handed, a Muslim warlord. Another rescue operation sent the Ark back to Lake Tana, where it was kept on the island of Daga Stephanos. In about 1635, it was returned to Axum, where a third St. Mary of Zion church was built. The last emperor of Ethiopia, Haile Selassie, ordered the building of a special chapel in which to keep the Ark, in 1965.

Over the past few hundred years only a few dozen people have been permitted to see the relic. These have been the Guardians of the Ark. The latest custodian in a long line is Abba Fameray, a monk in his fifties. He says the Ark is a gold-overlaid chest about four feet wide and two feet tall, with carrying poles.

Author Hancock says: "Tracing the route followed by the Ark over the past 26 centuries has taken me five years of intense research. I believe we can now say exactly what happened to this most sacred of relics."

Professor Richard Pankhurst of the Institute of Ethiopian Studies at the University of Addis Ababa said: "I find his arguments very convincing. He has a closely and well reasoned case. The Ark was one of the most important artefacts of the ancient world. What happened to it is therefore of very great historical importance."

But, to return to Moses. Our next glimpse of the celestial God-being is after Moses has angrily smashed the Commandment tablets at seeing his people worshipping the golden calf. He sets up a tabernacle outside the camp and the Lord appears in the form of a "cloudy pillar" that stands by the door, talking with Moses. Still, it seems, God is concerned about not being seen. Or could this "cloudy pillar" be simply, either a protection for those who approach, or even a controlled, localised, artificial atmosphere for the being to breathe while on Earth?

It is difficult to determine. But there is a later indication that God is simply concerned that no one shall see his face:

"And he said, Thou canst not see my face: for there shall no man see me and live." (Exodus 33:20)

Why? Various possibilities spring to mind. Either, he does not want Moses – or anyone, for that matter – to see that he is humanoid, like other men, or he is human only in body and manifestation and has a face so different, so alien, that the sight of it might frighten away his contact, his spokesman. On the other hand, he might even be wearing some breathing apparatus when not surrounded by the artificial atmosphere and to remove it would kill him.

Preposterous? Think of the shiny, reflective visors of the US astronauts on their Moon missions. Wouldn't they appear faceless to any sighted alien encountering them? And wouldn't it be impossible to remove such visors to show their faces?

Whatever the case, when Moses came down from the mountain again, bearing a freshly-hewn set of Commandments, some mysterious change had come over him. His own face seemed to shine:

"And it came to pass, when Moses came down from mount Sinai with the two tables of testimony in Moses' hand, when he came down from the mount, that Moses wist not that the skin of his face shone while he talked with him.

"And when Aaron and all the children of Israel saw Moses, behold, the skin of his face shone; and they were afraid to come nigh unto him...

"And till Moses had done speaking with them, he put a veil on his face.

"But when Moses went in before the LORD to speak with him, he took the veil off, until he came out [presumably, from the tabernacle]. And he came out, and spake unto the children of Israel that which he was commanded.

"And the children of Israel saw the face of Moses, that the skin of Moses' face shone: and Moses put the veil upon his face again, until he went in to speak with him." (Exodus 34:29, 30, 32–35)

To theologians, this phenomenon is usually taken to mean that Moses has been spiritually illuminated by the experience of meeting the Lord. But I believe it is equally reasonable to suppose that the cause of the effect was physiological. Whatever conditioning or treatment Moses had to undergo during his 40-day sojourn has brought about this change.

An interesting aside is that when Jerome (c.342–420AD), rendered this passage into Latin for the so-called Vulgate version of The Bible in the 4th century, he mistranslated the Hebrew word qaran, meaning "shone", as qeren, which means "horn". This is why representations of Moses, depicted so often in Christian art, holding the Tables of the Law, is shown with horns!

It is not until much later in the Old Testament that the occupants of what would seem to be extra-terrestrial craft make more straightforward, personal contact with humans – Ezekiel, for example. Perhaps the technology of the alien intelligences had not progressed sufficiently to allow for this in Moses' time.

5. Return Of The El

"For this record, I should have to state that my interviewing results dispose me toward acceptance of the existence of humanoid occupants in some UFOs."
James E. McDonald, Senior Professor of Physics, Department of Meteorology, Institute of Atmospheric Physics, University of Arizona

THE NEXT great prophet/avatar that I want to examine is Muhammad, who gave the Islamic world the infallible word of God (Allah) in The Koran. But it is not the text itself with which I am so much concerned as the manner in which Muhammad is said to have received it. In many respects, for reasons which should become obvious, The Koran parallels much of the Old Testament.

Muhammad was the son of Abdulah bin Abdul-Muttalib of the Quraysh tribe. He was born around 570AD at Mecca, but his father did not live to see him. Muhammad's mother, Aminah, also died when he was still a child. He was looked after by his grandfather and later by his uncle, Abu Talib. On his travels as a youth with the trading caravans that plied between Mecca and Syria, Muhammad came under the influence of both Jewish and Christian teachings,

He gained respect as a man of great wisdom and honesty and, at 25, married a rich widow 15 years older than himself. She was Khadija, daughter of Knuwailid.

At the time, the Arab religion was beginning to become enfeebled and showing signs of paganism. The Meccans, who claimed descent from Abram through Ishmael (in the Bible, later re-named Israel), worshipped not only the one supreme God, Allah, but several female deities, among them Al-hat, Al-Uzzah, and Al-Manat, who personified the Sun, Venus and Fortune. They were regarded as Allah's daughters.

But a group of worshippers called Hunafa had already rejected this form of idolatry and devised an ascetic religion of their own. Muhammad, it is believed, may have come under their influence, impressed as they were by the monotheism of the Jews and Christians.

One month a year, Muhammad would take his family to a cave at Hira, a desert hill outside Mecca, to pray and meditate. One night in 610AD during Ramadhan, the Muslim month of heat, Muhammad was deep in contemplation when the Angel Gabriel appeared to him and ordered him: "Read!" But Muhammad had never learned to read. Puzzled, he went outside the cave, the angel's voice still echoing in his ears, and again he heard the same voice speak:

"Oh Muhammad! Thou art Allah's messenger, and I am Gabriel!"

He looked up and saw the angel, "in the likeness of a man, standing in the sky, above the horizon". The angel repeated its message and Muhammad stood transfixed, turning his face away from the brilliance of the vision. But whichever way he turned, the angel was confronting him. After a long time, the angel disappeared and Muhammad went to his wife in a state of shock.

But the angel's words had become inscribed in his heart and eventually, he became convinced of the truth of his vision and, although he never claimed to perform miracles, Muhammad sincerely believed he was a messenger of God, sent forth to confirm previous scriptures. He was sure that the Jews and Christians, instructed by God through various prophets, had fallen off the true path of the Lord's intentions. In The Koran, which was revealed to Muhammad in a series of similar experiences at Al-Madinah and Mecca, the prophet denounces the Jews and Christians for breaking into rival sects and schisms; the Jews, he claimed, corrupted the Scriptures and the Christians went astray by worshipping Christ as the Son of God. It was Muhammad's task to bring the people back to the original purpose of God, as delineated by Abram: absolute submission to the will of Allah.

At first, the revelations of The Koran were memorised by professional holy men, then later written down on stones and palm leaves until eventually an "authorised" version was compiled. The Koran (Al-Qur'an) means "the reading" and is so-called because of the angel's order to the prophet who could not do so: "Read!"

So once again we have an intelligent man singled out for contact on a mountain by an unearthly presence. It is easy to assume that Muhammad might have invented or dreamt the whole story and re-hashed the Old Testament. But why? From all accounts he did not enjoy the kudos of being a prophet; he remained humble and devout throughout his life. And, remembering the example of Akhenaten, why should he, in setting himself up as a prophet, reaffirm already established teachings? Why not invent a totally new and different religion?

The answer is quite plain: Muhammad *was* chosen by an extra-terrestrial intelligence – the same entity that singled out Noah, Abram, Jacob, Joseph and Moses. The Old Testament names for God were El, Eloha, sometimes the plural Elohim and later, the personalised Yahweh. It does not take a genius to see the similarity between the earlier forms, El and Eloha, and that of Muhammad's God, Allah. Indeed, the angel who first approached him was Gabriel, which means "Man of God", signifying that he was an emissary from "El", which is why the names of many messengers from this being all have the same ending: Gabriel, Michael, Raphael, Uriel, Raquel, Saraqel and Ramiel, all of them "archangels".

So, it becomes apparent that the same Celestial Being – Eloha/Allah – was still seeking out suitable earthly spokesmen in the seventh century AD; someone who could carry out its purpose.

And there is plenty of highly suggestive evidence, apart from in the scriptures of the more orthodox religions, that these emissaries from beyond the Earth contacted mankind from time to time. The legendary *Book Of Dzyan*, a supposedly sacred, ancient Tibetan text, is full of references to "sons of flame" who visited the Earth in light-propelled flying "chariots". They were said to be of dazzling aspect and, after attempting to educate or enlighten the human race, abandoned the project, wiping out traces of their presence before departing into space. The book is allegedly so ancient that there is no record of its actual age and what remains of it are fragments translated into Sanskrit, Hindu, Chinese and Japanese. No one is certain where the original text may be, if it still exists, but there is a suggestion that it may lie hidden in some secret vault beneath one of Tibet's remote monasteries in the Himalayas.

Hindu texts, in particular the Mahabharata and the Ramayana, speak of vessels like "blueish clouds in the shape of an egg or a luminous globe" flying though the skies at the beginning of time. These craft, propelled by an "ethereal force", travelled on an undulating course, encircling the Earth. As they flew they made "melodious sounds" and were "like a shining light as bright as fire".

A Japanese tomb outside Yamaga City, Kumamoto, dated around 2000BC, shows an emperor holding his arms up in welcome to seven flying discs. The name of the suburb in which the tomb lies is, in ancient Japanese, Chip-san, which means "the place where the Sun descended".

A Russian physicist, Professor Matest Agrest, claims that in the caves of Bohistan, near Vladivostok, there are astronomical diagrams showing the positions of the stars as they were 13,000 years ago. Lines connect the Earth with the planet Venus.

References to lights, discs, eggs and chariots in the sky dot the literature of practically all races, as do the stories of gods coming down from the heavens. But what was their purpose? From the words of the various prophet/contacts, it would seem to instruct humankind in some way, to encourage an improved pattern of living; to point the human race on a correct course for self-advancement. Yet there are also other indications that this may not always have been the case; that humankind may not be quite so important in the scheme of things. Or at least, that *different* intelligences visited the Earth, each with quite different ideas about the future and usefulness of the human race.

6. War In The Air – 1400BC

"The United States and Russia from now on have the power to annihilate the entire world."
Charles Wilson, US Secretary for War, March, 1954

BETWEEN 1700 and 1200BC a tough, wandering horde with no cities of their own and few material possessions, invaded and conquered the Indus civilisation that sprawled from Rupar, at the foot of the Himalayas, to the Arabian Sea, west of Karachi. The invaders brought with them a rigid tribal formation – the roots of a caste system – and a tradition of gods that became the foundations of the Hindu religion. The Aryans, as this conquering race is known, worshipped gods from the skies whom they called *devas* – "the Shining Ones".

Father of the gods was Dyaus, whose family included:

Indra, god of the weather and of war, dragon-slayer, who rode into battle across the heavens with the spirits of the storm.

Surya, Sun-god, whose blazing chariot also raced across the skies.

The Asvins, Surya's twin grandsons, whose sky-patrols sought out the evils that afflicted mankind, and went to the aid of shipwrecked mariners.

Varuna, god of wisdom, punisher of wrong-doing, celestial king whose brief was to maintain order in the Universe.

Rudra, the archer, spreader of disease.

Pusan, protector of herdsmen and their flocks.

Agni, god of fire, a spirit of the household who, through Brahmana, the priest-musicians, was intermediary between men and the sky-gods.

Vishnu, also worshipped in his two earthly incarnations as Rama and Krishna and, along with Shiva, regarded in modern Hinduism as the supreme deity; each incarnation being thought of as a human, personal form of the Absolute.

From these Aryan roots, Hinduism has thus become a seemingly paradoxical mixture; a polytheism involving many gods and goddesses, and a monotheism, or belief in only one god. The many gods are regarded as diverse earthly manifestations of the underlying cosmic principle, the eternal *dhama* that governs the whole universe; the immutable law to which both men and gods are subject.

Among the enormous body of *Veda*, or "wisdom" – the name given to sacred Hindu literature – are two astonishingly rich and vast epics, the *Mahabharata* and the *Ramayana*. They are the Hindu equivalent of Homer's *Iliad* and *Odyssey* or, if you prefer, of the Old Testament.

In these great Hindu texts, the god Vishnu, in his earthly role as Krishna or Rama, takes a hand in the affairs of humanity in the same way that God frequently intervened in the guidance of the people of Moses, or the gods of Ancient Greece influenced the destiny of Odysseus and the outcome of the Trojan Wars, as related by Homer.

The *Mahabharata*, in a staggering 90,000 couplets, describes a great war between two neighbouring tribes of the Upper Ganges, the Panchalas and the Kurus, that took place around 1400BC. The text is an amazing amalgam of ancient philosophy, theology, social customs, human intrigues and heroic deeds, set against an historical background.

But more than this – *it describes aerial warfare over India, 14 centuries before Christ*.

As the story of the jealous rivalry between the two warring factions unfolds, the gods take note. When, for instance, sons from the two families gather as suitors to the princess of Panchala:

"And the gods in cloud-borne chariots came to view the scene so fair...

Bright celestial cars in concourse sailed upon the cloudless sky."
(Book II, chapter IV)

Again, when the eldest of the Panchala brothers, Yudhisthir, calls a meeting to proclaim his sovereignty over all the kings of India:

"Bright Immortals, robed in sunlight, sailed across the liquid sky,

And their gleaming, cloud-borne chariots rested on the turrets high."
(Book III, chapter II)

But when the various battles break out, the gods take a hand in their outcome, bringing into play fantastic weapons that are evocative of nuclear warheads and air-to-surface missiles. The *Bhisma Parva*, one of the epic's books, describes a "celestial weapon" used in the battle between Arjun, of the Panchala tribe, and Bhisma. In a translation commentary, in 1888, Protrop Chandra Roy wrote: "This Brahma-danda, meaning Brahma's Rod, can smite whole countries and entire races *from generation to generation*." (My emphasis).

Another of the books, the *Drona Parva*, describes what sounds like a squadron of flying spheres that fire powerful rays:

"In that dreadful battle, those shafts like the very rays of the Sun, in a moment shrouded all the parts of the compass, the welkin [sky] and the troops. Innumerable iron balls also then appeared like resplendent luminaries in the clear firmament."

Another section, the *Samsaptakabada Parva*, describes one of these flying machines in more detail and mentions another deadly weapon. In an account of a battle between Arjun and Rakshasas, reference is made to a "celestial car". The book goes on:

"...in the battle between the Gods and the Asuras in the days of old, it displayed a circular, forward, backward and diverse other kinds of motion...

"The son of Pandu [Arjun] blew his prodigious conch call, Devadotta. And then he shot the weapon called Tashtva, that is capable of slaying large bodies of foes together."

Similarly, the Ramayana describes flying machines and futuristic weapons, provided by the Celestials to aid those they favour on Earth. This epic tells of the trials and triumphs of Rama, whose bride Sita is kidnapped by Ravan, king of Lanka (Sri Lanka). Rama and Ravan engage in a mighty battle, Rama riding in a "celestial car", while Ravan drives his chariot on the ground below:

"Brave Matali drove the chariot drawn by steeds like solar ray,

Where the true and righteous Rama sought his foe in fatal fray.

Shining arms and heavenly weapons he to lofty Rama gave –

When the righteous strive and struggle, Gods assist the true and brave!

'Take this car,' so said Matali, 'which the helping Gods provide,

Rama, take these steeds celestial, Indra's golden Chariot ride.'"
(Book X, chapter X)

The battle is long and fierce, shaking the ocean, hills and surrounding countryside until:

"Still the dubious battle lasted, until Rama, in his ire,
Wielded Brahma's deathful weapon flaming with celestial fire,
Weapon which the Saint Agastya had unto the hero given,
Winged as lightning dart of Indra, fatal as the bolt of heaven,
Wrapped in smoke and flaming flashes, speeding from the circled bow,
Pierced the iron heart of Ravan, lain the lifeless hero low."

(Book X, chapter XI)

The whole of Hindu epic literature is dotted with references to flying machines, sometimes known as *vimana*, and to weapons of immense destructive power, brought into play when orthodox weapons of those times – bow, lance and spear – proved ineffective. And, occasionally, there is descriptive writing that once again evokes the aftermath of nuclear weapons.

The *Mausola Parva* talks of "an unknown weapon, an iron thunderbolt, a gigantic messenger of death which reduced to ashes the entire race of the Vrishnis and the Andhakas. The corpses were so burned as to be unrecognisable. The victims' hair and nails fell out; pottery broke without any apparent cause, and the birds turned white. After a few hours, all foodstuffs were infected."

In another part of the book, we are told: "Cukra, flying on board a high-powered vimana, hurled on to the triple city a single projectile charged with all the power of the Universe. An incandescent column of smoke and flame as bright as ten thousand Suns, rose in all its splendour." The vimana flying-vessel, when it comes to Earth, is described as being like "a splendid block of antimony", which suggests it had a metallic sheen.

Epics like the *Mahabharata* and the *Ramayana* are, of course, the relics of race memories that were first sung and related by wandering minstrels and poets, then later written down and no doubt embellished by later scribes and historians, the main bodies of the works being formulated around 1000BC. It would be easy, therefore, to explain away some of the more amazing and fabulous descriptive passages as pure romantic embellishment. But could a race of people, who traditionally fought their historic battles with swords, bows and spears, have conceived of such powerful weapons as those described in such vivid detail – without having actually *witnessed* such things? What did the Aryan races see in their skies that prompted them to think the gods were taking a hand in human affairs?

Before relegating these accounts to the realms of pure fancy, remember how often archaeology has confirmed mythology as fact. What about Troy, for example, of which Homer wrote? It was thought of as a mythical city until the 1870s, when its ruins were unearthed by the amateur archaeologist Heinrich Schliemann at Hissarlik, at the southern end of the Dardanelles. Similarly, little was known of the Minoan civilisation of 4500 years ago, until the archaeologist Sir Arthur Evans discovered the ruins of the great palace of Knossos, near Heraklion, Crete, in 1900.

The traditions of the great Hindu epics passed into some of the later rituals and beliefs of the Hindu peoples as the Aryan religion was assimilated into that of the Indus civilisation. One ritual in particular was noted by Sir J.G. Frazer, in his classic study of magic and religion, *The Golden Bough*.

From the Aryans, the civilisation that grew up in India inherited and adapted the old tribal class system that became the caste system of modern Hinduism. There were the *Brahmins* (priests), *Kstriyas* (warriors), *Vaisyas* (peasants) and *Sudras* (serfs). With these distinct and rigid social separations evolved a complex system of rules and observances, not the least of which was the way of life of the Brahmins, the highest caste. Among them were rules to be followed by a Brahman in learning a hymn of the ancient collection called the *Samaveda*. Of this, Frazer wrote:

"The hymn, which bears the name of the Sakvari song, was believed to embody the might of Indra's weapon, the thunderbolt; and hence, on account of the dreadful and dangerous potency with which it was thus charged, the bold student who essayed to master it had to be isolated from his fellow-men, and to retire from the village into the forest. Here for a space of time which might vary, according to different doctors of the law, from one to twelve years, he had to observe certain rules of life, among which were the following. Thrice a day he had to touch water; he must wear black garments and eat black food; when it rained he might not seek the shelter of a roof, but had to sit in the rain and say, 'Water is the Sakvari song'; when the lightning flashed, he said, 'That is like the Sakvari song'; when the thunder pealed, he said, 'The Great One is making a great noise.' He might never cross a running stream without touching water; he might never set foot on a ship unless his life were in danger, and even then he must be sure to touch water when he went on board; 'for in the water,' so ran the saying, 'lies the virtue of the Sakvari song.' When at last he was allowed to learn the song itself, he had to dip his hands in a vessel of water in which plants of all kinds had been placed. If a man walked in the way of all these precepts, the rain-god Parjanya, it was said, would send rain at the wish of that man."

The ritual, in which water plays such an important role, associated as it is with the thunderbolt of Indra, could well be a distorted race-memory harking back to the days of destructive weapons used by the sky-gods in the epics. The cleansing properties of water might have been seen as protective against the radioactive blight so clearly described in the *Mausola Parva*, when nails and hair fell out, birds turned white and food was infected. These rituals then could have been adapted symbolically as a form of imitative magic in which an initiate acts out a series of themes to achieve his purpose – in this case, causing rainfall. Early cave-dwellers used similar techniques. By drawing an image of a beast they wanted to hunt, the cavemen believed they could cause the creature to become easy prey.

It is my contention that the ancient Hindu epics, like the sacred texts of many other religions and races, contain accounts of visits by celestial beings. These stories, I believe, are the first eye-witness accounts of what have become known as UFOs or Flying Saucers – and of nuclear warfare.

7. The UFO Phenomenon

"We have well-documented sightings from every corner of the USSR. Illusions don't register clearly on photographic plates and radar."
Felix Ziegel of the Moscow Institute of Aviation, at a UFO conference in 1967

"We could lose more prestige in the scientific community than we could possibly gain by undertaking the investigation [into UFOs]... Our study would be conducted almost exclusively by non-believers who, although they couldn't possibly prove a negative result, could and probably would add an impressive body of evidence that there is no reality to the observations. The trick would be, I think, to describe the project so that, to the public, it would appear a totally objective study but, to the scientific community, would represent the image of a group of non-believers trying their best to be objective but having an almost zero expectation of finding a saucer..."
Robert Low, assistant dean of the University of Colorado's graduate school, on The Condon Report, in 1966

IN PRACTICALLY every age of mankind and in almost every area on Earth that humans have occupied there have been recorded sightings of unidentified flying objects – from the cave cultures of Northern Europe of about 15,000 years ago, to ancient Egypt, Greece, Rome, India, South and North America, Australasia and medieval Britain.

On the walls of caves at Lascaux and Rouffignac, in France, and at Altamira, Spain, among the realistic paintings of bulls, bears, bisons and other animals, are flying discs. These drawings were made by Cro-Magnon men, a race of extremely artistic hunters who moved northwards as the polar ice cap retreated some 12,000 to 15,000 years ago.

A papyrus attributed to the annals of Pharaoh Thutmosis III (c.1500BC), now believed to be in the Vatican Library, talks of a "circle of fire coming in the sky... and the hearts of the scribes became terrified and they laid themselves flat on their bellies". The papyrus was found among the effects of Professor Alberto Tulli, former director of the Vatican's Egyptian Museum, and was translated by Prince Boris de Rachewitlz. It goes on to say:

"Now after some days had gone by, behold, these things became more numerous in the skies than ever. They shone more than the brightness of the sun and extended to the limits of the four supports of the heavens."

The papyrus could well be describing a particularly dense swarm of meteorites peppering the Earth 15 centuries before Christ, except for a most intriguing reference, either to a giant satellite orbiting the Earth, or a "mother-ship" from which the fiery circles emanated:

"Dominating in the sky was [sic] the stations of these fire circles..."

According to the 4th century historian Julius Obsequiens, in *Prodigiorum Libellus*, the skies over ancient Rome were infested with "flying shields" in 100BC. And in 312AD Constantine the Great and his army on a march to Rome saw a "fiery cross"

---

in the sky, recorded in the Life of Constantine by Pamphilius Eusebius.

The Travels Of Panini, a Sanskrit work of 400AD claims its author and other chosen initiates were taken on flights to the inner planets by beings from outer space.

The Venerable Bede, Anglo-Saxon historian of the seventh century, in his *Historia Gentis Anglorum*, (Book 4, Chapter 7) describes a strange celestial light that flew over a group of nuns in the cemetery at Barking on the River Thames, then hovered over the monastery, before disappearing into the skies.

In *Historia Ecclesiastica Francorum*, St. Gregory of Tours, who was appointed bishop of Auvergne in 573, reported: "a very bright sphere flew over French lands in 583."

The "flying shields" turned up again in 776AD to rescue the knights of Charlemagne at Sigisburg from the attacking Saxons. (*Annales Laurissenes*, Saeculum IX, Migne).

The Anglo-Saxon Chronicles state that "in 793 in Northumbria, the inhabitants were scared by powers appearing over them... there were dazzling gleams like lamps and red dragons were seen flying in the air."

Three years later "globes were seen flying around the sun by people in several parts of England," according to the Benedictine monk, Roger of Wendover.

Throughout the Middle Ages unusual flying objects were reported by various chroniclers in Europe.

Sightings continued throughout the ensuing centuries:

• 1548: a "fireball" exploded above Thuringia, (central Germany), dropping a red, sticky substance, like blood.

• 1557: glowing "machines" overflew Vienna and green and red "suns" were seen over Poland.

• 1558: an aerial battle between two circular objects was seen over Austria, while three "rings of light" soared above Zurich. The Swiss engraver Wieck made blocks depicting the flying discs.

• 1697: northern Germany, particularly Hamburg, was treated to the sight of a "round machine with a sphere at the centre and extremely luminous" flying through the air.

These and many other ancient historical references serve to show that, far from being a phenomenon of the technological post-war years of the jet engine and atom bombs, UFOs have been around for a long time; probably as long as man himself – perhaps even longer.

There have been countless books and newspaper and magazine articles describing the re-emergence of these inexplicable aerial phenomena and space prohibits a full resume of the modern history of UFOs. But for those unfamiliar with the rise in frequency of these occurrences, I will outline a few cases regarded as "classic" by UFO researchers, including some particularly pertinent to this text.

Generally speaking, the modern Flying Saucer story began in June, 1947, with the experience of an American businessman and flyer, although some reports of unusual objects in the skies had been made in the US earlier. Kenneth Arnold, then 32, owned a fire-control equipment company in Boise, Idaho. On June 24, 1947, he took off in a light, single-engined aircraft from Chehalis airport, Washington State, to join a search in the Cascade mountains for a missing Marine C-46 transport plane. A $5,000 reward had been offered for finding it.

The skies were clear as, after an hour's flying, he approached Mount Rainier. Suddenly, a bright flash reflected on the wings and bodywork of his plane. He looked around. The only other plane in sight was a DC4 some distance away on his left, to the rear. There was another flash and, left towards the north, he spotted nine bright objects flying line astern, heading south.

Arnold had plenty of experience flying over mountainous regions, which tended to lend credence to the account he later gave to newsmen and told in more detail in the book he co-authored with Ray Palmer, *The Coming Of The Saucers* (1952).

The nine objects approached from the direction of Mount Baker and swooped and swerved among other mountain peaks. Their swift manoeuvres enabled him to estimate their speed. It is 47 miles between Mount Rainier and Mount Adams. The objects covered that distance in one minute, 42 seconds. This works out at 1,656.71 miles per hour – three times faster than any man-made aircraft of that period.

Arnold said the objects appeared to have wings, but no tailplanes. One seemed crescent-shaped and had a small dome between its wings. The others, he added, were "flat like a pie pan and so shiny they reflected the sun like a mirror". He likened their mode of flying to that of speedboats plying rough waters, and "flying like geese in a diagonal chainlike line, as if they were chained together". To newsmen at Pendleton airport, Oregon, he later said, "They flew like a saucer would if you skipped it across the water." It was this phrase – originally used by William Bequette, a reporter on the *Pendleton East Oregonian* – that caught the attention of subeditors as the story went out over the national teleprinter networks and on the radio – and the description "Flying Saucers" passed into the popular domain, later to be replaced by the more generally accurate term Unidentified Flying Objects.

Because of his experience as a pilot and his reputation as a respected businessman, Arnold's account was taken seriously – and spurred official U.S Air Force and general public interest in the UFO phenomenon. To my knowledge, the Arnold experience has never been satisfactorily explained.

Since that June day in 1947, seeming epidemics – called "flaps" by UFOlogists – have cropped up in most parts of the world, almost akin to children's seasonal crazes for marbles, the yo-yo and other fads.

Whatever attitude one may take towards the many and varied stories about the phenomena, they cannot *all* be dismissed as hallucinations, hoaxes, mirages; nor can they be mistaken for sightings of perfectly natural phenomena such as freak, or lenticular (lens-shaped) cloud formations, weather balloons, marsh gas, meteors, reflections on inversion layers, flocks of migrating birds or even the oft-mooted planet Venus. Apart from having been seen, UFOs have been photographed and filmed – with a predictable quota of fakes – tracked on radar, heard and felt in various ways. They are said to cause a variety of effects, from panic in animals, paralysis, radiation sickness, memory lapses, blindness in humans, burns, chemical changes in soil, the scorching and burning of the earth, the stalling of car engines and what are known as corn circles.

Numerous governments, including most of the South American countries, along with Mexico, Norway, Sweden, France, Spain, Italy, Germany, the Philippines, Canada, Australia and New Zealand, have, at some stage and in varying degrees of caution, admitted to the possible reality of UFOs. The U.S. and British authorities, meanwhile, have tended to deny officially their reality, other than as phenomena with probable, but as-yet unknown, "natural" explanations. Russian scientists have taken note of the reports of such objects and their comments have been reported in official Soviet news media.

It is worth noting here, however, that while Britain does not *officially* recognise UFOs, there is a strict, official procedure to be carried out within sectors of the Civil

---

Service – airport control personnel, for example – after sightings or radar trackings of unidentified aerial phenomena.

It is this kind of Orwellian doublethink that has engendered an equally absurd and sometimes ridiculous, quasi-scientific sector among the more fanatical element of UFOlogists. Whatever the official attitude towards UFOs may be, the incidence of sightings has been sustained over a remarkably long period for a supposedly ephemeral, "make-believe", "imaginary" or even mistakenly interpreted phenomenon.

A 1976 poll reported that around 15 million American citizens had seen UFOs at some stage and that by far a wide majority believed they were "real".

If UFOs are, as their detractors think, simply products of the imagination, or hallucinations, then the human race has had a particularly repetitive and somewhat unimaginative nature since the days of our cave-dwelling ancestors.

The Venus Skytrap

A widely-publicised UFO report that emerged in 1973 came from none other than the US President, Jimmy Carter. But Carter was referring to a sighting he claimed to have experienced some years earlier, before he was governor of Georgia.

Few UFOlogists bothered to investigate the case in depth, seemingly being happy to have such a distinguished person confirming what those who were definitely pro-UFOs chose to believe all along. However, the sceptical but highly thorough and reliable investigator Robert Sheaffer *did* research the Carter case and published his conclusions in 1977.

Checking through lists of Carter's speaking engagements, Shaeffer was able to establish that, although Carter originally mentioned his experience in October 1969 – though a report was not filed until four years later – the encounter must have taken place on January 6, 1969, after Carter left a Lions Club meeting at Leary, Georgia, where he had given a speech.

When Shaeffer used a planisphere to check the elevation and bearing of Carter's description of a light, "as bright as the Moon" that appeared to recede and draw closer alternately, he found that the brightest body in the sky on that night was the planet Venus.

Carter had claimed that there were no fewer than ten other witnesses to the phenomenon. But when Shaeffer questioned many members of the Leary Lions Club, only one recalled the event. He told of seeing a light in the sky which he took to be a weather balloon. He could not confirm Carter's version of the phenomenon's apparent motion.

Venus – named after the Roman goddess of love – has often been cited as the "fall gal" in explaining away many alleged UFO sightings over the past few decades. To such an extent has Venus been invoked, in fact, that some UFOlogists call the planet the "Queen of UFOs".

Indeed, as French-born veteran investigator and author Jacques Vallee has remarked: "No single object has been misinterpreted as a 'flying saucer' more often than the planet Venus." According to the Centre for UFO Studies at Evanston, Illinois, such mistaken identifications of Venus for a UFO, have run into millions of reports.

Even seemingly reliable, highly-trained astronauts have mistakenly thought Venus to be a UFO. One was Michael Collins who was on the first manned Moon-landing mission. Collins, who later went to work for the Smithsonian Institution in Washington, D.C., was taking star photographs on the July 1966 Gemini-10 mission, as it passed over Australia.

He reported by radio to ground control: "The sun is just beginning to come up. Also, to the east, we see an extremely bright object. I believe it's too bright to be a planet. It's north of Orion about six or eight degrees. Is it the Gemini-8 Agena? [an already-orbiting satellite]."

But later, Collins admitted: "I think I was fooled by the planet Venus." Checks with star maps established that, exactly where Collins had report his "object" at the time, was the planet Venus.

The Mantell Case

I gave a resumé of this case, once regarded as "classic" by UFO buffs, in *The Zarkon Principle*, using information available by the mid-1970s. Since then, however, further facts have emerged that have tended to colour the case somewhat differently.

At 2.45 pm on January 7, 1948, Captain Thomas Mantell, a young US National Guard pilot, was leader of a flight of four F-51 fighters, three of which chased a UFO that "looked like an ice cream cone topped with red" and had been sighted over Godman Air Force Base, at Fort Knox, Kentucky, by a number of both civilian and military witnesses.

There was a low, broken cloud ceiling. Three of the F-51s began to close in on the object and one pilot described it as metallic and "tremendous" in size. Another said it was "round like a teardrop and at times almost fluid". Mantell reported that the object was moving at half his speed at twelve o'clock. He climbed above the cloud layer radioing: "I'm closing in now to take a good look. It's directly ahead of me and still moving at half my speed."

The other pilots, still beneath the cloud layer, left Mantell to continue his chase while they returned to Godman.

At 3.15 pm Mantell reported: "It's going up now and forward as fast as I am – that's 360 mph. I'm going up to 20,000 feet, and if I'm no closer, I'll abandon chase."

It was his last transmission. The radar blip of Mantell's fighter suddenly disappeared from the screen, while the UFO zoomed out of range. Hours later, searchers found the fragments of Mantell's plane strewn across a field. Mantell's decapitated body was found in the wreckage.

The other fighters landed at Godman five minutes after Mantell broke formation with them. One of them resumed the search a few minutes later, roving to the south at altitudes of up to 33,000 feet, but discovered nothing.

An investigation initially identified the object of Mantell's pursuit as the planet Venus. But more detailed checking proved that, at specific intervals, the position of the planet – elevation and azimuth – did not tally with that of the object. Azimuth is one of the co-ordinates of a heavenly body, measured from the south or north point of the horizon, westward or eastward respectively, from 0 to 360 degrees. It was also suggested that Mantell died of suffocation, having blacked out from lack of oxygen at 20,000 feet.

Four years later in 1951 records of a gigantic, secret, stratospheric spy balloon – Project Skyhook – capable of climbing to 70,000 feet, became declassified information. It had been launched upwind of Godman Air Base a few hours before the Mantell chase. Designed to send up automatic cameras over Russia, the balloons were in a top secret programme that not even the Air Force had been notified about.

The balloons could expand to a 100ft diameter and would travel at between 175 and 400 mph in jet-stream, high altitude winds. They could appear metallic or even multi-coloured as sunlight reflected from their plastic envelopes and, in gusty conditions, could move quite erratically.

In his book, *The Report On Unidentified Flying Objects*, (Gollancz 1956) Captain Edward J. Ruppelt, former head of Project Blue Book, the U.S. Air Force investigative body into UFO reports, added this to the Mantell dossier:

"Not long after the object had disappeared from view at Godman AFB, a man from Madisonville, Kentucky, called Flight Service in Dayton. He had seen an object travelling southeast. He had looked at it through a telescope and it was a balloon. At four forty-five an astronomer living north of Nashville, Tennessee, called in. He had also seen a UFO, looked at it through a telescope, and it was a balloon."

Most UFO sightings are of a much more mundane – if that is the right word – nature than most. Someone sees an object or objects in the sky, usually performing unusual aerial manoeuvres, then they either fly away or disappear inexplicably. Little more than that. Indeed, when one considers the vast number of UFO reports logged – psychologist David Saunders of the University of Colorado had collected more than 60,000 by the mid-1970s – one wonders how many observers may have kept silent for fear of ridicule.

Now, if these objects are the same kind of phenomena reported, say, in the *Mahabharata*, or even the Old Testament, it may be asked why those seen today are not associated with similar events to those outlined in the ancient texts. Well, given the flexibility of interpretation – of how people of those times might regard such events, compared to more modern observations – they can be and frequently are.

For instance, in the *Mahabharata* and the *Ramayana*, celestial craft are reported as being involved in historical battles and conflicts. What is assumed to be poetic licence even attributes the outcome of such conflicts to the intervention of these objects.

Unidentified Flying Objects have, in fact, been sighted in modern war zones, apparently taking some interest in the proceedings. Towards the end of the Second World War, for example, there were reports from Allied military bomber and fighter personnel about UFOs which became known as "foo fighters". These objects – also called *kraut* balls and *Feuerballs* (fireballs) – were described as small balls of bright light, estimated at between a few inches to a few feet in diameter. They followed, caught up with and seemed to taunt pilots and were sighted over Germany and on Pacific bomber routes to Japan.

The foo-fighters tag is said to have derived from a popular contemporary comic strip called Smokey Stover, in which the catchphrase "where there's Foo, there's fire" was featured. Another theory is that the word derived from *feu*, French for "fire".

One of the earliest recorded appearances was on October 14, 1943, when 384 Bomb Group – on coded Mission 115 – was flying over an industrial installation at Schweinfurt, Germany.

Ahead of them, the bomber pilots reported a cluster of tiny discs about three inches in diameter. One of the B-17 bombers – number 026 – tried to evade the objects as they approached and reported that one wing passed clean through a cluster of the objects but did not sustain any damage.

Another early report was in November, 1944, from the pilot and crew of a B-29 bomber of 455 Night Fighter Squadron, based at Dijon, in eastern central France. The squadron went in search of German aircraft in an area straddling the Rhine, north of Strasbourg in eastern Germany. On November 23, the B29's observer/intelligence officer Lieut. Fred Ringwald saw what he first took to be starlike objects in the far distance. But the eight or ten "stars" rapidly transformed into spheres of orange light which flew "at a terrific speed". But whatever they were, they did not show up on either ground-based, or the aircraft's own, radar.

The spheres suddenly disappeared, only to re-materialise further from the bomber, then disappeared after a few minutes.

Another account of foo-fighter sighting in German airspace was reported two years after the end of the War by 23-year-old former B-17 pilot Charles Odom, of Houston, Texas. Odon, in a July 1947 newspaper interview, said the objects flew within 300 feet of his bomber group, then seemed "to become magnetized to our formation and fly alongside" never getting closer than 300ft. "After a while, they would peel off like a plane and leave." Although most foo fighter encounters were reported to have taken place at night, Odom claimed he saw them by day. He described them as resembling "crystal balls, clear, about the size of basketballs".

On January 24, 1965, a retrospective account of USAF experiences of foo-fighters during wartime appeared in the *Sunday News* of Manchester, New Hampshire. In it, a former Second World War correspondent recalled a gathering of about a dozen journalists at the Scribe Hotel in Paris, where they were celebrating V-E Day on May 7, 1945.

A War Department colonel joined them and was rather upset when the journalists poo-poohed his report of the Nazis working at a heavy water plant in Norway, in an attempt to produce an atom bomb. "Everybody had secret weapons coming out of his ears," the ex-war correspondent recalled, "V-1s, V-2s, and the rest of Hitler's grisly stable."

The colonel indignantly retired to another table and his place was taken by a U.S. Air Force major, who said he was a B17 pilot with 50 missions to his credit.

"Hey you guys," he said, "are you war correspondents? Then why haven't you told the folks back home about the flying saucers." That, at least according to the account, was the phrase the major is said to have used – long before the Kenneth Arnold sighting was reported, using the term.

"The last five or six [missions] were over Berlin," said the major, "and on every one of them these things popped up out of nowhere. Suddenly they'd be on our wing, six or eight of them, flying perfect formation.

"You turn and bank; they turn and bank; you climb, they climb; you dive, they dive – you just couldn't shake 'em. Little, dirty grey aluminium things, ten or twelve feet in diameter, shaped just like saucers; no cockpits, no windows, no sign of life. Now isn't that a story and why haven't you put it in the papers?"

Asked what his men thought the objects might be, he said: "Some of us think they're more of Hitler's V-weapons, something the Germans were only able to get up in the closing days of the war. Some of the boys think they're Russian... some think they must be from outer space because they manoeuvre so uncannily and fly at such superhuman speeds."

The journalists were no more impressed than they had been by the WD colonel's remarks about Nazi interest in the atom bomb. Then, said the ex-correspondent, in the following August, the Americans dropped their atom bombs on Hiroshima and Nagasaki – and he and his colleagues started to wonder about the "flying saucers".

About two years later the correspondent met a man who had been connected with Supreme Headquarters Allied Expeditionary Forces (SHAEF G2) in Paris, towards the war's end. When he asked him about the sightings, the man said: "Oh sure, SHAEF knew about those reports. There were any number of them, very well attested. They were considered so secret they were in the "eyes only" file. That means you couldn't make a copy of them. You want to know something else? Those flying saucers were reported, in the closing days of the war, over Tokyo.

As will be noted, these particular reports, including the size and behaviour of the sighted objects, and despite the "flying saucer" tag, do not resemble those of other alleged UFO encounters and none of the reports seems to have assumed the spheres were in any way from extra-terrestrial sources.

In December 1945, in an article in *The American Legion Magazine*, Jo Chamberlin wrote: "The foo-fighters simply disappeared when Allied ground forces captured the area East of the Rhine. This was known to be the location of many German experimental stations." This was to some extent backed up 24 years later by an Italian aircraft engineer, Renato Vesco who, in August 1969, wrote an article for the magazine *Argosy*. In it, he suggested that "experts" came to believe the objects were "German inventions of a new order, employed to baffle radar".

Vesco added: "How close they had come to the truth they only learned when the war was over and Allied Intelligence teams moved into the secret Nazi plants. The foo-fighters seen by Allied pilots were only a minor demonstration, and a fraction of a vast variety of methods to confuse radar and interrupt electro-magnetic currents. Work on the German anti-radar *Feuerball*, or fireball, had been speeded up during the fall of 1944 at a Luftwaffe experimental center near Oberammergau, Bavaria. There, and at the aeronautical establishment of Wiener Neustadt, the first fireballs were produced. Later, when the Russians moved closer to Austria, the workshops producing the fireballs were moved to the Black Forest. Fast and remote-controlled, the fireballs, equipped with kliston tubes [Vesco is probably referring to klystron tubes, that is, electron tubes that employ velocity modulation of an electron beam, and are usually used at high frequency for either the amplification or generation of high-frequency waves] and operating on the same frequency as Allied radar, could eliminate the blips from screens and remain practically invisible to ground control."

On February 19, 1952, the U.S. Air Force, through the United Press wire service, reported that the crews of two American bombers had seen "flying discs" over Korea. Several orange globes, giving off blue flashes, flew parallel to two B29 super-fortresses, at midnight over Wonsan, and a few hours later over Sunchon. No satisfactory natural explanation was ever given.

In April 1953, Lieutenant Julius Morgan was on a reconnaissance mission in a light plane over Panmunjon, near Pork Chop Hill, when he reported a "mysterious, shiny, white object", flying at about 80 mph, 100 feet over Communist territory, within only a few miles of the Western Korean battlefront. Three other Air Force officers also claimed to have watched the craft from other aircraft before it left the area.

Ancient observers, seeing flying discs during the course of a battle might easily have assumed that the sky-gods were taking a hand in their earthly conflicts.

Remembering the story of the two "angels" who temporarily blinded the lascivious men of Sodom outside Lot's home, let us now consider the case of rancher James Flynn, of Fort Myers, in Florida. On March 12 1965, Flynn was out on his swamp buggy with his four dogs, hunting in the Everglades. When three of the dogs took off after a deer and did not return, Flynn followed in his buggy.

At 1AM he saw a brilliant light above some cypress trees about 1½ miles away. When he went to investigate, he saw a 3032-foot, luminous, cone-shaped disc, 64 feet in diameter, metallic in appearance, hovering about four feet over the swamp.

Flynn estimated its size by comparing it to the nearby, 25-feet tall cypress trees. Moving closer, to within a few yards of the edge of the dull yellow glow given off by the object, Flynn waved towards what he thought were windows in four tiers around its circumference. Flynn's only remaining dog became agitated and began trying to tear its way out of its cage on the swamp buggy. Suddenly, a beam of light darted out from somewhere on the disc and struck him between the eyes. He lost consciousness. When he woke up he examined the area and found a perfect circle of burnt ground vegetation near his buggy. The dog had almost succeeded in escaping from its cage. Several cypress treetops were burned. Flynn then discovered tracks near his buggy suggesting that he had crawled around the area, although he could not recall doing so. He drove his buggy back to his original campsite, cooked himself eggs and bacon and ate. Then he made his way to the Big Cypress Indian reservation, some 18 miles east of Fort Myers, and found a friend, a Seminole Indian, Henry Billy, who took him part way towards his home town. Flynn had trouble getting along – his right eye was blind and he had only partial, blurry vision of the left one – but persuaded his Indian friend he could make it the rest of the way.

Five days after his experience in the Everglades, Flynn walked into the office of Dr. Paul Brown, an ophthalmologist in Fort Myers, and sought treatment. According to Dr. Brown, Flynn's eyes were puffy and bloodshot and he could scarcely see. Dr. Brown contacted Flynn's wife, who took him to Lee Memorial Hospital, where he was under observation for five days. It emerged that, after his encounter, Flynn had been unconscious for at least 24 hours.

Flynn's personal physician, Dr. Harvey Stripe, who had known him for 25 years and affirmed the rancher's honesty and reliability, made the following report:

"The eye condition was haemorrhaging into the anterior chambers of the eyes, apparently traumatic. The only abnormal findings were neurological."

The diagnosis went on to say that Flynn's tendon reflexes did not respond to stimulus, although they gradually returned in a week. In the centre of Flynn's forehead was an abrasion one centimetre in diameter. Four weeks later he was still being treated for lack of abdominal reflexes and cloudy vision of his right eye.

In a separate statement made to the Aerial Phenomena Research Organization (APRO) in April, 1965, Dr. Stripe said: "I have known Mr. Flynn for 25 years and have always considered him a reliable, emotionally stable individual."

Whatever Flynn saw in the swamp that night, his reaction to it was very real. And inexplicable.

On January 18, 1956, a glowing, saucer-shaped object splashed down into 25 feet of water, 75 yards off Redondo Beach, California. The object was seen by a night watchman and a handful of local residents. They described it as "frothing", before it sank beneath the waves. Captain Bill Stidham of the local lifeboat station organised a search, but nothing was found in the area where the saucer went down.

Further along the UFO record of strange experiences, we find an astonishing parallel to an event in ancient times. Remember, if you will, from Chapter Four, *Voices In The Sky*, the peculiar tale of Abram when he laid out samples of meat and food and curious lights passed by as he allegedly slept.

At 2.30AM on November 6, 1967, Karl Barlow, of Dawley, Shropshire, was driving a lorry on the A338 near Fordingbridge, in the New Forest area of Hampshire, when he saw a bright object approach from some trees to the right of the road ahead.

As it came within a quarter-mile of his truck, the vehicle's lights went out, the radio went dead and Barlow pulled to the roadside. The shining "egg-shaped" object stopped, hovering over the centre of the road about 45 feet away and, as Barlow watched, a tube like the nozzle of a vacuum cleaner emerged from an aperture and began to suck up samples of grass, gravel and leaves from both sides of the road. Barlow later told police that the object was an "out-of-this-world" green colour about 15 feet across and, after gathering its samples with a high-pitched whining noise, flew off in the direction from which it had come. Another driver, in a white Jaguar saloon, also saw the incident. His car stalled and his lights went dead ahead of it, the opposite side to Barlow's approach.

An interesting aside to this story is that later, both vehicles were checked by mechanics and found to be in working order – except that their batteries had been drained. This was odd in Barlow's case, since his lorry's battery had been charged only a few days beforehand. In confirmation of Barlow's account, a police spokesman said: "There is no explanation. But we have no reason to suspect the informant's story."

Now, could the sample-gathering "egg" have been of the same order as that which picked up Abram's offering of meat to the Lord? And was whatever caused the strange changes in the two vehicles a similar force to that which caused Abram to fall into his unnatural sleep with its "great horror of darkness"? It is, perhaps, worth noting here that one of the accessories designed for unmanned interplanetary exploration in the U.S. space programme was a "Wolf-trap" – a sample-gathering device similar to the one Barlow described. This equipment, it should be pointed out, was invented several years *after* Barlow's weird experience.

The next seeming Biblical parallel I noted took place in Maryborough, a town about 100 miles from Melbourne, Victoria, Australia. On April 4, 1966, steel contractor Ronald Sullivan was driving home when his car headlamps suddenly bent to the right. (Impossible as this sounds, it is a fact that light waves can be bent – by gravity, for example, as in part of Einstein's theory.) Sullivan managed to stop his car without careering into a roadside fence and ditch, then noticed that his deflected headlamp beams were shining on an object in a nearby field. It was an inverted cone-shaped, cloud-like column of light, 25 feet high, with a diameter of three feet at its base and 10 feet at the top. Sullivan said its cloudy mass shone, ranging through all the colours of the spectrum. As he looked, the cone rose silently and vanished at tremendous speed. His car headlamps were restored to normal and when he had them checked at Maryborough, they were correctly aligned.

Three nights later on the same stretch of road at about the same spot, 19-year-old Gary Taylor was found dead in his crashed car. In the nearby field was a circular indentation five inches deep and about five feet in diameter. A blood alcohol analysis on the dead youth proved negative, the road was dry and perfectly straight and there was no apparent cause of the accident. Unless, that is, Taylor had experienced the same, headlamp-bending phenomenon as Sullivan and, unlike his predecessor, had been unable to hold his car on the road. It may be significant that on the night Taylor died, it was overcast and pitch black, while on the night of Sullivan's experience, there was a bright Moon. Recalling the pillar of fire that guided the Israelites across the Red Sea and took off the Egyptians' chariot wheels "that they drave them heavily", one is tempted to wonder if that same, strange force might have driven Taylor off the road.

Another UFO "classic" case occurred in New Guinea. On June 21, 1959, Stephen Moir, a teacher at the Boinai Mission, Papua, reported to an Anglican priest, the Rev. Father William Gill, that he had seen a bright, shining object in the sky which, as it hovered overhead, was disc-shaped.

The minister was sceptical about UFOs, believing that they were probably caused by some electrical freak of nature. But on the night of June 26, Father Gill saw something that moved him to write to his friend, the Rev. D. Durie, of St. Aidan's College, Dogura: "I have changed my views..."

At about 6.45PM on the 26th after dinner, Father Gill stepped out of his mission house and looked towards the west, looking for Venus, which he knew should have been visible. "I *saw* Venus," [my emphasis – Author] he said, in his later account to a colleague. "But I also saw this sparkling object, which to me was peculiar because it sparkled and because it was very, very bright, and it was above Venus and so that caused me to watch it for a while; then I saw it descend towards us."

What he saw was originally hovering at about 500 feet. He estimated the object's diameter as about five inches at arm's length. (Later he altered his angular size factor to "five times the Moon's diameter".)

Just before 7PM, as he was taking notes and making sketches of the object, he saw a figure, like a man, standing on top of the saucer-shaped vessel. Shortly afterwards, two or perhaps three other humanoid figures joined the first and appeared to be moving about the upper surface of the disc, apparently doing some task.

For the next three hours, the priest and several of his companions at the mission watched fascinated as the "men" moved to and fro atop the hovering vessel. From it, a blue beam of light stabbed upwards to the clouds, which formed an overcast at about 2,000 feet. Two other similar saucers were seen moving about nearby, one over the sea, the second over the village. Shortly afterwards, a third appeared. All three were "coming and going through clouds, casting a light halo..." Around 9.30PM, the large, hovering object moved rapidly away over the bay towards Giwa.

This strange object, with its pillar of light reaching upwards, is evocative of the vision that Jacob had of a ladder reaching up to heaven and "angels" moving to and fro. But that was not the end of Father Gill's odd encounter.

The following night the same, or a similar object appeared once more, hovering over the mission and again, three figures appeared to be going about some task on the "deck". The appearance of the object was first reported to Father Gill by a Papuan medical assistant, Annie Laurie Borewa. As a small crowd of about a dozen of the mission's teachers and residents gathered below, one of the figures moved to the edge of the disc and looked down on them as if he were leaning on the rail of a ship. Father Gill waved – and an uncanny feeling ran through the group on the ground when, to their amazement, the figure waved back. Next, one of the teachers, named only as Ananias in Gill's account, raised both arms above his head and this time, two of the figures on the saucer repeated the gesture. Again, Father Gill and the teacher made the same movement – and all four of the figures on the disc responded in the same way.

As it grew dark, Father Gill began to signal with a flashlight he had sent for and, as if in answer, the object grew alternately larger and smaller as though it were moving closer and further away. Eventually, the figures on board moved out of sight and the observers below went off to attend church services. When they returned the object had gone. Father Gill estimated the object to have been some 35 feet across with a 20-foot diameter dome on top. Mr. Peter Norris, a Melbourne lawyer and investigator for the worldwide UFO watchdog group, the Aerial Phenomena Research Organisation, investigated the case and attested to the integrity of Father Gill and the other witnesses.

Saucerian Side Effects

Those who have made extensive studies of UFOs – and these include astronomers like the late Dr. J. Allen Hynek, former astronomy department chairman at Northwestern University, Dr. Charles P. Oliver, president of the American Meteor Society and biophysicist Dr. Leslie K. Kaeburn of the University of Southern California – have noted the recurrence of specific phenomena common to many sightings and experiences.

One, for example, is for internal combustion engines to go dead when UFOs are in close proximity. Another is the presence of inexplicable "electrical" effects. Yet another, and one that is particularly intriguing, is the phenomenon of what UFOlogists have come to call "angel hair".

Angel hair is strange material, as yet unidentified analytically, with the appearance of the white, silicon fibrous material used as artificial snow in Christmas decorations. It has been observed falling from the sky shortly after UFO activity. It tends to dissolve or disintegrate soon after its contact with the ground or, more particularly, when handled. There have been numerous cases involving the discovery of this diaphanous, fleecy substance, one typical example being the following:

After several witnesses in the San Fernando Valley, California, had watched a silvery ball follow three USAF jets, a fluffy substance began to fall from the sky. The observers at first thought the "ball" was a target of some kind, being towed by the fighters, but the jets peeled off from formation while the silvery object kept flying until it was out of sight. It followed an undulating course and, before disappearing, a long entrail of white material issued from it. The white stuff drifted to earth. Experts from three aeronautics companies went to inspect the substance but it quickly disintegrated to their touch.

Could it have been something akin to this material that the Israelites fed upon and called "manna" during their desert sojourn? No modern human being, so far as is known, has ventured to taste the substance.

No examination of the UFO phenomenon would be complete without some reference to the electric effects with which they have become associated. Again, case-histories are numerous, but I have chosen what I regard as two of the most puzzling to give an idea of this peculiar effect.

The first – on August 19, 1952 – involved a scoutmaster, D.S. Desvergers, of West Palm Beach, Florida. On the way home from a meeting that evening, Desvergers and three of his scouts, saw strange lights glimmering from a thicket by the roadside. Desvergers, thinking that an aircraft might have crashed, told the boys he was going to investigate. If he did not return in 20 minutes, he said, they were to go for assistance. When the specified time went by and Desvergers did not re-emerge, the three boys called out Sheriff Mott Partin. Just as he arrived on the scene, Desvergers staggered out of the trees in a state of shock.

The scoutmaster gasped that he had gone through the bushes carrying his flashlight and machete and had suddenly found himself in a clearing but realised he could not see by the night sky above. It then occurred to him that he was standing beneath an object that was hovering. Then, a glowing red ball with a misty outline emerged from the underside of the hovering body and floated towards him. He lost consciousness and, when he came to, the object had disappeared.

USAF investigators who searched the area took grass and soil samples from the spot and discovered that the roots of the grass were charred, while the blades of grass themselves remained undamaged. They discovered that the only way to simulate this effect was to run an electrical charge through the soil. But what caused such a charge at the site of Desvergers' encounter has never been determined. Was it a similar danger that caused God to warn Moses and his people not to approach too close on Mounts Horeb and Sinai?

Even more bizzare than Desvergers' experience was an incident on the morning of November 3, 1957, at Itaipu Garrison, near Santos, Brazil. Two sentries were making their rounds in the early hours, when one of them saw a bright orange glow approaching from the ocean. By the time the object was hovering over the garrison, the sentries were terrified. The thing – about 300 feet above – was bigger than a DC-3 transport aircraft.

Next, the men heard an eerie humming noise, then were blasted with an intense wave of unbearable heat. One collapsed, while the other dragged himself under a gun emplacement to shelter and began to scream hysterically. Inside the fort, the power suddenly failed and when an emergency generator was switched on, it also malfunctioned. By the time the men got outside to the sentries, the orange light was receding, back towards the ocean.

Both sentries, who later said that they had felt that their clothes were on fire when the excruciating heat hit them, were found to have second and third degree burns on their bodies – but only over the areas that had been covered by clothing. No satisfactory explanation was ever given by the Brazilian military authorities for the incident.

Dr. Olavo T. Fontes, a teacher of medicine and hospital consultant who, until his death in May 1968, was regarded as a leading authority on UFOs, did, however, put forward a theory. Dr. Fontes, of Rio de Janeiro, who personally investigated the Itaipu incident and many other cases, suggested that UFOs might utilise a high frequency, long-range, electro-magnetic force concentrated into a powerful, narrow beam, like a laser. This beam, he said, would ionize air particles, wherever it was directed, thus making the air itself a conductor of electricity. In addition to causing electrical failure, Dr. Fontes suggested, such a beam might also, through ultra-sonics, or high frequency sound waves, produce the heat effect, generated between different substances, i.e., between the flesh and the clothing of the afflicted sentries. The beam, he added, might not necessarily be a weapon, but a highly sophisticated scanner device whose undesired effects upon man and animals might merely be side effects.

Such a device would account for the numerous Biblical instances of people being paralysed or struck dead in seemingly magical ways by the power of the Lord.

So, although our manner of describing inexplicable phenomena may be more scientific, it seems that men are still subject to similar incidents that the scribes of the Bible and other ancient scriptures have recorded in what seems to us a fanciful way.

8. UFOs Ancient And Modern

"Who are these that fly as a cloud and as the doves to their windows?"
Isiaah 60:8.

LET US NOW consider one of the most bizarre of all cases – and it happened about 593BC. The observer was the prophet Ezekiel, whose "vision" in terms of modern experiences, has become regarded as one of the best-documented UFO sightings in the whole of the Old Testament. It is also what UFOlogists would call a "contact" case or a "close encounter of the third kind", because not only did Ezekiel meet the occupants – he even went for a flight in the vessel. Some might even classify it as an "abduction" case, although the text gives no indication that Ezekiel was taken aloft against his will.

Ezekiel was a priest, the son of Buzi. Around 597BC he had been among a number of Jews deported by King Nebuchadrezzar (Nabu-kudur-usur, in its Babylonian form), from Jerusalem to Tel-Abib, just south of Babylon. At the age of about 30, Ezekiel was on the banks of the Chebar River and, he says:

"And I looked, and, behold, a whirlwind came out of the north, a great cloud and a fire infolding itself, and a brightness was about it, and out of the midst thereof as the colour of amber, out of the midst of the fire.

"Also out of the midst thereof came the likeness of four living creatures. And this was their appearance: they had the likeness of a man.

"And every one had four faces, and every one had four wings.

"And their feet were straight feet; and the sole of their feet was like the sole of a calf's foot; and they sparkled like the colour of burnished brass.

"And they had the hands of a man under their wings on their four sides; and they four had their faces and their wings.

"Their wings were joined to one another; they turned not when they went; they went every one straight forward.

"As for the likeness of their faces, they four had the face of a man, and the face of a lion, on the right side; and they four had the face of an ox on the left side; they four also had the face of an eagle.

"Thus were their faces: and their wings were stretched upward; two wings of every one were joined to one another, and two covered their bodies,

"And they went every one straight forward; whither the spirit was to go, they went; and they turned not when they went.

"As for the likeness of the living creatures, their appearance was like burning coals of fire, and like the appearance of lamps: it went up and down among the living creatures; and the fire was bright, and out of the fire went forth lightning.

"And the living creatures ran and returned as the appearance of a flash of lightning.

"Now as I beheld the living creatures, behold, one wheel upon the earth by the living creatures, with his four faces.

"The appearance of the wheels and their work was like unto the colour of beryl;

and they four had one likeness: and their appearance and their work as it were a wheel in the middle of a wheel.

"When they went, they went upon their four sides: and they turned not when they went.

"As for their rings, they were so high that they were dreadful; and their rings were full of eyes round about them four.

"And when the living creatures went, the wheels went by them: and when the living creatures were lifted up from the earth, the wheels were lifted up.

"Whithersoever the spirit was to go, they went, thither was their spirit to go; and the wheels were lifted up over against them: for the spirit of the living creature was in the wheels.

"When those went, these went: and when those stood, these stood; and when those were lifted up from the earth, the wheels were lifted up over against them: for the spirit of the living creature was in the wheels.

"And the likeness of the firmament upon the heads of the living creature was as the colour of the terrible crystal, stretched forth over their heads above.

"And under the firmament were their wings straight, the one toward the other: every one had two, which covered on this side, and every one had two, which covered on that side, their bodies.

"And when they went I heard the noise of their wings, like the noise of great waters, as the voice of the Almighty, the voice of speech, as the noise of an host; when they stood, they let down their wings.

"And there was a voice from the firmament that was over their heads, when they stood, and had let down their wings.

"And above the firmament that was over their heads was the likeness of a throne, as the appearance of a sapphire stone: and upon the likeness of the throne was the likeness as the appearance of a man above upon it.

"And I saw as the colour of amber, as the appearance of fire round about within it, from the appearance of his loins even downward, I saw as it were the appearance of fire, and it had brightness round about.

"As the appearance of the bow that is in the cloud in the day of rain, so was the appearance of the likeness of the glory of the LORD. And when I saw it, I fell upon my face, and I heard a voice of one that spake." (Ezekiel 1:4–28)

It is not difficult to see an allusion to a flying vessel when Ezekiel's account is examined closely. Indeed it is, apart perhaps from the strange reference to the four-faced "living creatures" with wings, a much more detailed and lucid account than those given in earlier sections of the Old Testament about Moses' encounters in the mountains.

But when it came to interpreting and analysing Ezekiel's experience in more detail, I had my work cut out for me – thanks to Josef F. Blumrich, then an engineer with the National Aeronautics and Space Administration. Born in Steyr, Austria, Blumrich was chief of NASA's systems layout branch and was co-builder of the Saturn V rocket. Shortly before 1972, Blumrich became fascinated by Ezekiel's description of a wheel within a wheel and turned his engineer's mind to speculating as to what it was that the prophet might have been describing. Then he remembered a space-shuttle design by a fellow engineer, Roger A. Anderson – and saw in it a perfect key to the prophet's "vision". Not only would Anderson's design fit Ezekiel's non-technical, but nonetheless detailed, specifications, but a model of the vessel was actually built and tested in a wind tunnel and found to be an ideal design for use as a shuttle between an orbiting space-platform and the surface of a planet. Anyone interested in the more technical information about the Anderson-Blumrich craft, should read Blumrich's fascinating book on the subject, *The Spaceships Of Ezekiel*. It is necessary for our purposes here only to give a rough outline of the shuttle's appearance to demonstrate how Blumrich's concept ties in with that of Ezekiel.

The Anderson craft's main body is shaped like a child's spinning top of the humming variety, with a rounded dome on top that is the command capsule. Attached to its tapering sides are juxtaposed four cylindrical, upright units with helicopter blades that are capable of being folded. The main unit would be nuclear-powered, while the helicopter blades would power the vessel for soft landings and for general local flight in an atmosphere. The rotor blades can be feathered so that they would not be damaged by the immense heat from the nuclear core that has provided braking power as the shuttle descends. Then, as the rotors gently set the vessel down, retractable, telescopic legs can be set down, with multi-directional wheels for easy movement on the ground. These wheels are, in fact, the invention of Blumrich, who took out a patent on the design. They allow the wheel to roll forwards and backwards in the normal way, but also afford sideways movement through a segmented arrangement of individual rollers.

In Blumrich's interpretation, Ezekiel first sees the vessel as it comes in to land, flames belching from its engine with loud thundering noises. As the object descends, Ezekiel sees the cylindrical helicopter units with their straight legs and round, "calf's" feet and takes them to be living creatures. Cowling that houses various equipment could form bumps and depressions on these units that might have suggested the four "faces" to the awestruck prophet.

Short bursts of tiny, directional rocket tubes mounted on these cylinders, to make flight corrections as the craft descends, give the prophet the impression of lightning, while the whirling rotor blades explain his phrase, "their wings were joined one to another". The feathering or folding of the blades nearest the reactor cowling on the body of the ship would account for the later observation, "two wings of every one were joined to one another and two covered their bodies".

The allusion to the four "living creatures" moving straight forward without turning would be Ezekiel's way of noting that wherever the craft itself moved, so the rotor units went without appearing to change direction. As the retractable wheels unfold, Ezekiel then becomes fascinated by the way they can move in several directions without appearing to swivel – thus his wheel-within-a-wheel concept. Atop the vessel, Ezekiel sees a transparent dome – clear like crystal or the sky and arched like a rainbow – under which sits a man in a "throne"; obviously the pilot or commander of the craft.

Of course, Blumrich's interpretation may not necessarily be the only correct one. Other interpreters might suggest that Ezekiel saw a flying disc, part of which revolved within its outer framework, thus giving the impression of one wheel inside another. But Blumrich's suggestions are remarkable in that (a) they account for practically all that the prophet describes, and (b) they are technically viable and aerodynamically sound in terms of contemporary space technology.

However, the exact nature of the vessel is not terribly important, rather the simple fact that Ezekiel, as did some of his forerunners, saw something that suggests extra-terrestrial visitors.

The prophet goes on to describe how the figure from the "command module" atop the vessel gives him a scroll and takes him on a flight to Jerusalem to study the iniquities into which his people have fallen. About a year later, Ezekiel encounters the strange vessel again.

There is a parallel to the experience of Ezekiel, recorded on clay tablet fragments excavated at Nineveh, in the Library of King Assurbanipal. The tablets describe how Etan, king of the Babylonian city state of Kish, was taken for a trip aboard a "flying shield" about four centuries before the Christian era. The vessel, with a fiery exhaust, landed in a square behind Etan's palace. Tall, blond men in white suits descended from the ship and invited the king aboard. According to the fragments, they took off in a whirlwind of flames and smoke and the king went so high that the Earth appeared "like a loaf in a basket", then became lost to view altogether.

After two weeks, King Etan's court officials had given him up for lost and were beginning to cast around for a successor, since he had no heir of his own. Then the flying shield returned and touched down, again with its circular fiery plume. King Etan and the mysterious blond strangers alighted and these beings – "handsome as gods" – stayed as guests in the royal palace "for some days".

One of the big questions that is inevitably asked when the possibility of alien spaceships having visited the Earth is raised is: why are there no relics, no artefacts, to prove it? Another is: how come one of these UFOs has never crashed, leaving wreckage?

It is my belief that these extra-terrestrials who, as we have suggested, visited many parts of the Earth at various times, *did* leave something that affirms their presence – knowledge. Knowledge, albeit distorted, even idealised by the distance of time and by humans' inability to interpret accurately, for example, how the Earth was formed, how human life came from clay: secrets that no early civilisation was in a position to deduce scientifically.

Whether that knowledge was imparted deliberately, as part of some great scheme these entities were undertaking, or whether it was coincidental to their purpose, is not clear. But supposing that man was only a bystander in some great, intergalactic machinations on the part of these visitors. Why should they leave *objects* to confirm their presence? In any case, what good would a computer or some such equipment have been, say, to a Moses or an Ezekiel? Whether or not they left some surviving artefacts of their visits, intentionally or otherwise – as some other writers have asserted – I think the accounts of so many people around the world in times ancient and modern is sufficient testimony to such visitations from beyond.

As an exercise, however, let us examine some of the alleged evidence that extra-terrestrial objects, possibly spacecraft, *have* crashed on Earth.

Just after 7AM on the morning of June 30, 1908, the inhabitants of the remote Jenissi district of the Tunguska region of central Siberia – mostly farmers, hunters and fishermen – saw what they later described as a gigantic ball of fire racing towards the Earth. Villagers at Vanovara saw the light, "more dazzling than that of the sun", streaking along the horizon. Suddenly, there was an enormous explosion that devastated a 770-square-mile area of forest, the size of Philadelphia, PA, or Birmingham, England, and caused seismic shock waves that were felt as far away as the British Isles. The explosion was heard as distant from Vanovara as 500 miles away in the village of Kansk, where a train driver, thinking that one of his freight cars had blown up, halted his train. A pillar of fire, visible for hundreds of miles, erupted into the sky and colossal black clouds rose 12 miles, and were followed by dirty black rain. A fierce hurricane swept out of the Tungus region above the forests (*taiga*), tearing off house rooftops and smashing windows.

A clipping from the Irkutsk newspaper, *Sibir*, was one of many collected by the scientist Leonid Kulik, who in 1921, was commissioned by the new Soviet Academy of Sciences to investigate the phenomenon. It read:

"In the village of Nizhne-Karelinsk in the northwest high above the horizon, the peasants saw a body shining very brightly (too bright for the naked eye) with a bluish-white light. It moved vertically downwards for about ten minutes. The body was in the form of a 'pipe' [cylindrical]. The sky was cloudless, except that low down on the horizon in the direction in which this glowing body was observed, a small dark cloud was noticed. It was hot and dry and when the shining body approached the ground it seemed to be pulverized and in its place a huge cloud of smoke was formed and a loud crash, not like thunder, but as if from the fall of large stone, or from gunfire, was heard. All the buildings shook and at the same time, a forked tongue of flame broke through the cloud. The old women wept, everyone thought that the end of the world was approaching."

Nizhne-Karlinsk, it was later determined, was 200 miles from the actual epicentre of the explosion.

The next day, observers throughout the Asian continent and in Europe saw high altitude clouds that appeared to be glowing. The shock waves were recorded on barographs in London. In the same capital, the sky was so bright it was possible to read items in small print in *The Times*; photographs taken in Stockholm during the night looked as if they had been taken in bright daylight; in Holland the brightness hampered astronomers from making normal observations, and in Heidelberg, Germany, brightly shining clouds appeared and lasted until morning. From the fishing village of Brancaster, Norfolk, England, golfers wrote to *The Times*, saying that they could have quite easily played a game at 2AM. In the Antarctic on the far side of the Earth, the British explorer Ernest Shackleton reported ionospheric disturbances and bright aurora lights in the sky immediately before and after the explosion. The incident subsequently became referred to as the Great Siberian Meteor.

The explosion, later calculated to be the equivalent of a 30 megaton blast, devastated hundreds of square miles of forest, reportedly killing herds of reindeer and sheering off treetops like matchsticks. Perhaps significantly, the felled trees lay flat and pointing away from a central area. In that region, assumed to be the epicentre or seat of the explosion, some trees still stood upright, indicating that the explosion took place in the air directly overhead.

Initially scientists, who did not go into the region until the 1920s, after the Russian Revolution, thought that the explosion might have been caused by some kind of meteorite but, since no fragments could be found, later supposed that a comet might have been responsible. No crater was found. At the time it was uncertain as to the exact, physical nature of comets – none ever having been known to strike the Earth – so the theory remained unquestioned.

Then, nearly 40 years later in the 1947–1959 period, after fresh investigations and their resultant findings and data analyses, it was speculated that the explosion was that of an alien vehicle which was trying to land on Earth. In the latter year, two Russian scientists, Professors Aleksandr Kazantsev and B. Lapunov, announced that they were certain that the object that caused the explosion was an alien spacecraft. Kazantsev apparently first formulated his idea that the "fireball" might not have been a meteorite or comet shortly after the bombing of Hiroshima.

Just after the end of the Second World War, Professor Kazantsev, who visited

Hiroshima after the atomic blast, declared: "An atomic explosion took place in Siberia at a height of one and a half miles."

Born in 1906 in Siberia, Kazantsev studied at Omsk and Tomsk, graduating from the latter's Technological Institute in 1930. He joined one of Moscow's scientific research institutes and, in the 1940s, was appointed head engineer of one of Russia's defence complexes, working on the development of new weaponry.

In an article for a Russian science magazine, Professor Kazantsev reconstructed the effects of the Tunguska incident:

"The explosion wave rushed downward, and the trees directly below the point of the explosion remained standing, having lost only their crowns and branches. The wave burned the points of those breaks on the trees and hit the permafrost, splitting it. Underground waters, responding to the tremendous pressure of the blow, gushed up as those fountains seen by natives after the explosion. But where the explosion wave struck at an angle, trees were felled in a fan-like pattern."

At the moment of the explosion, the temperature rose to tens of millions of degrees. Elements, even those not involved in the explosion directly, were vaporized and, in part, carried into the upper strata of the atmosphere where, continuing their radioactive disintegration, they caused that luminescent air. In part these fell to the ground as precipitation, with radioactive effects.

It was in 1951 that Kazantsev teamed up with Lapunov and they formulated the idea that an atomic-powered vessel had exploded while trying to land.

Around 1958 the Czechoslovakian newspaper *Prace* quoted a book by an aerodynamics expert called Manotskov, saying that after the explosion, people living in neighbouring regions had died from a mysterious disease. The affliction later became known as radiation sickness. The article also noted that the explosion's biggest impact was some distance from its centre, a feature that had been observed in atomic explosions. But while no crater or meteoric fragments have been discovered, neither have any remnants of the supposed spacecraft. However, fresh evidence collected in post-Second World War investigations have discovered tiny particles of magnetite and silicate – both of which are extra-terrestrial – embedded in trees and buried in the soil. The magnetite particles contained some rare earth elements, such as ytterbium and too much nickel to be terrestrial, while the silicate held bubbles of gas similar to those detected in other meteoric fragments.

The comet vs. spacecraft arguments that have continued ever since the investigation of the Tunguska incident, may be summarised as follows:

The spacecraft detractors argue that the object's trajectory on approach was almost head-on which, if it had been an alien vessel, would seem irrational. (Presuming, of course, that it was either piloted or remotely-controlled. But this does not preclude the possibility that it was out of control.)

Evidence of most witnesses was not gathered until 20 years or more after the event, thus devaluing its accuracy and reliability.

In 1977, British scientists showed that a natural explosion of non-radioactive material could, through its immense temperature, produce a small amount of radioactive fallout. This, it is argued, would explain radiation traces found the previous year by the Russian scientist Aleksey Zolotov.

Based on more up-to-date research on the nature of comets, the anti-spacecraft lobby argues that the object could have been a small, carbonaceous chondrite comet because its ice and dust particles would have soon evaporated and its "orbit" before it hit the Earth was typical of observed comet behaviour.

The glowing cloud seen above Europe could have been dust lit by the sun, rather than the incandescence of radioactive material.

As for the reports of reindeer being killed, investigators have suggested that local allusions to "burned reindeer" really refer to the destruction of a warehouse, containing "reindeerloads of flour".

Those who favour the spacecraft hypothesis, on the other hand, assert that many witnesses described the object as cylindrical, highly suggestive that it was manufactured.

They also point to the fact that the object appeared to reduce speed before it exploded, and that its trajectory was erratic in a zig-zag path. They claim that the pattern of the blast was irregular, suggesting the explosion of a hull by some interior detonation.

Other pro-spacecraft arguments assert that there was evidence of radiation sickness and a rise of radiation levels in the Northern Hemisphere, measured by carbon-14 in trees; a marked acceleration of tree growth in the region following the blast, would be consistent with nuclear fallout.

Further outstanding questions include: if the blast were not a nuclear one, how was such energy generated, and why wasn't such a large comet seen long before it came to Earth?

The comet-theory supporters insist that such energy could have been generated in a natural explosion of a cometary body and that, since the comet appeared out of a dawn sky, its tail would have trailed *away* from the Sun, accounting for the extremely bright nights throughout Northern Europe.

In 1973, at the Center for Relativity Theory at the University of Texas, researchers A.A. Jackson and M.P. Ryan suggested that the object must have been a miniature black hole. They calculated that this would have moved right through the Earth and emerged on the opposite side, between Iceland and Newfoundland. Russian investigators checked ships' log books and local Icelandic and Newfoundland newspapers around the date of the explosion, but could find no evidence of the kind of disturbance an emerging black hole might have made.

Another, alternative suggestion was later made by Clyde Cowan and Hall Crannell, of the Catholic University at Washington, D.C., and C.R. Atluri and W.F. Libby, of the University of California, Los Angeles. They suggested the Earth might have been struck by a particle of anti-matter. But despite elaborate calculations and a complex method for working out the increase in radiation which should have succeeded such a collision, no hard and fast conclusions were put forward.

In 1980, Arthur C. Clarke pointed out that it wasn't until the development of radio astronomy that meteor swarms occurred that had hitherto gone undetected. And he pointed out that one of the most noticeable using this technique, a stream called the Taurids, encounters Earth every year on the same date: June 30, the date of the Siberian incident. (The Taurids were discovered by the British radio astronomer Sir Bernard Lovell and his colleagues at Jodrell Bank in 1947).

Clarke wrote ominously: "...perhaps the most important lesson from Tunguska is that what happened once will (not may) happen again. Almost all our planetary neighbours bear evidence of repeated bombardments from space... The only reason why it has taken so long to recognize such stigmata on our own planet is because weathering, and geological processes, have largely obliterated them.

"Early in 1980, American scientists produced evidence that the extinction of the dinosaurs, some sixty-five million years ago, was triggered by the impact of a heavenly body far larger than the Tunguska object. Perhaps that gave us a chance to evolve; and perhaps a similar event will open the way to our successors.

"It may not happen for a million years. Or it may happen... much sooner."

However, notwithstanding all the arguments on either side, the Siberian incident continues to baffle experts and generates controversy to this day.

A fragment of surprisingly pure magnesium, of a purity beyond human metallurgical techniques of manufacture, was one of three samples sent to *O Globo*, a newspaper in Rio de Janeiro, Brazil, in September 1957. They were received by one of the journal's columnists, Ibrahim Sued. With them was a letter claiming that the fragments had been gathered after a group of fishermen had seen a flying saucer over Ubatuba, a village in Sao Paulo province. It said that the UFO had exploded in the air, scattering fragments like the samples enclosed.

Analysis of one of the fragments, known as Sample No. 1, was made by Dr. Luisa Maria A. Barbosa, of the spectrographic section of the Mineral Production Laboratory of the Brazilian Ministry of Agriculture. She confirmed that it consisted *entirely* of the element magnesium.

A second fragment of the same Sample was confirmed as pure magnesium after analysis by Mr. Elson Teixeira of the Mineral Production Laboratory. After further tests on fragments of Sample No 1, it was found to be of an unusually high density of 1.866 [these included Debye-Scherrer-Hull powder pattern X-ray diffraction analysis, radiation tests and density measurements].

The last two remaining fragments of Sample 1 were passed on to the Brazilian Army and Navy, but if any analyses were carried out, no information was released.

The analyses carried out by Dr. Barbosa and Mr. Teixeira involved destroying the fragments, so at this point, no further ones of Sample No. 1, were left for further examination.

Pro-UFO enthusiasts, however, have pointed out the importance of the latter's findings in suggesting the material's extra-terrestrial nature – in human terms, it is impossible to manufacture any element that is utterly pure on spectrographic analysis.

Sample Nos. 2 and 3, also in Mr. Sued's possession, were sent to the Aerial Phenomena Research Organisation in Tucson, Arizona. One of APRO's reports said that the metal, on analysis, turned out to be highly purified magnesium. Its surface was found to be marked in such a way as to suggest that it had been subjected to intense heat – as in an explosion – then had suddenly cooled, as if immersed in the sea.

Sample No. 3 was lent for analysis to the University of Colorado UFO Project during the mid-1960s. The Project was contracted by the U.S. Air Force Scientific Advisory Board to investigate UFO phenomena and, under Dr. Edward U. Condon, was operative from November 1, 1966 until October 31, 1968.

Physical chemist Dr. Roy Craig submitted it to neutron activation analysis at the National Office Laboratory, Alcohol and Tobacco Tax Division of the Internal Revenue Service. It was concluded that it was not as pure as that reported for Sample No. 1. But the analysis also showed that it contained an impurity not found in terrestrial magnesium – a surprising level of strontium. Metallographic and micro-probe tests at the Dow Chemical Metallurgical Laboratory confirmed this fact.

It may be significant, in noting the lesser purity of Sample 2, that the University of Colorado team at no time had access to fragments of Sample No. 1, which the Condon Report failed to note when published in January 1968.

In the early 1970s, fragments of the magnesium from Ubatuba were allegedly subjected to laser impact studies by the Australian Commonwealth Scientific and Industrial Research Organisation. Then, midway through the same decade, samples were available for mass-spectrographic examination at Stanford University. But, so far as is known, results from neither of these two sources were made available.

So, like the Tunguska incident, a final solution to the origin of the Ubatuba magnesium has never been satisfactorily forthcoming.

The Spitzbergen Island Case

Like many researchers at the time, I gave an account of this case in my chapter on UFOs in *The Zarkon Principle*. Since then, however, it has emerged that the whole incident was a hoax perpetrated by a West German magazine, aimed at boosting circulation.

In 1952, the story went, European news agencies reported that a Norwegian Air Force pilot had spotted what appeared to be the wreckage of an aircraft on the island of Spitzbergen. Norwegian military officials were flown in to investigate and it was alleged that the US Air Force and other NATO representatives were invited to take part, but nothing further was reported. Pro-UFO buffs and conspiracy theorists, perhaps predictably, seized upon this as yet another instance of a CIA cover-up.

Shortly after the Norwegians went into Spitzbergen, however, it was reported that one official was quoted as saying that the "aircraft" had turned out to be an object "commonly known as a flying saucer". It had been seriously damaged.

The West German magazine even claimed that log books were found in the wreckage which indicated that the vessel could fly only 30,000 kilometres without refuelling, a factor scarcely conducive to interplanetary voyages. Nor was it explained how the log books – if extra-terrestrial – could be *read*, although curiously the magazine never said the object was an alien vessel. Rather, it claimed that the aircraft was Russian in origin and the log books and instrument panel markings, were actually in Russian!

However, once the magazine was published, further, obviously poorly-researched newspaper accounts, added fuel to the UFO-believers' arguments.

For example, on September 4, 1955, the *Stuttgarter Tageblatt* reported the following, datelined Oslo:

"A board of inquiry of the Norwegian General Staff is preparing publication of a report on the examination of remains of a UFO crashed near Spitzbergen, presumably early in 1952. Chairman of the board, Colonel Gernod Darnbyl, during a lecture to air force officers stated: "Some time ago a misunderstanding was caused by saying that this disc probably was of Soviet origin. It has – this we wish to state emphatically – not been built by any country on Earth. The materials used in its construction are completely unknown to all experts who participated in the investigation.

"According to Colonel Darnbyl, the board of inquiry is not going to publish an extensive report until some sensational facts have been discussed with US and British experts."

Researchers such as the arch-UFO-debunker, the late Edward U. Condon (1902–74) and, at the other end of the scale, author John A. Keel, became so incensed that they suggested that, since the Spitzbergen case had no grounding in reality, all references to it should be deleted from UFO archives everywhere.

I have given a resumé of it here, however, to show that in this and in many other fields, such as parapsychology, fakes and hoaxes are present and tend to devalue the work of serious investigators.

Despite hoaxes and cover-up stories, some of which may well have some substance, not to mention lunatic-fringe claims about imminent Martian invasions, it is clear that something quite extraordinary and inexplicable has been taking place in our skies and around our planet for centuries, even millennia.

And not all of the accounts can be explained away.

And yet, at the conclusion of the two-year study into the phenomenon at the University of Colorado – the Condon Report, issued on January 8, 1969 – Edward U. Condon, its director, made this statement:

"Our general conclusion is that nothing that has come from the study of UFOs in the past 21 years has added to scientific knowledge. Careful consideration of the record as it is available to us leads us to conclude that further extensive study of UFOs probably cannot be justified in the expectation that science will be advanced thereby."

Yet at one count, no fewer than 26 astronauts in the U.S. space programme alone had seen, photographed and filmed unidentified flying objects while in orbit around the Earth, beginning perhaps in 1962 and including personnel aboard Skylabs I, II and III. It would be pointless and tedious to catalogue here the long list of such sightings. But it is worth quoting at length the late James E. McDonald, (1920-71), former senior physicist at the Institute of Atmospheric Physics and professor at the department of meteorology, of the University of Arizona, Tucson.

McDonald, who studied in depth more than 1,000 UFO accounts and interviewed witnesses running into several hundreds, was critical of the U.S. Air Force's investigative Project Blue Book, and of the methods and findings of the USAF's University of Colorado UFO study project. With permission, he analyzed every single case in the Colorado project's Condon Report and decided that many of its "explanations" were unsoundly based.

In a prepared statement to the Committee on Science and Astronautics, a U.S. Congressional body, in July 1968, he declared:

"My own present opinion, based on two years of careful study, is that UFOs are probably extra-terrestrial devices engaged in something that might be termed surveillance. For this record, I should have to state that my interviewing results dispose me toward acceptance of the existence of humanoid occupants in some UFOs."

Professor McDonald added: "Occupant sightings must be carefully distinguished from elaborate 'contact-claims' with the Space Brothers; I hold no brief at all for the latter in terms of my present knowledge, and interviewing experience. But occupants there seem to be and contact of a limited sort may well have occurred, according to certain of the reports."

As an atmospheric physicist, in 1971, MacDonald was called before a House of Representatives committee which was studying the proposed US supersonic transport plane. MacDonald gave evidence based on his atmospheric research, expressing the opinion that he believed SSTs would damage Earth's ozone layer and thus would cause an increase in skin cancer. (This, of course, is today widely accepted.)

During the questions that ensued, the discussion somehow turned its attention to the subject of UFOs. MacDonald, who even had a National Academy of Sciences grant to support his research into UFOs, asserted his belief that there is a connection between sightings and electrical power failures. His statement was later used to ridicule his testimony on the effect of SSTs on the ozone later. MacDonald committed suicide later that same year.

The great pioneering psychiatrist Carl Gustav Jung, shortly before his death in 1961, began to take an interest in the UFO phenomenon and wrote a treatise on the subject, *Flying Saucers: A Modern Myth Of Things Seen In The Skies*. Far from being a sceptical essay – despite the word "myth" in his title – Jung had some fascinating observations to make. His conclusions are more or less summed up in these passages:

"These rumours, or the possible existence of such objects, seem to me so significant that I feel myself compelled, as once before when events were brewing of fateful consequence for Europe, to sound a note of warning. I know that, just as before, my voice is much too weak to reach the ear of the multitude. It is not presumption that drives me, but my conscience as a psychiatrist that bids me fulfil my duty and prepare those few who will hear me for coming events which are in accord with the end of an era.

"As we know from Ancient Egyptian history, they are symptoms of psychic changes that always appear at the end of one Platonic month and at the beginning of another. [A Platonic month is 2,150 years]. They are, it seems, changes in the constellation of psychic dominants, or the archetypes, or 'gods' as they used to be called, which bring about, or accompany, long-lasting transformations of the collective psyche. This transformation started within the historical tradition and left traces behind it, first in the transition from the age of Taurus to that of Aries, and then from Aries to Pisces, whose beginning coincides with the rise of Christianity. We are now nearing that great change which may be expected when the spring point enters Aquarius. It would be frivolous of me to conceal from the reader that reflections such as these are not only exceedingly unpopular, but come perilously close to those turbid fantasies which becloud the minds of world-improvers and other interpreters of 'signs and portents'. But I must take this risk, even if it means putting my hard-won scientific judgment in jeopardy. I can assure my readers that I do not do this with a light heart.

"I am, to be frank, concerned for all those who are caught unprepared by their incomprehensible nature. Since, so far as I know, no-one has yet felt moved to examine and set forth the possible psychic consequences of this foreseeable change, I deem it my duty to do what I can in this respect. I undertake this thankless task in the expectation that my chisel will make no impression on the hard stone it meets."

In his investigation of the UFO phenomenon, Jung found that many people somehow intuitively expected the modern wave of Flying Saucers – indeed, many even welcomed the idea. What worried him was the possibility of a mental regression, both moral and intellectual, that might accompany the sudden realisation by man that he is not the sole intelligent life in the Universe and, indeed, might be of an inferior strain. Jung was thinking, no doubt, of the results that this kind of confrontation had brought about in primitive societies on Earth, when faced with other, more civilised groups. Far from learning from advanced cultures, primitive peoples have been seen to become disenchanted by such contact; demoralised to such an extent that their societies have degenerated, lost all their distinctive cultural features and even ultimately become utterly enfeebled and then extinct. While anthropological traits are not a main theme of this book, it would be well to consider Jung's hypothesis in relation to modern society, anaesthetised as it is by such mass-level preoccupations as television, fashion, pop music and other ultimately directionless or goalless pursuits. (Goalless, that is, perhaps, except for amassing wealth.)

The late Canadian philosopher, Marshall McLuhan (1911–80), impressed by our sophisticated communications systems and the way in which the world has been shrunk by the link-ups of television, has called the Earth a "global cathode village". But would our "village" be able to cope with the psychological implications if an alien race, capable of journeying any number of light years across space, were to cease its surveillance and, as in Moses' time apparently, make contact?

When Orson Welles did his famous *War Of The Worlds* dramatisation on American radio in 1938, it created panic. At the thought of an invasion by Martians, people ran into the streets in terror, jammed highways with their cars as they fled aimlessly; others barricaded themselves in their homes or rushed out to churches to pray; there were even some suicides. If a mere radio broadcast could cause such disruption then, what would the reality of an alien confrontation mean to our planet now, especially now that it is instantly linked by satellite communications? And what, we may well wonder with some trepidation, would be the purpose of such a confrontation?

A study set up by NASA in the late 1950s consulted a broad spectrum of experts about their projections of the longterm effects of space exploration. In part the report, subsequently submitted to the federal government, said public hysteria could not be ruled out even if alien contact were made only by radio communication.

It recommended further studies to determine how people would emotionally react to such contact and how previous societies in the past had fared when faced with unfamiliar and disturbing events. The first encounters of the Spanish conquistadors with South American Indians, immediately springs to mind, for example – the Incas had never seen a man on horseback and at first were terrified, thinking that they were seeing one creature.

How, the study members asked, should the public be informed – if at all – if an alien encounter took place? Since the majority of science fiction stories, novels, movies and television series depict aliens as hostile, it is possible that public reaction would be a mixture of fear and, perhaps, unfairly grounded, mutually reciprocal aggression.

I should like the reader to keep such considerations as this in mind, as their relevance may become all too clear later.

9. Extra-Terrestrial Life-Search

"Hang up! Look what happened to the Indians."
Dr. Albert Hibbs, of Caltech Jet Propulsion Laboratory, Pasadena, California, when asked how Earth should reply to the first message from an alien source

"To consider Earth as the only populated world is as absurd as to assert that in an entire field sown with millet only one grain will grow."
Metrodorus (4th century BC)

EVIDENCE THAT "intelligent" beings exist upon Earth now pervades our galaxy, the Milky Way. This information is streaking through the galaxy at such speed that it may be reaching other solar systems that may be inhabited at the rate of one a week.

By the end of the 1970s, the American astronomer Dr. Frank Drake, of Cornell University, New York, was telling a Unesco conference on "Life in the Universe" that the Earth was already surrounded by a sphere of space with a radius of 30 light years, filled with television and other signals that had been broadcast over the previous 30 years.

And at the rate at which this sphere of outputs was expanding, Dr. Drake said, within another decade it would be reaching two new stars a week. This meant that knowledge of the existence of the human race and its liking for soap operas and Westerns was becoming available to a constantly increasing number of hypothetical extra-terrestrial civilisations. There was, Dr. Drake said, nothing mankind could now do to conceal our "cultural" tastes.

What chances were there, then, of intelligences on other planets orbiting the stars within this expanding sphere being capable of detecting our existence? Another radio astronomer, Dr. Jill Tarter, of the University of California, said the odds were by no means negligible.

She pointed out that within a radius of 80 light years from Earth, were about 600 stars of roughly the same age, size and stability as our Sun, a proportion of which could have inhabited planets in orbit.

The question that must – and indeed has – arisen from such considerations, of course, is that of communication between ourselves and other-worldly civilisations. Many scientists believe that, in the long run, it is inevitable. But, as may be seen from the first quotation at the head of this chapter, not all of them are in favour of such dialogues.

Indeed, there were those at the 1979 Unesco conference who claimed, for differing reasons to those of Caltech's Dr. Hibbs, that there would be little point in starting two-way radio communications with other civilisations. For a start, the detractors point out, we might wait thousands of years for a reply to one of our radio messages.

Dr. Pierre Connes, of the French National Research Council, told the Unesco meeting: "One may argue that much of the fun in sending letters lies in expecting answers. But a time delay of millennia would be too long." It would, he said, be more worthwhile to concentrate on digesting an original alien message to Earth.

Within scientific and lay circles, the argument – should we call them or let them call us? – has occupied countless hours of debating time and reams of carefully considered papers on the subject. In this chapter, I review the various developments in what has become known as SETI – the Search for Extra Terrestrial Intelligence.

Some UFO researchers believe that what appear to be signs of alien surveillance in various sightings throughout the world are actually follow-ups of previous, abortive attempts to make remote communication. There are many instances of signals picked up on Earth already recorded in the annals of UFOlogy, which are highly suggestive that such attempts have already been made in the past.

One of the earliest examples was that of the electronics pioneer and unsung genius Nikola Tesla, who received unusual signals at his laboratory in Colorado Springs – in 1899.

Born in 1856, in Smiljan, in the Austro-Hungarian border province of Lika, Croatia, Tesla arrived in the United States in 1881 or 1884, depending on which authority is accepted. A visionary, fascinated even as a child by electricity, Tesla had an eidetic memory: that is, he could visualise his ideas and inventions in his head, mentally testing them out, seeing their components from all angles, before he actually committed them to paper.

A proponent of alternating current, he worked for a time with Thomas Edison, who had a vested interest in direct current and who, along with many others, came to welch on promises of financial rewards for ideas stemming from Tesla's unquestionable genius.

Throughout his life, Tesla see-sawed between poverty and wealth and poured out a staggering number of ideas and inventions, some of which came to fruition, some of which did not. Often, others got the credit.

Among the things he devised that became accepted and implemented were the use of polyphase currents and dynamos to generate them, the rotating magnetic field, the alternating current motor, the principles of radar, radio control, an electronic tube for use as a detector in a radio system, X-ray therapy, lamps without wired connections, hydro-electric power, robotics, the bladeless turbine. He described guided missiles, what may have been lasers, wingless aircraft and may have discovered cosmic rays and X-rays. His name is commemorated in the Tesla coil, for generating very high frequency currents at high potential. In all, he patented some 1,200 of his inventions. In many cases, he literally gave away ideas he could have patented and cashed in upon.

Yet on January 7, 1943, Tesla died alone in his room at the New Yorker Hotel in Manhattan. Even before his body had been removed, FBI agents took away all his papers which, even though he was a legal immigrant, were then sealed by the Custodian of Alien Property. (It is said that in 1937 he had offered to the American and British governments a particle transmitter, sometimes, perhaps erroneously, described as a "death ray", which would put an end to all wars. But his idea was met with utter indifference. Other accounts have described the device as an "anti-war machine" capable of remotely detonating bombs anywhere, causing them either to explode on site or when they approached within 200 miles of Tesla's "machine". More latterly, it has been speculated that what Tesla was proposing was a particle beam weapon, capable of projecting high energy particles over vast distances to destroy or knock out ballistic missiles or enemy satellites.)

Today, there is a steadily growing cult to his memory, to such an extent that, in the

---

summer of 1990, the latest addition to the many theme parks – Biblical, historical, zoological – was opened: Teslaland, at Colorado Springs, high in the Rockies, on the former site of his laboratory. Among its attractions is the Tesla Coil – a giant spiral roller coaster which, as its carriage descends, shoots off spectacular sparks.

In 1899 in his Colorado laboratory, Tesla was using extremely dangerous high voltages to try to transmit energy, without the need for wires, by radio – one of his more cherished aims. In an almost Frankensteinian setting, on the hot summer nights, he fired artificial lightning bolts from a 200-foot tower into the sky, in a patterned sequence.

In this way, Tesla managed to make the electrical equipment and lighting of his lab function without any wiring circuits. Then, inexplicably, his radio equipment began to pick up signals. In them, he later claimed, he could detect "a clear suggestion of number and order not traceable to any cause then known to me".

Tesla became convinced the signals he received were transmissions by intelligences somewhere in space and that superior extra-terrestrial intelligences were attempting to make contact.

As a learned scientist, he was well aware of natural forces that might have been responsible, such as magnetic earth currents, sunspots or the aurora borealis. Instead, he said: "The feeling is constantly growing on me that I had been the first to hear the greeting of one planet to another."

In the very summer of the same year, 1899, the great radio pioneering genius Guglielmo Marconi (1874–1937), was shading into similar ideas to those of Tesla. While Tesla was pondering the possibility of signals from another civilisation, Marconi was working on his attempts to make radio a way of communication across the globe. He was transmitting the Morse signal for the letter V – dot-dot-dot-dash – to colleagues some 50 miles away. Around 22 years later, he made it public that he also had received seeming replies to his signals in what he suspected was some form of a cipher. Incorporated into the cipher was a repetition of the Morse for V which he had been sending out in 1899.

The *New York Times* of September 2, 1921 carried a news item stating that Marconi believed that some of the enigmatic "answers" to his outputs might possibly have been transmitted from the planet Mars. It went unnoticed that Tesla had also claimed to have picked up transmissions, having sent out his own signals in the same year of 1899.

Both researchers' pronouncements passed without much attention until 1924. It is possible that the lack of interest stemmed from the fact that, while Tesla was intent upon trying to send electrical impulses without the use of wires, Marconi was more concerned with using Morse code to send radio messages. But in 1924, Mars was at its perigee, that is, its closest orbital approach to Earth. At that time, the Jenkins radio camera, which could transform radio impulses into visual images, was being considered by the British astronomer David Todd, for examining Mars for signs of life.

Todd's proposed experiment was picked up by the news media and, because it necessitated complete silence from the Earth's radio transmitters, many governments cooperated in monitoring the attempt, something that would be virtually unthinkable with today's countless commercial broadcasting stations and radar installations.

As the great "listen-in" progressed, so strong were the signals received that even amateur, or ham, radio operators reported receiving them. On August 28, 1924, the *New York Times* gave a description of what had been picked up by the Jenkins technique:

"...a fairly regular arrangement of dots and dashes along one side, but on the other side at almost evenly spaced intervals are curiously jumbled groups, each taking the form of a crudely drawn face."

In 1927, Taylor and Young, a couple of American researchers, attempted to pinpoint the origin of the peculiar signals. They had measured a 0.01-second periodicity, seemingly emanating from 1,800 and 6,250 miles and tried to match them against the signals Marconi had received.

Other scientists began to take an interest. Jurgen Hals of the electronics giant Philips laboratories in Eindhoven, Holland, had noted three-second delays between signals received on his experimental transmitter. He and Professor Carl Stormer of Oslo, capital of Norway, conferred on the subject. A year later, another Philips employee, Dr. Balthasar van der Pol, reported that he, too, had picked up strange signals at the same time each morning when he planned a series of transmissions. Van der Pol concluded, judging by the time lapse between his outputs and the return of their echoes, that the signals could not possibly be reverberating from the Van Allen belt, bouncing off layers of ionised gas or even returning from the Moon.

For some reason, anomalous "signals", especially on the 30,000 metre wavelength, were picked up from time to time throughout two decades, continuing into the 1930s, when a series of reports of unidentified flying objects were logged in northern European countries and in Scandinavia. Simultaneously, operators of short wave radio receivers picked up sudden bursts of weird voices, some of which sounded like cries. Rough translations, though not always grammatically accurate, appeared to demonstrate some deliberate pattern, although not necessarily intelligible. Some of these signals seemed to consist of an amalgam of Swedish-sounding words, mixed up with other, unknown speech patterns.

In the early part of 1960, the American radio astronomer Dr. Frank Raymond Drake made what is accredited as the first ever attempt to detect a message or messages from an extra-terrestrial civilisation. He aimed the 85-foot diameter dish antenna of the National Radio Astronomy Observatory at Green Bank, West Virginia, at the stars Tau Ceti and Epsilon Eridani.

Drake selected these individual stars – about 11 light years away – because they seemed to be similar in type to our own Sun, and might have their own orbiting planets, one of which may be life-supporting. Drake called his venture Project Ozma, after a princess in the L. Frank Baum stories of the fabulous Land of Oz.

Director of the Green Bank observatory, Dr. Otto Struve, at a press conference to announce the project estimated that there must be at least one million inhabited planets in our galaxy. (The scientist and prolific author Isaac Asimov, through careful calculations, put the estimate for civilisations in the Milky Way at 530,000, in his 1980 book *Extraterrestrial Civilisations*.)

After three months of listening and waiting, the project lapsed – no signals from an alien civilisation were picked up by the telescope. There was, however, one seemingly hopeful hiccup during the project. At one point the recording needles of Drake's monitoring equipment were knocked off the scale by an eight-pulse-per-second signal. Drake and his team were listening in the 21 centimetre or 1420 MHz region – the frequency of radio waves emitted by hydrogen. The signals sustained for five minutes. The Naval Research Laboratory later admitted that it, too, had recorded similar impulses over the previous six months, but had determined that they were not of extra-terrestrial origin. And Drake's researchers discovered several weeks later that the signals had come from a military installation engaged on radar research.

But, according to Major Donald E. Keyhoe, who from 1957 to 1970 was director of the National Investigations Committee on Aerial Phenomena (NICAP), Project Ozma continued to operate secretly, under the eye of the Air Force Office of Scientific Research.

Surprisingly, immediately after Ozma was officially "closed", Dr. Struve appeared to backtrack on his original statements. He said it was folly to listen for messages from other worlds. And he added that, even if signals were received, it might be unwise to answer. Asked when the project might be reopened, he told newsmen: "Come back in a thousand years."

In his book, *Aliens From Space*, (Panther 1975), Major Keyhoe, who after his retirement from NICAP became a champion against an alleged government cover-up conspiracy on UFOs, wrote:

"What could have caused this noted scientist to expose himself to ridicule with such a strange performance? Inevitably, there was conjecture that the Tau Ceti message had been deciphered – and that it had caused sudden, deep fear... something powerful was involved in Struve's sudden reversal. The proof of this is the development which followed, perhaps the most unbelievable of all."

Major Keyhoe claimed that in November 1961, a secret meeting of scientists gathered at Green Bank to estimate the number of planets capable of communicating with Earth. Among those at the meeting, he said, were Dr. Struve, Dr. Melvin Calvin,, Dr. John C. Lilly, Dr. Drake and Dr. Carl Sagan. Following "long, careful discussions and calculations", according to Keyhoe, the whole group approved a secret estimate, known as the Green Bank Formula:

"There are between 40,000,000 and 50,000,000 worlds which are either trying to signal us or are listening for messages from Earth."

Since then, claims Keyhoe, Project Ozma has continued monitoring for space signals, at the Arecibo observatory in Puerto Rico.

"The true story of the Tau Ceti incident may never be revealed," he said. "It seems almost certain that Dr. Struve was persuaded to conceal the facts in the best interests of the public, though it meant a humiliating ordeal.

"Whatever happened, it was apparently the cause of the fear which still affects some space scientists. A few warn that it is dangerous even to listen to space messages. Arthur C. Clarke, the highly-respected space-travel authority, believes that a malevolent super-race might transmit vicious, compelling information which could cause us to destroy ourselves.

"Fear of contacting an advanced race has also extended to communicating with UFO beings. Some of the scientists know the evidence, the secret AF conclusions and the attempts to capture the UFO spacecraft. Even though there is no strong evidence of hostility, a few scientists have warned that we must not expect all space beings to be friendly – our visitors might enslave or destroy us. Dr. Thomas Gold, in a similar warning, added that such space beings might even consider us food."

As for the cover-up conspiracy, Keyhoe pointed an accusing finger at the CIA as the main instigators. He wrote:

"The Central Intelligence Agency is the power behind the UFO secrecy. Though it is not widely known, the CIA has authority over the Intelligence departments of all the military services. It has strong influence with the heads of the Army, Navy, Air Force and Marine Corps. It can exert pressure – though it does not have full control – on the Federal Aviation Administration, the Coast Guard, the Federal Communications commission and most other government agencies – except the FBI.

"The CIA take-over of the Air Force investigation occurred in 1953. Since then, the Central Intelligence Agency has used its power to guide and support the Air Force deception of Congress, the press and the public."

About the same time he launched Project Ozma, in 1960, Dr. Drake became the first astronomer to devise a system whereby messages could formulated for interstellar radio transmission. He pioneered the development of binary coded messages from which information-carrying "pictographs" could be decoded. Using this method, he constructed the first-ever interstellar radio-transmission aimed at reaching any extra-terrestrial civilisations. Drake's transmission became known as the Arecibo Message of 1974, because it was sent out from the world's largest 1,000-foot antenna radio telescope at Arecibo, Puerto Rico, at 1.30PM on Saturday November 16 of that year. So far, it is one of three messages, employing the techniques devised by Drake, to be sent into space. The other two are the Pioneer 10 and 11 plaques, (of which, more later), designed by Drake, Dr. Carl Sagan and his wife, Linda Salzman Sagan, and the Voyager Record, also the brainchild of Drake, with contributions by others.

Drake's historic message was aimed at a galaxy, M-1, a globular cluster 25,000 light years away. It contains some 300,000 stars. It took three minutes to transmit 1,679 pulses consisting of two alternate variations in the signal. Drake described it as "an anti-puzzle... a code designed to be easily broken".

It formed a pictograph made by arranging the 1,679 pulses in an format of 23 by 73 characters. These are the only two numbers by which 1,679 can be divided. The message was in a binary language, in which there are only two numerals – 0 and 1. The "on" pulses were coloured, while the "off" ones were left white.

The top row of the message demonstrated how to count from 1 to 10; the next line gave the numbers 1, 6, 7, 8 and 15 – the atomic numbers of the elements hydrogen, carbon, nitrogen, oxygen and phosphorus, all of them needed for the development of life on our planet.

Two rows followed giving the components of nucleic acids: a phosphate grouping, a molecule of deoxyribose, and the formulae for thymine, adenine, guanine and cytonsine. Together, these form DNA. A statement issued by the Arecibo observatory pointed out that "knowledgeable organic chemists anywhere should be able through rather simple logic to arrive at a unique solution for the molecular structures being described here." In the centre of the message were patterns representing the double helix in which DNA is found and a block of squares within the double spiral gave the binary number for four billion – the number of pairs of nucleotides in human DNA.

There follows a crude pictograph representation of a human figure, beside which on the right is a line from its head to feet and the binary number 14. This indicates that the figure is 14 units tall. Whoever decodes the message is assumed to understand that the unit is the wavelength of the transmission – 12.6 centimetres – which would make the human 5 feet 9½ inches tall. To the left of the figure is a binary representation of four billion, representing Earth's population at the time of the transmission.

A crude sketch of the solar system follows, with some indication of the relative sizes of the planets. The third planet from the Sun is inclined slightly towards the human figure to indicate that Earth is our home. Finally, the message ends with an outline of a radio telescope and binary representations of its size: 1,004 feet.

The Arecibo observatory statement said: "This information tells indirectly, when taken with the strength of our signal, a great deal about the level of our technology. If the message is transmitted repeatedly, a desired impression is made that the message emerges from the telescope."

To some observers, the project was something of a *fait accompli*. After the message had been transmitted, there was some dissent from the international SETI membership, because they had not been consulted in advance. And in 1976 a Soviet source indicated a hope "that there will be further international discussions on the subject before such a programme of transmissions is launched" – there had been a formal agreement at an international conference in Armenia five years earlier that no single nation should begin trying to communicate with other civilisations independently.

Dr. Drake somewhat countered these reactions by pointing out that the message was seen as more of a symbolic gesture than a serious attempt to communicate with extra-terrestrial sources. And, despite the observatory statement, the message was beamed only once. He added that it would take some 50,000 years to reach its destination, be received and answered, so any breach of Earth's security was not serious.

Seven years after the inception of Project Ozma, in 1967 a group of astronomers at England's Cambridge University, picked up a radio signal from space, which they at first thought might be from an extra-terrestrial civilisation. The signals were weak, but were transmitted at precise intervals of 1.33730113 seconds, "as regularly spaced as a broadcast time signal".

Members of the team, headed by Professor Anthony Hewish, were initially so excited by the signals, first noted by undergraduate Jocelyn Bell, that they called the source LGM-1, the initials standing for "Little Green Men".

They did not think they had actually received a coherent message, but there was the possibility that the signals could have been an impulse from some kind of interstellar beacon that an advanced civilisation might use to guide its interstellar vessels. However, the transmission eventually turned out to be that of a pulsar, a star – in this case mid-way between Vega and Altair – which emitted regular, natural bursts of radio energy. (Later, when Nobel prizes were awarded for the discovery of pulsars, many individuals in academic circles were disappointed, if not annoyed, that Jocelyn Bell was not among those credited.)

As more astronauts began to venture into space, further unexplained occurrences were reported by various individuals. When one of them, Gordon Cooper, was in orbit over Hawaii in his Mercury capsule on May 16, 1963, talking to mission control, unscheduled transmissions cut in. Carefully analysed later on tape recordings, the speeches did not appear to be in any Earthly tongue.

The same phenomenon happened on December 21 that same year, after UFOs had been sighted orbiting the Moon. The strange voices interrupted transmissions between mission control and the Bormann-Lovell-Anders Apollo VIII mission.

What was disturbing to both the astronauts and the controllers on Earth was that the frequency they were using was almost inaccessible to any private, amateur radio operator. The interferences posed something of a security risk.

The first Earth space project designed to leave the solar system, Pioneer 10, was launched on March 3, 1972, bound first for the giant planet Jupiter. Towards the end of the previous year, science writer Eric Burgess contacted the astronomer Carl Sagan, drawing to his attention the fact that, since the unmanned vessel would leave our system, it could bear a message to any alien intelligence that might encounter it.

When Sagan contacted NASA, suggesting the idea, he was surprised to find that there were no objections. After consultation with fellow-astronomer Dr. Drake and his wife, Linda Salzman Sagan, two plaques were designed and made within three weeks. Etched on gold-anodised aluminium plates measuring six by nine inches, the plaques were ultimately fixed to the antenna support struts of both Pioneer 10 and its successor, Pioneer 11, which was launched a year after the first.

The head of the plaque carries symbols of two hydrogen atoms, intended to depict that they are emitting 21-centimetre radiation. To the left centre is a network of lines radiating from a central point. Each line has a long binary number. They represent pulsars and the numbers represent the time lapses between radio wave emissions from each pulsar. The length of each line represents the pulsars' distance from Earth, at the centre of the radiating lines. This is designed to show the source of the message on the plaque and the time the probe was launched.

To the right of the plaque is a basic line drawing by Sagan's wife, of a male and female nude human figure, the man raising his right hand, as if in greeting. Behind them is a two-dimensional side elevation of the space vessel. To the right of this are binary representations of the size of the human couple.

At the foot of the plaque is a scale binary diagram of the solar system, with an image of the spacecraft originating from Earth and swinging outwards between Jupiter and Saturn.

Perhaps typically, some members of the supposedly "intelligent" race which launched the interstellar message objected, once it was publicised in the media. The nudity of the human figures on the plaque was condemned as obscene. Racially sensitive critics claimed the man and woman looked too Caucasian. Feminist elements, meanwhile, said it was unfair that the woman in the drawing was "passive" while the man was "active" – waving his hand in greeting.

Finally, and perhaps more to the point, there were those who claimed that an alien intelligence encountering Pioneer 10 would not necessarily be able to make sense of the plaque's markings. Would these hypothetical aliens, for example, have stereoscopic vision? Could they interpret a two-dimensional representation of a man and a woman as depicting living, 3-dimensional sentient beings?

Since Pioneer 10, once it had examined Jupiter and left the solar system, is actually heading nowhere specifically, the chances of it being found and interpreted by extra-terrestrials are infinitesimally tiny. Even if the spacecraft were aimed at the nearest star to our own, it would not reach its destination for around 80,000 years. As in the case of Drake's beamed Arecibo message, that gives Earthlings plenty of time to prepare, should any aliens who might encounter it turn out to be hostile. If, that is, the human race can survive that long. (In 1976, the Nobel laureate Sir Martin Ryle wrote to Dr. Drake and the International Astronomical Union suggesting an international treaty *not* to send out interstellar messages. He feared that a superior civilisation might be led to Earth by such broadcasts with the view to taking over.)

Be that as it may, as the Pioneer message's main instigator Carl Sagan pointed out, the project was simply "good fun".

Whatever public opinion may have been, NASA saw fit to repeat the venture – in a much modified form – when two Voyager missions were launched to Jupiter and Saturn in 1977. This time, the "message" was on a 16 2/3 rpm, 12-inch copper audio disc.

It carries a series of signals which can be decoded to form images. It shows the planets of our solar system, then zooms in on Earth. Then there are images of living cells, the DNA structure and human anatomy, although the reproductive act is not depicted. In the original plan, the process of reproduction was to be simply indicated by the image of a man and a pregnant woman and a diagrammatic representation of the position of the unborn foetus. However, the NASA committee in its wisdom (?), perhaps still embarrassed by the criticism of the Pioneer plaques, decided against actually showing the sexual act. Curiously, though, as if it would be of any interest to alien intelligences, the recording did include the names of all members of the House and Senate committees concerned with space exploration!

The first inter-galactic disco show also includes: Continental Drift, diagrams of Earth's interior structure, scenes of the American West, flora and fauna, pictures of different ethnic groups, the Great Wall of China, picturesque sunsets, the Arecibo radio telescope... and the Sydney Opera House.

There are various linguistic selections in alphabetical order, including the ancient Sumerian language of Akkadian (pronunciation arbitrary), greetings from President Jimmy Carter and Kurt Waldheim, UN Secretary General; these are followed by various "sounds of the Earth", such as the call of a whale, birdsong, a volcanic eruption, rain falling, crashing ocean waves, a train whistle, a kiss, the noise of medical instruments (!!) and recordings of pulsar emissions. Music provides the finale: the first movement of Bach's Second Brandenberg Concerto, Javanese, Senegalese, Mexican and other music of various cultures and culminating in the Cavatina from Beethoven's 13th String Quartet.

Carl Sagan described it as a "launching of the bottle into the cosmic ocean", adding that it "says something very hopeful about life on this planet".

However, whether humankind will survive long enough to receive any reaction to the message – or by then will recall to what it is an "answer" remains to be seen. Voyager 1 did not move out beyond the orbit of Pluto and off into the reaches of outer space until 1987, with Voyager 2 a couple of years on its tail. It will be another 40,000 years before either craft passes within one or two light years of even a minor star and another 147,000 and 525,000 years after the launch that they will make close approaches to other suns.

Ten years after astronaut Cooper's experience – on March 29, 1972 – a 27-year-old astronomer of Troon, Ayrshire, Scotland, Duncan Lunan, addressed a special meeting of the British Interplanetary Society at London's Caxton Hall. The following month an article, outlining the content of his speech, was published in *Spaceflight*, the Society's journal. Lunan had for years been studying the reports of Hals, Stormer, and those of van der Pol. Lunan claimed that the anomalous radio echoes came from an unmanned alien space probe, orbiting somewhere within range of Earth.

Plotting the signals on a graph, aligning the echo delay times with the sequence in which the original transmissions were made, Lunan concluded that they originated from the double star system Epsilon Bootis, some 200 light years distant in the northern hemisphere constellation of Bootes, the Herdsman. The brightest star in this system is Arcturus.

In an interview with Jack Stoneley, former Fleet Street editor of a Sunday newspaper, in 1973, for the *National Enquirer*, Lunan said:

"To my astonishment, the resulting dots on the graph made up a map of an easily recognizable constellation of Bootes in the northern sky. The curious pattern of delayed echoes was actually a pattern of star positions."

The same newspaper also quoted Professor Ronald N. Bracewell, of Stanford University, California: "The map of Bootes constructed by Lunan's analysis could be interpreted as a method of communication from another planet. If I wanted to tell you where I came from, and I couldn't speak your language, I could show you with a picture. Naturally, I am pleased to hear that the British Interplanetary Society is investigating these echoes. Their investigation could result in a shattering discovery.

"The space probe Lunan describes could never be seen from Earth, not even with the most powerful telescopes. We can't even see our own space vehicles circling the Moon."

In Lunan's graph-generated "star map", however, the binary star Epsilon Bootis is placed outside the six other main bodies in the system. It is separated by a horizontal straight line of seven dots, with Epsilon Bootis to its left and the others, Beta, Delta, Gamma, Alpha (Arcturus), Zeta and Eta to its right. (Two other stars in the system, designated Rho and Mu, are for some reason omitted.)

Lunan's hypothetical interpretation of the "message" of the star-map was: "Our home is Epsilon Bootis, which is a double star. We live on the sixth planet of seven... our probe is in the orbit of your Moon."

Lunan calculated that Epsilon Bootis is placed on his graph as it would have been positioned 13,000 years ago, which he suggests may have been when the probe entered our solar system. He expressed a belief that the Bootis civilisation may have sent out many probes to different parts of the galaxy to find a new home before their own planet became uninhabitable. He saw clues in the radio signals that the intelligences of the original planet, the second from its parent sun, had already moved outward to the sixth planet before launching their pathfinder probes.

But there are various flaws in Lunan's arguments. In fact, by the year following his first publication, both Professor Bracewell and Anthony T. Lawton, an English electronics expert and writer/lecturer on interstellar communication, had begun to have their doubts about Lunan's theory. And in 1981, the American UFO-sceptic, mathematician and astronomer Robert Merrill Shaeffer, in his 1981 book, *The UFO Verdict: Examining The Evidence*, pointed out that Lunan's star-map does not accurately tally with the echoes recorded by van der Pol. "One would not think it too difficult," he wrote, "for an advanced, space-faring civilization to make its interstellar probes capable of transmitting its star maps correctly."

According to Jack Stoneley who, with Anthony Lawton, co-authored a book on the Lunan claims, *Is Anyone Out There?* (Star Books, W.H.Allen, 1975), the reason Lunan gave for Epsilon Bootis' omission from the star-map is that it is meant to indicate that it was the "home" star of the intelligences that originally launched the probe.

To reply to the signal, Lunan suggested, Earth should transmit the star map with Epsilon Bootis in its rightful position, thus indicating that we are intelligent enough to understand the message.

To investigate whether Lunan's hypothesis about the 1928–29 delayed radio echoes actually issued from an extra-terrestrial probe or were caused by some natural effect, Lawton compared them with more recent delayed echoes, whose monitors believed did have a natural explanation. He even tried to "answer" Lunan's supposed messages by beaming powerful radio pulses from a large antenna in his back garden at Shepperton, Middlesex. He even arranged for scientists at the Stanford Institute for Plasma Research in California to monitor any possible replies. At the time, around 1974, he told me: "If we receive echo sequences like those heard in the 1920s, it will be difficult to state that the probe does not exist."

However, he was eventually forced to conclude from his researches that the recent echoes certainly were attributed to (1) signal reflection and amplification due to upper ionospheric conditions and (2) plasma interactions in the ionosphere, a slowing-down effect as a radio wave encounters plasma, or gas-cloud.

Stoneley writes: "The most common LDE [long delayed echo] times reported over the years are those of three and eight seconds. The former could well be caused by reflection from the surface of the moon. One American researcher, C.R. Clarke, has noted that the frequency of these three-second reports appear to be associated with the moon's zenith angle. Lawton, in a paper for the Russian conference on extra-terrestrial communication in the autumn of 1973, also suggests they may be coming back to us from the Lagrange or Trojan areas of the moon (areas sixty degrees ahead and sixty degrees astern of the moon) which could collect sufficient dust, gas and debris to act as reflectors of our transmitted signals – especially at higher frequencies."

Finally, another fact that tends to weaken Lunan's theories, is his tendency to switch direction rather acutely when criticisms arise. At one point, he protested that if his star map did not show the constellation Bootes, maybe it was the constellation Cetus, the Whale. This is a large constellation at the celestial equator, one of whose stars, Omicron (o) Ceti or Mira Ceti is a long-period variable. And while Epsilon Bootis is a binary or double star, Tau Ceti is a single sun – a feature that ought to be quite clear in an accurate and detailed star map.

For some 30 years now, Russian scientists have been concerned with the search for artificial, or alien, signals from space. Indeed, the Soviet Academy of Science's Council on Radio Astronomy set up a subsection devoted to the topic. The first national congress on the subject was held at Byuratam Astrophysical Observatory in 1964, and in 1971 the Soviet Union was host to the first International Conference on Problems of Communications with extra-terrestrial civilisation.

A report of the USSR Academy of Sciences Board of the Scientific Astronomy Problem Area, which was printed in the journal *Soviet Astronomy* in 1975, said:

"Efforts to detect extra-terrestrial civilisations should proceed smoothly and systematically, and should extend over a prolonged period... It would be a great mistake to build a programme in contemplation of rapid and easy success."

The report advocated continuous monitoring by Earth-based installations, backed up by two galaxy-scanning satellites. It added that "the possible discovery of probes sent from extra-terrestrial civilisations and now located in the solar system or even in orbit around the Earth warrants particular attention."

It may be a mark of Soviet thoroughness and determination in these research fields that the Russians have also, on their own admission, seriously investigated such areas as extra-sensory perception as a tool in trying to discover extra-terrestrial life. Indeed, in 1977, *Los Angeles Times* correspondent Robert Toth was put under arrest by the KGB for several days after he had been given various papers by a Russian parapsychologist. Apparently, though, after a careful study of ESP, the Russians concluded that it was useless for military purposes.

In the United States, the SETI movement, which largely owed its inception to a paper published by the physicists Philip Morrison and Giuseppe Cocconi, of Cornell University, in the respected British science journal *Nature*, in September 1959, had long been active in such areas. And in 1971 – the same year as the Russian conference – a report was issued proposing a major SETI undertaking named Project

Cyclops.

Now within the ranks of SETI are two main factions, known as "travellers" and "listeners". The travellers' lobby firmly believes that ultimately, humanity will have to send out space probes to other planetary systems to search for life. This, they concede, will necessarily cost vast amounts of money and may not be feasible for many decades. The listeners' lobby, on the other hand, points to the comparable economy and relative simplicity either of monitoring and listening for interstellar broadcasts or beaming out messages in the hopes of an answer.

But even the latter course is not quite as simple as it sounds on the surface. One complication arises in choosing a suitable frequency at which to transmit or to listen. For a start, the entire cosmos is permeated with a breathtaking range of frequencies of electro-magnetic radiation. Shining, twinkling stars, infra-red radiating planets, radio wave emitting galaxies and other stellar bodies giving off X-rays and gamma waves. Even the tiny molecules adrift in space itself put out their own forms of radiation.

The question of selecting suitable frequencies was treated by Morrison and Cocconi in their *Nature* article. At the time that they attacked the problem, emissions from hydrogen particles in space had recently begun to be detected by radio astronomers.

The hydrogen emission line of 1420 MHz happens to fall in what is on Earth considered the most relatively "quiet" band, or "window" of low atmospheric noise, between about 1000 MHz and 10,000 MHz. So, too, does the 1662 MHz emission line of the hydroxyl ion which, when joined with a hydrogen atom, forms a molecule of water (H_2O).

Thus, when SETI was casting about for a suitable frequency range at which to listen and/or broadcast, one of its members, Bernard M. Oliver, of the Hewlett-Packard Corporation, proposed this region.

"The Cyclops team feels that this band, lying between the resonances of the two dissociated products of water, is the foreordained interstellar communication band," Oliver said. "What more poetic place could there be for water-based life to seek its own kind than the age-old meeting place for all species: *the water hole?*"

The problems arising from attempts at interstellar communication are vast. Even if other life-forms exist, they may be utterly unimaginable to us. And even if other civilisations have developed under similar biological conditions, they need not have followed identical evolutionary patterns to those of terrestrial life. Would their laws of nature and logic be the same as ours?

Some pro-communicator theorists, however, believe that if another civilisation has developed radio communications equipment, they should have some parallel phases of that development to our own. Most members of SETI – an organisation pioneered and jointly founded by Dr. Frank Drake and cosmologist Carl Sagan – believe that although the exact sequence of developments that led to the human race may have been a one-off affair, the general evolutionary pattern leading from primitive life-forms to intelligent human beings could be common throughout the Universe.

The work of the American biologist John Lilly, who for decades has conducted intensive research into the intelligence and language of dolphins, has been suggested as an area of good experience and perhaps even a springboard for the problem of communicating with alien life forms. However, it has been pointed out that, since dolphins are non-technological creatures, knowledge of their intelligence has little bearing on the problem of extra-terrestrial communication. The late scientist and prolific author Isaac Asimov, speculated that the evolutionary pattern on any inhabited alien world was almost certain to be so similar to that of Earth that its denizens would have a general resemblance to humans. The value of having a brain, arms, manipulative hands and legs for mobility, he said, were so important that this format was likely to be found wherever there is intelligent life.

From the early beginnings of SETI and its allied projects, by around 1978, there were eight continuing search programmes: six in the United States and one each in Canada and the Soviet Union. But then, towards the end of the 1970s, such work seemed to lose impetus, largely through lack of cash – its funding was finally cut off by Congress in 1982 – and was allowed almost to lapse. However, one independent project worthy of notice was initiated in late 1977.

Under the supervision of the astronomer Professor Stuart Bower, of the University of California, Berkeley, a team of graduates aimed at an extremely low-cost programme that required the minimum of effort. It was called SERENDIP, initials of Search for Extra-terrestrial Radio Emission from Nearby Developed Intelligent Populations. (Serendipity is, of course, the faculty of making pleasant and unexpected discoveries accidentally. It was coined by Horace Walpole for his tale, *The Three Princes Of Serendip*, which was the ancient name for Ceylon.)

The students built a system hooked into the 85-foot radio telescope at Berkeley's Hat Creek Observatory, near Mount Lassen, northern California. It cost a mere $4,000. It incorporates a computer, a tape recorder and a noise analyser. As the observatory antennae performs its routine scanning work, the noise analyser and computer check 100 different frequencies for out-of-the-ordinary signals. Anything unusual triggers the tape recorder, noting both the time of reception and the location of the signal. Once a month, the tape went under review at Berkeley, to decide if any of the anomalous signals might be from an extra-terrestrial source.

In early February 1983, it was reported that SETI was to be revived, after a $1.5 million budget boost to NASA from Congress to re-start the programme.

Scientists at Stanford University and NASA's Ames Research Centre announced that they were developing an instrument capable of scanning 74,000 radio frequencies simultaneously and, it was hoped, of detecting transmissions from intelligent sources elsewhere in our galaxy.

NASA also announced that the multi-channel spectrum analyser being built for SETI's revival was merely the prototype of more powerful monitoring equipment, capable of listening for alien transmissions on up to 10 million channels at one time. It planned to install this equipment at no fewer than six radio telescopes around the world within the ensuing five years.

The re-establishment of SETI was the result of lobbying by NASA officials and Dr. Drake and Carl Sagan.

The new equipment would sift out signals of a natural or human origin, while the residue would be analysed to determine whether they contained any extra-terrestrial messages.

Despite such an ambitious programme, it had its scientific minority detractors. Mr. Frank Tipler, of Tulane University, in a letter to the journal Science, wrote: "SETI will only become a science when its proponents tells us what observations will convince them that it is reasonable to assume that we are alone."

But the programme's director, John Billingham of Ames, said confidently: "We believe on many different grounds that intelligent life is widespread in the Universe."

Three years after SETI's financial shot in the arm, in December 1986, Soviet scientists announced that they too were seeking in earnest for signs of extra-terrestrial intelligence – concentrating on lasers. A team of astronomers, under Dr. Viktor Shvartsman at the special astrophysical observatory of the Academy of Sciences, in the Caucasus, announced they were concentrating on looking out for laser transmissions from other planets. Their stance was that any more advanced civilisation than our own would probably not use the radio spectrum to send out messages, but rather the high density information channel provided by lasers.

The Russians admitted that contemporary equipment was not yet sufficiently sophisticated to allow researchers to join in a "hypothetical interstellar laser dialogue". But they claimed that their 6-metre optical telescope could eavesdrop on such "conversations", if they are taking place.

The Russians' first problem was to decide on which potential sources of radiation to aim their telescope. They ultimately agreed that stars in the same class as our Sun could have life-supporting planets – and chose representative samples all of which are 65 light years distant.

10. Secret Seekers Of Wisdom

"Anything can happen; anything is possible and likely"
August Strindberg (1849–1912)

PARIS, JUNE 1937: It is two years before the eruption of that cauldron known as the Second World War; five years before the setting up of the highly secret Manhattan Project; eight years before the awesome and deadly mushroom cloud of the first atom bomb rose above the desert of New Mexico at Alamagordo.

A mysterious stranger, smartly dressed, urbane, well-spoken, appeared to physics researchers in Europe. He bore the following dire warning:

"The research in which you and your colleagues are engaged is fraught with terrible dangers, not only for yourselves, but for the whole human race. The liberation of atomic energy is easier than you think, and the radioactivity artificially produced can poison the atmosphere of our planet in the space of a few years. Moreover, atomic explosives can be produced from a few grammes of metal powerful enough to destroy whole cities."

The stranger was not a chemist, not a physicist, not even a scientist. He was an alchemist. Not only that, one of the physics researchers to whom he spoke, later the French scientific writer Jacques Bergier, believed that he was in the presence of the remarkable man known only as Fulcanelli, Master Alchemist, who disappeared without trace shortly after the outbreak of the Second World War. Even in 1937, Fulcanelli was reputed to be 97 years old, although he never looked more than 50. And there were those who believed he was still alive a mere 20 years ago.

Preposterous? Absurd? Beyond belief?

Perhaps... and yet... Fulcanelli was not the first exponent of the strange and secret art of alchemy said to have lived for a remarkable number of years without seeming to age.

But to comprehend this, to begin to understand the amazing implications of such cases, we must first know something about the "forgotten" art or science itself.

Just what is alchemy? To many, even since the so-called "occult boom" of the 1960s and 1970s, it belongs with sorcery and witchcraft in some vague, mist-shrouded period of the past; an Age of Ignorance when men believed in dragons and the medicine and magic of travelling mountebanks; a forgotten, pseudo-science pursued by bearded old cranks and charlatans, who groped around in the dinginess of incomprehension, just as they fumbled about their dank and gloomy cellar laboratories.

Of all the branches of magic and the occult, it is the most easily relegated to the scrapheap, a deluded dodo that refuses to realise it is extinct. Even those who concede that, by accident rather than by purpose, it laid the foundations of early chemistry, tend to dismiss it, like a dead language.

But if alchemy is a dinosaur, it is one that will not lie down. For there are men and women in the world today who still indulge in what is thought of as an arcane art.

Most modern reference books describe alchemy as, at best, the trial-and-error

---

forerunner of chemistry; at worst, a false science based on an erroneous notion that base metals could be transmuted into gold; that life could be indefinitely prolonged by some eternally elusive Elixir.

In fact, nothing could be further from the truth.

As we shall see, alchemy has more in common with philosophies that have gained ground in the Western world over the past three decades – meditation, Buddhism and Yoga, for example – than it has with orthodox science or the seeking of material wealth by magical chemical processes.

And, like so many branches of the occult that I deal with in this book, it is only one of many ways in which humankind has sought to learn more about the self, the Universe and, ultimately, the powers that have long been thought of as God and the Devil. I will go so far as to suggest that, in common with many of its brother-occult arts, it might even contain germs of knowledge passed on to humanity by unearthly entities who visited this planet centuries, even millennia ago. Knowledge that has become shrouded in mystery and secrecy, dulled and distorted by faulty transmission and misunderstanding over the passage of time.

So far as history can tell us, alchemy grew up partly from the metalworking techniques of the ancient Egyptians, although there are indications that it developed on vaguely parallel lines in the Far East, in China in particular.

The oldest known alchemical work was written by Bolos of Mendes in Egypt, around 200BC, and was entitled *Physika Kai Mystika* in Greek translation, although the art is clearly much older than that. It is likely that men like Moses, Aaron and Solomon were to some degree versed in its more elementary forms, which is probably how they managed to perform such seemingly miraculous feats and why they lived so much longer than the average human span of today. But, to return to what history says...

Egyptian craftsmen had achieved high standards in metallurgy, even managing to produce alloys of silver and copper that had all the appearances of gold. A papyrus from the ancient capital of Thebes, dated around 300AD, describes the methods of changing the colours of various metals to make them appear like gold or silver. It boasts that these methods will foil all expert tests to detect the true nature of the treated metal. It was, perhaps, evidence of deliberately deceptive practices such as this, which continued down the ages, that prompted many historians of alchemy to suggest that so little was known of metal analysis outside the craft that any yellow-coloured substance of the correct weight and texture could in those times easily have been passed off as gold.

But to plumb the true nature of alchemy, it is necessary to delve into the old alchemical texts themselves which, couched as they are in deliberately obscure language and symbolism, are enough to daunt most investigators. And that was their precise purpose.

Why? There are many reasons. But perhaps the main one was that true alchemy could lead to such knowledge that would be a menace in the wrong hands – utterly disastrous, deadly, not only to the errant practitioner, but to the whole of humanity.

Hence the warning of the mysterious stranger in Paris in 1937. Another reason for secrecy, particularly when the Church had gained immense, absolute power in the Western world, was that alchemists – often bracketed with witches and sorcerers – could lay themselves open to charges of heresy and be put to torture and the stake. One such victim was Giordano Bruno (1548–1600), put to the stake by the Inquisition.

Perhaps for this reason, many alchemists would, in the process of their experiments, make direct appeals to God for assistance towards their goal. This made their operations uncomfortably close to blasphemy in the eyes of the clerical hierarchy, since it was only through them that direct appeals to the Almighty were sanctioned. Monopoly and Control are nothing new...

The alchemists hinted guardedly that the knowledge they sought was not entirely of this Earth, but could come only with the aid of other-worldly powers. Higher Intelligence, raised consciousness, call it what you like.

How could they explain this to anyone who caught them at work, without being at risk of imprisonment or execution? God, via the intercessory authority of the Church, was the only acceptable way.

Besides, they seemed to be all too aware of the terrible dangers implicit in their quest, as demonstrated in this passage from *The Ordinal Of Alchemy*, by the 15th century alchemist Thomas Norton, of Bristol:

"This art must ever secret be,
The cause whereof is this, as ye may see:
If one evil man had thereof all his will,
All Christian peace he might easily spill,
And with his pride he might pull down
Rightful kings and princes of renown."

What the alchemists truly sought was Ultimate, Perfect Knowledge. They wished to raise themselves to the highest possible levels of consciousness and understanding.

This would include, of course, such deadly knowledge as that of nuclear fission – the splitting of the atom.

The whole search for Cosmic Wisdom was veiled behind what they called the *Summum Bonum*, the Magnum Opus, the Great Work – the search for the Philosopher's Stone.

To discover this was to find the key that would unlock all nature's great mysteries. But to do so involved a lengthy, complicated, meticulous, deliberately mysterious and often materially unrewarding process. To put off unwanted prying eyes, they invented copious complex symbols and procedures. To gain the favour of patrons such as kings, landowners and aristocrats who would sponsor them and finance their researches, many of them pretended – or in some cases, believed – that their main aim was to manufacture gold. That, in itself, would be a relatively simple matter – if it were possible to discover the whole of the secrets of nature.

Yet, as he wrought chemical changes in his crucibles and glass vessels, the true alchemist believed that he would also bring about great changes in himself. In a similar manner to that by which a yogin, through sitting in various postures, by specific exercises and carefully controlled breathing, believes that he will become spiritually enlightened, so the alchemists were convinced that their operations would bring about transformations in themselves that would raise them to new, hitherto untapped, levels of consciousness.

Alchemy was a path towards a hidden reality that contained all the underlying truths of life, religion, beauty, love, hate, death and the Universe. This, the practitioners believed, could only be attained if the human consciousness were altered or transmuted like the metals with which some of them worked, from its everyday, base level of perception (represented by lead) to an infinitely more sublime plane of spirituality (represented by gold).

They wanted to penetrate the secrets of Life and Death, of Nature, of Oneness, of Eternity and Infinity. They were men and women who aspired to walk with the gods.

It is easy to shrug off all this striving as the kind of high idealism that has driven many religious thinkers, philosophers, sociologists, politicians and scientists. But behind the strange symbolism of alchemy – motifs like the red dragon, the king, the grey wolf, the black crow, the green lion, the phoenix, unicorn, the Abyssinian and many, many others – lie glimpses of the true nature of man, of Being.

In fact, the legendary father of alchemy – the alchemists' patron saint, so to speak – Hermes Trismegistus, said to have been an Egyptian, expressed theories very similar to those of modern scientific theories about such subjects as creation, DNA heredity (his chief symbol was a double helix – the caduceus), and the notion of evolution through natural selection, or trial and error. The famous and fabled *Tabula Smagdarina*, or Emerald Tablets of Hermes, whose other name means "Thrice Blessed", which form the corner-stones of alchemy, state:

"It is true without lie, certain and most veritable, that what is below is like what is above and that what is above is like what is below, to perpetuate the miracles of one thing.

"And as all things have been, and come from One by the mediation of One, thus all things have been born from this single thing by adaptation."

The practical alchemists even called the spherical glass vessel, or alembic, that they used, the Philosopher's Egg, not simply because of its shape, but because the Philosopher's Stone would hopefully emerge from it in the same way that the stuff of the Universe emerged from a cosmic egg, or primal atom. One of the prime symbols of the Great Work itself was a giant serpent, the Ouroboros, swallowing its own tail, signifying the great cycle of the universe, of life and death, of perfect stillness and perfect motion. The tail-swallower also symbolised the idea that alchemy began and ended at the same point – with man, or Man. The alchemist was the instigator of the Work, the seeker of knowledge. He was also its "raw material" and, if he was successful, his perfected, enlightened self was the finished product. One of the alchemists' mottos, therefore, was: *Ars totum requirit hominem* (The art requires the whole man).

The alchemists believed that, because all matter sprang from a single substance – the matter which, in a state of chaos, was the primal atom, or egg – all substances were different combinations of the four principal elements: fire, air, earth and water. The first task, then, in trying to unravel the physical laws of matter, was to try to reproduce it artificially; like a Creator, to start from scratch. So they combined the four principal elements and called the resultant mixture First Matter (*prima materia*).

Now each of these elements, they believed, had two of four principal qualities: hot, cold, dry and wet. Fire was hot and dry, earth was dry and cold, water wet and cold and air hot and wet. They reasoned that to change one element into another, all that was needed was to alter one of its principal qualities. So, if a fire was allowed to die out and lost its quality of heat, it would become earth (dry and cold) as it turned to ashes. Similarly, water (cold and wet), when heated, could change into air (hot and wet) as it evaporated.

In this way, by heating and cooling, drying and melting in a crucible, the alchemists believed that they could alter the qualities of any metal with which they chose to work. Each metal was allied to one of the seven bodies of the solar system known at the time: gold (the Sun), silver (the Moon), mercury (Mercury), copper (Venus), iron (Mars), tin (Jupiter) and lead (Saturn). They believed that because the universe came from one thing (the primal atom), elements of all these planets were present in the

Earth in varying amounts and that the planets themselves influenced the "growth" or formation of their respective metals in it.

These, then, are the basic principles of physical alchemical operations. The actual details of the process to which various metals were subjected are extremely complicated and are made even more difficult because each alchemist tried his own experiments and therefore each alchemical treatise is different or varies from the others. Some alchemists, for example, believed that there should be seven stages in the Great Work, because there were seven planets and seven days of Creation, etc. Others asserted that there ought to be 12 stages, linked to the months of the year and the signs of the zodiac.

These 12 processes were known as calcination, solution, separation, conjunction, putrefaction, coagulation, cibation, sublimation, fermentation, exaltation, multiplication and projection.

But whether the alchemist used seven or 12 stages, they all saw them as symbolic of the cyclic nature of things: of the formation, development, destruction and re-creation of the Universe; of the annual birth, growth, decay, death and rebirth of the Earth; and of the birth, life, death and rebirth of man.

We can see from this that the alchemists had some rudimentary idea of how the Universe functions. What they then tried to do was to probe its deeper mysteries; they tried to discover the details and particulars of why it functioned in this way, and what made it do so.

Before passing on to the individual alchemists themselves and whether any of them actually achieved their object, however, I shall now attempt to outline the basic stages of the Great Work and what they represent. It provides a fascinating insight into humanity's eternal grappling with the unknown. It should be remembered, however, that alchemical texts themselves vary greatly in style and content.

One of the greatest problems facing anyone who decides to attempt a physical alchemical operation occurs right at the very beginning of the Work. Not only are the operations long, costly, tedious, complicated and confusing, but it is extremely difficult to determine exactly what the alchemists began with. What, exactly, constituted what they called First Matter. Without this knowledge it is simply impossible to begin the Work.

Alchemical writers throw up many barriers designed to baffle and deter the outsider. For example, a 17th century alchemical volume describes First Matter in the following, enigmatic manner: "...a stone which is not a stone... like thick, curdling milk but it is not milk; like mud, but not like any other mud. It resembles a green, poisonous thing, because frogs crouch beneath it, but it is not a poison, it is a medicine. In sum, it is the earth from which Adam was fashioned." Another practitioner of the same period, Johannes Isaac Hollandus, talks of First Matter as "vitriol" which, taken literally, is sulphuric acid. But characteristic of all alchemical writings, vitriol is not meant to be interpreted literally. It is a cipher: the initial letters of the Latin phrase *Visita Interiora Terrae Rectificando Invenies Occultum Lapidem*, which means, "visit the interior of the earth and by purifying you will find the secret stone".

A German historian of alchemy, Hermann Kopp, was totally perplexed by the meaning of First Matter: "Substances from the mineral kingdom, different plants and saps, the secretions and excretions of the animal world, even the most disgusting things were subjected to a thorough examination... They tried milk, but with little faith, and then saliva to see if that was the materia prima and frequently made use of human faeces and urine in their operations."

Thus, all outsiders and would-be dabblers who tried to unravel the secrets of the alchemical art were baffled at the very first step. One suggestion is that First Matter was something like the primordial mixture that made up the original cosmic egg. Besides, alchemists believed that all matter had three components – mercury, sulphur and salt. But these were "philosophical" elements, not the common variety and were sometimes referred to as "our mercury", or "our sulphur", to distinguish them from the familiar ones. They saw these as symbols of the spirit, body and soul of man; as the Father, Son and Holy Spirit in Christian doctrine and, in Eastern terms as *Sunyata* (formless void), *Maya* (creation), and *Prana* (life force).

First, the alchemist reduced his First Matter mixture of mercury, sulphur and salt to a liquid state, in the process known as solution. We can perhaps begin to see here a parallel between the chemical operations and the cyclic process of creation-evolution-destruction-re-creation of the Universe and the birth-life-death-rebirth of Man that the alchemist hoped would occur within himself on a spiritual plane. Once the First Matter was reduced to liquid, according to some texts, it was poured over horse manure and buried "in the belly of the earth" during which time it would darken. This process, symbolised by a black raven, was known as *nigredo*, or "blackening". It symbolised a state of limbo in a formless void. The alchemist hoped it would act as a kind of cleansing process on his mind and spirit, wiping away all his preconceived ideas and notions, putting him back into a state of total innocence, ready for the great re-awakening.

Next, the matter had to be reconstituted within the vessel. This most critical state of rebirth was symbolised by the black raven transforming into a white dove and was known as *albedo*, or "whitening".

If this stage went wrong, as the alchemist added and subtracted his chemicals, raised and lowered the heat, the whole process had to be started all over again. The highly delicate stage of the operation was allegorically described in an "Alchemical Mass" by the 16th century Hungarian astrologer royal, Nicholas Melchoir:

"Then will appear in the bottom of the vessel the mighty Ethiopian [nigredo], burned, calcined, bleached, altogether dead and lifeless. He asks to be buried, to be sprinkled with his own moisture and slowly calcined till he shall arise in glowing form from the fierce fire... Behold a wondrous restoration of renewal!"

If this stage is successful, the material in the alchemist's "egg" should turn red (*rubedo*), "like a red dragon tearing itself to pieces". This clearly symbolises the mighty cosmic explosion of the primal atom that regenerates the Universe once more. With it, should come the enlightenment of the practitioner, a new awakening to a fresh world of ultimate reality, of pure, absolute truth. If sulphur, mercury and a minute quantity of gold are then added to the mixture in the vessel and subjected to intense heat from the furnace, the result should also be the *lapis philosophorum*, the Philosopher's Stone, with which it should be possible to transmute base metals into gold, or to obtain the Elixir of Life. But was this simply further symbolism, designed to disguise the true quest of the alchemist in his long hours of poring over difficult texts, and the repetitious and precise manipulation of alembics, retorts, chemicals and furnaces? Did the Philosopher's Stone truly exist? From the evidence, the answer would seem to be yes.

In fact, while their methods and techniques differ, the alchemists' descriptions of the stone tally on the whole, identifying it as a brilliant, ruby-coloured crystal in its solid state, and as saffron-coloured in its powdered form. In describing the final steps

---

of the Great Work, an English alchemist of the 16/17th centuries, George Starkey, quoted a standard text, *The Stone Of The Philosophers*:

"Having thus completed the operation, let the vessel cool, and on opening it you will perceive your matter to be fixed into a ponderous mass, thoroughly of a scarlet colour, which is easily reducible by scraping, or otherwise, and in being heated in the fire flows like wax, without smoking, flaming or loss of substance, returning when cold to its former fixity, heavier than gold bulk for bulk, yet easy to be dissolved in any liquid, in which a few grains being taken its operation most wonderfully pervades the human body, to the extirpation of all disorders, prolonging life by its cure to the utmost period."

11. A Glimpse Of Immortality

"Man is not body. The heart, the spirit, is man. And this spirit is an entire star, out of which he is built. If therefore a man is perfect in his heart, nothing in the whole light of Nature is hidden from him... The first step in the operation of these sciences is this: to beget the spirit from the inner firmament by means of the imagination."
Paracelsus (1493–1541).

THE IDEA of an Elixir of Life – a potion that will cure all ills and prolong the human lifespan indefinitely – harks back to the legends of the gods of Olympus, feasting on nectar and ambrosia and thus enjoying immortality. In ancient civilisations, it was believed that such elixirs – from the Arabic *aliksir* – could be made from earth's precious elements, such as gold and silver, or from rare jewels such as pearls and diamonds.

There are many stories of early practitioners in the alchemical art producing such an elixir. The Chinese master Wei Po-Yang, of the second century AD, for example, is said to have become immortal by swallowing a carefully prepared potion. The underlying theory of such a panacea was that all sickness was caused by impurity in the body, which led to corruption and death. Alchemical practice, therefore, sought to introduce some element that would purify and purge the system.

Many alchemists claimed that they had perfected the elixir, among them the physician and philosopher, Paracelsus. Born Phillipus Aureolus Theophrastus Bombastus von Hohenheim, at Einsiedeln, Switzerland, in 1493, he named himself after the Roman physician, Celsus.

Educated at Ferrara in northern Italy, Paracelsus travelled widely in Europe and earned himself a reputation both for great medical ability and for possessing an irritable, impatient and intolerant nature. He did not, it seems, suffer gladly those he considered fools. This passage from his book *Paragranum*, shows the contempt in which he held his contemporaries and what he considered to be their out-of-date methods:

"Avicenna, Galen, Rhasis, Montagna, and all the rest of you, after me and not I after you! You people from Paris, Montpellier, Swabia, Meissen, and half a dozen other places, after me and not I after you! Even in the most distant corner there will not be one of you on whom the dogs will not piss. But I will be the king and mine the kingdom."

Paracelsus did, however, have something to crow about. He wrote the first detailed treatise on the causes, symptoms and treatment of syphilis, taught that epilepsy was a sickness and not a form of madness or demonic possession, was one of the first to identify bronchial complaints as industrial disease in mining communities, and is regarded as the father of modern wound surgery, homoeopathy, antisepsis and micro-chemistry.

He also wrote two important texts that deal with, among other matters, alchemical work: *De Occulta Philosophia* and *Archidoxes Magica*.

Using what he described as a Physician's Tincture, Paracelsus claimed to have cured

---

many diseases, including epilepsy, leprosy and dropsy, through alchemical techniques. He is said to have cured dying patients simply by prescribing a strange powder which he always carried. He told one woman to give the powder to her husband mixed in warm beer – and the man recovered.

In his book, *De Tinctura Physicorum*, published in 1570, he revealed:

"This is the tincture by which some of the first physicians in Egypt and afterwards up till our times have lived for 150 years. The lives of many of them lasted for some centuries, as history clearly teaches, although this does not seem to be true to anybody; because its force is so miraculous, that it is able to enlighten the body... and to strengthen him to such a degree that he will remain free of all diseases and, although afflicted by his old age, will appear as he had been in his youth. Therefore the *tinctura physicorum* is a universal remedy which devours all sickness like a fire devouring wood. Its quantity is tiny, but its force is mighty!"

However, Paracelsus' delvings into alchemy do not appear to have helped him much materially, whether his interest in the Philosopher's Stone was as a prolonger of life, or an aid to the manufacture of gold. He died in poverty at Salzburg on September 24, 1541.

Throughout the Middle Ages, ruling powers of Europe sought after the alchemists' gold. When the finances of Venice were dwindling in the late 16th century, the Senate hired an alchemist from Cyprus in the hope that he would bring solvency. But the venture failed.

Both James IV of Scotland and England's Charles II are said to have dabbled in the secret art, albeit unsuccessfully.

An alchemist transmuted copper and tin into gold in 1675 before the Emperor Leopold I and turned a silver medallion into gold two years later. When it was assayed in 1888, the medallion was found to have a specific gravity of 14.9 – halfway between that of gold and silver.

One of the most intriguing cases of alleged transmutation was reported by the Dutch physician Helvetius, whose real name was Johann Frederick Schweitzer.

Helvetius was extremely sceptical towards alchemy and occult matters. On December 27, 1666, a stranger with a pockmarked face visited Helvetius at his home and began to talk about the Philosopher's Stone. From a small box, the stranger produced three tiny lumps of a sulphur-coloured substance. He refused to give any to the physician, but Helvetius managed to scrape off a minute quantity with his fingernail. After the stranger left, Helvetius dropped the particles onto molten lead, but all that happened was that "almost the whole mass of lead flew away and the remainder turned into a mere glassy earth".

Three weeks later the stranger called on Helvetius again and, at length, the doctor-philosopher confessed that he had stolen a fragment of the substance his visitor called the Philosopher's Stone and told him what had happened. The little man gave Helvetius a tiny piece of the material and when he complained that it was too small, cut it in half and threw half away, assuring Helvetius that that was more than enough for his purposes. He also warned his host that in using the stone, he should wrap it in wax before dropping it into the molten lead so that it would not vaporise. The stranger left, promising to return, but was never seen again.

Helvetius, however, performed the experiment and, as he described in his book, *Golden Calf*, "I cut half an ounce, or six drams, of old lead, and put it into a crucible in the fire which, being melted, my wife put in the said Medicine made up into a small pill or button, with presently such a hissing and bubbling in its perfect

---

Armageddon 2000

operation, that within a quarter of an hour, all the mass of lead was totally transmuted into the best and finest gold, which made us amazed..."

Helvetius consulted a goldsmith who confirmed that the resultant substance was pure gold and, indeed, so Helvetius claimed, portions of this gold, mixed with nitric acid and silver produced even more quantities of gold.

Like many of the cases of Unidentified Flying Objects, the stories of alchemists are beyond orthodox, rational explanation, yet they cannot all be dismissed as pure invention.

The remarkable Comte de Saint-Germain was said to have known the secret of the Elixir of Life, to which, along with his strict diet of oatmeal, groats and white meat of chicken, he attributed his astounding longevity. Even by accepting only the most reliable sources of the Count's career and activities, such as those in the British Record Office, he appears to have frequented the highest social circles of Europe for at least 100 years. And yet, he reputedly never looked more than about 45 or 50 years old. Some stories say he was more than 2,000 years old and that he was either the fabled Wandering Jew or the strange hybrid son of an Arabian princess and a giant salamander. This latter, of course, could have been a veiled, allegorical hint at his alchemical pedigree – the salamander is an alchemical symbol and the alchemical art was developed and practised by various Arabic masters.

The Count himself added much fuel to these stories through his apparent habit of reminiscing about his past, name-dropping such acquaintances as Cleopatra and the Queen of Sheba. At a party in Paris, he is said to have talked about "an old friend", Richard Coeur de Lion, then turned to consult his personal manservant for corroboration of a minor point. The valet answered: "You forget, sir, I have been only five hundred years in your service."

It was said that he was a guest at the wedding in Cana when Jesus turned water into wine and in the mid-18th century, the Count was a favourite of Madame de Pompadour to whom he gave a sample of his "water of rejuvenation". In 1760 he was at one of Madame de Pompadour's parties when he was asked by an aging dowager, the Countess de Gergy, if his father had been in Venice 50 years earlier, in 1710.

The Count replied: "No, Madame. It is very much longer since I lost my father, but I was living in Venice myself at the time. I had the honour of paying my respects to Madame then."

The dowager pointed out that the Count de Saint-Germain she had met in Venice when her late husband was ambassador there, had been at least 45 and that the man to whom she was speaking could not be more than that age.

The handsome Count assured the lady that he was very old.

"But then you must be nearly a hundred," she said.

"That is not impossible," he said. He then went on to remember minute details of their meeting in Venice, finally convincing the Countess that he was the same man she had met half a century previously.

The Count de Saint-Germain was supposed to have died in Germany in 1784, but there were records of him having represented French Freemasonry the following year at Paris and at Wilhelmsbad, in Germany. Mme d'Adhemar, former lady-in-waiting to Marie Antoinette, claimed that in 1788 the Count vainly tried to warn Louis XVI and his queen of their possible fate. She also reported having met the Count on subsequent occasions in 1813. He was frequently mentioned as having turned up in various European capitals throughout that century, including London. The late English businessman, Christian mystic author and custodian of the Chalice Well at Glastonbury, Wellesley Tudor Pole, claimed he met Saint-Germain while travelling to Constantinople on the Orient Express in 1938. Various other modern students of the occult swear that Saint-Germain is still alive today.

Whatever the truth about men like the Count and about alchemy and its supposed achievements, it is worth noting that the psychologist Jung came to see the art not as the forerunner of chemistry, but as the precursor of modern psychology. In his autobiographical *Memories, Dreams, Reflections*, Jung admits that his first reaction on attempting to read an alchemical treatise was that it was utter rubbish. But he quickly revised his views, believing that he had "stumbled upon the historical counterpart of the psychology of the unconscious". Jung, who spent some ten years collecting alchemical volumes and studying the subject, said it was one of the greatest intellectual discoveries of his life.

He came to the conclusion that alchemy was an attempt to penetrate the great mystery of the Universe. He determined that the ultimate aim of the alchemists was to attain a godlike state or, as some occultists express it, "to become more than human".

We can gather something of what is meant by this in the *Occult Philosophy* of Henry Cornelius Agrippa, the 16th century German alchemist, philosopher and magician. Agrippa says that the soul gains prophetic power when it transcends its normal bounds and escapes from the body to spread over space "like a light escaped from a lantern". The experience, he says, comes through "continued yearning heavenward from a pure body" which carries the soul out of the body, pervading all time and space.

Similarly, another German alchemist and a pupil of Paracelsus, Gerhard Dorn, talked of "freeing the spirit from its fetters".

The alchemists were striving towards a goal that is the same throughout all history, all philosophies, all religions – the liberation of the human spirit and, most of all, immortality. By becoming godlike, they believed, they would transcend the limitations of the flesh and inherit the qualities of the godhead, including that of eternal life.

And while their ideas may have been focused towards the right aims and objects, their methods must have been dogged by imperfection. It will become apparent later in this volume that the alchemists envisioned, although perhaps did not achieve, the type of immortal projection that could well be the only escape clause in mankind's future destiny. This does not, however, involve the attainment of life everlasting within the confines of human existence as we know it, but a higher, more transcendental state than man has ever envisaged in any of his ceaseless quests for absolute truths.

12. Alchemy Lives On

"The initiate is eternally individual; he is ineffable, incorruptible, immune from everything. He possesses infinite wisdom and infinite power in himself."
Aleister Crowley (1875–1947)

DESPITE ITS many failings and imperfections, some of alchemy's followers have contributed to modern science. And in spite of its associations with antiquity, the art has survived to the present day.

It was an alchemist, Hennig Brand, for example, who in 1674 discovered the element phosphorus. Johann Baptist van Helmont, who lived from 1577 to 1644, meanwhile, spent 35 years trying to prove that there was a third state of matter, apart from solids and liquids – gas. So devoted to alchemy was van Helmont that in 1609 he refused a university professorship to continue his researches and named his son Mercury in honour of his beloved art.

Curiously enough, the suggestion that there was a fourth state of matter three centuries later by the scientist and psychical researcher Sir William Crookes, resulted in an accidental confirmation of one of the basic tenets of alchemical teachings. The fourth state of matter is known as plasma, a state more gaseous than gas and not to be confused with blood plasma.

Plasma, like gas, contains molecules and atoms, but some of them have been ionized, or electrically charged. Plasma is present in everyday life in the brilliance of the Sun and in the form of neon lighting. Yet plasma is different from gas in many more complex ways than its ionized particles. For instance, whereas gas will diffuse or expand outwards into any given space or retaining shape, plasma can be controlled under laboratory conditions to a confined area. It can contract into a vapour, called a plasmoid, that will repel any other plasma vapours.

Scientists believe that the many solar systems that dot the Universe were made up of huge plasma vapours before suns and planets were formed as the gases condensed. Now, curiously enough, it is possible to create plasmoids for brief moments in laboratory conditions. They give off light, are about half-an-inch in diameter and about two inches long. When photographed during the split seconds of their existence, they look exactly like spiral galaxies. Hermes Trismegistus, it seems, knew precisely what he was talking about when he made the "as above, so below" analogy.

Yet another remarkable story about the prophetic nature of alchemists, although there is no way to confirm its validity, concerns Albertus Magnus, who lived from 1206 to 1280. Albertus, Bishop of Regensburg, was an accomplished physician, mathematician, astronomer and chemist. He is said to have been first to define the Milky Way as a dense cloud of distant stars. He is also accredited with having built the first mechanical man, or robot.

In his autobiography, Albertus says that it took him more than 20 years to build the man "of metals and unknown substances according to the stars". The automaton, he claimed, could walk and talk and was used to carry out the menial tasks of a manservant. However one day, the story goes, the incessant chatter of the robot so annoyed Thomas Aquinas, a disciple who lived with Albertus, that he lost his temper, ran at it with a hammer and smashed it to smithereens.

The great English scientist Sir Isaac Newton appears to have believed that the secrets of alchemy and other arcane knowledge was passed from person to person along a chain of selected adepts sworn to secrecy and dating back to great antiquity.

Indeed, in July 1946, the nuclear physicist Da Costa Andrade, in addressing the Newton Tercentenary Celebrations at Cambridge University, hinted that Newton might even have been a link in the chain of initiates and had, perhaps, given only a fragment of his learning to the scientific world.

He said: "I cannot hope to convince the sceptical that Newton had some power of prophecy or special vision, had some inkling of atomic power; but I do say that certain passages do not read to me as if all he meant was that the manufacture of gold would upset world trade.

"Because the way by which mercury may be so impregnated has been thought fit to be concealed by others that have known it, and therefore may possibly be an inlet to something more noble not to be communicated without immense danger to the world, if there should be any verity in the Hermetic writings" – and a little further on – "there being other things beside the transmutation of metals (if those pretenders brag not) which none but they understand."

The physicist commented: "In pondering what these passages may import, consider the no greater reticence with which he speaks of his optical discoveries."

Despite the seeming antiquity and remoteness of alchemy, there are, surprisingly enough, people today who still practise the art in the hope of unravelling the immense tangle of allegorical and symbolical mysteries of the old masters.

One of these was the late Armand Barbault, who spent 12 years perfecting what he calls "vegetable gold" or Elixir of the First Degree in his book, L'Or Du Millième Matins (Gold Of A Thousand Mornings, Paris, 1969; Neville Spearman Ltd., 1975). Barbault claimed that his elixir was tested and analysed by Swiss and German laboratories and was found to be of great value in treating serious kidney and heart complaints. But the experts who examined the material could not give a complete analytical breakdown of its composition, nor could they reproduce the material synthetically. The scientist declared it a new state of matter with mysterious and, perhaps, deeply significant qualities. Barbault, was pressing on with his alchemical work, striving to perfect the Third Degree, until his death in 1981.

France seems to be the most active headquarters in the world of modern alchemists. One was Eugene Canseliet, who spent more than 50 years trying to perfect the Great Work. On his own admission, only four times during the 20-year period up to 1974 did he manage to reach and attempt the critical stage of the albedo, each time ending in failure. Canseliet, who died in 1986, blamed his disappointing results on atmospheric conditions and his own ineptitude, but expressed his determination to carry on with the Work.

Canseliet was, in fact, the closest surviving link with one of the most mysterious and fascinating figures of modern alchemy – the man known as Fulcanelli, to whom I referred earlier as the man who warned against the dangers of nuclear research. Reverting to Da Costa Andrade's allusions to Newton's possible awareness of nuclear secrets, it is worth quoting from Walter Lang's introduction to Fulcanelli's first published manuscript, Le Mystère Des Cathédrales.

To begin with, let us look at Lang's modern assessment and definition of alchemy:

"Alchemy is a total science of energy transformation... The creation of matter from energy and the creating of energy from matter is alchemy. *God is an alchemist.*

"The decay of radium into lead with the release of radioactivity is alchemy. *Nature is an alchemist.*

"The explosion of a nuclear bomb is alchemy. *The scientist is now an alchemist.*" (My italics throughout).

Now, perhaps most importantly, Lang goes on to say:

"All such energy transformations are fraught with great danger and the secrecy which has always surrounded Hermeticism is concerned with this aspect among others.

"Nuclear energy was undoubtedly foreseen thousands of years ago. Chinese alchemists are said to have told their pupils that not even a fly on the wall should be allowed to witness an operation. 'Woe unto the world,' they said, 'if the military ever learn the Great Secret.'"

One man who clearly knew the nature of the Great Secret was (or is?) Fulcanelli. One day in 1922, the pupil Canseliet, still working under the instruction of this Master Alchemist, was handed a manuscript by his teacher, who then disappeared. For more than 50 years, private individuals have tried to track down Fulcanelli – and failed. An international intelligence agency – the American Office for Strategic Services, forerunner of the CIA – also tried without success.

Yet before he disappeared, Fulcanelli handed to Canseliet a tiny amount of what was described as the "Powder of Projection". In September, 1922, Canseliet successfully transmuted 100 grammes of gold, using the powder.

Even more remarkable is that 30 years later, Canseliet received a message from his former Master, arranging a clandestine meeting with him. Fulcanelli was 80 years old when Canseliet worked under him as a 20-year-old neophyte. Yet, on this meeting, 30 years later, Canseliet said: "He appeared to be a man of fifty. That is to say, he appeared to be no older than I was."

Again, Fulcanelli disappeared without trace. The only other reported contact with Fulcanelli was on the occasion I have already mentioned – by the French scientific writer Jacques Bergier, although he had no proof that the man he met was indeed the Master Alchemist. One day in June 1937, Bergier was called to a test laboratory at the Paris Gas Board, by the physicist Andre Helbronner, later murdered by the Nazis. In *The Morning Of The Magicians*, the remarkable and thought-provoking book that Bergier co-authored with Louis Pauwels, an account of the conversation that took place is given. The supposed Fulcanelli did most of the talking:

"M. André Helbronner, whose assistant I believe you are, is carrying out research on nuclear energy. M. Helbronner has been good enough to keep me informed as to the results of some of his experiments, notably the appearance of radioactivity corresponding to plutonium when a bismuth rod is volatilised by an electric discharge in deuterium at high pressure. You are on the brink of success, as indeed are several other of our scientists today. May I be allowed to warn you to be careful? The research in which you and your colleagues are engaged is fraught with terrible dangers not only for yourselves but for the whole human race. The liberation of atomic energy is easier than you think, and the radioactivity artificially produced can poison the atmosphere of our planet in the space of a few years. Moreover, atomic explosives can be produced from a few grammes of metal powerful enough to destroy whole cities. I am telling you this as a fact: the alchemists have known it for a very long time."

Naturally, talk of alchemy in 1937, especially in connection with nuclear physics, was preposterous to Bergier. He was about to answer the stranger with some sarcastic rejoinder, when "Fulcanelli" interrupted:

"I know what you are going to say, but it is of no interest. The alchemists were ignorant of the structure of the nucleus, knew nothing about electricity and had no means of detection. Therefore they have never been able to perform any transmutation, still less liberate nuclear energy. I shall not attempt to prove to you what I am now going to say, but I ask you to repeat it to M. Helbronner: certain geometrical arrangements of highly purified materials are enough to release atomic forces without having recourse to either electricity or vacuum techniques. I will now read you a short extract. [He then picked up *The Interpretation Of Radium* by Frederick Soddy (1877–1956); an English chemist, in 1912 Soddy elaborated the theory of isotopes and, with Rutherford, stated the displacement law of radioactivity.]

"'I believe that there have been civilisations in the past that were familiar with atomic energy, and that by misusing it they were totally destroyed.'

"I would ask you to believe that certain techniques have partially survived. I would also ask you to remember that the alchemists' researches were coloured by moral and religious preoccupations, whereas modern physics was created in the 18th century, for their amusement by a few aristocrats and their wealthy libertines. Science without a conscience... I have thought it my duty to warn a few research workers here and there, but have no hope of seeing this warning prove effective. For that matter, there is no reason why I should have any hope."

Bergier told "Fulcanelli" that in his own investigations into alchemy, he had found nothing but charlatans and impostors, and asked what researches his strange visitor was currently following. The man replied:

"You ask me to summarize for you in four minutes four thousand years of philosophy and the efforts of a lifetime. Furthermore, you ask me to translate into ordinary language concepts for which such a language is not intended. All the same, I can tell you this much: you are aware that in the official science of today the role of the observer becomes more and more important. Relativity, the principle of indeterminacy, show the extent to which the observer today intervenes in all these phenomena. The secret of alchemy is this: there is a way of manipulating matter and energy so as to produce what modern scientists call a field of force. This field acts on the observer and puts him in a privileged position, vis-a-vis the Universe. From this position he has access to the realities which are ordinarily hidden from us by time and space, matter and energy. This is what we call the Great Work."

Asked about the Philosopher's Stone, "Fulcanelli" remarked: "These are only applications, particular cases. The essential thing is not the transmutation of metals, but that of the experimenter himself. It's an ancient secret that a few men re-discover once in a century."

Bergier asked: "And what becomes of them?"

"I shall know, perhaps, one day," said the mysterious stranger.

Bergier never saw him again, but remained convinced until his death in November 1978, that the man was Fulcanelli. Whoever he was, he seemed well versed in the inner knowledge of alchemy. But why should such a brilliant man disappear without trace and without offering any explanation?

There are various possibilities. If, as is alleged, Fulcanelli possessed the secrets of transmutation, of retaining youth and of nuclear energy, there would have been many powerful sectors of society ready to snap him up and exploit him for their own greedy and possibly even evil purposes. Unscrupulous speculators could have used him to create artificial imbalances on the world's money markets for their own gain as, indeed, they sometimes do now, without the aid of a Master Alchemist. World powers, at that time striving to win the race to perfect the atomic bomb, would have seized Fulcanelli and put him to work. Any other enterprising parasite could have made a fortune, marketing his elixir.

Imagine the awesome responsibility of possessing such knowledge and knowing the terrible abuses to which it would be subjected if it were made widely available. And in such a case, remember, it is not a matter of knowledge falling into the "wrong hands" – they are *all* wrong hands.

In any event, Fulcanelli disappeared. His going seems to have been an entirely voluntary affair, as if he had deliberately planned it. As for his warning to Bergier, it would be interesting to learn whether any other young physics researchers got a similar call from a stranger around the summer of 1937. Whether or not they did, the warning went unheeded. The first atomic bomb was tested by the U.S. in the desert of New Mexico on July 17, eight years later. A month afterwards, it was used on Japan.

13. The Secret Language Of Architecture

"I have found among my papers a sheet... in which I call architecture frozen music."
Goethe (1749–1832)

JUST AS ALCHEMY is a secret art – the remnants of wisdom given by celestial intelligences to provide humanity, as Fulcanelli put it, with "access to the realities which are ordinarily hidden" – so architecture is another way of preserving that half-forgotten knowledge. Even the most cursory examination of The Bible is sufficient to indicate that, in transmitting knowledge to humankind, a great significance was placed by the Hebrew God upon architecture and form. From the precise instructions given to Noah for building the Ark, the meticulous details outlined to Moses for his portable tabernacle, to its "permanent" form, the supreme Biblical edifice, the Temple of Solomon, a great deal of emphasis is placed on the materials, dimensions, locations, orientation, fittings and finishings of these structures. Superficially, it appears that the God of the Israelites wished to establish these projects as distinctive and set aside from any of mankind's earthly architectural creations. They are (with the exception of the purely functional Ark of Noah) places that signify the presence of God; structures that provide a semi-permanent reminder of his contact and covenants with humanity; buildings where people could commune with the Supreme Being. In Biblical terms, holy places.

But on more careful examination, it becomes clear that religious architecture – and not only that of the Hebrews – is much more than that. It is a method of storing hidden knowledge.

Through distinct signs, symbols and hieroglyphs, man could lock his knowledge and arcane secrets into his buildings to be discerned only by those who were meant to understand. These are facts that have been known for centuries to certain pockets and sects within society, including the alchemists and groups like the Illuminati, the Rosicrucians and, perhaps to a lesser degree, by the Freemasons. Before elaborating on this theme, however, let us now look briefly at the instances in the Old Testament where important buildings are designed to the original specifications of God. Noah's Ark was, as I said, for a specific functional purpose – that of saving selected human beings and animal life from the Great Deluge. Nonetheless, it was God himself that gave the detailed instructions for its dimensions and purpose.

Next in chronological order, comes the tabernacle made by Moses from orders given to him during the 40-day stay on Mount Sinai. Outlined in Exodus 26, this is seen as a portable temple that really amounts to little more than a rather opulently appointed tent. Even so, the instructions about its size, hangings, accessories and orientation are quite precise, as anyone who cares to read the appropriate chapter will discover. There are hangings of specific length, boarded walls and gold and silver fixtures. Even the colour scheme is delineated, as is the clothing that the appointed priests who will officiate in the tabernacle should wear. Moses is told to "rear up the tabernacle according to the fashion thereof which was shewed thee in the mount." A blue, purple and scarlet veil, with fine twined linen "of cunning work" is stipulated, to be hung on four pillars, and to be used to enclose the Ark of the Covenant. Note the use of the word "cunning" – obviously implying that the decorative needlework employed in adorning the Veil of the Temple should itself contain some message as to its purpose in protecting or enclosing the Ark. It may even, recalling my earlier speculations about the nature of the Ark, have been intended to convey instructions for the use of this most mysterious object; instructions, perhaps, that only selected initiates might be able to decipher and understand. For it was through the Ark, remember, that God said he would communicate with Moses and his elders.

There is also some significance in the way in which Moses is instructed to align his tabernacle, great care being taken to designate what objects should be placed in it and where: "twenty boards on the south side, southward... for the sides of the tabernacle westward thou shalt make six boards... and the candlestick over against the table on the side of the tabernacle towards the south: and thou shalt put the table on the north side."

Exactly what purpose these alignments may have served is not clear, but the fact that God made a point of outlining these instructions in such detail indicates that they must have been of paramount importance. We have lost the key to these secrets and, at this distance in time, can only speculate about their significance in most instances. In view of our earlier assessment of the Ark as some type of communication device, however, it may be reasonable to speculate that these directional alignments were important in that connection. The alignment of modern TV satellite dishes and radio aerials springs to mind as perhaps analogous.

Many Biblical scholars have said that the tabernacle of Moses, which the Children of Israel carried about with them on their wanderings, was the prototype or blueprint for the great Temple of Solomon. Having established themselves in Jerusalem and temporarily given up their nomadic life, the Israelites were in a position to seek a more permanent edifice to the glory of their God. It was, in fact, David, Solomon's father, who first suggested the idea of building an opulent temple to replace the much-travelled tabernacle containing the Ark of the Covenant. But when he conferred with God, David was told that he might not build the temple because his hands were tainted with the bloodshed of the many wars that the Israelites had fought. It was, however, acceptable for one "sprung from his loins" to embark upon the project. Solomon, it turned out, was particularly fitted to this task.

One of the most fabulous and fascinating figures in Biblical history – he reigned over Israel during the 10th century BC – he is also one of the most paradoxical. On the one hand he is renowned for his unbelievable wealth and incomparable wisdom; a stainless upholder of God's law, husband of the Queen of Sheba and of a reputed 300 other wives and 700 concubines. On the other, he emerges as a master magician, consorter with demons, supposed author of some of the most arcane texts dealing with the "Black Arts". How are the two to be reconciled?

It is quite possible that Solomon embraced both these widely diverse facets – his Old Testament image and his other, darker, extra-Biblical nature. The Book of Kings shows quite clearly that in Solomon's time the Israelites tended to live a dual religious life, worshipping old Canaanite gods such as Baal, while at the same time paying obeisance to Yahweh. Indeed, sometimes they appear to have combined the two.

The younger son of King David and Bathsheba, Solomon appears to have seized for himself the best of both worlds, first by choosing wisdom when Yahweh asked him what gift he desired, while at the same time becoming an initiate in the arcane secrets of magic. In addition to his Biblical persona, he is said in Rabbinical lore and tradition to have possessed a magic ring with which he could control all demons, including their king, Asmodeus. In *The Testament Of Solomon*, an ancient magical work attributed to the king, are listed all the names and powers of these various demons and a description of how Solomon tricked Asmodeus and his legions into building the Temple of Jerusalem for him.

Asmodeus, though, had his revenge on Solomon when he managed to seize Solomon's magical ring and fling it into the sea. But Solomon was clearly a more powerful magician than the demon imagined; the wily king caught a fish which he split open. In its stomach was the ring. With it, Solomon managed to banish Asmodeus and his hordes.

It is interesting to note that in the *Lemegeton*, another grimoire attributed to Solomon, Asmodeus is said to have three heads – that of a ram, a bull and a man, corresponding in part with Ezekiel's description of the "living beings" that he saw flying by the River Chebar. Could Solomon then have had some experience of the same, other-worldly beings; an event now only preserved in his case in allegorical legend? *The Testament Of Solomon* says that Asmodeus was "born of angel's seed by a daughter of man".

Most of these magical grimoires attributed to Solomon can only be traced back to the 16th/18th centuries, although the *Testament* is said to have first been written down in the first century AD. Almost as if to confirm the Solomonic influence, the dual approach to religion that is suggested in the Old Testament is reflected in these magical tomes. In the same breath that the texts give their elaborate directions for the summoning of demons, they also persistently urge the practitioner to call upon God for assistance.

One of the most important of magical works is the *Key Of Solomon*, a 12th century Greek version of which is in the British Library. It is an exceedingly rare volume, classified as qabbalistic, after the Qabbalah, a tradition of "secret" Hebrew knowledge and wisdom that was passed down by word of mouth, as opposed to the written scriptures. The book is a complex manual of instructions to the magician on how to summon up spirits and demons and contains an elaborate system of esoteric symbols. Both the Jewish historian Josephus, of the first century, and the 13th century magician Roger Bacon made references to Solomon's powers as a sorcerer and, indeed, another magical work attributed to Solomon, *Le Livre De Saloman*, was burned by order of Pope Innocent VI in 1350.

Such were the powers attributed to the great king that many later grimoires, such as the 18th century *Grimorium Verum* and the French, 17th century *Le Grand Grimoire*, were based on Solomon's rituals and mystical teachings.

Bearing in mind, then, the importance of seals, sigils and symbols in connection with the magical arts of Solomon, let us now examine the building of his temple and its significance.

Solomon knew that the men of Tyre and Sidon, in the eastern Mediterranean, were experts in woodwork, for as he says (I Kings:5–6), "there is not among us any that can skill to hew timber like unto the Sidonians." So he asked Hiram, King of Tyre, to provide timber from the cedar forests of Lebanon and to carry out the necessary woodwork for the Temple. Solomon recruited 30,000 men to work on the project, alongside Hiram's men, sending them to the forests at the rate of 10,000 a month, working for one month, then resting for a month. He also had 70,000 men on his supply lines ("those that bear burdens") and 80,000 stonemasons, working in the quarries of Zeredathah, an Ephraimite city to the northwest of Jerusalem, hewing out the stone for the Temple. There were also 3,300 overseers.

Once again, precise dimensions were outlined for the House of the Lord: 60 cubits long (about 90 feet, taking the cubit as 18 inches), 20 cubits wide (30 feet), and 30 cubits in height (about 45 feet). There was also a porch 20 cubits long and 10 cubits wide. Various chambers were to be constructed within the building, in particular, an outer, middle and inner chamber, this latter sanctum to be a reliquary for the Ark of the Covenant.

Perhaps most interesting of all, in I Kings 6:7:

"And the house, when it was in building was of stone made ready before it was brought thither: so that there was neither hammer nor axe nor any tool of iron heard in the house, while it was in building."

In Front of the Temple, Solomon put up two enormous pillars of bronze, named *Jachin* (Establishment) and *Boaz* (Strength). They stood 27 feet tall and were 18 feet in circumference, with ornate capitals on top.

The whole incredible project took a total of seven years. And so magnificent was the Temple of Solomon that it has, at various times throughout history, been proposed as the Eighth Wonder of the Ancient World.

While there is little archaeological proof of the actual historical existence of the Temple (although some of its stones are said to be in the Wailing Wall, in Jerusalem), there have been various excavations in Palestine, giving every indication that it might have been a glorious reality. Apart from the alleged discovery of the famous "Stables of Solomon" in 1928 at Megiddo, southwest of the Sea of Galilee, between the Jordan and the Mediterranean, Solomon's smelting and metalworking plants have been unearthed at Ezion-Geber, on the Gulf of Aqaba. There, Dr. Nelson Glueck, professor of the Biblical Archaeology department at the Hebrew Union College, Cincinnati, Ohio, found the site of what he *thought* was an amazing smelter-refinery.

Blasted as the area is by the windblown sands from the north, the site provides natural conditions for a furnace and Dr. Glueck, during excavations in the 1930s, found air channels and flue systems so aligned as to take advantage of the powerful winds. There, thousands of skilled workers would produce ingots of pure copper and iron from raw ore, which would then be transported by ship or caravan to the various parts of Solomon's kingdom and, via the port of Joppa (Jaffa), to the site of the Temple.

Sadly, neither the stables nor the copper refinery turned out to be correctly identified.

Although the workings at Megiddo – partitioned buildings – seemed remarkably similar to modern stables, later excavations showed that they were built a century after Solomon's time and belonged to that of Ahab, king of Israel from 875–853BC. In addition, further digs at Beersheba unearthed the same building plan, but there was also evidence that the premises were used as a storehouse, not stables.

Twenty-five years after his findings at Ezion-Geber, the over-enthusiastic Rabbi Glueck admitted that the "flues" for what he had thought were a form of Bessemer furnace were in fact holes in walls left by the decay of wooden beams in what was actually a granary, not a smelting plant.

In the 1950s, however, some evidence of Solomon's building works was excavated. Israeli archaeologists unearthed the massive, elaborate city gates of ancient Hazor, which Kings 9:15 says Solomon built. The team also found evidence that Hazor was utterly destroyed by Joshua in the second part of the 13th century BC and was only rebuilt by Solomon three centuries later.

The Temple is supposed to have been built over the rock upon which Abraham offered up his son Isaac in sacrifice and which is now the site of the Muslim Mosque of Omar, the Dome of the Rock. Because this is a most holy Islamic place, where Muhammad is believed to have ascended to heaven, there is no possibility of it being excavated to find the remains of Solomon's Temple.

It was around this still-buried edifice that the whole of the Craft of Freemasonry evolved. What is Freemasonry? Perhaps the best description, used by members of the Craft themselves, is that it is "a system of morality, veiled in allegory and illustrated by symbols".

There is no simple way, short of writing a separate volume, of explaining exactly what the Brotherhood is. It allegedly grew out of the medieval guilds of craftsmen who, travelling about to perform large building operations such as cathedrals, would protect their interests by a code of secret signs, marks and passwords to recognise each other as genuine master craftsmen. This is known as Operative Masonry by those in the Craft today. Eventually, during the 17th century, outsiders, not necessarily associated with the building profession, were admitted and the various oaths of fraternity and fidelity were adapted to encompass a brotherhood with ideals of free-thinking and toleration that became known as Speculative Masonry.

Although popularly regarded as a secret society, Freemasonry will, in fact, admit any man of good reputation whatever his professional, religious or social standing, provided, that is, that he admits to a belief in a Supreme Being. "We are a society with secrets," Masons often say. Nor is the organisation supposed to recruit its members. In theory, they are expected to discover the existence of the Craft by chance, usually through making friends with a member who will then introduce them to a Lodge if they show an interest.

This sketchy background of Freemasonry is pertinent in helping to point up the significance of Masonic tradition in relation to the Temple of Solomon. In sum, then, Freemasonry is basically a philosophic fellowship that performs many charitable works, often unpublicised and unrecognised, that purports to admit men of all creeds and religions, provided they believe in a Supreme Being.

Freemasons meet in Lodges that are specially designed and furnished to represent, symbolically, the Temple of Solomon. In Masonic legend, according to the early historians of the Craft, Freemasons themselves date back to the actual building of the Temple. A similar association in France, the *Compagnonnage*, also claims descent from Solomon's builders. The three pillars that "support" a Masonic Lodge, therefore, are said to represent Wisdom, in the figure of Solomon himself, Strength, personified by King Hiram of Tyre, who supplied the materials, and Beauty, symbolised by Hiram Abiff, superintendent of the work.

Lodges themselves are dedicated to King Solomon – "he being the first Prince who excelled in Masonry, and under whose royal patronage many of our Masonic mysteries obtained their first sanction". The chessboard-style flooring of a Lodge is said to represent the "ground floor of King Solomon's Temple", and the building itself, being aligned due east and west, is oriented in the same way as the original Temple.

Thus, in Masonic Catechism, we find the following question-and-answer material:
"Q: Where was the first lodge?
A: In the porch of Solomon's Temple.
Q: How stands your Lodge?
A: East and west, as the Temple of Solomon.

Q: Where was the first Lodge kept?

A: In Solomon's Porch; the two pillars were called Jachin and Boaz.

Q: What do they represent?

A: Strength and stability of the Church in all Ages."

And, perhaps most interesting of all, the Masonic explanation of the Temple being constructed without the ringing of the hammer or axe, nor the noise of any iron tools:

"Q: Why were metal tools prohibited?

A: The better to show the ingenuity of the Craft in those days, for tho' the materials were prepared at so great a distance when they were put together each part fitted with so exact a nicety that it seemed the work of the G.A. of the U. than of mortal man. [G.A. of the U. is a Masonic abbreviation for Great Architect of the Universe.]"

Charles A. Conover, a Masonic writer, in a paper on the Temple, described the Queen of Sheba's astonishment when Solomon first showed her the building:

"Tradition informs us that when she first beheld this magnificent edifice, which glittered with gold, and seemed from the nice adjustment and exact accuracy of all its joints, to be composed of a single piece of marble, she raised her eyes and hands in an attitude of admiration and exclaimed: 'Rabboni!' signifying 'A Most Excellent Master had done this!'"

The Jewish historian Josephus, in his *Antiquities* (VIII, 3:2) commented: "Now the whole structure of the Temple was made, with great skill, of polished stones, and those laid together so very harmoniously and smoothly, that there appeared to the spectators no signs of any hammer, or other instrument of architecture, but as if, without any use of them, the entire materials had naturally united themselves together, that the agreement of one part with another seemed rather to have been natural, than to have arisen from the force of tools upon them."

It becomes obvious that however Solomon constructed his Temple, his idea was to make it quite clear that it symbolised not the work of humans, but of an Unearthly Intelligence. True, there are in Masonic legends and traditions, many discrepancies between the traditions of the Craft and those details in The Bible. But these are easily explained. In the Middle Ages when there were no comprehensive histories or encyclopaedias, scholars would compile their own reference books which were known as *polychronicons*, from any writings they could find. Thus some Biblical references in ancient Masonic manuscripts contained ideas introduced second-hand.

There has been a great deal of speculative discussion in Masonic writings about the meaning of the two pillars that Solomon placed outside his Temple and which are represented in the various Lodges. They are, in Masonic circles, usually highly ornamented and hollow, being used as repositories for important documents.

One suggestion is that Solomon's Pillars represented the pillars that shepherded the Children of Israel out of Egypt – the pillar of cloud by day and the pillar of fire by night, the former being, it will be recalled, the same type of pillar seen in the doorway of Moses' tabernacle.

In *The Perfect Ceremonies Of Craft Masonry*, (London, 1926), A. Lewis wrote:

"They were set up as a memorial to the Children of Israel of that miraculous pillar of fire and cloud, which had two wonderful effects: the fire gave light to the Israelites during their escape from their Egyptian bondage, and the cloud proved darkness to Pharaoh and his followers when they attempted to overtake them. King Solomon ordered them to be placed at the entrance of the Temple, as the most proper and

---

conspicuous situation for the Children of Israel to have the happy deliverance of their forefathers continually before their eyes, in going to and returning from Divine worship."

Intriguingly, though, there is reference to another form of pillar symbolism in Masonic tradition. These are known as the Antediluvian Pillars, believed to have been made by the third son of Adam, Seth. Somehow, Seth like Noah had advance warning that the Earth was to be destroyed by God and made two pillars, one of marble to withstand fire and one of tile that would float. On them he inscribed the whole of man's knowledge of the arts and sciences and, it is said, when the Flood subsided, one was found by Hermes Trismegistus, father of alchemy, the other by the Greek philosopher-mathematician, Pythagoras (c.580–500BC). Josephus also makes reference to these Pillars of Seth. The Babylonian historian Berosus, however, in an idea also attributed to the Persian prophet Zoroaster of the 6th–7th centuries BC, said that there were two sets of pillars, seven of brass and seven of brick upon which the liberal arts were inscribed.

And so we find in an 18th-century Masonic "working":

"Q: Where was the noble art or science [Masonry] found when it was lost?

A: It was found in two pillers [sic] of stone, the one would not sink and the other would not burn."

Students of occultism, on the other hand, give a completely different meaning to the Pillars of Solomon, interpreting them as the "opposites" of Universal Law, the space between them representing the gateway to Ultimate Truth. It is noteworthy also that in many versions of the oracular Tarot deck, the trump card numbered two and known as the High Priestess or Female Pope, depicts a noblewoman seated on a throne between a black and white pillar, representing the opposites. The card, among its many interpretations, is seen as symbolic of the gateway to heaven.

However, Helena Petrovna Blavatsky, the 19th-century teacher of modern occultism and Theosophy, saw the whole Biblical story of the building of Solomon's Temple as purely allegorical. In her two-volume work, *Isis Unveiled*, she wrote:

"...if, following the ingenious exoteric description of the Bible, there are yet Masons who persist in regarding it as once an actual structure, who, of the students of the esoteric doctrine will ever consider this mythic temple otherwise than as an allegory, embodying the secret science? Whether or not there ever was a real temple of that name, we may well leave to archaeologists to decide; but that the detailed description thereof in I Kings is purely allegorical, no serious scholar, proficient in the ancient as well as medieval jargon of the kabalists and alchemists can doubt. The building of the Temple of Solomon is the symbolical representation of the gradual acquirement of the secret wisdom or magic; the erection and development of the spiritual from the earthly; the manifestation of the power and splendour of the spirit in the physical world, through the wisdom and genius of the builder. The latter, when he has become an adept, is a mightier king than Solomon himself, the emblem of the Sun or Light himself – the light of the real subjective world, shining in the darkness of the objective universe. This is the 'Temple' which can be reared without the sound of the hammer or any tool of iron being heard in the house while it is 'in building'."

Be that as it may, there is no reason why the building of Solomon's Temple should not have been an actual, physical event that symbolised both the Celestial Intelligence of the Hebrew God and the spiritual enlightenment of the Master Architect and Magician himself, in the same way that the Great Work of alchemy is both a physical and spiritual achievement.

As to the Biblical account, the words of the archaeologist Professor W.F. Albright, who devoted himself to digging up evidence of the Old Testament's historicity, are most significant:

"The excessive scepticism shown toward the Bible by important historical schools of the eighteenth and nineteenth centuries, certain phases of which still appear periodically, has been progressively discredited. Discovery after discovery has established the accuracy of innumerable details, and has brought increased recognition of the value of the Bible as a source of history."

A surviving example of the practice of Operative Masons of incorporating profound symbolism into their work can be found in the heart of the French capital. Notre Dame Cathedral, among many other examples of religious gothic architecture in Europe, is pointed to by none other than the great Master Alchemist Fulcanelli as a veritable textbook of the alchemical arts. His own book, Le Mystère Des Cathédrales, consists of a guided tour of several of these important edifices, a tour upon which he points out the alchemically significant features that often go unnoticed by the casual visitor or the orthodox student of architecture.

It would be fruitless to go through Fulcanelli's exhaustive catalogue of symbolism here, but to illustrate the profound nature of this "hidden knowledge", the following pointers should suffice. Fulcanelli notes that the ground plan of these gothic structures take the form of a Latin cross, which itself is the hieroglyph of the alchemical crucible in which the First Matter "dies" to be resurrected, purified and transformed.

The semi-circular apse on one of the arms of this groundplan cross, he points out, forms the Egyptian ankh or crux ansata, symbol of the Aten and which signifies to the alchemist universal life concealed in matter. This, in turn, is the hermetic and astrological glyph for the planet Venus, whose corresponding metal is copper. The Greek word for copper is the same as that for ordure, dung, manure or muck. Thus, an alchemical saying was: "The wise man will find our stone in the dung heap, while the ignorant will not be able to believe that it exists in gold."

Various quatrefoils bearing relief pictographs that adorn the walls of cathedrals like Notre Dame take the alchemist symbolically through the various steps on his search for the Philosopher's Stone. Thus, says Fulcanelli, the plan and design of a Christian building points the alchemist towards the First Stone – that upon which Jesus built his church. (It need hardly be pointed out that the name that Jesus gave to his disciple Simon was Peter, meaning a stone.)

14. Waiting For The Gods

"The pyramids themselves, doting with age, have forgotten the names of their founders."
Thomas Fuller (1608–1661)

IF, AS I HAVE tried to show, some forms of architecture contain a secret, encoded form of writing, what are we to make then of the greatest-ever monuments in stone and only surviving example of the Ancient World's Seven Wonders – the Pyramids? To attempt an answer, we must try to transcend the 45 centuries or more of mystery that has enshrouded these engineering marvels.

Mesopotamia, the fertile strip between the Tigris and Euphrates, which forms the present-day borderland between Iraq and Iran, became a focus for migrating settlers: Sumerians and Elamites from southern Persia, Assyrians from the western deserts and the invading Kassites from the mountains to the north.

Between 3000 and 500BC, the many city-states of Mesopotamia built hundreds of ziggurats – stepped towers, not unlike the pyramids of South America. These temples of the old Mesopotamian civilisations took the form of towers built on square bases. On the extremely flat plains that these peoples inhabited, such structures would be the most prominent objects to be seen for miles. So far, no satisfactory explanation has been given by archaeological research for these square, tiered towers, rising in stages. Once again, any attempt to understand their significance must remain, in part at least, in the realms of speculation. Yet most of the evidence for the appearance of God in the days of the ancient Sumerians and Israelites, initially took place on the tops of mountains, and it has been suggested that the founders of the Mesopotamian civilisations, in moving from the east to the flat plains where they settled, raised their temples as imitations of "holy" mountains where they had seen and communed with their gods.

In Genesis, after the story of Noah, we see some reference to this reaching for the celestial God in the account of the Tower of Babel. It could be then, that the stepped towers, or *ziggurats*, as they are known, were thought of either as ways of trying to reach the sky-gods, or symbolic means by which they may be persuaded to descend to Earth. It is known that at the top of each ziggurat – which means "pinnacle" – was a shrine known as *Shakuru*, which translates as "the room of transit", or even "the waiting room".

According to Genesis, the Mesopotamian cities of Babel, Erech and Accad (Akkad), were built in the land of Shinar. Erech, or Uruk, was southeast of Babylon and featured a great temple. At this site, archaeologists have found the earliest known forms of writing, dating back to the fourth millennium BC. No trace has been found, however, of Akkad, although researchers believe it may have stood near modern Baghdad. It must certainly have existed, because remaining fragments of its Akkadian tongue show that it was a Semitic language, akin to Hebrew.

Together with Babel (Babylon), the three cities made up the original kingdom of Nimrod, "a mighty hunter before the LORD". (Genesis 10:9)

There was no stone in the deep fertile plains of Mesopotamia. Its people made bricks of mud, baked them and cemented them together with bitumen, an asphalt found naturally near the earth's surface.

As Genesis 11:4 relates:

"Come, let us build ourselves a city, and a tower with its top in the heavens..."

Shamayim, Hebraic for "heavens", also means "sky".

The most notable of all the ziggurats was that at Etemenanki, the one mentioned in the Bible as the Tower of Babel. Little more than a heap of rubble today, its outlines can still be seen from the air: its massive, square base made of earthen embankments, now overgrown with vegetation, pitted by hollows and dotted with palm trees.

A tablet from Esagil, the temple of Marduk at the base of the structure, describes Etemananki as "the foundation house of heaven and earth". It says that the base of the building was 295 feet long on each side and that the tower rose to the same height.

The actual Biblical name given to the tower – Babel – stems from the Hebrew verb *bal-li*, which means "to confuse". But its real meaning is from *Bab-li*, which in the Babylonian language meant "Gate of God" – another suggestive clue to its purpose as a place where a celestial being or beings might descend to commune with humans.

In his *Histories*, the Greek Herodotus (c.484–424BC) describes his visit to the site of Etemananki:

"It has a solid central tower, one furlong square, with a second erected on top of it and then a third, and so on up to eight. All eight towers can be climbed by a spiral way running round the outside, and about half way up there are seats for those who make the ascent to rest upon."

In fact, archaeological excavations have established that the ziggurat had *seven* stages or terraces – Herodotus was probably counting either the earthen base platform or the shrine at its summit as an eighth.

He described the sanctuary at the top as "a great temple with a fine large couch in it, richly covered, and a golden table beside it. The shrine contains no image and no one spends the night there except (if we are to believe the Chaldeans who are the priests of Baal) one Assyrian woman, all alone, whoever it may be that the god has chosen. The Chaldeans also say, though I do not believe them, that the god enters the temple in person and takes his rest upon the bed."

At the end of the Babylonians' new year festival, a ceremony called *Akitou*, the symbolic marriage rites of the god Marduk, chief of the pantheon, were enacted, with a priestess playing the role of the god's wife, Zarpanit. It is believed that the goal of this sacred rite was to ensure the fertility of the land and its people.

Some centuries before the time of Herodotus, the tower had been damaged by the fierce Assyrians. Beginning with Nabopolassar (625–605BC), the kings of the ensuing Babylonian dynasty undertook its restoration. An inscription ascribed to Nabopolassar says that "gold, silver and precious stones from the mountains and from the sea were liberally set into its foundations. Oils and perfumes were mixed with the bricks...

"I made a likeness of my royal self carrying the brick basket, and I carried it into the foundations. I bowed my head before Marduk. I took off my robe, the sign of my royal rank, and carried bricks and clay upon my head. I had my eldest son Nebuchadrezzar, who is so dear to my heart, carry clay and offerings of wine and oil..."

Nebuchadrezzar takes up the story in another inscription: "As for Etemananki,

---

Nabopolassar had set its foundations and built it to 30 cubits [about 45 feet], but he had not built the summit. I set about doing this. With pure hands I cut great cedars from the splendid forest of Lebanon and used them in the building. I made the tall gates to the enclosure and work of splendour, dazzling as the day itself, and I put them in place."

There are Babylonian reliefs depicting the building operations, with the king and his family carrying baskets of bricks and other materials on their heads and carrying tools and surveying instruments. According to yet another inscription, to swell his work force, Nebuchadrezzar recruited "the various peoples of the Empire, from north to south, from the mountains and the coasts".

The opulent temple of Marduk lay beside the great tower. Herodotus recorded that inside was a 22-ton (800 talents) golden statue of the god seated upon a throne. Within the great enclosure of the Tower, according to one inscription, there were no fewer than "53 temples of the great gods [An, Enki and Enlil; Anum, Ea were the Akkadian names of the first two], 55 chapels to Marduk, 300 chapels for the earthly deities, 600 for the heavenly deities [Nannar, Utu, Innin or Inanna; Sin, Shamash and Ishtar in Akkadian]".

In 331BC, when Alexander the Great ventured into Babylonia, he too considered trying to restore the massive ruin of the Tower. But the colossal job was never to see completion. As Strabo (c.63BC–22AD), the Greek geographer and historian recorded, preliminary clearance of the site alone took 10,000 workers two months to carry out.

Several ancient authors, including Strabo and the Greek historian Diodorus Siculus, who flourished in the late 1st century BC, have offered various ideas about the purpose of the ziggurats. Diodorus thought they might have been observatories, while Strabo suggested that the Etemenanki tower was the mausoleum or a cenotaph of Marduk. But the general, later consensus of opinion remains that these mighty edifices were places where the gods could descend and bestow wisdom and blessings upon humankind.

To the west of Mesopotamia, with the growth of the Egyptian civilisation, similar buildings to the ziggurats were modified and used as tombs, called *mastabas* – rectangular, brick structures whose walls sloped inwards over their underground vaults. By the Third Dynasty, the buildings became larger and larger until, in the reign of the Pharaoh Zoser, around 2700BC, the master architect and engineer Imhotep designed and built a huge mastaba, 200 feet square by about 26 feet in height at Saqqara (Sakkara), west of Memphis. But as Imhotep worked on this tomb for the pharaoh, Zoser continually intervened with modifications. Extra layers of stone were added to its walls, then it was decided to convert it into a step pyramid, with four mastabas, each smaller than the one beneath, built one atop the other.

Eventually, Zoser's tomb was completed as a six-tiered step pyramid, rising to a height of 200 feet from its 358 by 411-foot base, and surrounded by a wall.

A few decades later, the first prototypes of the true pyramids were built – one at Maydum and two at Dashur, sites south of Saqqara. The one at Maydum began as an orthodox step-pyramid of eight levels, but was completed by the filling in of its steps with limestone casings, so that its sides rose smoothly to an apex, although this work has now deteriorated, leaving only the second storey rising from an untidy pile of fallen rubble.

One of the two at Dashur is known as the Bent Pyramid because about halfway up its sides, the angle of its slope suddenly changes as if, for some reason, its builders could not maintain the same angle of inclination. But the other pyramid at this site, that of the Pharaoh Seneferu, was the first "perfect" pyramid shape.

It is, however, at Kafr es-Samman, near Giza, that the most interesting and intriguing of Egypt's pyramids stand, along with that other most enigmatic structure, the Sphinx. Here, the Great Pyramid of Khufu (Cheops in Greek), the mightiest and most awesome of a group of three, stands on the levelled rock plateau that divides the lush, cultivated banks of the Nile from the dry, barren deserts beyond. It stands 450 feet high (originally 480 feet before its outer stones and capstone were plundered) and, with its 2,300,000 blocks, weighing an average of 2½ tons, covers an area of 756 square feet, forming an almost perfect square base. The sides of the base are carefully aligned within less than one-tenth of a degree of true north and south and within two minutes (two sixtieths of a degree) of east and west.

It is made of local limestone and was originally cased in finer limestone from quarries on the opposite banks of the Nile, although this outer finish has been cannibalised over the centuries, particularly by medieval Muslims. It is also widely accepted that the missing capstone may have been gilded.

The most popularly propagated idea about the purpose of the Pyramid is that it was an elaborate tomb for the Pharaoh Khufu, so designed as to be impregnable (so the pharaoh thought) to robbers. While this may well have been part of its purpose, the Pyramid may also have had a much more profound purpose.

Long before the edifice reached its finished height and shape, when construction work had reached the Grand Gallery that leads into the so-called King's Chamber in the heart of the Pyramid, it was used as an observatory by Khufu's astrologers. Shortly before the turn of the century, the British astronomer Richard A. Proctor put forward this idea, saying that the huge, square platform that the structure formed at this stage in the operation, would have made an ideal place from which to study and record the movements of the stars. Not only that, the Descending Passage, which abuts onto the Grand Gallery, is inclined at an angle of 26 degrees 17 minutes – the perfect inclination, in view of the orientation of the Pyramid's base, to be aimed at the celestial Pole Star. Astrologers would position themselves at different levels of the Gallery to watch the passage of stars in a mirrored surface at its junction with the Descending Passage, through the critical gap it formed, in the same way that the telescopes of modern optical observatories are trained through the narrow transit gaps in their domes.

When the Pyramid was built, the Pole Star was Thuban in the constellation of Alpha Draconis, the Dragon. But because the Earth bulges slightly at the equator, the gravitational influences of the Sun and Moon make it wobble slightly, over a period of 25,800 years. This phenomenon causes what is known as the precession of the equinoxes. Thus, the Pole Star, which is a point at which the imaginary axis of the Earth is aimed, changes during this period. Today it is Polaris in Ursa Minor. In some 12,000 years, it will be Vega in the Lyre. Although the Egyptians may not have known this, so perfect was their alignment of the Great Pyramid, that whichever way the inclination of our planet's axis shifts, the Descending Passage will always remain aligned on the Pole Star.

No one is absolutely certain how the Egyptians managed to locate true north with such precision, although it could have been discovered by bisecting the angle formed by the rising and setting point of any northern star in relation to the centre of the platform from which it was observed. This technique is known as using an artificial horizon and seems the most likely method.

Further confirmation of the Giza pyramid complex's connection with the heavens was offered early in 1994 with the publication of *The Orion Mystery*, by Robert Bauval and Adrian Gilbert (Heinemann.) Bauval, a construction engineer born in Egypt, spotted an aerial photograph of the three Giza pyramids while visiting a Cairo museum. As a man used to reading architectural plans, he noticed that the smaller of the three was not geometrically aligned, but was offset from the southwest siting of the other two.

A year later, while working in Saudia Arabia, Bauval took his wife Michele and their four-year-old daughter Candice camping a few miles from Riyadh. Lying in his sleeping bag on the desert sands, the engineer looked up at the Milky Way, to the west of which lay the constellation of Orion. When he awakened a yachtsman friend, along for the trip, the star Sirius appeared brightly over the horizon. Bauval's friend pointed out that, to locate Sirius, one had merely to follow the pointer of the three stars forming Orion's Belt. Then he added: "Actually, those three are not perfectly aligned. The smallest, at the top, is slightly offset."

Immediately, Bauval realised he was looking at a star configuration that matched precisely the alignment of the three Giza pyramids. Not only that, the stars' intensities matched the sizes of the three pyramids.

After ten years' further research, Bauval and his co-author were able to put forward his theory in their book. In it, they suggest that the pyramids were built to mirror the three stars which pointed the way to the ultimate resting place of a pharaoh – the star Sirius. He found confirmation of this in the so-called Pyramid Texts, comprising hieroglyphics on the walls of a pyramid at Saqqara. Pharaohs were thought of as reincarnations of Horus, son of Osiris. Throughout the texts, it is repeated: "O king, you are this Great Star, companion of Orion... behold, Osiris has come as Orion... O king, the sky conceives you with Orion."

Research by another engineer and archaeologist, Rudolf Gantenbrink, who examined the so-called "ventilation shafts" of the Great Pyramid, also tended to corroborate Bauval's conclusions. When the Pyramid was built, he calculated, these shafts were aligned at the stars in Orion's Belt, presumably so that the soul (*ba*) of the dead pharaoh could wing its way directly there.

During the mid-19th century, an entire cult, known as Pyramidology, grew around the Pyramid of Khufu, triggered off by Colonel Howard Vyse, who used gunpowder to blast his way into its inner chambers. On his return to London, Colonel Vyse published the various measurements that he had taken of the Pyramid's internal and external dimensions and a publisher, John Taylor, derived from these a series of amazing theories, among them that the Pyramid had been built with divine guidance by Noah and his sons. He suggested that the structure was a textbook of Universal Law and Wisdom and backed this up with such roundabout theories as one proposing that, if the length of its perimeter were divided by double its height, the result would be the value of *pi*. As every schoolboy knows, *pi* is the ratio of a circle's circumference to its diameter (3.14159... approximately 22/7). But in fact, only an approximation of this mathematical figure results when Taylor's theory is put into practice.

Nonetheless, Taylor's ideas were picked up by the Scottish astronomer royal, Charles Piazzi Smyth, who travelled to Giza to measure the Pyramid himself and, on his return, prepared a paper for the Royal Society. It was, however, rejected.

The whole of Smyth's analytical hypothesis was based around what he described as a "pyramid inch" – 1.001 English inches, an idea which he appears to have invented for his own purposes and a measurement that the Egyptians certainly did not use. The perimeter of the base, he suggested, was 36,524 pyramid inches – or 100 times the number of days in a year. He claimed that the mass of the Pyramid was one trillionth that of the Earth, that its height was one billionth of the distance from the Earth to the Sun and many other highly improbable and contrived snippets of information that, in any case, would seem of dubious value to the Egyptians, even if they had been aware of them in the first place.

Despite the dismissal of Smyth's wild, wonderful and "occult" calculations, many people found juggling with the Pyramid's supposed dimensions fascinating and jumped on the bandwagon. Thus, in 1865, another Pyramidologist named Robert Menzies claimed that each pyramid inch represented a solar year and developed an entire system of symbolic history and prophecy based on his findings. The Second Coming of Christ, for example, was variously predicted for 1911 and 1936, by those who took up Menzies' theories. But the entire fabric of Pyramidology was, despite its frustrating complexity, full of holes.

Indeed, in 1888, some 14 years after reading Smyth's weird and wonderful book, *Our Inheritance In The Great Pyramid*, (London 1864), the great archaeologist W.M. Flinders Petrie went to Egypt to make an exhaustive examination of the Pyramid. He discovered that most of the so-called measurements were falsified and inaccurate, as well as being illogical. The base of the Pyramid was not, as the theorists suggested, 9,140 inches, but 9,069 inches. A discrepancy of 71 inches may seem negligible – but not when one inch was supposed to represent one year. Petrie lost no time in determining that there were no mysteries or secrets of Biblical prophecy enshrined in the Pyramid's dimensions.

However significant the figures may have seemed to the adherents of the Pyramidology cult, they had certainly not been of any interest to the builders. Since then, the cult has declined, although there are still some groups who persist in manipulating figures which, as most people know, can be made to demonstrate all kinds of wonderful, albeit groundless, ideas.

Two of the greatest puzzles surrounding the Pyramids are the way in which they were built and the reason why Khufu eventually located his supposed tomb where he did. The first question has now largely been satisfactorily resolved by the deductions of archaeologists, architects and surveyors.

From ancient Egyptian art, literature, the remains of tools, the evidence of quarrying and ramp-building, it is now almost certain that the Egyptians used little more than resourcefulness and sheer hard work. A series of mastabas, whose remains have been discovered near the Pyramid site, seem to have housed the permanent labour force of 4,000 who worked on Khufu's Pyramid, supplemented by gangs of farm labourers, who were redundant during the annual flooding of the Nile Valley. Limestone from local quarries and finer quality limestone from Troyu, across the Nile, was hewn out by further gangs of stonemasons. One of the methods used, bearing in mind that the Egyptians did not have any metal tools apart from copper, was to drive wooden wedges into notches that the masons made with copper saws. These wedges would then be soaked with water, causing them to expand – thus fracturing the rock. Using levers, ropes, ramps, sleds and rollers, these blocks could then be hauled, floated, dragged and pushed to the building site by gangs of labourers or teams of oxen. Ramps, built up to the height of the level in progress, ascended with the Pyramid as it rose to its apex. When the job was finished, the ramps were dismantled.

The claims of many writers that the Pyramids were built using some occult power – "floating" the blocks through the air by telekinetic or some other magical means – are not only absurd, but completely unnecessary. A team of eight or ten men could easily drag blocks that weighed an average 2½ tons, assisted where necessary with the heavier ones by extra manpower or by beasts of burden.

Neither is it impossible that the Egyptians took full advantage of the flooding that occurred and floated their blocks on small canals to the actual site of the levelled platform on which the Pyramids were being built. None of this is to say, however, that the Egyptians did not exercise their occult knowledge in other directions – only that it was not necessary for the physical task of building the Pyramids.

On completion, the Pyramid served yet another purpose: as a giant clock and calendar. It was the French astronomer Jean Baptiste Biot who in 1853 visited Giza and remarked that the Great Pyramid was like an enormous sundial "which marked annually the periods of the equinoxes with an error less than a day and three-quarters". Meanwhile, Moses B. Cotsworth, a Yorkshireman, built a number of models to prove that a pyramid, as opposed to a cone or an obelisk, was an ideal shape for measuring in its shadow the time of day, the week and the month, along with the seasons of the year.

Now, however, let us deal with the other intriguing question: that of the location of Khufu's supposed burial chamber within the Great Pyramid. When work first began on the structure, the customary underground chamber was constructed beneath the ground level of the Pyramid, a location chosen by the designers of other, earlier pyramids for a sepulchre. But during the progress of the work, Khufu appears to have changed his mind twice. Firstly, it seems, he rejected the idea of being laid to rest in an underground chamber, then again, when the probably erroneously-labelled Queen's Chamber was constructed as an alternative, about one-sixth of the way up the centre of the Pyramid. Khufu may then have settled for the third and highest enclosure, called the King's Chamber, about one-third the way up the core of the Pyramid. Why? The answer may lie in the strange properties of the Pyramid itself.

In 1959, Karel Drbal, a Czechoslovakian radio engineer, secured a patent at Prague (No. 91304) for a revolutionary new type of razor-blade sharpener. It was shaped to the same scale as the Khufu Pyramid.

Drbal got the idea from a Frenchman named Bovis who, while visiting the Great Pyramid, had discovered that a cat and a few small desert rodents that had died inside the King's Chamber were in a remarkable state of preservation, despite the apparent humidity. Bovis, wondering if the Pyramid itself, rather than the mummification process used by the Egyptians, had anything to do with this phenomenon, made a scale model of the Khufu Pyramid, and positioned it with the base-lines oriented to north-south and east-west.

In the position where the King's Chamber would have been proportionally located, Bovis placed a dead cat. After several months the cat became dehydrated, almost mummified. Similar experiments with other dead creatures brought the same results of amazing preservation. There was, and is, no complete scientific explanation.

Next, Bovis remembered an old superstition that razor blades would go blunt if left in the rays of the Moon. Curious, he left one in the model pyramid after shaving with it several times. When he took it out he found it was even sharper than before.

The only theory that comes close to suggesting an answer to this mystery is that the crystals which comprise the edge of a razor blade actually "grow" organically and that the Moon's polarised light (light that only vibrates in one direction, being the reflected light of the Sun), could somehow break down and destroy crystals. But why the shape of a pyramid should have the opposite effect and promote the reproduction of those crystals is not known. It has been theorised that a pyramid, being similar in shape to the crystals of a razor blade, somehow builds up a protective magnetic shield.

In any event, Drbal tried out Bovis' seemingly improbable razor-sharpener, found that it worked and managed to market the idea, made of cardboard, later of plastic. The important factor seems to be that the pyramid must be a scaled down replica of the Khufu Pyramid, with its sides and the positioning of the "sharpening spot" in proportional position to the King's Chamber. The four sides must be isosceles triangles with their two equal sides in the ratio of 15.7 to 14.94 to the base, and the razor blade should be placed 3.33 units of the way up inside the pyramid. The sides of the pyramid should be aligned to the cardinal points of the compass and the edges of the blade should face east-west. The pyramid should also be kept away from any electrical equipment. Larger versions of the device can be made in which food can be stored for remarkably long periods without perishing.

To comprehend why Khufu should want his body placed in such an environment, perhaps we should recall a few points made earlier. The Egyptians appear to have been in contact with extra-terrestrial intelligences, whom they recorded as flying in egg-shaped or discoid vessels. Traditionalist theory meanwhile is that the Egyptians believed that their afterlife could be enjoyed only so long as the body was in a perfect state of preservation, which is why they practised mummification.

But, taking into account all the factors – the "mountain" symbolism of the Pyramids, the preservational qualities of the burial chamber, the "room of transit" of the ziggurats, the food and worldly treasures that were entombed with dead rulers – isn't it more likely that the pharaohs were maintaining a tradition, in some distorted form, that they would themselves expect to join their sky-gods in their afterlives?

To re-cap the hypothetical stages of this tradition's development: first, objects are seen in the sky. Contact is made on mountains with selected human beings. It is clear that these visiting celestials are superior to humankind and have probably travelled inestimable distances to Earth. They teach humans how the Universe was created from a primal atom (suggesting perhaps that they themselves preceded this process) and how the human race evolved from the print-out of clay patterns. Humans, being unable to appreciate this explanation in its scientific sense, interpreted this as meaning that the celestials themselves had created the Universe and made humans from clay. The celestials also explain that they can journey many light years across space, journeys that take hundreds, perhaps even thousands of Earth years and necessitate a process of suspended animation in their vessels as the centuries slip by.

Again, such concepts are perhaps beyond the comprehension of the ancient peoples and eventually become interpreted as a need to preserve the body after death in order to "join" these sky-gods through emulation. The celestials then promise to return.

In the meantime, a whole philosophy evolves over the ensuing centuries that to attract these beings, who first manifest on mountains, man must build his own mountains, mountains that are so geometrically perfect that the sky-gods will immediately see them as "reception rooms" on their return. Next, the idea of lying in a preserved state within these mountain-tombs becomes a prevalent necessity to await the skygods. The pharaohs upon their deaths are mummified and are then entombed in their mighty, man-made capsules, edifices that indeed seem to have a preservative quality.

But, as we have seen, the sky-gods did not always return to the same peoples. The Egyptians waited in vain. Eventually, because of their vulnerability to plunder, the

Egyptians abandoned the Pyramids and removed the bodies of their rulers to the labyrinthine vaults in the Valley of the Kings, at Luxor. But the idea of an afterlife among the gods persisted and remained as the traditional Egyptian concept that we know today, reverting to its old order of underworld gods and rituals that are described and depicted on the walls of Egyptian tombs, and in coffin texts.

15. Watchers Of The Skies

"No field of inquiry is more fascinating than a search for humanity, or something like humanity, in the mystery-filled happy lands beyond the barriers of inter-stellar space."
Harlow Shapley (1885–1972)

"There is nothing new except what has been forgotten."
Attributed to Marie Antoinette's milliner, remodelling a hat for the Queen

THE BIBLE makes many references to the way that mankind has always considered stones to be of some sacred significance – objects of reverence. Following most major events in the Old Testament, the central figure almost invariably sets up a crude altar or stone to mark the occurrence and its importance in the affairs of humanity is recorded for those that follow. Jacob, for instance, after seeing the ladder with its ascending and descending "angels", set up a stone at a place he called *Beth-el* (House of El or, if you prefer, the Lord), to commemorate his experience. When Joshua made the children of Israel renew their Covenant with God, he did the same, this time placing his monument near an oak tree. In the New Testament, Jesus symbolically re-names Simon, his disciple, Peter (*petra* in Greek – a rock, or stone), denoting the stone upon which he will build his Church.

And 1,000 years after the building of the Great Pyramid, before the Israelites went into bondage in Egypt, saw the beginning of work upon another of the world's fascinating enigmas – the towering stone columns of Stonehenge. This mighty, broken circle of huge rocks, on Salisbury Plain in Wiltshire, has an air of sombre, brooding mystery that, in its own way, is as compelling and seemingly unfathomable as the Pyramids.

For centuries men have speculated as to the identity of its architects, its manner of construction and, most puzzling of all until relatively recently, its purpose. Its dark secrets have been said to have included human sacrifice in the pagan rites of the ancient Druids, magical machinations involving the legendary Arthurian sorcerer Merlin and the Devil himself, and even today, a modern sect of so-called Druids gather there on Midsummer's Eve to wait for sunrise and practise their rituals and observations as the first rays of the sun strike the "Heelstone".

Thus has the true nature of this historic site been obscured in rites and stories which, albeit fascinating, bear little relationship to Stonehenge and its builders. One legend, for instance, says that Merlin had the stones magically transported from Ireland, as a memorial to a number of ancient British nobles treacherously murdered by the Anglo-Saxon warrior Hengist, who flourished around the end of the 5th century AD. Another says that the Devil devised and arranged the rocks of Stonehenge to annoy and puzzle man for evermore, but was caught in the act by a snooping friar. As he ran off to tell of the Devil's mischief, Satan hurled a great stone and pinioned the friar by the heel – hence the name Heelstone, given to the great, leaning monolith outside the circle.

Even today Stonehenge is popularly associated with the Druids – although it has been established by researchers that the Druidic cults did not arrive in Britain until more than 1,000 years after the giant stones were erected. The Druids may have utilised Stonehenge in their rites, but there is no proof; they are known to have preferred woodland groves for their religious ceremonies, centred around "sacred oaks".

The modern sect of neo-Druids do not help matters. Somehow, these practitioners whose order was not founded until the 18th century, have persuaded the authorities to permit them to use Stonehenge on Midsummer's Eve and Day for their highly inventive, elaborate, but equally highly unauthentic rites, so contributing to the popular misconception that Stonehenge was built by and for the Druids.

The only common and often repeated statement about Stonehenge that in truth turns out to be more than figurative is one which describes it as "England's answer to the Pyramids". Those who drew this parallel rarely suspected how close they were to the truth.

Now, some facts and scientifically-based conjectures. Archaeology has shown us that Stonehenge was built over a period of about 300 years, between 1900 and 1600BC – from the time of Abram to the bondage of the Children of Israel in Egypt.

People of the Neolithic, or New Stone Age, who arrived in ancient Briton in about 3000BC, began the work by constructing a large, circular mound about 380 feet in diameter. The circle, hewn from a ditch outside its perimeter, is so well constructed and geometrically precise that it was probably begun by first marking out the ground with a sharp stone on the end of a piece of rope, tethered to a central axis stake. It is only in retrospect that the purpose of Stonehenge's various features have become more obvious and it is now clear that this large circle was intended as an artificial horizon to record the movements of the stars, in the same way that the Egyptians must have used one to calculate the position of the Pole Star.

The same people, who appear to have constructed similar earthworks elsewhere in Britain, are also thought to have raised the large megalith known as the Heelstone, which lies 100 feet outside the circular bank and marks from its centre the direction of Midsummer sunrise. Four "Station Stones", only two of which remain, may also have been positioned by these Neolithic people, forming a rectangle with its corners touching the inner edge of the circular bank, although some archaeologists claim they were erected later.

The next phase of building was undertaken by a race known as the Beaker People, so-called for their manufacture of pottery cups or beakers which have been unearthed in their graves in the area. They began the modifications to Stonehenge about 1700-1750BC. This consisted of a staggering physical operation comparable to the building of the pyramids. The Beaker People who, it appears, had one foot in the Stone Age and the other in the Bronze Age, came from Spain and began to set up a double circle of what are known as the Bluestones, about six feet apart and some 35 feet from the centre of the circle. These stones came from the Prescelly Mountains, east of Milford Haven, in Pembrokeshire, Wales – 130 miles in a direct line from the site of Stonehenge, but about 240 miles along the route that the stones must have been transported. The stones weigh an average of five tons.

Using similar techniques to those of the Egyptians, the Beaker folk hauled the massive rocks – which are found only in the Prescelly Mountains – using tree-trunk rollers and wooden rafts, down to Milford Haven, floated them into the Bristol

Channel, then, by raft on river and sled or rollers overland, managed to convey them to the site.

But before the double circle of these stones was complete, a further modification took place. The Bluestones were uprooted and an inner horseshoe of "trilithons" – two uprights with an overhead, connecting lintel – was constructed by the Wessex People, another group of European origin, who appeared around 1700BC and took over the work around 1750, going on to complete the third and final stage of the project. The trilithons they built were of sarsen stone from some 20 miles away at Marlborough Downs. Next, an outer circle of sarsen trilithons was made, about 97 feet 4 inches in diameter and the fancifully, but inaptly named Slaughter Stone was put up by the "Avenue" entrance to Stonehenge, to the north-east, in a line with the Heelstone. To demonstrate something of the skill with which Stonehenge was constructed, it is worth mentioning that the uprights of the trilithons of the inner horseshoe weigh about 45/50 tons each, while the 30 sarsen megaliths, or single uprights, average 25 tons.

Since no evidence of sufficiently large earth excavations has been traced in the area, it is assumed that the uprights were raised with ropes and wedges, while the overhead lintels were put into position using platforms of notched logs that could be built up in steps, the stones being rocked from one step to another until they reached the desired height.

To complete the picture, three concentric circles of holes were also dug, outside the ring of sarsens. Fifty-six holes – known as the Aubrey Holes, after their discoverer, the 17th century antiquary John Aubrey – are just inside the circular, earthen bank. Next, 30 holes designated "Y" by archaeologists, make a circle about 35 feet outside the sarsens, and inside this is a ring of "Z" holes, of which there are 29, between 5–15 feet outside the sarsens.

The so-called Avenue, a processional route to Stonehenge, leading from the direction of the River Avon, was also lined by single standing stones.

The entire project – considering the work involved, the precision achieved and the purposes to which the edifice was put, and also taking into account the cultural development level of the builders – has been compared to the American space programme.

Now having set the stage, let us look at the possible purpose and meaning of Stonehenge. It was a British-born astronomer, Professor Gerald S. Hawkins, who first truly unlocked the mystery of the uses to which the ancient monument was undoubtedly put. Hawkins, on a visit to Salisbury Plain, became fascinated by the structure, in particular by the fact that, when standing at various points within the inner horseshoe, and looking out through the narrow gateways formed by the encircling trilithons, his attention was directed to specific segments of the sky. What, he wondered, did the builders of this hitherto enigmatic device expect to see? Hawkins fed into a computer known as Oscar (an IBM 704) the layout of Stonehenge, its dimensions and its exact geographic location. He then asked Oscar to project the possible "lines of sight" of its stone gateways into the skies to discover the various combinations of what might be seen. He also got the computer to calculate astronomical positions as they would have been seen from that location around 1500BC.

The results were uncanny. A combination of the computer's calculations, plus

---

Professor Hawkins' own reasoned deductions about Stonehenge, led him to the amazing conclusion that the edifice was none other than an incredibly accurate almanac, calendar and astronomical computer.

By various observations from select positions within the giant stones, its Bronze Age astronomers could work out the extreme positions of the Sun and Moon – the equinoxes and solstices. And through the careful use of the various circles of holes, using stone marker pegs moved around in precise sequence, they could make accurate predictions of solar and lunar eclipses. In all, an astounding demonstration of the ancient Britons' astronomical and mathematical knowledge and awareness, particularly considering the time that they lived and the limited resources with which they worked.

The advantages of such a device are obvious. It would be useful in guiding the people on the most effective times for crop-planting, allowing them to divide the year into seasonal quarters. The ability to predict eclipses would have been of immense value in maintaining the priests' hold on their influence and power. (Two Chinese astrologers, Hsi and Ho, are said to have been executed in 2136BC for failing to predict a solar eclipse accurately).

It would also have enabled them to make many other observations and predictions of celestial events – making Stonehenge an observatory much more sophisticated in fact than that formed by the alignments of the Great Pyramid, being as Stonehenge was, an open air, 360 degree observation post on the heavens, with many more precise gradations and alignments than the Great Pyramid. Anyone interested in learning the precise details of Hawkins' findings, should read his excellent book, *Stonehenge Decoded*.

But what made the ancient Britons take such a detailed interest in the heavens in the first place? They could have noted the movements of the Sun and Moon with a much less complex structure, and kept records of days, months and years to work out the periodicity of solar and lunar eclipses without having to manhandle and align such massive and enormously heavy rocks into such precise positions. Why did they need an all-year-round shift system, watching every segment of the skies in a complete circle? Hawkins thinks that, having established the basic framework of the observatory to the satisfaction of the priests and farmers, the Bronze Age adepts then became fascinated by its possible improvements and refinements and from then on looked upon it as a kind of intellectual game of calculation and discovery.

But another pointer to the answer can be suggested. There is strong evidence that the builders of Stonehenge had contact with the earlier Mediterranean civilisations, including Egypt and Mesopotamia; people who had noted strange objects in the skies and had recorded occasional contacts with sky-gods. In fact, cautious as they are, archaeologists have been tempted to wonder whether the builders of the final stage of Stonehenge might not have received instruction from a master architect who travelled from the eastern Mediterranean for that specific purpose.

The Greek poet Homer did not wonder – it seems that he *knew*. In the *Odyssey*, (Book 17, lines 282–86), he remarks:

"Who pray, of himself ever seeks out and bids a stranger from abroad unless it be one of those that are masters of some public craft, a prophet or a healer of ills, or a builder, or a divine minstrel... for these men are bidden all over the boundless earth."

We are reminded here of the traditional idea of the Operative Masons; of expert craftsmen travelling abroad, seeking out only fellow masters in their craft and keeping the inner mysteries of their knowledge and the more valuable aspects of their skills

---

a secret. But why, it might be asked, didn't the ancient Britons adhere to the earlier, established concepts of, say, the pyramid format, or even the ziggurat? In part answer, it might equally be asked: why didn't the Egyptians? Could it be, perhaps, because those configurations had ultimately been demonstrated to be unsatisfactory? Or that, by the time that Egypt was invaded by Greeks and Arab influences, its priesthood had become enfeebled and had lost the real keys to such mysteries?

We know, for instance, that the pyramids did not serve their purpose of protecting their contents. But the ancient Britons were not seeking to build tombs to safeguard their dead – they built long earthworks called barrows for this purpose, many examples of which have been discovered around Stonehenge.

It seems rather that the ancient Britons were merely interested in watching the skies. And the advantages of the clear, precise and all-round view that the circles of Stonehenge provided, over the one-position, narrow-angled aspect of the Pyramid of Khufu, are obvious. True, the seasons and the crops were vital. An ill-timed planting and a bad harvest might result in famine... but somehow, life continues. An eclipse is an important and, to the ancients, sometimes an awesome, or even frightening event. Miscalculate one and a priest loses his credibility, his power, his self-esteem, his livelihood, perhaps even his life. Still, the world goes on. There are always others to succeed him.

An alternative hypothesis suggests itself: that the ancient Britons were looking for something in addition to the obvious advantages that the astronomical computer of Stonehenge could provide; something that they had been told about by visitors from the Mediterranean regions, something that the Mesopotamians and Egyptians had experienced personally.

They were keeping a watch for extra-terrestrials. They were waiting for the sky-gods to appear. The gods that had appeared to the Sumerians and the Egyptians, in their circles of flame and shiny, golden, ovoid craft and had, ultimately, seemingly deserted them.

Other similar stone circles – not, of course, as sophisticated as Stonehenge – and rows of standing stones, menhirs and cromlechs, have been found as far north as Scotland and in areas of northern France, such as Carnac [c.f. Karnak, in Egypt], in Brittany, which have confounded archaeologists. But European UFOlogists have insisted that all these formations of rock lie in patterns, on distinct lines along which UFOs have been sighted in modern times, describing them in fact, as regular "flight paths" of alien vessels. The town of Warminster, to the west of Salisbury Plain, in particular was the seeming focus of considerable alleged UFO activity during the late 1960s and throughout the 1970s.

So, perhaps the people who built Stonehenge were merely doing what thousands of UFOlogists are still doing today – watching for the coming of the saucers. It may even be that in describing these craft to the people of Bronze Age Britain, a Mediterranean emissary unwittingly suggested the circular configuration of the Stonehenge sky-watching project. Author and Earth-mysteries researcher John Michell has noted the similarity in shape of Stonehenge to a flying disc in his book *The Flying Saucer Vision*, (Abacus, 1974). There is also evidence that the architects who designed and built Stonehenge may have first experimented with various ideas of a circular configuration at a nearby site known as Woodhenge, two miles to the north-east of the great stone observatory.

But, it would seem, as the Sumerians and Egyptians eventually discovered, the wait was in vain. Apart from the spasmodic sightings of UFOs during the Middle Ages mentioned earlier in this book, the sky-gods apparently did not make themselves known in person to the ancient Britons.

Why? One can only speculate. Perhaps it was because the gods' search for an ideal representative, a suitable human contact, to transmit or carry out their purpose on Earth had so far proved unsatisfactory. After investigating the Mesopotamians, the ancient Aryan-Hindu races and the Egyptians and finally abandoning them and, while Stonehenge was still under development, the Israelites were being selected as the next people to be given intensive attention, as we have seen.

However, the ensuing form of "divine" intervention took an even more mystical and sophisticated form than occasional manifestation and experimental covenant...

16. Jesus Christ – Sorcerer

"Therefore the LORD himself shall give you a sign; Behold, a virgin shall conceive and bear a son and shall call his name Immanuel."
Isaiah 7:14.

NO HISTORICAL or legendary figure fits the prophecy of Isaiah, of a Saviour in the form of a suffering Servant of the Lord, more than the man known as Jesus-bar-Joseph, Yeheshuah, or Jesus of Nazareth, despite the Hebrews' rejection of him as the foretold Messiah. (The name Jesus stems from the Greek form of *Yeheshuah*, which is Hebrew for Joshua, and means "Yahweh is salvation".) But it is fairly easy to see how the Jews, still longing for liberation from the afflictions that had dogged them throughout their entire history, found the events that followed the coming of Jesus did not live up to their expectations. After persistent assurances from various prophets that the Messiah would once and for all punish and rid them of their transgressors, then reign in a Golden Age as the Prince of Peace, the actual spiritual effect of Jesus upon society must have seemed something of a let-down. The largely pacifistic, non-revolutionary and *laissez-faire* attitudes of the man that John the Baptist had so dynamically publicised in advance – "He shall baptize you with fire" – paled beside the God in whom they had previously set their faith. That was the God, Yahweh, who had led them out of Egypt, smitten their enemies mercilessly and manifested himself dramatically with fire, smoke and thunderings, as his spacecraft descended to Earth before men like Moses, Jacob and Ezekiel.

The humble, plainly-spoken healer, orator and son of a carpenter, who resignedly went to his death on the cross for sedition must have seemed to have borne no relation to the God of Abram, Isaac and the other patriarchs. Yet while he lived, Jesus gained many followers; so many, in fact, that his popularity was what made the authorities worried and led to his eventual arrest. And in looking at the overall character, life and general story of Jesus of Nazareth, it would seem that he might well have been the instrument of some extra-terrestrial or unearthly power, whether or not he lived up to the Messianic claims that became associated with his name.

Throughout the course of his contact with the Israelites, the god Yahweh seemingly experienced great difficulty in making them understand and adhere to his purpose. All along the long, weary route from Babylon, Egypt and Canaan, to Jerusalem, they had fallen by the wayside, reverted to older, pagan pursuits, needing continual reminding of the laws and rules that they should follow to remain in his favour. A fresh approach – in the form of the actual permeation or overshadowing of a suitable human body and spirit – would seem to be the next obvious step in trying to establish a more satisfactory rapport with humankind.

Something of the nature of this new experiment or approach was obviously conveyed to the prophets, Isaiah in particular, and although it was a difficult concept to put over, an inkling of the project, albeit in stylised, prophetical language, was grasped. "Behold," Isaiah wrote, "a virgin shall conceive and bear a son and shall call his name Immanuel." (*Immanuel* means "God [or *El*] with us".)

Many explanations have been suggested for the strange phenomenon the Star of Bethlehem, which is said to have heralded the birth of Jesus and to have guided the Magi to the place of his nativity. One is that the three "wise men" as they are popularly known, saw a comet, or shooting star (meteorite) in the heavens and interpreted it as a great portent. Another suggests that a supernova – an exploding star – burst forth over Palestine, coinciding with the birth of Jesus. There are even suggestions that the Star of Bethlehem was an Unidentified Flying Object or spacecraft, which guided the Magi to the birthplace of Jesus.

In December 1976, Dr. D.W. Hughes of Sheffield University, in a paper in the scientific journal *Nature*, suggested that what the Magi saw was a triple conjunction of the planets Saturn and Jupiter in 7BC. (Allowance was made for errors that occurred when the BC/AD calendar was established in 525AD). In that year, Dr. Hughes said, the three conjunctions, when the planets approach most closely to each other, occurred on May 29, September 29 and December 4. If, Dr. Hughes argued, the Magi's preparation and journey took four months, the first conjunction would have inspired their departure from Babylonia, the second would have confirmed their prediction as they approached Jerusalem and the third, following their audience there with Herod, would have led them five miles south to Bethlehem.

According to the journal's report, cuneiform tablets found at Sepharvaim in the former Babylonia, record the calculation and prediction of the Saturn-Jupiter triple conjunction, in the constellation of Pisces. In rabbinical tradition, Pisces had an affinity for the Jewish people, Saturn was the protector of Israel and Jupiter was considered a royal and lucky star.

A year after Dr. Hughes' announcement, three astronomers – John Parkinson of the Mullard Space Science Laboratory, Dorking, Surrey, Richard Stephenson of the University of Newcastle and David Clark of the Royal Greenwich Observatory – disagreed with him. From astronomical records of ancient China and Korea, they determined that the Star of Bethlehem was more likely a nova – a thermonuclear explosion on the surface of a white dwarf star. They placed the date of the event at 5BC.

But the argument against all these suggestions is quite simple. If such a distinct and bright light had been seen over Palestine, if it were some kind of physical, celestial phenomenon, why didn't more people see it? Only the gospeller Matthew, in fact, mentions the Star. Why didn't Herod himself see it? Why did he have to ask the Magi about it? The answer is plain: *because there was no visual, physical celestial phenomenon*.

A nova or supernova, for example, would have been seen by everyone, not only in Bethlehem, but in adjacent countries of the Middle East, for several days, as was one recorded by the Chinese in 1054AD, in the Crab Nebula. Similarly, a large comet would have been seen and noted by more than three or four people. (Jesus was, according to Luke, born at the time of the Imperial Census and tax-gathering under the Emperor Augustus, which historians have calculated to have been around 4BC. The closest time that Halley's Comet – which has been one serious suggestion put forward – appeared to the assumed birthday of Jesus was in fact in 11BC and the comet recurs only every 75 years).

So what was the Star of Bethlehem? The key to this mystery lies in the fact that those who reported it were Magi – the plural of *magus*, (Greek, *Magoi*) which means one who is adept in the occult arts and sciences. This would, of course, include astrology. What the Magi doubtless meant when they said, "We have seen His star in the east", was that they had, in attempting to plot a horoscope for the expected Messiah, seen an important star in a birth chart. To astrologers, a heavenly body in the "ascendant", (rising in the east) would be the most important factor in the astrological combination of stars and planets under which a person was born. Not being versed in astrology himself, Herod was compelled to consult the advice of the Magi, traditionally identified as savants from Mesopotamia or Persia and named as Caspar, Melchior and Balthasar.

There is plenty of independent, extra-Biblical evidence that the Jews practised astrology at this period. Among some of the more mystical documents of the Dead Sea Scrolls of the Jewish Qumran sect, was one outlining the zodiacal signs, their symbols, meanings and relationships to the months of the year. Another, in a secret code, shows how the stars and planets influence the destinies of those born under the 12 signs of the zodiac. It suggests a system of "parts" – from the "House of Light" and the "Pit of Darkness" – which a person might inherit as a result of being born under particular signs. A person born under the sign of Taurus the bull, for instance, would be expected to have long, lean thighs and narrow toes, according to the Scrolls. He would be of a balanced nature, with six elements of good spirit to every three elements of bad spirit, and would be humble. The more "good" elements a person "inherits" in this way, the better will be his spirituality.

In fact, the Scrolls speak of a Teacher of Righteousness expected by the Qumran Sect, who has been associated with John the Baptist by some scholars, and a Prince of Light, who was the anticipated Messiah. In his book, *The Dead Sea Scrolls*, the scholar John Allegro goes so far as to suggest that the initiates at Qumran were undoubtedly searching the skies and plotting astrological charts, seeking the signs and portents that would tell them in advance the time and birthplace of the coming Saviour.

Which brings us back to the Magi. To anyone reading the gospel according to Matthew, it will be noticed that, although King Herod seeks the advice of the Magi in trying to find the birthplace of the Christ-child, the three magicians do not in fact divulge the information. On the contrary, the child's parents, Joseph and Mary, are enabled to flee to Egypt to escape the edict of Herod ordering the death of every boy child of two years or less in Bethlehem. Although Matthew does not mention it and was probably not aware of it, the reason for this should be obvious. It was essential that the Magi find the child. The Bible suggests that Joseph and Mary were "warned" in a dream of the danger, but it was almost undoubtedly the three Magi who told them. Why? Because the Magi also had been warned "in a dream" that Herod planned to murder the child. The Magi may have been astrologers from or associated with the Qumran Sect and needed to arrange to make contact with the parents of the "Prince of Light" so that, when he was of a suitable age, they could take him away to be initiated in the secret arts and be readied for the role for which he had been destined.

The actual year in which Jesus was born has been a puzzle to researchers, both theological and secular. The gospel of Matthew suggests (2:1–12) that the birth occurred during the latter years of Herod, who died in 4BC. Luke, meanwhile (1:5), placed the annunciation of John the Baptist's birth also under the same ruler. Since Jesus was allegedly born about six months after the Baptist (Luke 1:36), presumably Herod was still in power. The fact that Jesus may have been born in a year now designated BC is explained through an early medieval calendrical miscalculation.

But Luke (2:1–7) also records that Jesus was born during a census taken in the time of Quirinius, governor of Syria. However, historical evidence shows that the census actually took place in 6/7 AD – and that, during Herod's rule, Quirinius was not the governor. Some scholars have suggested that the census may have been undertaken in two stages, the first being taken around 4BC.

It is a curious fact that nowhere in any of the four gospels does it mention what happened to Jesus between the ages of 13 and 30, when first he appeared to John the Baptist. Why? Because for all those years, Jesus was away, travelling in the East, learning the arts of the Magi: meditation, yoga, levitation, healing, alchemy, divination and magic; arts that he would need when his time came to fulfil the prophecies.

In short, by the time he was 30 and baptised by John, Jesus was a fully-fledged Magus himself; a powerful sorcerer/magician of the first magnitude.

While I realise that this statement in such bold, straightforward terms may seem blasphemous and might shock and offend some people, it is nonetheless true. To practise the magical arts does not necessarily mean that someone is evil. But to be as powerful a magician as Jesus appears to have turned out to be, he must have been totally versed in all the arcane secrets, whether they are considered black or white. And besides, the evidence of his amazing powers is there in the gospels for everyone to read. There is also further, external proof. But first, the gospels themselves.

Apart from Matthew, Luke is the only other one of the four gospellers who deals with the actual birth of Jesus. And it is Luke who lends fuel to the alternative idea that the Star of Bethlehem might have been a spacecraft. For it is Luke who reports (Ch. 2:8–9):

" And there were in the same country shepherds abiding in the field, keeping watch over their flock by night.

"And lo, the angel of the LORD came upon them, and the glory of the LORD shone round about them: and they were sore afraid."

The passage goes on to describe how the "angel" told them of the miraculous event – that the Christ-child had been born. But the key phrase in the account is "the glory of the Lord" – the exact, selfsame phrase used by Ezekiel in his attempt to describe the celestial vessel that he saw on the banks of the River Chebar. At no time, however, is the Star of Bethlehem mentioned in connection with the angel, nor is it associated with this particular phrase. What the shepherds saw might well have been a celestial vessel. But what the Magi saw was more likely an astrological sign that foretold of the imminent birth of the Messiah. Otherwise Herod could have followed the Star himself.

It is also Luke who gives us the last account of the boy Jesus' activities before his mysterious disappearance from the gospels – and who provides a clue to his whereabouts during the 17 or 18 unaccounted years. Here are the key passages (Chapter 2: 40–47) after the return from Egypt when Herod was dead:

"And the child grew, and waxed strong in spirit, filled with wisdom: and the grace of God was upon him.

"Now his parents went to Jerusalem every year at the feast of the passover.

"And when he was twelve years old, they went up to Jerusalem after the custom of the feast.

"And when they had fulfilled the days, as they returned, the child Jesus tarried behind in Jerusalem; and Joseph and his mother knew not of it.

"But they, supposing him to have been in the company, went a day's journey; and they sought him among their kinsfolk and acquaintance.

"And when they found him not, they turned back again to Jerusalem, seeking him."

So far, it emerges as the common experience of most parents; "losing" a child on some outing involving crowds of people. Then:

"And it came to pass, that after three days, they found him in the temple, sitting in the midst of the doctors, both hearing them, and asking them questions."

"And all that heard him were astonished of his understanding and answers."

When Joseph and Mary quizzed the boy, asking – in a typical situation of child-parent misunderstanding – what he meant by causing them such consternation and worry, the boy answered in a casual, matter-of-fact way that absolutely confounded his worried and angry parents:

"...wist ye not that I must be about my Father's business?"

This reference to his "Father" simply did not make sense to them and Jesus was packed off home to Nazareth. The last reference that Luke makes, before his account of John the Baptist and the "temptation" of Jesus in the desert, is that Jesus "increased in wisdom and in stature and in favour with God and man".

Now many people assume that the next years of Jesus' life were spent fairly uneventfully, learning the trade of his father, a carpenter, until he was ready to proclaim God's message. But there is no evidence of this. Whether Luke knew it or not – and his phraseology suggests that he might have had some idea – what almost certainly happened was this. During the stay of Mary and Joseph in Jerusalem to observe the Passover, Magi, possibly from the Qumran Sect, made contact with the child and examined him, to see if his potential was developing sufficiently for his future role. For three days he was quizzed and interviewed and, shortly after his return to Nazareth with Joseph and Mary, he was summoned away, the Magi being satisfied that he was ready to begin his initiation.

First, however, a word or two here about the epithet Jesus of Nazareth would seem in order. The title is actually wrongly translated – practically all the Greek manuscripts use the name Jesus the Nazarene (*nazarenos*). In fact, this epithet, along with Nazarite (*nazoraios*) and Nazorene (*nazorenos*), were all used of Jesus. Nazarene derives from *nazar*, which is Aramaic for "to keep watch" or "to observe". And, in keeping with Jesus' other title *Chrestos*, the Anointed, as a noun it means a diadem – the symbol for one who is annointed, chosen, or elect. One branch of the Qumran Sect of the Essenes, were the Nazaria, one of several gnostic cults which practised healing and magic. Finally, the name Nazarenes was used of non-ascetics among such sects, to distinguish them from Nazarites, who did not cut their hair or drink wine.

As I have already pointed out, the next Biblical record of Jesus is on his appearance before the Baptist. Now it is impossible within the limited confines of this work to enumerate, step by step, the events and achievements of Jesus after his reappearance. But anyone familiar with, or who cares to take the trouble to read the relevant accounts in the four gospels, can see quite clearly that the Jesus that re-emerges has mastered a whole range of esoteric arts during his absence and operates with considerable confidence, which can only point to some kind of deliberate study and training. If these faculties are carefully analysed, it will become apparent that there are many influences. He is a healer of extraordinary potency – curing the lame, the sick, the blind, the leprous. He is also an exorcist, casting out devils and ridding the possessed of their personal demons. He demonstrates a form of necromancy, making the dead walk and talk again. (It should be borne in mind here, however, that even today there is still some dispute about the true clinical definition of death.)

He is also prone to long periods of prayer, fasting and meditation, such as the 40 days in the desert when he is said to have been tempted by the Devil. This, I believe

– and I will elaborate upon this theme later – was perhaps an attempt by another alien influence to thwart the efforts of the extra-terrestrial power under whose influence Jesus was already being guided.

As I intimated earlier, this is not to suggest that Jesus was some kind of itinerant healer and mountebank – none of his "miracles" bore the kind of ostentatious flair that Moses and Aaron demonstrated when they challenged the pharaonic priesthood. On the contrary, when Jesus was challenged to prove he was the Son of God by performing some act of magic that many expected of him, he refused. His magic was more of a spontaneous phenomenon, usually motivated by compassion, by a desire to do good, rather than to show off his powers and satisfy doubters and sceptics.

Indeed, he even shows some impatience with those who demand signs and wonders to prove himself. He is what would have been considered a natural thaumaturge, emitting a personal power or force through the strength of an inner faith that excels that of others. In rabbinical tradition, he is even described as "mad", which seems to indicate that he is highly emotionally charged, a characteristic that has been frequently noted in shamanism.

There is no record of him conducting elaborate rituals to perform his magical acts. He simply appears to exude the force necessary to achieve his aim. Perhaps the key to such powers is more than hinted at in a passage in which Jesus suggests that everything is possible to man, provided there is utterly unshakable faith:

"Have faith in God. For verily I say unto you, That whosoever shall say unto this mountain, Be thou removed and be thou cast into the sea; and shall not doubt in his heart, but shall believe that those things which he sayeth shall come to pass; he shall have whatsoever he saith.

"Therefore I say unto you, What things soever ye desire, when ye pray, believe that ye receive them, and ye shall have them."

All of these abilities, then, would point to the conclusion that Jesus had come under the tutelage of Magi, outside the scope of those within Judaea, except perhaps for the Essenes.

At the wedding at Cana, and at Bethsaida, where he fed 5,000 on five loaves and two fishes, Jesus demonstrates powers akin either to the alchemical arts of transmutation that came out of Egypt, or a great talent for mass hypnosis, which itself would be a pointer to Hindu influence, recalling such contemporary accounts of effects like the so-called Indian rope trick, snake-charming, levitation, etc. Indeed, his walking upon water appears to have all the hallmarks of fakir studies.

Similarly, Jesus' propensity for illustrating his attitudes and lessons through parables is not a device confined solely to Christianity; Judaism, Hinduism, Buddhism and many other religious philosophies rely upon this technique of conveying a complex, ethical message through a simple, easily understood analogy.

It is my contention, therefore, that the so-called "lost" years of Jesus – the 17-year period unaccounted for in the gospels – were spent travelling through Persia, Afghanistan, northern and southern India, taking in Tibet, absorbing the essence of all kinds of religions and mystical teachings, before his final return to fulfil his role in Palestine. There is even the possibility that he was influenced by the mystic Persian ideas that came to fruition in the Sufi movement, who have an age-old tradition of transmitting knowledge through "teaching stories", akin to the parables of Jesus. On his return to Judea, I would suggest, he then made contact once more with the Magi who had paid him such close attention as a youth and, at the Qumran Community's monastery, in the north-western corner of the Dead Sea, went, as it were, through "finishing school".

As to my suggestions about Jesus' "missing years", in 1973, the Rev. Canon John D. Pierce-Higgins, then vice-chairman of the Churches Fellowship for Psychical and Spiritual Studies, and an active and prominent member of the Society for Psychical Research, told me:

"Jesus had all the gifts of the spirit – healing, clairvoyance and precognition – and although He was not a medium in the modern sense of the word, He does appear to have revealed powers and qualities claimed for Indian Yogis.

"Like the Yogi, He spent hours in prayer and meditation and with His disciples and His pattern of teaching was not dissimilar to that of the Hindu holy man."

There is a strong suggestion that the man who paved the way for Jesus' reappearance – John the Baptist – was a member of the Essenes (meaning physicians, healers), with which the Qumran Community has become associated. Members of the sect practised baptism. As well as being a lone wanderer in the deserts in that particular corner of Judaea where the Qumran monastery was located, John was described as wearing the simplest garments of "camel's hair and a leathern girdle", and living on a basic diet of locusts and wild honey. (Matthew 3:4). Both these requirements are found in the "Food Laws" outlined in a portion of the Dead Sea Scrolls known as the "Damascus Document".

Another indication is that, like both Jesus and the Baptist, the Scrolls bitterly denounced the "establishment" priesthood in Jerusalem, for defiling the Temple and allowing the people to stray from the true path indicated by God's laws.

Which brings me to my next point. Bearing in mind, meanwhile, that I am far from suggesting Jesus was an extra-terrestrial, but rather a human being born of woman, there are also the political aspects of his life to be considered. And these, perhaps, more than his seeming supernatural powers, are what led eventually to his betrayal, arrest and execution.

While on a spiritual level Jesus appears to have advocated a policy of pacifism and mutual love and trust of one's fellow man, on a more mundane level he seems to have transcended these ideals, becoming quite vehemently ensnared in the more immediate issues confronting his people. His flamboyant last entry into Jerusalem, for example, appears to have been an attempt, despite his pacifism, to encourage the insurrectionist tendencies of the Zealots, an activist group who would not submit to Roman rule and who, indeed, instigated the Maccabean revolt of 66AD.

It should not go without notice that one of Jesus' followers was known as Simon the Zealot which, while indicating that the other disciples were not necessarily of that political persuasion, also suggests Jesus' tolerant, sympathetic attitude towards them.

On his arrival in the city with a large demonstration of public support that must have been daunting both to the Roman military authorities and to the powerful Jewish priests of the Temple, Jesus then proceeded to challenge the priestly hierarchy by denouncing their financial interests within the Temple, which itself was possibly even an attempt or incitement to seize the building and overthrow its corrupt controllers. This having failed, despite a parallel attack by the Zealots, led by Barrabas, Jesus and his followers moved off unmolested to a clandestine meeting at Gethsemane, in Galilee.

Obviously the Roman authorities, seeing the massive public approval and support that the man enjoyed, hesitated to act – and seized the less popular groups associated with Barrabas and the Zealots. It is interesting to note that, almost as if he anticipated trouble, Jesus made sure that his men were armed before the rendezvous at

Gethsemane. Luke 22:36, tells us:

"Then he said unto them, By now, he that hath a purse, let him take it, and likewise his scrip: and he that hath no sword, let him sell his garment and buy one."

And so, while Barrabas and the Zealots were rounded up, Jesus and his entourage passed into the Garden of Gethsemane. He was betrayed by Judas and arrested, but not without some armed resistance, on the part of Simon, who hacked at a Roman with his sword, severing his ear.

At first, Jesus was handed over to the Temple authorities, the *Sanhedrin*, who interrogated him intensively. Because of his challenge to their authority, he was a supreme annoyance to be despatched as quickly as possible. He had consorted with social outcasts, such as money-lenders and prostitutes, he had interpreted the Jewish law in his own unique way, suggesting that it was more important to love God and one's fellow man than to observe food taboos, or to put human needs before such rules as observation of the Sabbath. He would, he made it clear, feel no conscience in healing on the Sabbath. But most of all, he had taken it upon himself to forgive sins and spoke of himself as the Messiah.

Yet despite all these transgressions in the eyes of the Temple hierarchy, they could not have him executed without Roman sanction. And the only offence that the Romans would consider as justifying the death sentence, was a challenge to their authority. In other words, political resistance or insurrection.

Jesus could scarcely have been convicted of revolutionary acts simply in ejecting those who changed foreign currency into Temple currency, and so he was finally tried and dealt with on the charge of claiming that he was King of the Jews, as stated in Latin, Hebrew and Greek on the plaque that was affixed to his cross. To the Romans, who did not see this claim of kingship as a mere spiritual one, he was clearly guilty of flouting the authority of the emperor. To the priesthood, he was guilty of blasphemy.

He had, therefore, on his conviction, satisfied all those whom his attitudes and teachings had alienated, including the political factions within the Jewish community: the priesthood for usurping their authority; the Zealots for failing to be sufficiently activist; the Pharisees because of his unilateral interpretation of the laws, and the Sadducees, because he derided their pacifistic policy of collaboration with the Romans. To the Romans... well, another trouble-making Jewish orator had been dealt with.

But what of his followers? What of the great masses of people who had triumphantly welcomed him into the city, waving and strewing palms? To them, the big test was to come. Would this man, who had gone among them performing miracles, preaching mutual love and understanding and professing to be the Messiah, fulfil the prophecies? Would he survive the Cross?

17. A Photograph Of Jesus?

"No pain, no palm; no thorns, no throne; no gall, no glory; no cross, no crown."
William Penn (1644–1718)

CRUCIFIXION, AS A form of execution, was probably one of the most agonising tortures imaginable. The normal manner employed by the Romans in carrying out such an execution, was simply to tie the victim to a cross or a basic wooden upright with a horizontal bar, often shaped not like a cross, but like a T. The condemned man thus hung only by his arms, his only support being if he could push upwards against the vertical wooden beam with his feet to relieve the weight of his body, the whole of which would otherwise be supported by his arms. Victims, frequently crucified in great numbers, would normally hang this way for days in excruciating pain, passing from consciousness to unconsciousness and back again before death, from asphyxia, caused by muscular contraction exerting constriction upon the lungs. Some would, of course, have died from heart failure. Occasionally, the "luckier" victims would have their legs broken so that the total weight of their bodies depended upon their arms, which would bring unconsciousness and death much more quickly.

To be tortured to death in this way – for that is what it amounts to – is one of the most unimaginably horrific forms of execution ever devised by man. Pain, caused by muscular constriction, would spread slowly from the arms and shoulders to the chest, abdomen, back and legs. These constrictions would in turn cause serious restriction of the circulatory system, making the pain even worse. Under the searing sun of the Mediterranean and the Middle East, followed by the chill temperatures of the night, the victim would hang, his mouth and throat parched, his whole body racked with unbearable pain, every breath a further torment. It was cruel, agonising and lingeringly fatal.

Yet the execution of Jesus, it appears, was unusual, if not unique. Although recent excavations near Jerusalem have unearthed part of the skeleton of a man, including the bones of the lower leg and the heels. Both legs had been broken – and the feet had been pierced by a metal spike more than four inches long. The remains were dated to the 1st century AD.

Like this unknown victim of crucifixion, Jesus was not tied to his cross but nailed – through both hands and feet. But at no time, according to the four gospels, did he ever exhibit any signs of the agony that such a form of crucifixion must have caused. If the accounts of Matthew, Mark, Luke and John are accurate – and, comparing their four descriptions, there is no reason to suspect that they are not – Christ did not so much as cry out in pain during the whole time of his execution. Indeed, he was even able to make several coherent statements, conscious most of the time of those who were there to witness. He spoke to his mother, Mary, to his disciples, to the two thieves crucified with him and to the God that he appeared to have feared had forsaken him in his final hour. He called out that he thirsted and, as the Roman soldiers diced for his garments, one of them proffered a sponge soaked in vinegar on the end of a pole.

At the end of the ninth hour – and three of the four gospellers, Matthew, Mark and Luke, confirm this period – Jesus "gave up the ghost". According to John, the Roman soldiers then broke the legs of the two thieves who were crucified beside him, but did not break Jesus' legs. Instead, a centurion pierced his side with a spear "and forthwith came there out blood and water". (John 19:43)

The actual date of the crucifixion of Jesus has traditionally been held to have fallen sometime in the year 33AD. And it may be worth recording that, in 1983, two Oxford dons claimed to have established it more precisely as Friday April 3 of that year. Colin Humphreys and Graeme Waddington, of the Department of Metallurgy and Science of Materials at the University of Oxford, published a paper in *Nature* in December 1983. In it they explained how they had reconstructed the Jewish calendar for the period, amending earlier versions. They concentrated, however, on a reference in the Acts of the Apostles (2:14–21) in which Peter says that the forecast of the prophet Joel was fulfilled on the night of the crucifixion: "the sun shall be turned into darkness and the moon into blood".

Backing up their thesis with mediaeval and biblical annals, the two Oxford dons said this would have indicated an eclipse of the Moon caused by the Earth's shadow. Although the Moon is in shadow, sunlight still reaches it by refraction in the Earth's atmosphere, eliminating the blue end of the spectrum. Their calculations were based on astrophysical data, which identified only five possible dates, four of which they managed to eliminate.

Hitherto, practically every year of Pontius Pilate's 10 years in office as Judaean procurator – from 26 to 36AD – had been suggested as the crucifixion date. It was also the time of the Jewish Passover, held at the time of a full Moon. But Humphreys and Waddington emphasized that the reddening of the Moon was the vital clue in their pinpointing of the date.

They said: "It is surprising that the link between the Crucifixion and a lunar eclipse does not appear to have been made before".

Following the crucifixion, Joseph of Arimathea begged the body from Pilate and, once satisfied that Jesus was dead, the governor assented.

"And there came also Nicodemus, which at the first came to Jesus by night, and brought a mixture of myrrh and aloes, about one hundred pound weight.

"Then they took the body of Jesus and wound it in linen clothes with the spices, as the manner of the Jews is to bury." (John 19:39–40)

Jesus was laid in a sepulchre and with slight variations in the four accounts, was seen again, apparently alive and walking, his hands and side scarred by the wounds of the nails and the spear, three days later.

Now despite the great emphasis often laid upon the so-called Ascension, only two of the four gospels actually make reference to this event. Matthew reports having last seen Jesus on a mountain in Galilee but makes no mention of any "ascension" or any other mode of departure for that matter. Mark says that, after appearing to the disciples as they sat at supper, Jesus was "received up into heaven". Luke says Jesus' final appearance was at Bethany: "And it came to pass, while he blessed them, he was parted from them and carried up into heaven." John simply reports a final rendezvous with his Master as the disciples sit at supper by the sea of Tiberias.

The only positive conclusion we may draw from these conflicting accounts is that Jesus went away somewhere not clearly defined and was not seen by the disciples again. There are several possibilities as to what happened after the crucifixion. Either Jesus *did* die on the cross and was seen in vision, hallucination or in some other inexplicable, paranormal manner, in the same way that other dead people are said to be seen by those who knew them. He may, if we accept the supernatural nature ascribed to Jesus as the Son of God, have resurrected from the dead, as claimed by his disciples. Or, the whole account of his appearance after the crucifixion was sheer fabrication, designed to convince others of his divinity, by those who wanted to perpetuate his cause. The only remaining possible explanation now is that he *did not* die on the cross and was indeed seen in the flesh by his disciples.

Taking these possibilities one by one, it is first of all doubtful if the appearance of Jesus after his crucifixion was of a visionary or hallucinatory nature, nor is it likely that those who bore witness to these several appearances saw what is popularly thought of as a ghost or spirit. For this would hardly explain the puzzle of the empty tomb, the removal of the stone, the funeral raiments left inside the sepulchre. Besides, we have the word of three of the disciples – Matthew, Luke and John – that the Jesus they saw was corporeal, allowing them to touch him and see that he was real. He also, it appears, dined with them, an action not normally associated with hallucinations or ghosts. None of the accounts describes these appearances in anything other than an ordinary manner; there is no suggestion of the gospellers' experience being of a visionary nature.

There is no way to prove or disprove conclusively whether Jesus went through some process by which he was able to pass from the condition known as death to life again; but we do have indications that he demonstrated what seemed to be supernatural powers throughout his life. However, examination of the remaining possibilities points to a natural, rather than a supernatural, explanation for his "resurrection".

The third possibility – that the four gospellers invented the whole story of the resurrection – is arguably the most improbable of all. If the disciples were prepared to go to such lengths to perpetuate the idea of the divine qualities of their Master, it would surely have made more sense to collaborate on such a deception; to make their stories corroborate each other in the most minute detail. In fact, the stories vary quite considerably, but in a wholly natural manner, as indeed they do throughout the whole of the life of Jesus.

We are left, therefore, with one final possibility: that Jesus did not die on the cross and was seen in the flesh. And there are many points that would seem to make this the most reasonable and most likely explanation. To begin with, despite the unusual step of securing Jesus to his cross with nails, he remained on the cross for only nine hours. The following day, a Saturday, was the Hebrew Sabbath and it was against Jewish law to leave a man hanging crucified on that day. Hence the necessity of breaking the legs of the two thieves to accelerate their deaths and the piercing of Jesus after his "giving up the ghost" to make sure he was dead. Now, as I have suggested, during his "lost years", it is highly likely that Jesus learned the art of Yoga from teachers in India.

In its most advanced levels, yoga can be used to control the most spontaneous functions of the body, including those of the nervous system, the process of breathing and, indeed, the circulation. The fact that Jesus is not reported as showing any signs of acute agony while on the cross suggests that he utilised his abilities as a yogin to lessen the pain and intense discomforts of crucifixion. He might also, through a highly-developed control of his breathing, have managed to slow down his heartbeat to the point where it ceased. There is plenty of evidence that yogins, and even those accomplished in the art of self-hypnosis, have been able to do this for considerable periods. Yogins, it should also be noted, are able to maintain normally the most uncomfortable postures for days, weeks, even months on end, as part of their aspiration to higher levels of consciousness and perception.

If this is not an acceptable hypothesis to explain how Jesus endured the agonies of crucifixion, there is an alternative. It is possible that, constricted as Jesus' lungs were by the stretching of the arms, the tightening of the chest and body muscles, the fumes of vinegar on a sponge, caused him to suffer a temporary breakdown of his respiratory system, rendering him unconscious – in a cataleptic state. Since the clinical definition of death was vague and arbitrary in those times, this might have been assumed to have been the moment of expiry. (Anyone wanting to test the effect of vinegar on the lungs – although I don't recommend it – has only to try inhaling its vapours or taking a stiff swallow of the liquid.)

There remains, then, the piercing of the body with a spear by one of the centurions, by tradition a man named Longinus. His name is given in an apocryphal work, the *Acts Of Pilate*, as that of a captain who supervised crucifixions. This surely, on top of all the other tortures that Jesus had suffered, including a severe flogging before the crucifixion, would have been sufficient to kill him? Not necessarily. It is at this point, however, that we must turn to one of the most amazing, fascinating, enigmatic and, possibly most valuable, holy relics in the possession of the Christian Church – the Holy Shroud of Turin.

The shroud is a piece of ancient, yellowed cloth, 14 feet 3 inches long by 3 feet 7 inches wide, that is kept in a reliquary at the Cathedral of Turin. Every 33 years – the assumed age of Christ on his death – pilgrims flock to the Italian city to view the artefact as it is only at these times that it is exhibited. On it are various dark brown and reddish marks; stains and patches which, when examined carefully, appear like a photographic negative of the image of a man, back and front views, placed head to head.

In gazing upon the facial features of this figure, the faithful have for many years been convinced that they were looking at an image of the actual face of Jesus himself. It is believed by many that the cloth is the shroud in which Jesus was wrapped after his removal from the cross. By some natural process, possibly the oils, aloes and unguents with which the shroud was treated, plus the body's own secretions, it is thought that an image of Jesus was formed in a similar way to that on a photographic plate. What makes the shroud even more remarkable is that the image is most distinct not when viewed in the ordinary way, but when the shroud is photographed and the negative, rather than the positive, image is examined.

There emerges the imprint of a man, 5 feet 11 inches tall, with an extremely noble and dignified face, in the repose of death. He has long, straight hair, falling to the shoulders, a moustache and full beard. There are marks about the body indicating that the man was scourged with a three-tongued lash with stone or metal studs on the end of each "tail". There are stains around the head, from the brow upwards, as if it has been pierced by thorns. The hands are crossed, left over right (reversed, of course, on the actual shroud image) and the left wrist bears a dark stain as if pierced by a nail, with other marks suggesting rivulets of blood flowing down towards the forearm from an open wound while the arm was extended in the attitude of crucifixion. The feet, too, bear the signs of nail wounds and there is a large bloodstain and wound on the left of the chest near the lower ribcage and a smaller one over the right breast, suggesting the entry and exit points of a spear.

Many experts from various fields have examined and photographed the shroud at various times and were fairly unanimous, first of all, in declaring that it is too perfect a representation, not simply of a human body, but of one that appears to have undergone muscular changes and suffered wounds consistent with crucifixion, to have been manufactured. Indeed, two Italian artists, Cusetti and Reffo, copied the shroud during its exposition in 1898. But when their work was photographed, the negative images were completely distorted and did not in any way resemble the negatives of actual photographs of the shroud. In other words, it was suggested, it was virtually impossible to paint the image so that it showed up so clearly in photographic negative, as the man on the shroud does.

There are also too many seemingly authentic details – bruises, wounds and muscular distortions – for any artist, even the most carefully versed in anatomical study, to have been able to invent so accurately a representation of a body racked by beating, scourging and crucifixion.

What then is the historical evidence for the authenticity of the shroud? The actual object that is kept at Turin can be traced as far back as 1353, when it was owned by Geoffroy de Charny, Lord of Savoisie and Lirey (now Turin). But writers dating back to 120AD mention the exhibition of a shroud of "the Lord" in Jerusalem, that bore the imprint of the body of Jesus. It was written about by St. Braulion of Seville that year, by the French bishop Arculph (670AD), by St. John Damascene in the 8th century and by several other writers down through the centuries. From Jerusalem, the shroud was taken to Constantinople and kept in the chapel of Our Lady of Blachernes until it was eventually removed to France by crusaders, when it is believed to have passed into the possession of the Dukes of Savoy, who eventually placed it in the care of the cathedral authorities at Turin.

So, there is fairly sound circumstantial evidence tracing the shroud back to Jerusalem. But what is the official attitude of the Church towards the relic? While the Church in fact leaves proof of the authenticity of holy relics to archaeologists, palaeontologists and other scientific experts, the general nature of the shroud as being that in which Jesus was wrapped, was more or less taken for granted – unless proved otherwise. Indeed, pontifical acts by the Popes Paul II, Sixtus IV and Julius II, sanctioned the cult of sindonologists (students of the shroud) which had grown up around the article. It should be made clear, however, that until very recent times the shroud was never allowed to have been submitted to complete scientific examination and testing, such as the radiocarbon-14 dating process. But this test, apart from involving the destruction of a portion of the material, has also been shown to have a margin of error of about 500 years either side of the determined age. Over a 2,000-year-period, the margin of error is sometimes given as 50 years.

In May 1978 – three months before the shroud was due for its regular public exhibition – a request to allow carbon-14 testing, under the supervision of Dr. Walter McCrone of Chicago, was turned down. The Rev. David Sox, secretary of the British Society for the Turin Shroud, announced that the scientific commission which advised the Archbishop of Turin, the Most Rev. Anastasio Ballestrero, had rejected the suggestion. The commission said: "A re-study in depth of the carbon-14 test [should be] postponed for the present since we do not have a consensus among the experts on the 100 percent efficacy of this test in the specific case of the shroud."

However, the commission indicated that further tests, including examination of the bloodstains on the cloth and of the reverse side of the shroud, might be allowed.

In October 1979 scientists at Los Alamos, New Mexico, once more requested permission to carry out radio-carbon 14 tests – this time, on only "two or three threads" of the shroud, rather than a handkerchief-sized piece which earlier, less sophisticated tests, would have required.

The following month, Thomas D'Muhala, president of a nuclear technology company in Amston, Connecticut and head of the 40-member international scientific team investigating the relic, announced that he believed the image on it might have been caused by a brief burst of radiation from the body at the moment of death.

In July 1980, another shroud-investigator, the Rev. Francis L. Filas, a professor of theology at Loyala University, Chicago, said that he had identified tiny marks over the eyes of the image as impressions of a Roman coin. Photographic negative enlargements showed small marks resembling a staff and four Greek letters forming part of the inscription "Of Tiberias Caesar". Numismatists confirmed that the staff, known as a *lituus* in Latin, appeared only on coins minted between 30 and 32AD, during the rule as governor of Judaea of Pontius Pilate.

Then, two months later, Dr. McCrone created a stir in an interview with the *Catholic Herald*, in which he declared the shroud a fake. He claimed to have discovered considerable quantities of iron oxide, a constituent of red ochre, on the cloth – an artists' pigment which pointed to its forgery. He estimated that a carbon-14 test would show it to have been manufactured around 1356. "A major portion of the image is in artist's pigment," he said. But he added: "How he did it I cannot say."

There were complaints about the "leak" to the Press from officials of the British Society for the Turin Shroud, but they also confirmed that doubts had been raised about the relic's authenticity. Other interested parties, including Thomas D'Muhula, disputed Dr. McCrone's claims.

But the real bombshell dropped when, in August 1988, various newspapers prematurely announced that, based on improved carbon-14 tests, scientists involved in its investigation had determined that it was a 14th century forgery. Again there were complaints about a leak – this time from the Turin authorities, who had not planned to make any announcement until the end of September that year.

Those experts who, until recently, had spent most time assessing the shroud, determined that it was a genuine imprint, made by a combination of oils and unguents and natural bodily secretions on a linen strip. Secondly, whoever the man was that the shroud contained, he was crucified in a most unorthodox manner – by nails driven through the wrists and insteps. This in itself seemed to point to the shroud's authenticity. Apart from the fact that Jesus' execution deviated from the more common procedure – by nailing rather than tying to a cross – the wound marks on the shroud show quite distinctly that the nails were driven through the wrists, not through the fleshy part of the palms. The thumbs, which are not visible, seemed to have retracted, to have been pulled back by the piercing of the nails and the closed eyelids indicate that coins were placed over them – a common Jewish burial custom. The nail that pierced the feet – and careful examination of the shroud's imprint has suggested that only one nail was used – similarly, went through the instep and not through the centre of the foot. Practically all artistic depictions of the Crucifixion show Christ's hands and feet pierced, a seemingly erroneous notion. Indeed, if the Shroud were an artistic forgery, it was argued, by some unknown genius whose talents must have equalled or even surpassed those of Michelangelo or Leonardo, it would seem more reasonable to expect that these same errors would have been repeated on the relic. The other important point in this connection is that medical experts have established that nails through the wrists would be a much more effective method of crucifixion, since the fleshy part of the palms would quickly tear with the weight of the body upon them, allowing the victim to fall forward, probably wrenching out the nailed feet also. As the Romans were experienced executioners, it can safely be assumed that they would not make this mistake.

Further examination of the shroud indicated that the spear entered the left-hand side of the chest, between the sixth and fifth ribs, at an angle of approximately 29 degrees, its point of exit being above the right breast, at the position of the gap between the second and third ribs. This would mean that the spear would in fact have missed the heart, although piercing a lung. To pierce the heart, the spear would have had to have been thrust in horizontally, an impossible angle for a soldier, reaching up from the ground to the upper body of a crucified man. The piercing of the lungs would be consistent with the report in John's gospel account of blood and "water" (pleural fluid) issuing from the wound.

Finally, the marks of wounds, as if from thorns, from the forehead upwards, suggests that the supposed crown of thorns was not in the form of a circlet, as shown in most Christian art and copied in many motion pictures, but a kind of dome-shaped skullcap that covered the whole of the top of the head. It has been pointed out that anyone trying to forge the shroud image would almost certainly have adhered to the orthodox ringcrown depiction of Christian iconography.

All in all then, looking at the markings on the shroud, its supporters were forced to ask where, other than in the gospels, is there an account of a man being brutally flogged, crucified with nails, pierced in the side with a spear, and crowned with thorns? The only conclusion that could be drawn was that the man whose image appeared on the shroud must have been Jesus of Nazareth.

One man who refused to accept the shroud's rejection as a fake simply on the grounds of a radio carbon 14 test, was Group Captain Leonard Cheshire VC, vice-president of the British Society for the Turin Shroud. Group Captain Cheshire, who had first alerted my own interest in the relic in the late 1950s, pointed to the precision of the anatomical details of the image:

"So exact that no 14th century artist could have got them right," he commented in August 1988. He also pointed out that no authority had disputed the medical details.

"Every detail seems right," he said. "The scourge marks are diagonal at shoulders and seat, horizontal at the midriff, exactly as they should be.

"They show incisions shaped like dumb-bells. We know now that the Roman or flagrum had small lead weights shaped like dumb-bells tied on its thong

Next, he drew attention to the bloodstains on the image's forehead: "A had bound the Crown of Thorns to his head. The bandage arrested the flo as is evident on the shroud. Another small touch of realism."

He continued: "The wound in the hand is critical. Every artist until th showed the Crucifixion with the nails going through the palms. No a body would tear away if nailed by the palms. The nails were d wrists — just as the wound on the shroud depicts.

"And a nail through the wrist makes the thumb curl in thumb-print on the shroud. No artist-faker could have know could have known that the spear-wound should slant at the All medieval artists showed that wound horizontal. Only th right."

As to the image having been painted, Group Captain C

A Photograph Of Jesus?

cannot see the image if you are closer than five feet. Was it painted, then, with a five-foot paintbrush?"

He also observed that wrapping a paint-smeared effigy model of a human figure in a cloth would merely result in a distorted image, whereas the shroud bears sufficient visual "information" to allow computers to generate three-dimensional projections of it.

Finally, he said: "I cannot accept that one scientific test on its age can invalidate all that scientific evidence in its favour.

"Those who claim it is a fake must show how that fake was made. That seems to me the most difficult question. So difficult, in fact, that I personally believe no answer can be found."

Despite such considerations, at least one observer suggested that Leonardo da Vinci might have been the forger. An art expert and antique dealer, Jerome Lynch, claimed that, being well versed in anatomy and fascinated by optics, Leonardo would have been capable of producing a negative image.

But there is one flaw in Mr. Lynch's suggestion: Leonardo da Vinci was not born until 1452 – slightly more than a century after Geoffroy de Charny, the French knight who "discovered" the shroud, put it on display in 1350.

In connection with my suggestion that Jesus might not have died on the cross, there are some sindonologists who claim that the shroud proves this very fact. If, they say, Jesus was dead when removed from the cross, then the blood of his wounds would not have stained the shroud so markedly. The argument being that, once the heart stops beating, blood is no longer pumped through the body. That blood at the site of wounds would quickly congeal and air pressure would serve to hold the remaining blood in the veins.

I am inclined, up to a point, to accept this theory. True, the blood around the more serious wounds, such as those of the hands, feet and side, would be unlikely to have coagulated completely and would therefore be expected to leave a stain on the shroud. But what about the minor wounds – the pricks and scratches of the crown of thorns, the weals made by the lash more than nine hours earlier, the trickles of blood from the nail wounds in the hands? Signs of no fewer than 28 wounds that must have continued to bleed after the removal of Jesus from the cross, have been counted upon the shroud. Wouldn't these be more likely to have clotted and dried by the time the body was removed from the cross? And if, as we are told, Joseph of Arimathea took possession of the body on its removal from the cross, isn't it likely that he would have cleaned up the various wounds before laying out the body in its cerements in the sepulchre? The gospels also say that Nicodemus brought no fewer than 100lbs of aloes and myrrh for the preparation of the shroud and the body. Therefore, if this were done, how could bloodstains, quite distinct from those impressions left by the oils and ointments, come to be upon the shroud? Besides, we are also told that the marks other than the bloodstains were caused by the combined action of oils and unguents and natural bodily secretions. Does a dead man sweat? Finally, the condition known medically as rigor mortis usually begins to set in within minutes of death, leaving the body completely rigid within three to six hours, depending on localised temperature. High temperatures – as in Palestine – would make the process happen more quickly. Since Jesus was supposed to have remained on the cross for some three hours after his death before his body was removed, this condition could have been expected. However, since his body would have sagged after death occurred, his head dropped forward onto his chest and his knees would have been bent. Yet on the shroud, the figure was clearly laid quite flat, producing an undistorted, full-length image, back and front.

Three days later, the tomb was empty and Jesus was seen walking around. All these factors could point to only one reasonable conclusion:

Jesus did not die on the cross.

I would suggest that a combination of his yogic training, the coolness of the rock tomb, and the massive quantity of oils and unguents that Joseph and Nicodemus applied, helped to bring about his rapid recovery from the nine-hour ordeal on the cross. There have even been suggestions that some inexplicable surge of radiation may have been emitted by the body upon its revival – thus creating the image on the cloth. Whatever the case, within three days, Jesus was well enough to get up and leave the garden where he had been laid in a cave.

Remember also that Jesus was a thaumaturge, a magical healer. Isn't it possible that those of his skills that he passed on to his disciples might have been used to help him revive?

In putting forward these suggestions, I have no desire to discredit the beliefs of those who regard Jesus as the Messiah, or Son of God. Nor do I wish to suggest that in surviving the crucifixion he fulfilled the prophecies required of a true Messiah by the Jewish scriptures. Religious dogma plays no important role in the main purpose of this book.

I am merely putting forward the most likely combination of possibilities in seeking a rational and natural explanation for the hitherto unfathomable enigmas that surround the story of Jesus of Nazareth. But if Jesus did not die on the cross – and only two of his disciples affirm his "ascension" – where did he then go? I believe there is an answer to this question, which I address in the next chapter.

But first, some final words about holy relics. Apart from the shroud, three of what are perhaps the best-known examples of relics are undoubtedly products of over-pious imagination: alleged pieces of the "true cross", nails from the crucifixion, and the Holy Grail. There are probably sufficient pieces of the "cross" kept in various reliquaries throughout the Christian world to reconstruct Noah's Ark. And equally probably enough nails to hold it together.

However, one relic that has not been subjected to as many tests as the Turin shroud, is a ragged and bloodstained tunic, supposed to have been worn by Jesus on the day of his crucifixion. It is kept in the Basilica of St. Denys, in Argenteuil, France and put on public view only once every 50 years. On such occasions, thousands of pilgrims flock to view it, many hoping to benefit from its supposed powers of healing.

Scientific examination has shown that the tunic, made from pieces of reddish-brown wool stitched to white silk that with age has turned to the colour of ivory, was actually woven during the time of Jesus. And infra-red photographs have disclosed bloodstains on the back, where it might have been in contact with a wooden cross.

The last display of the tunic – in April 1984 – was marked by special celebrations. The previous December, the tunic had been stolen and a demand made for the release of three terrorists unless a large payment was made to the Polish Solidarity movement. However, in February 1984, the garment was returned to the Rev. Marcel Guyard by the thieves, on condition that their identities were not revealed. Believed once to have been owned by the Emperor Charlemagne, the tunic was vandalised during the French Revolution, when a local priest cut it into pieces and hid the fragments. However, it eventually reappeared and was deposited at Argenteuil. To this day, no one can be sure whether or not it is genuine.

18. After Calvary

"Who dreamed that Christ has died in vain?"
Edith Sitwell (1887–1964)

THE MANNER of Jesus' appearance to his disciples after the crucifixion is somewhat puzzling. If, as the scriptures claim, he had risen from the dead, it seems reasonable to wonder why he did not make more of his survival – not only to those already faithful and in sympathy with his teachings, but to those whom, it would seem, most required convincing that he was indeed the Son of God. Why not an appearance in Jerusalem to many people, similar to the triumphal entry that he made preceding his arrest? It more than suggests that Jesus wanted his presence known only to his disciples and immediate friends. Indeed, there is some suggestion that Jesus might have adopted some form of disguise so that, in moving about the country three days after his assumed death, he might be able to reveal his identity only to selected individuals. Luke, for instance, said that as two apostles were on their way to Emmaus, Jesus caught up with them, "But their eyes were holden that they should not know him". Only later, over supper, by the way that Jesus broke the bread, did the disciples recognise their Master.

John meanwhile tells how Mary Magdalene mistook Jesus for the gardener when she first encountered him near the empty tomb.

Obviously, Jesus on his reappearance wore unfamiliar clothes to the ones he normally wore. He quite likely wore a hood to shade his face. It is even possible that his face, still bruised and swollen from his beatings, made him look quite different in appearance. (The Holy Shroud of Turin image, according to medical experts, showed considerable disfiguration of the face – a swelling of the right cheek and bridge of the nose, severe bruising under the right eye, and grazes on the left cheek, lower lip and nose.)

The reluctance of Jesus to make his presence widely public may point to the possibility that he was, despite his apparent victory over death, quite human and would undoubtedly have been seized and killed most definitely by Pilate's men, after his failure to die on the cross. It was necessary for him, therefore, after saying his farewells to his disciples, to flee the country so that the authorities would not catch up with him.

The fact that two of the disciples claim Jesus "ascended" into heaven, while the other two make no mention of this event, also suggests some form of deception, designed perhaps to make Jesus' intended departure as confusing and secretive as possible. Perhaps "heaven" was where he merely told the apostles where he was going. He might even have arranged a mysterious departure, contriving to "vanish" into clouds wreathing the top of a mountain. It would have been foolish to tell all his disciples the truth, however much they could be trusted. If word got back to the Sanhedrin or the Romans that Jesus had been seen alive, the witnesses would have been quickly rounded up and no doubt made to divulge his whereabouts.

So, if Jesus fled Jerusalem, where did he go? The most likely place would seem to be one of the countries where he had spent most of his youth, learning the arts at which he had become so adept: Afghanistan, Persia, Tibet, India. Are there any clues?

In modern day Srinagar, holy city of Kashmir, is a small shrine in which is a plain, grey stone, coffin-shaped tomb. It holds the remains of a prophet named Jus Asaf, who is said to have died there some 1,800 years ago. *Jus Asaf* means Jesus the Collector and pilgrims who journey to the shrine to pray and meditate believe that Jus Asaf was none other than Jesus of Nazareth, the man the Romans crucified at Calvary.

Dr. G.F. Hassnain, head of Kashmir University's department of history, and an archaeologist, has sought – and been refused – permission to open the tomb to examine the remains. He wants to find out if there is any way of scientifically determining whether its contents can be linked with Jesus. "Nobody wants any trouble with the mighty Christian church," Dr. Hassnain said resignedly in 1973. Yet he intended to persist in his researches, despite strenuous opposition.

"Perhaps I can show the world that here lies Jesus," he said. "I am convinced that Jesus was not dead when He was brought down from the cross. He was nursed back to health.

"Then He fled from the Romans, across Persia and Afghanistan, to Kashmir, where many Jews had fled for refuge from Babylon and Assyria. He died there when He was about 115 years old."

Dr. Hassnain described his alternative post-Calvary scenario that he put together after years of research:

"In the ordinary way, the crucified lingered for three or four days on the cross, dying from exhaustion, hunger and thirst. Jesus was put on the cross on Friday, at midday, and by the ninth hour, He became unconscious. By then it was near to the Sabbath Day – and the Jews allowed nobody to hang on the cross on the Sabbath. A Roman soldier put a spear into Christ's side and blood and water ran. He was taken down."

Afterwards, Dr. Hassnain suggested: "Joseph and Nicodemus were allowed to take Him away. They carried Him off quickly because they did not wish the Romans to think He was still alive. But they had seen His blood flow and were certain He was still living.

"They placed Him in His tomb, treated Him with oils and creams, wrapped Him and hurried off, hoping He would recover.

"They made a risky plan. They bribed the guards outside the tomb, found Jesus still alive and carried Him away. On the third day, when Christ's mother and Mary Magdalene came, they found the tomb empty."

Referring to the gospel of Luke, Dr. Hassnain continued: "Who were the two men standing by the empty tomb and why did they say to the two Marys: 'Why do you seek the living among the dead?'

"Were they trying to tell the women that Jesus was still alive? According to the same Gospel, when Jesus reappeared among His followers, they thought He was a ghost, until He said: 'Behold my hands and my feet... handle me, and see; for a spirit has not flesh and bones as ye see me have.'

"After that, He said goodbye to His disciples on the mist-shrouded Mount of Olives. While they bowed their heads, He walked away.

"The empty grave started a massive search by the Romans. Saul was ordered to find the missing Christ and he found Him in Damascus. Saul was convinced of Christ's great mission and became His devoted servant, changing his name to Paul. Jesus was free. And started His journey to India."

Dr. Hassnain pointed out that Jesus had foretold that he would "preach to the lost sheep of Israel. They were in India. They were the persecuted Jews who had fled there for their lives. Jesus knew India well. He had been there before."

And there are other clues to the presence of Jesus in India. Dr. Hassnain also claimed to have found a 15th century work by a Turkish historian which says that Jesus "was first in Turkey, where He met His disciple, Thomas". It is commonly believed that Thomas did leave Palestine and died in Madras around 72AD.

A grave near Rawalpindi, in Pakistan, which Dr. Hassnain discovered, bears the intriguing inscription, "Mai Mari da Astahn" (Rest place of the Mother Maria). Could this be the tomb of the mother of Jesus? It is a fact that many Jews fled to India to escape the persecution of the Romans; their tombs and ruins of their temples are to be found throughout Kashmir.

Dr. Hassnain's evidence was building up. At the Institute of Oriental Studies, in Purana, Dr. Hassnain found the fragment of a book, once the property of the Maharajahs of Kashmir. Written in 115AD, it contains an account of a meeting between the King of Kashmir and "a light-skinned man in robes", who told the ruler he was Jus Asaf, born of woman, and who had journeyed from a far country to purify religion. When the king asked Jus Asaf to elaborate, he was told:

"O King, I come from a land far away, where there is no truth any more and evil knows no limits. Through me the bad people and the sinners had to suffer and I suffered through them."

Of his religion, the stranger said: "She is love, truth and pureness of heart. She teaches men to serve the Lord, who is in the centre of the Sun and the Elements and God and Sun are forever."

He added: "They call me Isa Masih." (The Messiah).

On his 1,800-year-old trail through India, Dr. Hassnain also came across a monastery near Ismuquam ("Rest Place of Jesus") where the monks keep and revere an ancient shepherd's crook which they claim belonged to Jus Asaf. Jus is spoken about as a kindly humanitarian, who travelled through Kashmir as a prophet and called those who followed him his "sheep", or his "flock". At the town of Bassaren, the professor encountered the sale of a special lotion known as "Jesus Cream". Locals told him it was the same mixture with which Jesus' wounds had been healed. Another town in Kashmir is called Pahlquam ("Town of the Shepherd"), after the wandering prophet Jus Asaf.

Over the Indo-Chinese border at the Tibetan monastery of Hemis Gumpa, Dr. Hassnain claims, are 1,500-year-old scrolls that provide more clues to the life of Jesus. As evidence, he cites an account by Nicolas Notovitsch, who visited the monastery in 1887. While there, Notovitsch got the Buddhist Lama of Hemis Gumpa to translate a portion of the scrolls. According to the Russian historian, they described the "Unknown Life of St. Isa". Isa is Arabic for Jesus.

The scrolls said: "Isa, at the age of 13, left His parents' home and joined a caravan travelling from Jerusalem to Persia and India. In India, He studied in the temples. He learned the use of herbs for medical treatment, studied mathematics and the Hindu religion and travelled in India for almost ten years. The people loved Him, but the priests were against Him and His arguments about life after death. The priests wanted to take His life for His interference in their beliefs and Isa was forced to flee to Nepal. He stayed there for many years until his return to Palestine by way of Kashmir and Persia."

There is even a suggestion that Jus Asaf, on his return from Palestine, took a wife, had children and lived to the age of 115. Basharat Saleem, an hotelier and poet of Srinagar, believes he is descended from the prophet, who is believed to have died around 111/115AD. Saleem proudly keeps a parchment that his family has had for centuries. It is a judgement, declaring that the tomb of Jus Asaf is genuine. It says: "After definite proof, in this place lies Jus Asaf, the prophet of Kashmir, who came to preach to the people."

The proof that Dr. Hassnain seeks may, of course, never be conclusive. But the information he has collected is far too coincidental to be dismissed entirely and is certainly no less valid than the accounts of other ancient religious historians, the gospels included. All the information seems to suggest, therefore, that Jesus of Nazareth was a human being, possibly motivated or inspired – even "overshadowed" – by some celestial force that has come to be regarded as God. It would appear to be a completely new phase in other-worldly contact with mankind, involving the use of a carefully selected individual, whose purpose was to interpret the message of God in an entirely fresh way. Could it have worked, or is the very nature of man incapable of assimilating the true intentions of the unearthly intelligence?

In the sense that Jesus passed on to mankind an improved code of morality and peaceful co-existence, the new approach might be said to have succeeded partially. But it is doubtful that the Celestial Intelligence intended the scheme to result in the many rifts and schisms that mankind has imposed upon itself through unintelligent, partisan, politically motivated, perverted and power-greedy interpretation and application of that code. True, the word of Jesus was spread over a large proportion of the world, often imposed by force upon innocent, so-called primitive peoples. But whether man can ever have been said to have lived by that Christian code is a highly dubious conjecture. It would seem that while the evangelicalism of Jesus' disciples worked, his own mission – to raise mankind to a higher moral and spiritual level – was a dismal failure.

Apart from the inspirational works of Muhammad, and an appearance to St. John the Divine, the Celestial power would not manifest itself in any other major way such as this again, up to the present time. Between then and now, however, man has tried to establish contact with the power that he calls God – or, in some cases, even the Devil – on his own initiative.

19. The Rebirth Of Magic

"I travelled through a land of men,
A land of men and women too.
And heard and saw such dreadful things
As cold earth wanderers never knew."
William Blake (1757–1827)

MEN HAVE always sought, and always will continue to seek out, a Supreme Intelligence, whether they think of this power as the God that manifested himself to selected, pre-Christian leaders, or the power that overshadowed Jesus, making him the Christos, the "annointed", or the evil influences of supposed demons or the Devil himself, associated with King Solomon and others. But in the centuries after Christ it seemed that if man were to reach some Cosmic Intelligence in order to try to understand himself and his relation to the Universe, the effort had to be 100 percent his own. To those who felt a growing dissatisfaction with the tenuous "proofs" of communion with God through the establishment churches and orthodox religions, other methods had to be found to re-establish contact with the Power that appeared to guide the forces of the Cosmos. These methods, whose practitioners and exponents were often condemned, shunned, discredited and even persecuted and executed in less enlightened times, have become known as Ritual Magic. They involved alternative routes to awareness of the powerful forces at work in the Universe and, in their eventual recognition of more than one driving influence and their fearless pursuit of any apparent "breakthrough" to greater understanding, appear much more intelligent and acceptable approaches than the blind, unexploratory acceptance of many of the more orthodox religious doctrines, based almost entirely on faith and indoctrination, or conditioning. Indeed, to the perceptive, it became more and more evident that organised religion was simply being used as a way of controlling, rather than enlightening, the people. To these alternative seekers, any and every path was worth trying, even if it eventually led up a blind alley; trial and error and personal experience was much more satisfactory than the sheeplike adherence to a system outlined by a corrupt priesthood that was anything but infallible. The efforts of these delvers were tirelessly persistent, involved immense physical and spiritual strength and, in some cases, achieved the most remarkable results. But, while some pattern of success emerges, there were always pitfalls, usually created by the inherent weaknesses and foibles of those who practised these alternative methods. The very condition of being human, it would seem, was a major barrier to complete understanding and enlightenment.

Yet there remains a curious and stubbornly unwavering outline; a vague similarity of the results of these many and varied schools of magic, that suggests flashes of truth, glimpses of an incomplete, but nonetheless discernible scheme of Cosmic Law. Imperfect, not totally satisfying hints at the nature of forces beyond the grasp of man. In my own limited experience, it seems that the deeper one delves into arcane knowledge and occult philosophy, the further it recedes into yet more tantalising mystery.

Before we take a look at these operators and their momentary partings of the veil, however, it is necessary to sketch in something of the advent, development and meaning of magic during the Christian era. The revival of the ancient magical arts in Europe paralleled the renewal of interest in the ancient classical world that was the major driving force of the Renaissance. In an attempt to recapture and reconstruct something of the imagined Golden Age enjoyed by the early Mediterranean civilisations, scholars also began to try to salvage some of the forgotten arts practised by the Ancient magi of Babylonia, Chaldea, Egypt, Syria, Persia, Palestine and Greece. The Church had carefully disguised the magical aspects of Jesus' character and emphasized his "divine" nature. But there were those who realised the connection between holy men such as Christ, Apollonius of Tyana, Simon Magus and others, and the astrology, alchemy, qabalism and sorcery in the half-forgotten teachings, ancient stone tablets and inscriptions, manuscripts and oral traditions of the ancient cultures. From these an attempt was slowly made to reconstruct an acceptable system of arcane knowledge and its application.

In hindsight, such knowledge was understandably piecemeal, imperfect, often garbled, deliberately confusing and difficult to organise and implement satisfactorily. But the roots of what had become known as magic are as old as mankind itself and where information was sparse, intuitive or inspirational awareness took over.

In its most basic sense, magic may be defined as a striving to control the powerful, unknown forces of the Cosmos, often seen personified or symbolised by magicians as demons, spirits and gods, rather than the lesser forces of Nature, involving the charms, potions and cures of "primitive" medicine men. Yet the underlying principles of ritual magic were in effect the same as those of the shaman-magician of early cave dwellers; that the observance of a set ritual – in the shaman's case, dressing up in animal skins and headdress, and performing a dance before an image inscribed on a rock – would order the forces dominating the object of that ritual. In other words, an animal would be influenced into becoming easy prey at a particular time and place. Man had seen that, like himself, animals went through regular rituals: courtship, mating, feeding, etc. He therefore coupled his knowledge of these with his own intuitive ceremonies to hunt and trap them. And man has not changed much in this respect: a look around at the prevailing preoccupation with ritual today – birth, christenings, coming-of-age, marriage, burial, religious festivals, even pop concerts and sporting events – shows how deeply rooted these prehistoric behaviour patterns became in human psychological development.

Behind the magical ceremonial of the early magicians and their successors was a profound conviction that, just as men could be impressed and influenced by moving, atmospheric rituals and ceremonials, so would the driving forces of the supernatural; the secret powers that control the Universe. In addition, those taking part in such impressive ceremonials could also be swept into feelings of mental and spiritual uplift, a frenzied or even passive state of ecstasy or attunement, that makes the participants themselves feel an almost superhuman power. Indeed, they might even reach a heightened state of spiritual insight in which they feel an affinity with the supreme powers of the Universe. In other words, they identify with and feel a oneness with, God, or a god.

The ultimate object, then, of any operation of High Magic became an attempt to penetrate, assimilate and know with utter conviction and certainty the secrets of the great driving forces of creation; and, in knowing to control them, to become godlike,

---

all-powerful and, in a sense, time-transcending and immortal. The path to this most lofty pursuit, however, was and is a complex and difficult one, fraught with many dangers. And those who formulated the principles and methods of such operations during the magical revival of the Renaissance and after, delved into all the byways and labyrinthine writings that they could discover in the teachings of the ancient master-magicians. Thus, elements of practically all the early Mesopotamian and Mediterranean mystical and magical philosophies – from the astrology of the Chaldeans, to the Dionysian and Eleusinian Mysteries of the ancient Greeks – were synthesized into European magical practice and teachings.

Into these reworked and reformulated doctrines of more ancient times – themselves gradually altered and influenced through the inter-relationships of different cultures – were also swept some of the mystical elements of Christianity, and remnants of early Jewish oral tradition, as in the esotericism of the Qabalah. And, as I pointed out earlier, the early grimoires or magical texts of Europeanised magic invoked Christ or the Hebrew God for aid in the success of the work. Indeed, the many names of God and Christ were even used as threats or coercements against reluctant or malevolent spirits or demons that were being summoned or dismissed. Thus, the *Key Of Solomon*, in outlining a method of conjuring up spirits to confer invisibility, contains the following:

"Come here then and stay, and consecrate this spell, for God Almighty, the Lord, has assigned you to this function!"

(It should be pointed out here that the real object of this operation is not to make the participant actually invisible, but to enable him to make those around him unaware of his presence. It is, in effect, the attainment of a curious state of mind that distracts the attention of others away from the subject. It is taught in many magico-religious doctrines, including in some schools of Tibetan Buddhism. The magician Aleister Crowley, of whom more later, claimed to have used the technique effectively. Modern psychologists would perhaps explain it as a psychological trick, but would probably be unable to explain exactly how it works. Yet work it does.)

Ritual magic places great importance upon several factors, designed to affect the state of mind of the practitioner, for the simple reason that in trying to attain "abnormal" effects and control paranormal forces, it is necessary to function in an abnormal state of mind. Thus, incantation, the burning of incense and herbs, the use of correspondences and flashing colours, the occasional sacrifice of a small animal or bird, or the self-inflicted wounding of the magician, along with precise movements and gestures using carefully designed and symbolic implements such as swords and wands, are designed to contribute to a desired mental state necessary to commune with and command the powers evoked or invoked. (Evocation involves the physical conjuration, usually outside a protective circle within which the magician operates, and inside a confining triangle, of the entity required. Invocation involves allowing a preferably benign intelligence to take over the self, as in certain magical orders in which the practitioner assumes a god or goddess-form themselves.)

During such ceremonies, the words spoken – incantations, mantras, adjurations, etc., – take on a considerable auxiliary importance. Even if the words are in some barbaric, forgotten or unknown tongue, their influential power can be considerable.

The Gospel of St. John emphasizes the power of the spoken word (John 1:1):

"In the beginning was the Word, and the Word was with God, and the Word was God."

John seems to be reaffirming the Old Testament tradition that it was the Word that

sublimation of ideas, etc.

began the whole process of Creation. In Genesis 1:2: "darkness was upon the face of the deep." Then the first words spoken (Verse 3): "And God said, Let there be light: and there was light."

It is easy to see, therefore, the reason for the emphatic insistence of magical practitioners that a word is more than simply a name of a thing: it *is* that thing; it evokes that thing. Egyptian pharaohs, besides the names by which they were known, also had secret names that only they knew. In this way, they hoped to protect themselves from others' malevolent magic. And so, as the powerful utterance of words can affect people – in oratory, drama, song and poetry, for example – the magus believes that the proper pronunciation, intonation and chanting or "vibration" of specific words of power can bring about the required conditions to achieve his goal.

I have given this necessarily sketchy background of the underpinnings of Western magical practice simply to set the scene for the more important examples of those who attempted to commune with the gods, or higher powers, through such methods.

20. Breakthrough To The Gods?

"...how trust historian and psychologist that have for some three hundred years ignored in writing the history of the world, or of the human mind, so momentous a part of human experience? What else had they ignored and distorted?"
William Butler Yeats (1865–1939)

IN MANY RESPECTS, the careers and interests of the leading lights of occultism and magic of the 19th/early 20th century that we are now about to examine, overlap. And, perhaps more important, so do some of the conclusions and results that they experienced. So much so that, despite the ever-present aura of doubt and the unshakable elements of fraud and charlatanism that have dogged the work of these personalities and their organisations, at their most effective, they were the witnesses of some strange, inexplicable powers.

They plumbed areas of the conscious, subconscious and possibly even a hitherto unknown ultra- or superconsciousness and explored fields in which there were no standards and no precedents. Totally outside the confines of accepted sciences, they were perhaps more brave and courageous than those explorers in the fields of more orthodox research. For the fruits of dabbling in the occult, however sceptical a view is taken, can often constitute the most serious and totally real dangers of mental aberration, breakdown, madness, even death.

Magic, unlike the disciplined pursuits of philosophy and science, involves the whole personality, the total mind on all its charted and uncharted and often uncontrollable and unpredictable levels and often the physical body, submitting all three aspects of the human make-up to the most rigorous and exacting trials and pressures. These daunting and formidable challenges, along with the constant scepticism of an ill-informed and antagonistic establishment, constitute one of the strongest arguments in favour of the veracity of the persistent and serious students of occultism. It survives despite vindictiveness, despite the inherent dangers it involves on a spiritual, mental and physical level to the practitioner.

The man perhaps most responsible for the modern revival of magic in Europe was born Alphonse Louis Constant, in 1810, the son of a Paris shoemaker. At first, Constant seemed to have a vocation for the church, but this can easily be seen in hindsight as an early sign of his inquisitiveness into the "how" and "why" of mankind and its position in the scheme of things.

After being educated at the instigation of a parish priest at the foundation of St. Sulpice, Constant began his training, took minor orders and became a deacon, but was never ordained a priest. There is no recorded reason, but at some unspecified date after 1835, he was expelled from the church and his interest in occultism became quickly apparent. It may have been his refusal to accept religious dogma unquestioningly that led to his movement away from the church and towards the occult, but that has to remain an assumption.

Adopting the name Eliphas Levi Zahed – his own name transliterated into Hebrew – he studied the works of such magical predecessors as Cornelius Agrippa and

Paracelsus, and came under the influence of a strange, semi-transvestite prophet named Ganneau. Ganneau and his wife believed they were the reincarnation of Louis XVI and Marie Antoinette and preached a doctrine of political illuminism whose object was to restore "legitimate truths". Here again, there is a hint that it was this kind of "legitimate truth" that Levi had been seeking and had not found in the teachings of the church. It also appears that Levi was a pupil of a little-known, Polish mathematician and occultist named Josef Maria Hoene-Wronski (1776–1853).

While he did not actually publish anything of an occult nature until around 1855, Levi's reputation as a magus began to spread and, in May 1854, after his marriage to a sculptress named Noeime Cadot failed, visited London, where he met the novelist Edward Bulwer-Lytton (1803–1873), who was also dabbling in the occult.

Lord Lytton was a Rosicrucian, versed in astrology and alchemy and had organised a society to study and practice magic. His lesser-known novels, *Zanoni*; *Vril: The Coming Race*; and the alchemical novel, *A Strange Story* – he is best remembered for *The Last Days of Pompeii* – attest to his study of the occult arts and his apparent belief in their underlying truths.

During his stay with Bulwer-Lytton, Levi claimed to have performed a rite to conjure up the spirit of Apollonius of Tyana, a wandering sage, prophet and religious mystic of the 1st century AD, an event he describes in his classic work, *Rituel Et Dogme De La Haute Magie* (translated as *Transcendental Magic*), published in 1856. Levi admitted, however, that the conjuring up of spirits was a subjective matter. This did not mean that the "demons" or "spirits" that were summoned were "all in the mind", but that the magus could tap areas of his psyche that put him in touch with hidden powers on a different plane. On the whole, he did not approve of putting on "performances" merely to satisfy the idle curiosity of outsiders and regarded magical rituals as particularly dangerous operations.

Indeed, after his own conjuration of Apollonius, for a wealthy and aristocratic lady – he described the experience as "a drunkenness of the imagination" – Levi noted: "...something of another world has passed into me; I was no longer either sad or cheerful, but I felt a singular attraction towards death, unaccompanied, however, by any suicidal tendency."

Back in Paris, Levi began to teach his own brand of Qabalistic magic, in which he linked the 22 paths of the symbolic Tree of Life of the Hebrew Qabalah (based on a diagram representing the ascendant qualities of God, man and the Universe as a series of spheres or planes), to the 22 major trumps of the Tarot deck. It is apparent that, through his qabalistic studies, Levi knew the true nature of the three Magi who attended the birthplace of Jesus and was aware of Jesus' status as an initiated magus. In *Transcendental Magic* he wrote:

"Among the sacred records of the Christians there are two texts which the infallible Church makes no claim to understand and has never attempted to expound: these are the Prophecy of Ezekiel and the Apocalypse, two Kabalistic Keys reserved assuredly in heaven for the commentaries of Magian Kings, books sealed as with seven seals for faithful believers, yet perfectly plain to an initiated infidel of the occult sciences... The original alliance between Christianity and the Science of the Magi, once demonstrated fully, will be a discovery of no second-rate importance, and we do not doubt that the serious study of Magic and the Kabalah will lead earnest minds to a reconciliation of science and dogma, or reason and faith, heretofore regarded as impossible."

And of the Tarot, the divinatory pack of "playing" cards believed by some to have been brought out of Egypt and spread through Europe by Bohemians, Levi said:

"There is also another work, but, although it is popular in a sense and may be found everywhere, this is of all most occult and unknown, because it is the key of the rest. It is in public evidence without being known to the public; no one suspects its existence and no one dreams of seeking it where it actually is. This book, which may be older than that of Enoch, has never been translated, but is still preserved unmutilated in primeval characters, on detached leaves, like the tablets of the ancients. The fact has eluded notice, though a distinguished scholar has revealed, not indeed its secret, but its antiquity and singular preservation. Another scholar, but of a mind more fantastic than judicious, passed 30 years in the study of this masterpiece, and has merely suspected its plenary importance. It is, in truth, a monumental and extraordinary work, strong and simple as the architecture of the pyramids, and consequently enduring like those – a book which can resolve all problems by its infinite combinations, which speaks by evoking thought, it is the inspirer and moderator of all possible conceptions, and the masterpiece perhaps of the human mind."

In another work, *La Clef Des Grand Mystères* (1861), Levi elaborated: "It consists of 22 allegorical letters [the major trump cards] and four series of ten hieroglyphics [the four suits: wands, cups, swords and pentacles or discs], corresponding to the four letters of the name Jehovah. [In occult circles this is written in Hebrew letters, with no vowels, as YHVH – Yahweh – known as the Tetragrammaton, the four-letter name. Long before the Christian period, Jews banned the pronunciation of this name, substituting *Adonai*, "Lord"; the Greek equivalent is *Kyrios*.] The diverse combinations of these signs and of the numbers to which they correspond form as many Kabalistic oracles, so that all science is contained in this mysterious book, a most simple philosophical machine, astonishing in the profundity and accuracy of its results."

While Levi never got around to publishing a complete manual on the Tarot, his work in that direction was most influential on other occultists and it is true to say that, almost single-handedly, Levi was responsible for the tremendous upsurge of interest in magic and the occult and the directions it would take during and after his lifetime. He died in 1875, aged 65.

One of the hypotheses that Levi put forward, apart from his veiled hints about the potential of the Tarot, was that there was a "Secret Doctrine" whose structure and details were known only to a small group of Adepts. And it was this idea that was to influence two of the most important occult groups that followed – the Theosophical Society and the Hermetic Order of the Golden Dawn.

Bulwer-Lytton, completely fascinated by the personality and teachings of Levi, incorporated some of them in his fictional works, such as *The Haunted And The Haunters* (1859), a short story, and in his alchemical novel, *A Strange Story* (1862). He also adapted Levi's notion of a magical ether – a separate state of matter that was the "conductor" of psychic energy – in his novel *Vril: The Coming Race* (1871). Lytton called it "vril" and his idea was later adapted by the Nazis. Levi called it the "astral light", which was the name used by the followers of the next most important occult influence, the Theosophical Society.

If Levi was the father of modern magic, the mother of the more general revival of occultism and mysticism was one of the co-founders of that society, Madame Helena Petrovna Blavatsky (1831–91), one of the most remarkable women of the last century. Theosophy itself was not new when Madame Blavatsky introduced it to the West after 1875. It was, as its name implies, a system based on a mixture of theology and philosophy and consisted of an attempt to achieve an awareness of God or Cosmic Intelligence by intuitive methods, rather than by conscious reasoning. Madame Blavatsky's version of it also claimed it was an attempt to reconcile science and religion.

The basic ideals behind its proposed kind of exercise in superconsciousness – of trying to commune with a universal consciousness through what is called the Overself – can be found in many areas: in the works of Swedenborg, Eckhardt and Paracelsus, and in the Hindu schools of philosophy centred around Vedanta and the Upanishads.

Madame Blavatsky, a well-travelled woman, claimed to have been initiated into these doctrines by Eastern Masters in Tibet and India – a similar concept to Levi's "Secret Doctrine" from the "astral light" – before her explosion into the world of Spiritualism in America in 1873, which was at that time enjoying a craze for seances and spirit-calling sessions.

HPB, as she became known, was the Russian-born daughter of Colonel Peter Hahn and a cousin of a Tsarist Prime Minister, Count Sergei Yulievich Witte. At 16, she married Mikifor Blavatsky, vice-governor of Erivan Province, Transcaucasia, but soon left him. Uneducated, she became a bareback rider in a circus in Constantinople, a piano teacher in Paris and London, ran a shop selling artificial flowers, and met and worked with the celebrated London Spiritualist, medium and levitationist Daniel Dunglas Home (1833–1886). During her travels in the East, her teachers are supposed to have included a Copt magician named Paulos Metamon and Sheikh Usuf ben Makerzi, an expert snake handler and mystic who lived in Cairo.

At the age of 42, in 1873, when 18 million Americans were being fascinated by the strange happenings at Spiritualist seances, HPB arrived penniless in New York. She had frizzy blonde hair, weighed 16st. and chain-smoked cigarettes which she rolled herself. She became involved in regular Spiritualist meetings at Chittenden, Vermont, where two brothers, William and Horatio Eddy, held regular sittings with an almost party-like atmosphere, at which they "materialised" the spirits of dead Civil War soldiers, children, American Indians and drowned sailors. Despite the enthusiasm of the followers of the craze, including HPB, the novelty eventually wore off when some mediums were discredited and exposed as frauds. It was at these sessions, however, that HPB met and formed a curious, lasting platonic friendship with Colonel Henry Steel Olcott, businessman, investigator of psychic phenomena and correspondent of a New York newspaper. It was Col. Olcott, through his columns, who put Madame Blavatsky in the public eye as a "Russian aristocrat" and a "medium of most extraordinary ability". Further articles about her began to appear in other American newspapers and it was not long before HPB had gained a wide following.

But when the interest in Spiritualism waned, HPB began to talk of "hidden masters" or mahatmas, god-like supermen who lived in a secret sanctuary in Tibet. They sent her messages, "precipitated" through the "ether" or "astral light". One night in 1875, HPB and the Colonel decided to found a society to investigate divine wisdom and the occult, and chose the name Theosophical Society. Next, HPB spent two years writing a most incredible book about this divine wisdom and the nature of God and the Universe. It was called *Isis Unveiled*.

She wrote of the secret brotherhood of adepts who imparted knowledge to selected initiates via the Astral Light or, in Sanskrit, *Akasha*. For centuries, Tibetan mystics have taught of this Akashic Record, a vast, almost cinematographic record of all knowledge and historical events, past present and future, that can be consulted like a library by those experienced adepts who can rise to the required plane of the

---

astral in spiritual form. This, she claimed – and in view of her lack of education one is tempted to wonder where else she got her incredible fund of knowledge – was how she managed to write her books, picking up quotations from any source she desired as she went along.

Through contact with the Arya Samarj (Society of Men of Goodwill), a Hindu organisation, Colonel Olcott and HPB eventually travelled to India to pursue their work, she declaring that ignorant Western society was not yet sufficiently mentally or intellectually attuned to appreciate such profound concepts as they were prepared to teach. Although their relations with the Arya Samarj did not go altogether smoothly, the pair were able to set up a highly successful monthly journal, *The Theosophist*, and gained a great following among both Europeans and Indians. Through her "hidden masters" HPB continued to impart arcane secrets and to perform strange effects of materialisation. The name Koot Hoomi – one of the secret brethren in Tibet – became well known to followers and this Master would regularly "write" to HPB and others through the strange method of "precipitation", his letters mysteriously appearing on tables and desks, or seeming to drop through the air.

In 1844 with a massive army of members, the co-founders of the Theosophical Society travelled to Europe and became the focus of interest for French mystics in Paris.

In England, the Society for Psychical Research decided to investigate, with her full approval, HPB's remarkable powers. But back at the headquarters the Theosophical Society had founded in Madras, on the banks of the Adyar River, trouble was brewing. Two of the Society's officials, whom HPB had befriended when they were down on their luck, Madame Emma Columb and her husband, having been ejected from the headquarters because of internal squabbling, decided to expose their founder as a fraud. Mme Columb informed Christian missionaries in Madras, who disapproved of the Theosophical Society, that all HPB's powers were fake. She claimed that her husband had constructed secret panels in the rooms of the headquarters whereby the appearance of "precipitated" letters could be produced. She said that she pushed the alleged letters from Master Koot Hoomi through cracks in the ceiling to make them appear that they came out of thin air, and that her husband, on the instructions of HPB, had made a dummy figure of Koot Hoomi that could be carried around at night to give the impression that his astral spirit was moving about.

Following a series of legal threats and wrangles and the final report of the Society for Psychical Research, HPB was somewhat discredited. After wandering around Europe she finally went to London, where she concentrated on her second monumental work, *The Secret Doctrine*. Unabashed, she gave an account of all the basic knowledge, from which all other fields – science, philosophy and religion – had derived. She truly believed that it was possible to look into a collective consciousness of all mankind for all time – the Akashic Record. Despite the unfavourable report of the SPR, which described her as "one of the most accomplished, ingenious and interesting impostors of history", the Theosophical Society survived. Its influence extended to some of the most respected intellects of its day, including Alfred Lord Tennyson the poet, Thomas Edison the inventor, Lord Crawford the astronomer, W.B. Yeats the Irish poet and later Mahatma Gandhi and Rudolf Steiner, the latter heading the German branch of the Society until he went on to form his Anthroposophical movement.

As for Mme Blavatsky being an impostor, another eminent Theosophist, the learned Western authority on Buddhism and former British High Court judge, the late Mr..

Christmas Humphreys, pointed out that Richard Hodgson, the Society for Psychical Research investigator who reported on the case, never saw the Mahatma letters, yet alleged they were false and never actually witnessed any of HPB's so-called "phenomena" – materialisations and apports, etc – and therefore claimed that they were fraudulent. Besides, the SPR does not hold corporate views and Hodgson's "exposé" was merely the opinion of one individual.

Perhaps the best vindication of HPB came from a little-noted source – a genuine Tibetan lama. In his Introduction to the *Bardo Thodol*, or Tibetan Book of the Dead, W.Y. Evans-Wentz says of its translator: "The late Lama Kazi Dawa-Samdup was of opinion that, despite the adverse criticisms directed against H.P. Blavatsky's works, there is adequate internal evidence in them of her intimate acquaintance with the higher lamaistic teachings, into which she claimed to have been initiated."

When HPB died on Friday, May 8, 1891 – she had suffered from Bright's Disease and acute bronchitis – her place was taken by Annie Besant, feminist, former atheist and committed Theosophist. Despite what had happened to HPB, Mrs. Besant declared that the Theosophical Society's inner meanings and teachings remained valid whether its co-founder was a fraud or not. Indeed, of Mrs. Besant, HPB herself had declared:

"She is not psychic or spiritual in the least – all intellect; yet she hears Master's voice when alone, sees his light and recognises his voice."

The Master who communed with Mrs. Besant was not Koot Hoomi, but another member of the secret brethren, known as Morya.

Although later, many Theosophists discarded the idea of the existence of HPB's Tibetan Masters, claiming that some of their letters were forged, Mrs. Besant continued to affirm their reality. In her *Autobiography*, she insisted: "...that the great Sages spoken of by H.P. Blavatsky exist, that they wield powers and possess knowledge before which our control of Nature and knowledge of her ways is but child's play."

In the early part of the present century, Mrs. Besant became more and more interested in Hinduism, having already published a translation of the *Bhagavad Gita* in 1895.

She came to feel that the time was approaching when God would incarnate upon the Earth. But the person determined upon as this avatar – discovered, in fact, by an ex-clergyman turned Theosophist, C.W. Leadbeater – eventually renounced all claims to being the Messiah.

His name was Jeddu Krishnamurti, and it was the Society's promotion of him that caused a great many members to fall away from the organisation, including Rudolf Steiner in 1912. Mrs. Besant drifted into a concern for Indian nationalism and in 1916 founded the Home Rule for India League. Likewise, C.W. Leadbeater also wandered away from Theosophy, eventually founding the Liberal Catholic church and enlisting many Theosophists. Mrs. Besant died in 1933 at the age of 90.

But the Theosophical Society still exists to a lesser extent today, its international headquarters the original building in Madras. In 1934 the man who took over leadership from Mrs. Besant, Dr. George S. Arundale, outlined the principles of life as related to Theosophy in the following way:

1. Life is essentially one and universal.

2. Life is within a great evolutionary process whereby an infinitude of life-units move from lowliest unconsciousness through innumerable stages of unfolding to heights of self-consciousness.

Good/evil (handwritten)

3. This irresistible movement is under beneficent and immutable law, order and purpose.

4. That all good and ill fortune, individual or collective, are signs of this evolutionary principle at work.

5. Each life-unit can hasten or retard the pace of its own evolutionary progress, through understanding or through ignorance.

Modern Theosophy, in modifying and adapting the core of these principles, now holds that the so-called evolutionary process exists in a Universal Creative Mind, both in the physical and spiritual worlds. Creation, the Theosophists believe – an ideal not dissimilar to the principle of a Pulsating or Cyclic Universe – is a continuous, cyclic development, not only among the stars and planets, but among men, supermen and animals. They believe that mankind dates back millions of years and has evolved through five of seven human types, each divided by great cataclysms – earthquakes, floods and ice ages – controlled by extra-terrestrial intelligences. Each individual person is thought to have an inner unit of divine consciousness; part of a Supreme One consciousness that willed to become many. Through a succession of incarnations, or lives, it is then possible to achieve an ultra-consciousness that will lead to an ultimate consciousness of unity with the Supreme One.

As with the theories of the Rosicrucians and men like Eliphas Levi, the end-product doctrines of Theosophy as they stand, point to the great depth behind the movement and the profundity of thought of its founder, Madame Blavatsky. Her apparently pointless and almost childish dabbling in "phenomena", deception and trickery apart, HPB was clearly intuitively aware of the inkling of some great universal truth, but was unable to grasp it fully. On at least two occasions, Mme Blavatsky is said to have confided that the effects she achieved – "precipitated" letters and "apported" objects such as flowers and teacups produced seemingly out of thin air – were of no importance. They were merely devices she regarded as necessary to titillate and maintain the interest of followers who demanded wonders and miracles.

The Russian journalist Vsevolod Sergeyevich Solov'yov, for example, claimed that Mme Blavatsky told him:

phenomena & person (handwritten)

"What is one to do when, in order to rule men, you must deceive them, when, in order to catch them and make them pursue whatever it may be, it is necessary to promise and show them toys? Suppose my books and The Theosophist were a thousand times more interesting and serious, do you think that I could have anywhere to live and any degree of success, unless behind all this there stood 'phenomena'? I should have achieved absolutely nothing and would long ago have pegged out from hunger. They would have crushed me, and no-one would have begun to consider that I, too, am a living creature, that I, too, must eat and drink. But long, long ago I understood these dear people whose stupidity gives me at times enormous satisfaction... If you only knew what lions and eagles in all the countries of the world have turned themselves into asses at my whistling and obediently clapped me in time with their huge ears."

On another occasion she confided in Moncure Conway, a Unitarian preacher: "It's all glamour. People think they see what they don't see; that's all there is to it."

illusion (handwritten)

Yet despite these admissions about her "phenomena", Mme Blavatsky remained adamant about the truth and reality of her secret brethren and the principles of Theosophy throughout her life. She undoubtedly possessed some occult powers, her showmanship and "glamour" not withstanding. Anyone who has taken the trouble to read the exhaustively monumental and encyclopaedic works, *Isis Unveiled* and *The*

Secret Doctrine, and noted the complex ideas and detailed, interwoven knowledge of ancient mythology, legend, folklore and philosophy, cannot fail to appreciate that here was a woman who approached levels of consciousness, spirituality and understanding that are rarely attained by anyone in the materialistic West. Beneath all the framework, the true Mme Blavatsky bore no relationship to the gullible, shallow and directionless table-turners and rappers with whom she was unfortunately associated in 19th-century America. And Mme Blavatsky was not the last to believe she had achieved a kind of breakthrough to the gods.

21. The Secret Chiefs And The Coming Of The Beast

"I am that I am, the flame
Hidden in the sacred ark.
I am the unspoken name,
I the unbegotten spark.
I am he that lifteth up
Life, and flingeth it afar;
I have filled the crystal cup;
I have sealed the crystal star.
I the wingless god that flieth
Through my firmamental fane,
I am he that daily dieth
And is daily born again."
Aleister Crowley (1875–1947)

ABOUT 14 YEARS after the beginnings of the Theosophical Society, one of the most important, complete and authentic magical systems ever organised, was formed in England. It was the Hermetic Order of the Golden Dawn. It grew up in a manner strangely similar to the Rosicrucian movement and indeed, adopted some of Rosicrucianism's traditions. In many respects, what has survived of Rosicrucianism today has similarities to the Craft of Freemasonry, although only in the form of its workings. While Freemasonry is based around the tradition of Solomon's Temple and the murder and resurrection of its supposed chief architect Hiram Abif, Rosicrucianism grew up as a result of the publication of three slim volumes between 1614 and 1616. The forms it eventually took – even today there are still a number of pseudo-Rosicrucian groups, particularly in the USA – bore little relation to its true origins.

The three books are the first traceable evidence of the Rosicrucian legend. They were published anonymously in Germany, the first two at Kassel, the third at Strasbourg. Their titles were:

Fama Fraternitatis.

Confessio Fraternitatis R.C.

Chymische Hochzeit Christiani Rosenkreutz.

In its introduction the first book outlined the need for a total reformation of humanity. It then went on to describe the life and travels of an individual named Christian Rosenkreutz who, after journeying to Palestine, Arabia, Egypt, Morocco and Spain, seeking out ancient wisdom, returned to his native Germany to found a fraternity which would help him record all his knowledge. Eventually, after compiling a vast library and formulating a code for their fraternity, the brethren split up, but remained committed to their ideals and rules. They were to practise only healing and medicine, never to accept any payment for their services, not to adopt any distinctive costume but to blend in with the fashion of whatever country they worked in, to meet once a year on the feast of Corpus Christi (the Thursday after Trinity Sunday), to use the initials R.C. as their seal and password and to be eternally on the lookout for someone suitable to succeed them when they died. The nature and identity of this brotherhood was also to be kept a secret for 100 years.

No one knew when Father R.C., as Rosenkreutz became known, died. But long after that time his body, still perfectly preserved and undecayed, was allegedly discovered in a secret tomb at the fraternity's "Sanctus Spiritus" headquarters, behind a door bearing the inscription: *Post Centum Viginti Annos Patebo* (After 120 years I will reappear.)

In addition were found secret repositories containing copies of every book of the brotherhood, magical equipment such as mirrors, lamps and bells – all hidden away so that the movement could be reformed if its members all died without being replaced; a sort of "time capsule."

This strange book, which was widely received, running to three reprints during 1615 and another in 1617, was followed by the *Confessio*, seemingly written by the same, anonymous author. This volume outlined the aims and objects of the brotherhood and encouraged its readers to join. It did not, however, say how this could be done. It attacked Islam, the papacy and the false alchemists and, following up the undated revelations of the first book, shed some light on the time that the mysterious Christian Rosenkreutz was supposed to have lived. The *Confessio* claimed that C.R. was born in 1378 and, since he was alleged to have lived until the age of 106, died in 1484. So, according to the claim of the inscription on his vault, that he would return in 120 years, his reappearance should have been in 1604, ten years before publication of the *Fama Fraternitatis*.

The third of the Rosicrucian books, translated as *The Hermetick Romance*; or *The Chymical Wedding*, contained an allegorical story of an old man, again named Christian Rosenkreutz, involving his invitation to a royal wedding, his investiture with the Order of the Golden Fleece and his accidental discovery of some books of wisdom. As a punishment for prying into these secrets, he is made to guard the entrance to the chamber where he found them.

The allegorical and dreamlike quality of this third volume, through its vivid symbolism, incorporates in an obscure and mystical form, allusions to alchemy, astrology and magic.

The result of the appearance of these three strange books in 17th-century European society was a great surge of interest in the Rosicrucian movement. But, since no one could be found who was legitimately connected with the brotherhood, as outlined in the texts, many people assumed membership and began to publish pamphlets and tracts, presumably hoping to attract the attention of true members. Despite the difficulties of interpreting the meaning of the three original books, men like Robert Fludd (1574–1637), an English alchemist and Hermeticist, began to develop and embellish the ideas of the Rosicrucian texts.

In 1710 the Order of the Golden and Rosy Cross was founded in Germany by a Sigmund Richter (*Sincerus Racatus*) and from then onwards, all kinds of groups and secret organisations began to emerge, flourish briefly and disappear, using the names Rosenkreutz, Rosy Cross or Rosicrucian, throughout Europe. But most of them were so patently spurious, contrived and over-inventive that the original legend became totally obscured by the made-up rigmaroles and rituals of such groups.

The whole object of recounting the origins, popularity and wane of this peculiar mythos is that it re-emerged, in its more traditional form, a century later, in the formation of the most authentic magical society – the aforementioned Golden Dawn. In 1880, an Anglican clergyman, the Rev. A.F.A. Woodford, claimed to have bought an old, 60-page manuscript written in a mysterious code, from a bookstall in Farringdon Street, London. Written on old paper – some of its leaves bore an 1809 watermark – in faded brown ink, the MS was probably a more recent production than it seemed, although its true pedigree will probably never be determined. But whoever was responsible was obviously knowledgeable about the recently revived Western occult tradition, possibly from the works of Eliphas Levi, and about Masonic ritual.

With it was a letter written in German, which said that whoever managed to decipher the document should communicate, through a Fraulein Anna Sprengel, whose magical name was *Sapiens Donabitur Astris* (The wise one will be ruled by the stars). The Rev. Woodford, himself an elderly Freemason, showed them to a couple of colleagues who were versed in the Qabalah and Rosicrucianism, Dr. William Robert Woodman (1828–91), a retired physician, and Dr. William Wynn Westcott (1848–1918), a London coroner. Transcribed by Dr. Westcott, the manuscript consisted of treatises on occult and qabalistic themes, plus an outline of five rituals, or degrees of attainment, for a magical order. These rituals were elaborated with the aid of another Freemason, Samuel Liddell Mathers, who later called himself MacGregor Mathers and the Hermetic Order of the Golden Dawn was formed in 1887. It had 11 degrees, divided into three groups. There was the Golden Dawn in the Outer, with five degrees; the *Stella Matutina*, consisting of the *Rosae Rubiae et Aurea Crucis*, each having three degrees; and the innermost order, known as the *Argentum Astram*, or Silver Star, had three degrees and was said to consist of "Secret Chiefs".

In the summer of that year, the founders were joined by the poet William Butler Yeats (1865–1939), who then helped to write the finished and polished versions of the rituals, involving Chaldean and ancient Egyptian rites, along with the influence of the prophetic poet William Blake (1757–1827) and the Christian Rosenkreutz legend.

As in the case of the Theosophical Society, most of the order's early "wisdom" and instructions, were received as spiritual communications by MacGregor Mathers' wife Moina, known as Vestigia, a clairaudient and clairvoyant. Once Dr. Westcott had been informed by the mysterious Sapiens Donabitur Astris in Germany that he could authorise any documents necessary for the order's constitution, no further communications are alleged to have come from this source. News was supposed to have been received, in fact, that Fraulein Sprengel had died.

There is a suggestion that somewhere in Europe a magical society, possibly Rosicrucian, had been in existence, which influenced the formation of the Golden Dawn, the Theosophical Society and the later teachings of Anthroposophical Society founder Rudolf Steiner. Another theory was that Eliphas Levi may have been one of the original members of the European sect – among the early manuscripts of the Golden Dawn is a coded note on "the Tarot Trumps and their attribution to the Hebrew Alphabet" and signed A.L.C. which, it will be recalled, were the initials of Alphonse Louis Constant, alias Levi.

For several years the order flourished, practising high ritual magic, and attracted a number of distinguished members, including the supernatural writers Arthur Machen and Algernon Blackwood, the mystic Allan Bennett who later became famous as a Buddhist monk, Bikku Ananda Maitreya, the scholar Arthur Edward Waite and Florence Farr the actress. Temples were formed in London (Isis-Urania), Paris (Ahathoor), Bradford, Yorkshire (Horus), Weston-Super-Mare in Somerset (Osiris) and Edinburgh (Amen-Ra). But eventually, as happens so often in mystical societies, as indeed occurred within the Theosophical Society, internal squabbles, personality clashes and power struggles interfered with the running and development of the order. MacGregor Mathers began to claim that he was the only member in true communication with the "Hidden and Secret Chiefs" of the Inner and Third Order, and in 1896 claimed that he had in fact been admitted to this select Order by the Magi themselves. He claimed that he met the Masters both on the astral plane and, occasionally, in the flesh.

He said: "For my part I believe them to be human and living upon this earth; but possessing terrible superhuman powers. When such rendezvous has been in a much frequented place, there has been nothing in their personal appearance and dress to mark them out as differing in any way from ordinary people except the appearance and sensation of transcendent health and physical vigour (whether they seemed persons in youth or age) which was their invariable accompaniment; in other words, the physical appearance which the possession of the Elixir of Life has traditionally supposed to confer.

"On the other hand, when the rendezvous has been in a place free from easy access by the Outer World they have usually been in symbolic robes and insignia."

He went on: "But my physical intercourse with them on these rare occasions, has shown me how difficult it is for a mortal, even though advanced in Occultism, to support the actual presence of an Adept in the Physical Body; and such meetings have never been granted to my own personal request, but only by their own special appointment; and usually only for some reason of special importance."

Elaborating on these experiences, Mathers said: "The sensation was that of being in contact with so terrible a force that I can only compare it to the continued effect of that usually experienced momentarily by a person close to whom a flash of lightning passes during a violent storm; coupled with a difficulty in respiration similar to the half-strangling effect produced by ether; and if such was the result produced in one, as tested as I have been in practical Occult Work, I cannot conceive a much less advanced Initiate being able to support such a strain even for five minutes, without Death ensuing."

It is significant how so many people have claimed knowledge of "secret masters" – supernatural or otherwise. Could these "Secret Chiefs" of MacGregor Mathers have been similar to the ones to whom Sir Isaac Newton referred as a "chain of initiates" when hinting at the knowledge of the alchemists?

It was not so much MacGregor Mathers' insistence on his sole contact with the masters, as his introduction in 1900 of Aleister Crowley to the Order that contributed to the divisions arising within the membership. MacGregor Mathers, then in Paris, sent Crowley to London to seize control of the Isis Urania Lodge. As a result, Yeats and other officials deposed Mathers in absentia. Mathers is alleged to have performed powerful magical rites in Paris, designed to blast his usurpers. Whether Mathers did indeed possess such powers or not, the order quickly began to disintegrate. Yeats and A.E. Waite quarrelled as to the purpose of the Order, Yeats wanting to adhere to magical pursuits, Waite inclining to the mystical.

A number of offshoot organisations were attempted at various times by several of the dispersed members, but not with any of the substantially authentic magical foundations of the original. A Dr. R.W. Felkin founded the Stella Matutina, or Order of the Companions of the Rising Light in the Morning, with a temple (Amoun) in London and one in Bristol, called the Hermes, a revived version of which was still operative in the 1970s. In Paris, Crowley quarrelled with MacGregor Mathers and formed his own Argentum Astram, introducing sexual, or Westernised tantric, rites

---

into the workings. Mathers died in 1917.

Another member, Violet Mary Firth (1891–1946), who became famous as the occult writer Dion Fortune, formed the Society of the Inner Light, which is, I believe, still functional today.

In 1930 a book by Christina Mary Stoddart, denouncing the Golden Dawn, appeared. In *Light-Bearers Of Darkness*, she said she believed that the Secret Chiefs were subversive and wanted to control the Earth and that Mathers was "doing political work under the Secret Chiefs" and was "mixed up in war and military matters".

I have some reasons for believing this to be close to the truth, although it is doubtful that Mathers himself was aware of the true nature of the powers he had invoked. Certainly, most other members of the Order regarded their work as beneficial and exploratory and any suggestion of "black magic" would have been met with indignant denial.

In fact, some of the Golden Dawn's papers affirm that, on the contrary, among its aims was "To establish closer and more personal relations with the Lord Jesus, the Master of Masters... the ultimate object of the teaching of our Order".

At the same time, however, there is no doubt that various aspects of the occult arts were thoroughly investigated and practised, including astral travel, astrology, geomancy, alchemy and scrying. The three main varieties of magic taught were those expounded in the notorious *Key Of Solomon*, the *Sacred Magic Of Abramelin The Mage*, and what is known as the Enochian System, described by the Elizabethan astrologer and magician Dr. John Dee (1527–1608). These were supplemented by rituals based upon the Rosicrucian story of the discovery of the Vault of the Adepts in which Christian Rosenkreutz's undecayed body was hidden. This ceremony, with its hints of necromancy, was said to represent the "rebirth" of the initiate from the confines of his mortality "by the power of the Holy Spirit".

To this end the Order had constructed a seven-sided vault, as described in the *Fama Fraternitatis*, complete with a circular pastos and a coffin. It walls were decorated with occult and Rosicrucian symbols and the dramatic moment of the ritual was when the initiate discovered the "body" of Christian Rosenkreutz, usually played by Mathers or Dr. Westcott, or some other Temple official, lying in the coffin.

It is not difficult, perhaps, to imagine the effect of such a dramatic piece of mummery on a candidate, with all its air of mystery, its atmospheric ceremonial and symbolism, and the carefully-devised dialogues of Mathers and Yeats.

For his own part, Yeats explained his interest in magic as follows: "It is surely absurd to hold me 'weak' or otherwise because I chose to persist in a study which I decided deliberately four or five years ago to make, next to my poetry, the most important pursuit of my life. Whether it be, or be not, bad for my health, can only be decided by one who knows what magic is and not at all by any amateur... If I had not made magic my constant study I could not have written a single line of my Blake book, nor would *The Countess Kathleen* ever have come to exist. The mystical life is the centre of all that I do and all that I think and all that I write."

Yet however well-intentioned and genuinely motivated the Golden Dawn's members may have been, I believe that their incursions into a mysterious and potentially dangerous art, with all its mixed influences, led to a quite genuine, spasmodic link with external powers of a very dark nature. I also feel that the only two members who realised this were Mathers and Crowley, who became one of the most notorious and feared magicians of contemporary times.

Crowley regarded the theatrical rituals of the Golden Dawn as weak and ineffective; watered-down ceremonials that satisfied the romantic nature of men like Yeats and Christian mystics like Waite, but which were not powerful enough to unleash the true forces of superior intelligences. Crowley suffered from an immensely inflated ego and an exploratory fearlessness that drove him much further than any of the Golden Dawn members would have been prepared to go. He, too, believed in other-worldly intelligences that could be contacted by magical ceremonial, but he made no bones about it: these intelligences were often of the Powers of Darkness, rather than of Light. He believed he made contact with a Secret Chief named Aiwaz or Aiwass, in 1903 in Cairo, who ordered him to record an important message to humanity.

Aiwass, whom Crowley claimed appeared on more than one occasion, identified himself as the minister of Hoor-PaarKraat, a Graeco-Egyptian god Harpakrad, describing himself cryptically as "a messenger from the forces ruling this earth at present". The result of his dictations was *The Book Of The Law* (*Liber Al vel Legis*) which, Crowley claimed, he did not fully understand at first, but which eventually became the basis upon which he founded all his subsequent work and his code of living: "Do what thou wilt shall be the whole of the law."

Crowley explained *The Book Of The Law* by saying that there had been, during the evolution of the world, two aeons. The first was the Age of Isis, in which woman dominated. The second was that of Osiris, the age of man and which encompassed the rise of Judaism, Buddhism, Christianity and Islam. Then, in 1904, began the Aeon of Horus, age of the crowned and conquering child. This involved, he said, an emphasis on Thelema, the Will – man's true self.

Eventually, however, Crowley's own ego seems to have overtaken him and we find him setting himself up as the New Messiah, but not on the side of Light. The Great Beast of the Apocalypse, 666, as he styled himself, would supplant Christ as the "Logos [Word] of the Aeon".

"Lo," he wrote, "Jesus of Nazareth, how thou art taken in my snare. All my life long thou hast plagued me and affronted me. In thy name – with all other free souls in Christendom – I have been tortured in my boyhood; all delights have been forbidden unto me; all that I had has been taken from me, and that which is owed to me they pay not – in thy name. Now at last I have thee; the Slave-God is in the power of the Lord of Freedom. Thine hour is come; as I blot thee out from this earth, so surely shall the eclipse pass; and Light, Life, Love and Liberty be once more the law of the Earth. Give thou place to me, O Jesus; thine aeon is passed. The Age of Horus is arisen by the Magick of the Master, the Great Beast."

Crowley may have been right about the aeon of Christ being passed. But he was wrong about himself as the New Messiah and he died, lonely, perplexed, drug-ridden and unfulfilled in 1947.

22. Behind The Crooked Cross

"Lo! thy dread empire, Chaos! is restored;
Light dies before thy uncreating word;
Thy hand, great Anarch! lets the curtain fall
And universal darkness buries all"
Alexander Pope (1688–1744)

IF ALEISTER CROWLEY was not, as he seems to have thought, the prophesied Anti-Christ, perhaps the only other man of our times that the title fits most snugly was Adolf Hitler. For behind the powerful political motivations of the National Socialism that he preached and which was an inspiration to the German people, lay a truly dark and sinister driving force of occultism of the darkest variety. In simple terms, Black Magic. Growing up in a country already steeped in occultism, in which magical societies and groups waxed, flourished and waned in practically all the major centres, Hitler could scarcely avoid becoming interested, let alone involved. He adopted ideas from many of them and rose to power on a premise that was already well established: a national self-certainty of racial superiority. The idea of being part of a super-race, destined to control the world, was part of the doctrines that many of the occult groups taught. Like Crowley, though, Hitler also came to believe in a hidden race of other-worldly intelligences – "forces ruling this Earth at present", as the self-styled Great Beast put it – and set himself up as the instrument of those powers. His persecution of the Jews was not only a way of keeping the imagined Aryan-Germanic race pure, but a way of striking a blow against the opposing cosmic forces; the powers on the side of Light that had helped the Israelites. Hitler believed that, like Moses, he was one of the Elect... except that he was working on behalf of a totally different celestial power. A power that many call the Devil.

It was no coincidence that the ceremonies of the Hitler Youth Movement resembled those of Christian Church services, with extracts from Hitler's speeches and from *Mein Kampf* being read out instead of the Gospels, and the red Nazi flag and the black swastika substituted for the sacrament. Symbolically, the Hitler Youth ceremonies were nothing less than a form of the Black Mass. Nor was it coincidental that the swastika itself – the *Hakenkreutz*, or "hooked cross" – was reversed. Originally, the centuries-old symbol, found in many of the pre-Biblical Mediterranean and Near Eastern cultures, as well as in those of Amerindians, had its arms pointing to the left, and was representative of fortune and well-being. Its very name derives from the Sanskrit word *svasti*, meaning good luck. It was also a motif signifying the cycle of rebirth to Buddhists and Hindus. But when the man who designed the Nazi emblem, Dr. Friedrich Krohn, took his idea to the Party in 1920, it was Hitler who insisted that the swastika symbol should be reversed. Even then, it seems, the potential Fuhrer knew whose side he was on.

So, too, it would seem, did Winston Churchill. It has been suggested that Churchill himself used his well-known V-sign as a potent cabalistic gesture to counteract the influence of the swastika – and that he adopted the sign following secret meetings with none other than Aleister Crowley.

One of the main earthly influences on Hitler was a fellow Austrian, Adolf Lanz, born in Vienna in 1874, although he did not receive the recognition he anticipated when the Fuhrer rose to power. Lanz, like Eliphas Levi, began his life in the Church – as a Cistercian monk at Heiligrenkreuz on the Austrian border, but was expelled at the age of 25 for "worldly and carnal desires".

Calling himself Dr. Jorg Lanz von Liebenfels and claiming he was the Italian-born son of a baron, Lanz set up his own pseudo-religious organisation, the Order of the New Templars. Lanz was convinced it was essential to preserve the "pure" German race, which he saw as a superior "Aryo-heroic" people with blue eyes, fair hair, high-bridged noses, narrow skulls and slender hands. To this end he suggested the setting up of centres where only the purest specimens of the race would breed – an idea echoed three decades later in Heinrich Himmler's diabolical *Lebensborn* or love camps as they were popularly known, where members of the SS mated with specially chosen "Aryan" girls; supposedly the pick of Germanic womanhood.

Lanz also advocated other measures to preserve the German "master race" that were later adopted by the Nazis: the castration or sterilisation of "undesirable" or "inferior" strains likely to pollute the pure Aryan blood. Lanz admitted only carefully screened members to his Order and began buying up old German castles as centres, or Temples. Among these was Burg Werfenstein, overlooking the Danube. He even adopted the swastika as emblem of his Order. At this time, Hitler was only 18 years old.

Initiates of the Order studied medicine, the Qabalah (despite its strong Hebraic origins), astrology and many other semi-mystical subjects, such as dietary techniques and phrenology – the assessment of personality by the examination of "bumps" on the skull. The brethren dressed in white robes and performed rituals and ceremonies written by Lanz himself, borrowed from Nordic legends and symbolism such as the Icelandic *Edda* and the story of the search for the Holy Grail in Wolfram von Eschenbach's *Parsifal*. He composed an enormous library of literature for the use of initiates, such as his ten-volume "bible", the *Bibliomystikon*, the *Hebdomadarium*, a prayer book, and the New Templars' *Breviary*.

It was during his period as a starving art student in Vienna that Hitler encountered Lanz and his teachings, when he called into the offices of the Order's magazine, *Ostara*. Hitler left with several back numbers under his arm to study. In February 1932, Lanz wrote to one of his associates: "Hitler is one of our pupils. You will one day experience that he, and through him, we will one day be victorious and develop a movement that makes the world tremble."

Lanz was off target on only one count. The movement that would make the world tremble would be Hitler's own National Socialist German Workers' Party and Lanz and his Order would not "through him" gain any status, credit or thanks whatsoever.

It was also at this time in Hitler's career that he fell under the influence – imagined or otherwise – of a symbol that provided a powerful, driving inspiration to him throughout his dictatorial life. One of the places that Hitler frequented during his time in Vienna was the Hofburg Museum, which contained the treasures of the Hapsburg Empire. On display there was an ancient spear, said to have been the Spear of Longinus, the Roman centurion who supposedly pierced the side of Jesus on Calvary.

The full story of this spear and its amazing hold over the future Fuhrer of the Third Reich is told in Trevor Ravenscroft's book, *The Spear Of Destiny* (Neville Spearman, 1974). According to Ravenscroft, who spent many years researching his work, Hitler

---

was whiling away his time in the museum when one day he heard a guide telling a group of visitors that a legend associated with the spear invested its holder with power over the whole world. Hitler, who had studied the works of Nietzsche, including his theories of the *Ubermensch*, or Superman, suddenly became obsessed by the relic. He would spend hours before the glass case in which it was kept, dreaming of a day when he would possess the spear and wield its power. He felt, on one occasion, the immediate surroundings of the building fade as he gazed on the lance and, according to Ravenscroft:

"I stood alone and trembling before the hovering form of the Ubermensch – a Spirit sublime and fearful, a countenance intrepid and cruel. In holy awe, I offered my soul as a vessel of his will."

Like Crowley, Hitler did not disbelieve in the power and divinity of Christ; he simply loathed and despised the passive and seemingly weak and insipid doctrines that to him Christianity upheld. Ravenscroft is not the only writer to note Hitler's fascination with the idea of hidden, supernatural forces. In his book of conversations with the Fuhrer, *Hitler Speaks*, Hermann Rauschning, former Gauleiter of Danzig, who later defected to the Allies, makes similar observations.

Once, while Hitler was talking about experimental mutations of human beings, Rauschning thought Hitler was referring to careful interbreeding of specially selected Germans.

"All you can do," the Gauleiter told Hitler, "is to assist Nature and shorten the road to be followed. It is Nature herself who must create for you a new species. Up till now, the breeder has only rarely succeeded in developing mutations in animals – that is to say, creating himself new characteristics."

Hitler began trembling, almost as if he were in the grip of some religious ecstasy and cried:

"The Superman is living amongst us now! He is here! Isn't that enough for you? I will tell you a secret – I have seen him. He is intrepid and cruel. I was afraid of him."

Rauschning also spoke of these conversations to an experimental psychologist, Dr. Achille Delmas who, in his book *Essai De Biographie Psycho-Pathologique* (1946), said Rauschning told him:

"A person close to Hitler told me that he wakes up in the night screaming and in convulsions. He calls for help and appears to be half-paralyzed. He is seized with a panic that makes him tremble until the bed shakes. He utters confused and unintelligible sounds, gasping, as if on the point of suffocation."

Although many historians and commentators have remarked that Hitler was subject to epilepsy, at this point it is worthwhile comparing these strange experiences of Hitler with those of MacGregor Mathers who talked of the "half-strangling effect produced by ether" as one of the effects when he was in communication with the "Secret Chiefs".

Rauschning went on: "The same person described to me one of these fits, with details that I would refuse to believe had I not complete confidence in my informant. Hitler was standing in his room, swaying and looking all round him as if he were lost.

"'It's he, it's he!' he groaned, 'He's come for me!' His lips were white; he was sweating profusely. Suddenly he uttered a string of meaningless figures, then words and scraps of sentences. It was terrifying. He used strange expressions strung together in a bizarre disorder. Then he relapsed again into silence, but his lips continued to move. He was then given a friction and something to drink. Then suddenly he screamed: 'There! There! Over in the corner! He is there!' – all the time stamping with his feet and shouting. To quieten him he was assured that nothing extraordinary had happened and finally he gradually calmed down. After that he slept for a long time and became normal again..."

To anyone with any knowledge of ritual magic who has achieved any degree of practical ability, or to anyone who has witnessed a voodoo ceremony, what was happening to Hitler will be fairly clear. He had somehow, knowingly or unknowingly, invoked an entity which had temporarily taken over him; an event that he perhaps had neither prepared for nor actively summoned, except through intense, obsessive concentration. Nor, once the experience had begun, could he control it or himself sufficiently to carry out the necessary banishment ceremony, if he was in possession of such knowledge. Aberrations and frightening experiences of this kind are relatively common among practitioners of ritual magic who fail to follow the correct procedures or are of insufficient strength of character to support them. There appears to be a kind of psychic kickback, often resulting in waking visions and horrific hallucinatory experiences, rather like the "bad trips" and recurrent "freak-outs" of people who dabble idly with impure strains of hallucinogenic drugs such as LSD, mescalin or peyote.

Often, these kinds of involuntary experiences in magic are the result of hours of preparation, including lack of sleep, sensory deprivational exercises and the self-hypnotic effects of repetitious magical ritual. Within a circle of protective symbols, the magus may often work alone for hours on end in conditions that all too easily can produce undesirable aftereffects such as nightmarish hallucinations.

During another of his interviews with Rauschning, Hitler declared: "A new age of the magic interpretation of the world is coming, an interpretation in terms of will and not the intelligence."

Precisely what level of attainment in the magical arts Hitler managed to reach is difficult to determine, but there is evidence of many different influences. His Deputy Führer Rudolf Hess, for example, studied and believed in the efficacy of astrology, while Heinrich Himmler had studied rune occultism. This is a form of magic involving ancient and powerful symbolic writing. On his rise to power as Chancellor in January 1933, Hitler on the surface appeared to show a contempt for occultism. But it was only a public front.

On his orders, newspapers were instructed to refuse all advertisements from astrologers, professional fortune-telling was banned in Berlin and police raided bookshops, confiscating all books on the subjects that in any way might be termed occult. An official censor was established by the Reich Chamber for Authors and Publishers, to deal exclusively with astrological works. Germany's two leading astrological magazines, *Zenit* and *Astrologische Rundschau* suddenly disappeared from the market without explanation in 1938, and branches of Madame Blavatsky's Theosophical Society were outlawed in Germany.

It looked outwardly as if the Führer was taking a strictly materialist line, stamping out any areas of superstition or speculative thinking. But quite the opposite was the case. Hitler was taking a deeper interest in the occult arts than was generally realised then, and even now, so long after his supposed suicide in 1945.

On November 8, 1939, an attempt was made to assassinate the Führer in a Munich beer cellar. Six days earlier a Swiss astrologer named Karl Ernst Krafft had written to Dr. Heinrich Fesel, who worked in Himmler's Reich Administration, saying that Hitler's life would be in great danger between November 7 and 10. At first, Dr. Fesel had thought nothing of the letter and quietly filed it. But when the assassination attempt occurred, Krafft sent a telegram to Rudolf Hess, telling him of the letter. Krafft was quickly arrested and rushed to Berlin.

He was put to work in Josef Goebbels' propaganda Ministry and it was, in fact, a letter from Krafft to the Rumanian Minister in London, M. Virgil Tilea, which eventually prompted the British Intelligence service to engage an astrologer, Louis de Wohl, as a counter measure against the Nazis' occult dabblings. Tilea knew that Krafft was an astrologer and suggested that the British should also consult one to try to find out just what the Germans were doing.

Heinrich Himmler, meanwhile, tried to identify Hitler's failed assassin through a trance medium in Vienna, while Goebbels busied himself searching the prophecies of the 14th century astrologer Nostradamus, looking for any significant information that could be applied to current events.

Further evidence of the Nazi interest in the occult came with the Rudolf Hess affair, known as *Aktion Hess*. Hess' surprise flight to Scotland in 1941 was followed by the sudden rounding up and arrest of hundreds of astrologers and occultists a month later. It was believed that Hess had timed his departure according to some astrological calculations and the Nazis wanted to find the astrologer responsible for helping him. The action was explained to the German public with the excuse that Hess had been very ill and had been consulting astrologers and hypnotists. Again, bookshops were raided for occult material and some private collections were seized. No scapegoat was ever found, although a number of the arrested occultists were put into concentration camps and never released. One was Dr. Hubert Korsch, who had written about Hitler's horoscope long before he ever came to power. Korsch died in Orianenberg, outside Berlin, in April 1942.

He was probably murdered. It is not unlikely that he made predictions as to Hitler's demise and the Führer was sufficiently unbalanced to accept any astrological advice that was favourable and conformed with his own ideas. Thus, if Korsch plotted a chart that predicted Hitler's failure, he would be an astrologer to be feared – and despatched.

More practical, although largely unsuccessful, application of the Nazis' occult researches came about in 1942, when a group of radiesthesists was assembled at what became known as the Pendulum Institute in Berlin. Radiesthesia is on a par with water divining, except that people or objects are attempted to be located by holding a pendulum over a map. From the way the pendulum swings, the operator is said to be able to find the object or person required. Captain Hans Roeder of the German navy directed the operation, trying to locate British convoys in the Atlantic so that they could be attacked by U-boats. A spate of British success in sinking many U-boats had led the Nazis to believe that the Allies were employing similar techniques.

Radiesthesia was successfully used by the Nazis in finding Mussolini in Naples after he had been arrested by the Badoglio government in July 1943.

On the surface, the Nazi involvement in the occult appears somewhat superficial, haphazard, amateurish and largely ineffectual. But there is reason to believe that Hitler and his more immediate confidants were much more deeply involved in the more esoteric aspects of the secret arts, and that the ministerial dabblings like the Pendulum experiment were, like the bookshop purges and arrests of occultists, simply covers. Before Hitler's rise to power there was formed in Berlin a secret society based around an idea in Bulwer-Lytton's novel *Vril:The Coming Race*. Lytton had written of a superior race of supermen living in secret, subterranean hideouts in the centre of the Earth. One day they would emerge to dominate the world.

The Berlin group which called itself the Vril Society or Luminous Lodge, believed that by careful mental training they could become those supermen. They believed that man had hidden reserves of superhuman energy and mental power called "vril" and that anyone who could tap the source of this power would be invulnerable and would, like Lytton's characters, dominate the Earth. From his conversations with Rauschning, it is clear that Hitler believed in a race of hidden masters, just as did MacGregor Mathers, Aleister Crowley, the Illuminati, the Rosicrucians and Madame Blavatsky.

But in the 11 amazing years of his rise and fall, it would seem that Hitler was unable to control the forces that he had invoked sufficiently to aid his own earthly ends. Nor did the Spear of Longinus, which he had ordered removed from the Hapsburg treasure house in Vienna to a secret hiding place discovered by the American liberation forces in Nuremberg in 1945, prove the symbol of absolute global power he believed it to be. Not in his hands, at any rate.

Once again an individual had tapped mysterious, unearthly powers, without fully understanding their nature, their *raison d'être*, their potential, or even the extent of their possible interest in mankind. Like the Power of Light – seen as the God of the Hebrews – those of Darkness also moved in mysterious, unfathomable ways.

Before leaving Hitler, let us look at yet one more fringe occult figure in whom he took more than a passing interest. Indeed, those of the Nazi hierarchy who knew Hans Horbiger declared him to be the Copernicus of his day. Horbiger, another Austrian, was born in 1860 and, after studying in Vienna and Budapest, became an engineer with an inspirational flare. And it was from his visionary doctrine of *Welteislehre*, or Theory of Eternal Ice, that the Nazis drew the basis of their cosmological view as members of the Vril Society. Horbiger envisaged a cosmos that was founded on opposites: Ice and Fire, attraction and repulsion. These opposites, he declared, ruled the whole of the Universe, including the Earth and all its organic matter, in a cyclic pattern. He believed the Universe was formed when a huge sun collided with an equally enormous block of ice floating in space – and exploded. The fragments flew off into space. Some fell back into the seat of the explosion, while others became the stars and planets in our galaxy.

Horbiger believed that the Moon and the major planets were icebound – the Martian "canals", he said, were simply cracks in the ice. The only body in our solar system that was not solid ice was Earth, where a recurring cycle, a struggle between ice and fire – evidenced in the various Ice Ages – goes on.

The Milky Way, he postulated, was a giant belt of floating ice fragments with stars beyond it shining through. Within our solar system, the heavenly bodies are subject to two laws: gravity, pulling inwards and the slowly fading inertia of the explosion thrusting outwards. Eventually, Horbiger theorised, all the planets will converge back into the Sun. This collision once again of ice (the planets) and fire (the Sun) will set off yet another explosion and the process will begin over again. A wild, theoretical cosmology, perhaps, but close enough to the idea of the Pulsating Universe theory to be highly significant.

What was perhaps most important, however, was Horbiger's hypothesis of opposites. For that – although neither he nor the Nazis appeared to realise it – may be one of the vital principles behind the secrets of the celestial powers of the entire cosmos.

23. The War That Shapes The Cosmos

"All the children of righteousness are ruled by the Prince of Light and walk in the ways of light; but all the children of falsehood are ruled by the Angel of Darkness and walk in the ways of darkness."
The Community Rules of the Dead Sea Scrolls

IT SHOULD BE possible now, after our long and circuitous journey through areas of the unknown, to formulate some ideas about the true nature of man, his limitations and, if he aspires to walk with the gods, his as-yet unrealised potential and his relation to the Universe. Also, we should get a clearer picture of the power that many have called God. Having sifted through the relevant evidence of archaeology, of religious texts, of mythologies, race memories and traditions, of the beliefs and doctrines of some of the most important mystical and occult thinkers and organisations, we should be able to arrive at some reasonable conclusions based upon the principles inherent in all these areas.

In basic terms, it should be possible to rewrite the Bible in a more understandable and more acceptable form. By this I do not mean simply the Old and New Testaments, the *Koran*, the Buddhist Scriptures or the *Vedanta*. I mean a true "bible" that sets out a revised exegesis of God, a new view of Creation, a new model of the Universe, a new overview of mankind and, perhaps most important of all, the cosmic purpose and what its future might mean for all humanity.

Before attempting a necessarily brief and sketchy outline of this, however, for the benefit of those who may not wholly accept the scriptural and traditional indications that there is indeed a cosmic purpose, let us examine what some areas of the most modern scientific thought indicates. One of the "new" sciences of our era is that of cybernetics. This is the science of systems; the analysis of patterns of control and communications in both animal life and in mechanics and can thus be applied to practically everything from corporate structure in business to the design and function of artificial limbs. It may also be applied to the structure of the Universe itself. Being a fairly "young" science – it was only formulated in its modern sense in 1948 by the American physicist Norbert Wiener (1894–1964) and takes its name from the Greek *kybernetes*, meaning a "governor" or "steersman" – its exponents are frequently reluctant to project their ideas too far. Like many scientists, cyberneticians are often cautious in expounding new theories and frequently anchor them with a network of "ifs" and "buts" and other qualifications. Yet there is a small pocket of cybernetic thought that points to a distinct purpose in the Universe – almost as if the whole structure had been "programmed" like a computer. The data of the Universe are all around us. The "programme" for life, as we have seen, is in the DNA molecules; the "programme" for a flower is contained in the chromosomes of a seed; the "programme" for matter is contained in the nucleii and electrons of atomic particles. In effect these data can be seen as coded ciphers that will eventually spell out quite complex ideas or "sentences".

The point is, however, that computers do not programme themselves. *Someone* has to feed in the information and request results.

The results, as we can see all around us if we observe carefully, are quite distinct and particular and are in no way random. The Universe and life on Earth are governed by laws – not all of them yet known to man, a delusion that persisted during the Victorian era – that ensure that these patterns and programmes are repeated.

More and more the notion of "accidental" development and evolution is being eroded away. We are virtually on the doorstep of "proving" that there is planning and purpose in everything. When that proof becomes conclusive and irrefutable, the only logical premise must be that *someone* or *something* carried out this programming. And, from its very nature, we must accept that whatever intelligence was responsible, it was of a much higher order than man.

Keeping this in mind, alongside what ancient scriptures and traditions tell us, it should be possible to sketch a New Genesis that may go something like this:

In the beginning there was formless matter in a state of absolute chaos that existed in total void. Amid that matter, through a specific arrangement of energy and particles, there evolved an Awareness that was intelligent and sentient, yet without form. Eventually that Awareness-Being became so intelligent and aware of its own existence, its own nature and its complete juxtaposition to the Not-Being of lifeless, purposeless matter from which it had differentiated itself, that it resolved to continue to exist by retaining the arrangement of its own being-ness.

That Being was and is what many call God. And, in its retention of its state of Being, the intelligence gained power – the ability to influence and manipulate matter and energy. It had also, in coming into existence from non-awareness and non-being, laid down the first principle of the Universe: the Law of Opposites. In a Universe initially composed of matter in void, Being had arisen from Not-Being. In the void was stillness and inertia and in the matter arose motion. Through the process of becoming, purpose arose from chaos. It is significant to note here that a more accurate translation of "I AM THAT I AM", which is what Moses was told to call the entity when he encountered the Lord on the mountain, is: "I AM THAT WHICH IS BECOMING."

The resultant upheaval caused the formless matter to inter-react, until an explosion blew it all apart, one of many that now occur in regular cycles of 80 billion years: the Pulsating Universe.

The pulsations may be likened to the breathing process of human and animal life; the filling and emptying of the lungs. An analogy of this is contained in references in the Hindu scriptures to the Breaths of Brahma. Yet this explosion did not affect Being, for this intelligent life-force was without form or mass. The explosion created the stars and planets of the cosmos and where there had been only void and darkness, there was now matter and light.

The life-force was now free to permeate matter in any and all parts of the Universe it had "created". It could influence or "programme" matter and allow it to evolve independently, subject to the Universal laws it had engendered and set into motion. It could assume corporeal form, or forms, at will.

Having grasped the idea of a first principle of the Universe, it becomes quite clear from an examination of the scientific, historical and philosophical evidence that this principle of opposites is what guides the Universe.

It was perceived many thousands of years ago by the legendary Hermes Trismegistus, figurehead father of alchemy, in the juxtaposition of the four principal elements.

It is the law of repulsion and attraction noted by Horbiger.

It is the self-balancing principle of love and hate observed by philosophers, poets and psychologists.

It is the scientific law encapsulated in the basic principle of physics: every action has an equal and opposite reaction.

This law is eternal and immutable.

It is absolute.

It is found on a macrocosmic scale throughout the entire Universe and in the microcosmic, miniaturised reflection of that Universe represented in man and on down to single-cell creatures.

It is heat and cold, wet and dry, harmony and discord, sleep and wakefulness, peace and war, life and death, forwards and backwards, positive and negative, matter and anti-matter, order and chaos, up and down, gravity and weightlessness, wisdom and ignorance, time and non-time, galaxies and black holes, motion and stillness.

It is reflected in the cyclic creation and destruction of the Pulsating Universe.

It is Light and Darkness.

And all these aspects of the Universal Law are interdependent: no one of them can exist, can have any meaning, without the other, its opposite.

Even the Supreme Intelligence, known by some as God, is subject to this law. The Good associated with the God of Moses, of Muhammad, is offset by the power of Evil, traditionally represented by the Fallen Angel, Satan, sometimes called, or miscalled, the Devil. The ancient Persian god of Light, Ohrmazd, is opposed by the Spirit of Darkness, Ahriman. The beneficence ascribed to Christian saints, Hindu holy men, Tibetan lamas and the incarnations of Buddha, is matched by the evil of black magicians, malicious voodoo priests and shamans, malevolent witchcraft practitioners and all those who seek to overcome its power.

The magus Eliphas Levi was aware of this cosmic law. In *Transcendental Magic* he wrote:

"If two forces are absolutely and invariably equal, the equilibrium will be immobility and therefore the negation of life... Thus contraries act on one another, throughout all Nature...

"God loves the void, which He made in order to fill it; sciences loves the ignorance which it enlightens; strength loves the weakness which it supports; good loves the apparent evil which glorifies it; day is desirous of night, and pursues it unceasingly around the world; love is at once a thirst and a plenitude which must pour itself forth. He who gives receives, and he who receives gives; movement is a continual interchange. To know the law of this change, to be acquainted with the alternate or simultaneous proportion of these forces, is to possess the first principles of the Great Magical Arcanum, which constitutes the human divinity."

Throughout the entire cosmos, since the emergence of Being, a perpetual war has been relentlessly waged through all eternity by the Powers of Light and Darkness. It was first represented by the struggle of awakening sentience against the inanimate, non-intelligence of initial matter in the void, from which the Universe was created. It evolved into two extreme polarities, its nature pervading opposing forces that took the form of intelligent beings after the first explosion of creation.

The reason for this struggle on an infinite, eternal cosmic scale is its very being. Without the conflict of opposites, nothing can exist.

Throughout history, many men and women on the opposing sides of both Light and Darkness have been aware to a greater or lesser extent of this cosmic struggle, reflected in the human race itself. I believe that, initially, it was not perhaps the intention of the Power of Light to involve humanity in this conflict, but that the Power of Darkness probably initiated it. This may be the key to the allegory of Man's "Fall" in the Garden of Eden. Adam, *adamah*, that is mankind as evolved from clay print-outs, became or was made aware: he tasted of the fruit of the Tree of Knowledge. Before that human beings had simply lived, content to exist without questioning the nature of that existence; living in an immediate sense only, unaware of a past, present or future; not knowing the "how" or "why" of their being. In this sense, to the original members of the human race, death did not exist. Then came awareness.

(To digress momentarily, it is an interesting speculation that the Biblical fruit of the Tree of Knowledge was not, as has been popularly imagined and depicted, an apple but more than likely a particular type of fig, known as *ficus religiosus*. This has been claimed as the same fig that grew upon the Bodhi-tree beneath which the Buddha sat for seven days and was "enlightened". It contains a chemical ingredient known as serotonin which, in a way not yet fully understood by science, has the effect of stimulating the pineal gland. This is an apparently useless, lenslike apparatus at the frontal portion of the brain. Modern biologists have been unable to define its precise purpose, but Tibetan monks and other mystics have claimed it is the so-called Third Eye, supposed to being heightened awareness. Some Tibetan sects have been claimed to have been able to perform an operation that opens this atrophied, extra-sensory faculty. With it, the enlightened are believed to be able to see the human aura, a hypothetical field of energy around the head and body in which it is claimed possible to "read" the character, health and emotions. This aura, it is claimed, has been photographed using heat-sensitive techniques – Kirlian photography.)

Once aware, man could not help becoming involved in the ripples, as it were, of the vibrationary waves of the great cosmic struggle sweeping the heavens. The race memory of this battle lingered in some branches of humanity, passing from generation to generation. Jesus appears to have been one man who was aware of this battle.

Apart from the New Testament references in which Jesus indicates that there are some things beyond the understanding of his disciples, evidence for Jesus' awareness of the principle of opposites may be found in a little-known work called the *Leucian Acts Of John*. This text, which dates from about the 1st century AD, contains a Mystery Play which was supposed to have been danced and sung by Jesus while his disciples moved around him in a circle. The dance itself is very ancient and similar to those performed by the Dervishes of the mystical Sufi following. The person who stands in the middle is said to represent the Sun, while those who move around him in complex, circular, revolving motions represent the planets. As this proceeds, according to the *Leucian Acts Of John*, the Master Jesus sings the following verses, in which the juxtaposition of opposites may be seen:

"We praise thee, O Father;
We give thanks to thee, O Light;
In whom darkness dwells not.

I would be saved and I would save
I would be loosed and I would loose
I would be wounded and I would wound
I would be dissolved and I would dissolve

I would be begotten and I would beget
I would eat and I would be eaten
I would hear and I would be heard
I would understand and I would be all understanding

I would flee and I would stay

I would be atoned and I would atone
I have no dwelling and I have dwellings
I have no place and I have places
I have no temple and I have temples
I am a lamp to thee who seest me
I am a mirror to thee who understandest me
I am a door to thee who knockest at me
I am a way to thee a wayfarer

Now, answer to my dancing. See thyself in me who speak and seeing what I do, keep silence on my mysteries...

As for me, if thou wouldst know what I was: in a word, I am the Word who did dance all things..."

It seems obvious that, by performing this "dance of the Universe" and intoning the verses, Jesus was, among other things, indicating that he knew the macrocosmic and microcosmic principle of opposites. Later in the text, he tells John of the title: "The cross of light is called by me for your sake sometimes Mind, sometimes Jesus, sometimes Christ, sometimes Door, sometimes Way, sometimes Bread, sometimes Seed, sometimes Resurrection, sometimes Son, sometimes Father, sometimes Spirit, sometimes Life, sometimes Truth, sometimes Faith, sometimes Grace. Now, those things it is called as towards men; but as to what it is, in truth, itself, in its own meaning to itself and declared unto us, it is the defining and limitation of all things, both the firm necessity of things fixed from things unstable and the harmony of wisdom.

"And as it is wisdom in harmony, there are those on the right and those on the left – powers, authorities, principalities, and daemons, energies, threats, powers of wrath, slandering – and the lower Root from which have come forth the things in Genesis."

Another who, to some extent, appears to have been aware of the cosmic struggle, was the magician Crowley. That was perhaps what he indicated when, in talking of the secret alien intelligence Aiwass, he said the being represented "the forces ruling this earth at present". The very way it is phrased suggests that the same forces do not always rule. Crowley knew that the Powers of Darkness were in the ascendant and took their side, setting himself up as the New Messiah of the New Aeon of Horus, in the form of an Anti-Christ. How close he was to the truth, with Hitler trampling over Europe!

The power of each of the mutually-self-perpetuating forces, as Eliphas Levi saw, is equal; otherwise one would eventually gain control and obliterate the other, and the cosmos would revert to its original state of oblivion and inertia – formless matter in the void. But although equal, these forces can each gain ascendancy at various times and places, either on a macrocosmic or on a limited microcosmic scale. The fluctuations of this cosmic struggle are all too obviously reflected in a localised form on Earth.

Thus the Dead Sea Scrolls of the Essenes, or Qumran Sect, indicated that they were expecting to take part in a great battle with the Powers of Darkness. From the first cave in which a portion of the Scrolls was discovered by an Arab shepherd boy, north of Khirbet Qumran, came a document outlining the order of battle for the expected conflict between the "Sons of Light" and the "Sons of Darkness".

The entire philosophical basis of the Essenes was a doctrine of Two Spirits in the Universe, of Good and Evil, or Light and Darkness. The members of the Sect believed that both these spirits were under God's supreme rule and that, after a long cosmic battle, He would eventually ensure that Light prevailed.

Anticipating modern psychology by centuries, they actually thought of man's dual nature of good and evil as an earthly reflection of this conflict. If a man could control or overcome his evil side, he was helping the Power of Light to gain more control over earthly affairs.

The Qumran Manual of Discipline declares:

"And He assigned to man two Spirits in which he should walk until the time of His visitation. They are the Spirits of Truth and Perversity: Truth born out of the Spring of Light, Perversity from the Well of Darkness. The dominion of all the children of righteousness is in the hands of the Prince of Light so that they walk in the ways of Light, whereas the government of the children of perversity is in the hands of the Angel of Darkness. The purpose of the Angel of Darkness is to lead all the children of righteousness astray, and all their sin, their iniquities, their guilt and their rebellious works are the result of his domination, in accordance with God's mysteries until His appointed time. And all their stripes and seasons of affliction are consequent upon the rule of his [the Angel of Darkness'] hostility."

The Manual continues:

"Until now the Spirits of Truth and Perversity struggle within the heart of Man, behaving with wisdom and folly. And according as a man inherits truth and righteousness, so will he hate Perversion, but in so far as his heritage is rather from the side of perversion and wickedness, so shall he loathe the Truth."

The Power of Darkness at this point in history was temporarily in the ascendant and the Essenes looked to the coming of the Messiah as a time when Light would regain power.

Darkness was also prevalent in the years leading up to the Second World War and the magician Crowley knew it. During the War, he was accused of disseminating pro-German propaganda, through articles he wrote in America while he was temporarily editor of a magazine. Crowley's excuse, however, was that he sought to discredit and ridicule the Nazi propaganda machine by making it appear totally ludicrous.

Darkness was also influential after the time of Jesus, thus contributing to the failure of the ultimate and true aim of the Jesus Experiment. It had earlier thwarted the attempt of the Power of Light to influence mankind through the Pharaoh Akhenaten, which was why his monotheistic system lasted only a few decades. It lost control during the leadership of Moses, enabling the Power of Light to help the Israelites and to take revenge on the Egyptians.

It was perhaps a mistaken association of some of the physical manifestations of the Powers of Darkness with those of Light, that resulted in the Old Testament God appearing tyrannical and cruel. Was it, for example, really the God of Abram who destroyed Sodom and Gomorrah? Or did the Powers of Darkness cause the cataclysm, leaving man to rationalise the event as a judgement of his debased morality?

If Yahweh and the various angels mentioned in the scriptures are seen as manifestations of the Powers of Light on Earth, what evidence have we for physical manifestation of the Powers of Darkness? The Babylonians seem to have been one of the main "contacts" with the evil forces in ancient times.

Berossus, high priest of the god Bel at Babylon during the 3rd century BC, wrote a history of Babylonian civilisation, fragments of which were preserved by the Jewish historian Josephus. Berossus claimed he had ancient papyrii covering 150,000 years of Babylonian history going back to the Creation, the dawn of humanity... and the coming of celestial beings to Earth. But these beings were not associated with El, Eloha or Yahweh of the Hebrews – they were known as the *Akpallus*. They were said to have appeared on Earth during the reigns of several kings of Ur of the Chaldees. Berossus' description of the beings may sound incredible, but it is not quite so unbelievable if, in comparing these creatures with the manifestations of Yahweh, one takes a detached view.

According to Berossus, they had the body of a fish, two heads – one "underneath" the other – human feet and a fish's tail. During the daytime these creatures appeared to the Babylonians, but were never seen to eat. They taught the people to write, to harvest wheat and the basics of the arts and sciences.

At night as the Sun went down, the beings dived back into the waters of the Persian Gulf. A total of seven of these creatures appeared over a period of seven reigns of Chaldean kings, from Abydenus to Euedoreschus. The entities were named as Oannes, Annedotus, Eudocus, Eneugamus, Enenboulos, Anementus and Odacon.

Let us look more closely at Berossus' description of these strange beings. Could their resemblance to fish have been inspired by the material of metallic space suits resembling silvery scales? The concept of them having two heads, one beneath the other, might suggest that one "head" may have been inside the other – as in the image of an astronaut wearing a pressurized helmet. The "fish's tail" could have been part of their breathing apparatus or life-support pack. The creatures appeared to live in the Persian Gulf. It may be significant that, in Sumerian tradition, it was shortly after the appearance of the last of the Akpallus that a Great Flood occurred – during the reign of King Xisuthros. Also, it may be remembered that Abram was told by Yahweh to leave Ur of the Chaldees before he could take up his mission of leading the Israelites.

It is possible that these "sea" creatures were representatives of the Powers of Darkness – the opponents of Yahweh and his minions. After trying to pervert and corrupt men, or to enlist them, they discovered that Yahweh was on his way to Earth. The Akpallus decided to destroy the Earth by flood – but Yahweh intervened and selected individuals like Utnapishtim, of the Gilgamesh Flood epic, Xisuthros, King of Ur, and Noah of the generations of Adam, managed to escape. The Akpallus were driven from the Earth. This scenario also provides an alternative possibility that Sodom was destroyed by Yahweh – as a reprisal against the Powers of Darkness.

Certainly the Babylonians appeared to have been aware of the evil purpose of the fish-like beasts that came out of the skies and splashed down in the Persian Gulf. An ancient Babylonian incantation says:

"Seven are they, seven are they. In the Ocean Deep, seven are they. They are reared in their home the Ocean Deep. neither male nor female are they. They are as the roaming wildblast. No wife have they, no son do they beget. They know neither mercy nor pity. They harken not unto prayers and supplications. They are the horses reared on the hills. The Evil Ones of Ea, throne bearers of the gods are they. They stand in the highway to befoul the path. Evil are they, evil are they. By Heaven be ye exorcised!"

The evidence of the Power of Darkness is acknowledged by Yahweh quite early in the Old Testament, in a begrudging sort of way. His insistence that he was the one and only God, for instance, implies some concern that the Hebrews might discover he had some real opposition. If the other "gods" were false and imaginary, He had nothing to worry about. "The LORD thy God is a jealous God," he admits. Jealous of what? Jealousy is an objective emotion. "Thou shalt have no other gods but me," he commands. If he is the one and only God there is little choice. His infallibility and omniscience is called into question by his own inferences. Surely, if he is a supreme being, his supremacy should be absolute, unchallengeable? But no – it is clearly very open to challenge, as he guardedly indicates.

Why, we may wonder, was Moses so angry when he descended from the mountain with the stone Commandment tablets, to find the Children of Israel worshipping the Golden Calf? If it represented merely an imaginary, non-existent power, it was harmless. But it did not. It represented Baal, a "pagan" bull god, and the calf or bull, like the serpent or dragon (Bel, the god of Babylon), was simply another symbol of the Power of Darkness. The winged bull, for example, turns up in Assyrian symbolic imagery, in Babylonian, Egyptian, Greek and Cretan tradition and eventually seems to have evolved into the Horned God of the followers of witchcraft: the Goat of Mendes. The Golden Calf constituted a symbol representing the alternate power of the Universe: Darkness.

"I have seen the Superman. He is here amongst us now!" screamed Hitler, centuries later. "He is intrepid and cruel." He had indeed apparently seen a frightening, unearthly power. The challenger had once again manifested upon the Earth, and was an inspiration to the evil-motivated purposes of the Führer. Yet the Power was thwarted. The balance was maintained.

Somewhere, then, out in the broad reaches of infinite space, there exist two branches of cosmic intelligence, one of Light, and one of Darkness. They are the forces that, together, brought about the very drive and essence of the physical Universe. One, a Supreme Mathematician and Architect, seeks to establish an ordered, stable Universe. The other, an ultimately Negative Force, a Lord of Chaos, seeks to unbalance and destroy it. Without the other, neither can exist; the result is the duality of both humanity and the Universe.

In their service, these two forces have hordes of materialised intelligences, semi-humanoid, not unlike human beings, but evidently far, far superior. Almost certainly, although creatures of an evolutionary process they, like the Powers they serve, have attained a form of immortality.

They probably inhabit planets like human beings, but are vastly advanced and can span the light years separating the countless galaxies and solar systems in their space vehicles. These beings from both warring camps have visited Earth as emissaries of the two Powers, and have brought the influences of the eternal cosmic struggle with them. They doubtless also visit the countless other inhabited planets of the Universe, wielding similar influence, so it is difficult to gauge the significance, if any, of mankind in the boundless pattern of these cosmic operations. We might, looking at the unimaginably huge canvas of our Universe, be quite insignificant. Yet at various stages in humanity's evolution, we have quite definitely been the object of the observations of these extra-terrestrial beings.

They came in various cycles and waves and in many different craft, as can be seen by the variant descriptions throughout history and in the less explicable cases of UFO sightings. The ancient Indo-Aryan races saw them engaged in battle in the skies, their celestial cars using fearful nuclear weapons. The Egyptians saw their golden fiery discs streaking through the heavens. The Israelites saw their spaceships belching smoke and flame, touching down in mountainous regions, met the men-like occupants and witnessed their mighty powers. The Babylonians saw the fish-like, diving-suited creatures that came out of the Gulf; creatures that perhaps gave rise to the myths of trident-wielding sea-gods such as Poseidon and Neptune and later the Horned Beasts that represent the Devil.

The influence of the Powers of Light remains in the essence of all the major, root-religions that display reasoned, humanitarian and generally beneficent traits. The influence of the Powers of Darkness remain in Satanic practices, Demonology, Goetia, Black Magic, some forms of witchcraft and all the associated cults and sects that promote malevolence, disorder, destruction, cruelty, unreason, madness and evil.

The cosmic battle goes on today and, while the influence of these forces can be felt in the fluctuations of good and evil that pervade life on our planet, these emissaries of Light and Darkness themselves are not overtly physically evident. There are signs, however, that we have been and perhaps still are, under surveillance. It may be significant that, as has been observed by others, an upsurge in the reappearance of discoid and other shaped objects in our skies coincided with the ushering in of the atomic era. And we may have been watched ever since. So far, man has only succeeded in reaching the Moon, while unmanned probes penetrate further and further beyond the outer reaches of our solar system.

When they consider the time propitious from their own point of view, the celestial beings will doubtless return. But the questions facing us all are: when and for what purpose? Will they be the Powers of Light – or Darkness?

24. The Master Plan Revealed?

"Characters of the great Apocalypse,
The types and symbols of Eternity,
Of first, and last, and midst, and without end."
William Wordsworth (1770–1850)

"There are flashes throughout the first part of the Apocalypse of true cosmic worship.
The cosmos became anathema to the Christians, though the early Catholic Church
restored it somewhat after the crash of the Dark Ages. Then again the cosmos
became anathema to the Protestants after the Reformation. They substituted the
non-vital universe of forces and mechanistic order, everything else became abstraction,
and the long, slow death of the human being set in. This slow death produced
science and machinery, but both are death products."
D.H. Lawrence (1885–1930)

AS SCIENCE HAS only in relatively recent times begun to discern some pattern in the cosmos – signs of a pre-determined, intelligent programming – it is almost impossible at this stage to make any positive projections of this apparent purpose on the vast, panoramic screen of time and space: past, present and future. But as we have seen, there have been human beings who somehow pierced the veil, if only momentarily, to gain a glimpse of the secrets of the Universe. Through intuition, visions, magic, meditation and other paranormal channels, we have so far seen fragments and inklings of cosmic laws and intention.

But one source that I have not yet examined is perhaps the most important of all because it does appear to give an idea of the celestial Master Plan, once stripped of all its intensively religious associations, its peculiar symbolism and its incredibly frustrating and complex structure. That source is the last book of the Christian Bible – the Revelation of St. John the Divine. For – all orthodox religious associations aside – it is my contention that the author of this book was perhaps given the deepest insight ever into the great unknown. As a result, he provided an account of his experience that has baffled many millions ever since. I believe – and I hope to show why – this man was selected by an extra-terrestrial agency to give to mankind a brilliant insight into cosmic purpose; the last of the Biblical writers to have direct contact with celestial intelligences.

I would suggest that, because of his nature, experience, character and particular leanings, some of his account is distorted – not deliberately or maliciously – and it is because of this that to date no-one has been able definitively to unravel the complicated tangle of his text satisfactorily. There have been countless interpretations of Revelation, but because of their failure to accommodate all those who approach them to their satisfaction, commentaries continue to be written, arguments and discussions continue to be stimulated by its enigmatic style and content.

My own interpretation given here followed a considerable amount of study and consideration. I hope that it may raise the veil a little more. As I have pointed out already, when touching upon other controversial areas of religious thought and belief, I have no desire to undermine or shatter, to mock or insult any person's religious convictions. I am merely concerned with trying to make some sort of sense – and, if possible, truth – out of the vast accumulation of knowledge available that has so far defied any satisfactory explanation.

If my interpretation is considered flawed or incorrect, I will merely have followed in the footsteps of many more learned than myself. It is, in fact, in the same insatiable spirit as the child's eternal "why?" that I have made these excursions into history, literature, religion, science, philosophy and metaphysics. And a child does not give up asking "why?" until he is answered satisfactorily... if ever.

Let those who are without courage or curiosity put down this book now. The remainder, I know, will follow in the same spirit of wonder with which I began these speculative and investigative writings.

It has been suggested by many scholars and students of mysticism that the Revelation or Apocalypse – from the Greek *apokalypsis*, meaning the unveiling or uncovering – represents one of the most impressive, yet abstruse systems of prophecy available. Like the Tarot and the Chinese Book of Changes, the *I Ching*, it is a mysterious and complex work, framed in a completely different set of references to these other two. Perhaps the key word in its assessment is system – a factor that has often been ignored in attempts at its interpretation. Scholars have tried to apply the pattern of the book to past history, such as the association of its ten-horned, seven-headed beast to a series of Roman Emperors, with Nero as the Great Beast whose number is given as 666. Others have seen the seven letters to the seven churches of Asia Minor as representing historical periods – Ephesus as the first century, Smyrna the period of Christian persecution, Pergamos the age of the Emperor Constantine, Thyatira the Middle Ages, and so on.

Yet others have applied the book's complex and bizarre symbolism of fantastical beasts, plagues, trumpets, swords, seals and bowls of wrath to our present time and the immediate future. Indeed, one of the inherent characteristics of Apocalypse interpreters seems to be that they invariably attempt to centre it around their own time, looking both backward and forward from that point.

A third school sees the book as a projection of "future history", outlining the End of the World and the Last Judgement.

A fourth suggests that Revelation is a symbolic picture of all time – past, present and future – from the Creation to Armageddon.

There are even those who believe Revelation has no significance whatsoever in our own scientific era.

The first four may each be valid in their own ways. For, as I have said, Revelation is a system of prophecy and as one would expect of any system, should be applicable in part to any period or set of circumstances of the past, present or future with reasonable effectiveness. Alternatively it should, as a whole, be applicable to all three simultaneously. In other words, like a mathematical formula, it would remain valid and useful for as long as the laws that shape the cosmos apply. In fact, John's book can be applied in this way. Thus the "Babylon" that crops up in the text can be seen as a reference to the corrupt and decadent city of the Old Testament Babylon, to the equally corrupt and decadent Egypt of Moses' time, the Rome of John's own era or to any modern city or nation whose main motivation is greed and where the true qualities of life have been sacrificed in favour of more temporal, hedonistic pursuits and pleasures.

But before examining the book's message, let us look at the man who wrote it and the way in which it is thought to have been conceived.

While some scholars have subscribed to the view that the writer of Revelation was the same as the Apostle John, son of Zebedee, to whom the Fourth Gospel and three epistles are accredited, there is no absolute evidence for this. These are largely matters of linguistics and style, however, and do not concern us here. All that is really known is that Revelation was written by someone who called himself John, a Jewish Christian, on the island of Patmos, off the coast of Asia Minor (Turkey), possibly in exile, some time between 54 and 95AD.

In his opening, John states that Revelation was given to him by God through an angel and the book begins with a series of letters to seven churches on the mainland: at Ephesus, Smyrna, Pergamos, Thyatira, Sardis, Philadelphia and Laodicea, all of which existed. Each letter summarises the moral and spiritual state of each individual church and hands out admonitions, warnings and advice for improvement. But then the book begins to present the greatest difficulty to those who attempt to interpret it. Thousands have given up – but I believe there is great truth and wisdom in it.

Traditionally it represents a series of "visions" that come in seven pairs, the first of each pair apparently being a vision of "heaven", the second being relevant to events on Earth.

Whether John had his "heavenly" experiences all at one time, followed by his collective visions of Earth, and then arranged them in pairs as a form of literary style, is always a great stumbling block to those to try to dissect the book. But I suggest that in fact they probably occurred in the order given for a specific reason: because John was singled out by an unearthly intelligence and may have had access to what occultists call the Akashic Record. As I have mentioned previously, this is envisioned as a vast, cineramic account of all time – past, present and future – that mystics, such as Tibetan Buddhists, have claimed they could consult on the "astral" plane.

The name Akashic derives from a Sanskrit word, akasa, meaning sky, but also indicating the imponderable and intangible "life spirit". In Syria, Palestine, India and Greece, this became known as As, pronounced "Ah", and came to mean life. The ancient Hebrew tribes knew it as Iah or Ya and it meant breath, the wind, or air in motion. Thus it is that the God of the Old Testament is described as the spirit moving on the face of the waters and tells Moses that his name is Yahweh, a double aspirant, denoting the breath of life. The "breath" is indicated by the Hebraic spelling without vowels, YHVH. This came to be translated as "I Am that I Am", or Being. Although a more accurate rendition would seem to be: "I am that which is becoming", as I have already pointed out.

The Akashic Record then, is the eternal record of the "life-spirit" that pervades the Universe. And it was an experience of this which John was granted.

With these considerations in mind, let us now look at the evidence for celestial intervention. At the outset of his strange experiences, after he has been instructed by the "angel" to take down the seven letters in a book, John's descriptions begin to bear a striking resemblance to those of Ezekiel when he saw the extra-terrestrial vessel. In fact, some of John's phrases are almost identical. When, for example, Ezekiel is apparently taken for a flight in the spinning top-shaped vehicle, he says, "the spirit took me up", obviously being unable to find words to describe the experience in any other way. He would obviously not, for instance, like a modern airline passenger who is familiar with the concept, say that he himself was "flying" for fear of being misunderstood. Besides, not knowing anything about aircraft or engines, his words make it clear that he felt that same "spirit" was the power source of the strange vessel that he saw. "Whithersoever the spirit was to go, they went, thither was their spirit to go; and the wheels were lifted up over against them; for the spirit of the living creature was in the wheels," Ezekiel says.

Also, it may be remembered he talks of a throne (the pilot or commander's seat) above the vessel, over which was what looked like a "rainbow" (probably a transparent bubble over the control room) under which sat a manlike being, with some kind of brilliant aura about him; reflections off the transparent canopy, perhaps.

Here is what John says, at the beginning of his "heavenly" experience:

"After this I looked, and, behold, a door was opened in heaven [Ezekiel called it a whirlwind]; and the first voice which I heard was as it were of a trumpet talking with me, which said, Come up hither, and I will shew thee things which must be hereafter." (Revelation 4:1)

The carefully-phrased reference to a trumpet would appear to indicate simply that the voice was loud, shrill, possibly metallic, like an intercom or a loud-hailer.

"And immediately I was in the spirit; and, behold, a throne was set in heaven, and one sat on the throne.

"And he that sat was to look upon like a jasper and a sardine stone [shiny, metallic clothing]: and there was a rainbow round about the throne, in sight like unto an emerald [transparent, plexi-glass dome or canopy]."

Now either John was guilty of cribbing from Ezekiel or he shared a very similar experience. But whereas Ezekiel actually described the craft that picked him up, John somehow is one minute on the ground, the next in a strange place which he assumes to be heaven on account of its totally unfamiliar, necessarily daunting and awesome, alien nature. In fact, today it sounds as though he is aboard some vast ship in orbit around the Earth; a place that makes him, being of a religious and mystical nature, naturally think he is in "heaven".

Whatever it was that John saw, it was much bigger and elaborate than Ezekiel's "shuttlecraft" orbit-to-surface vessel:

"And round about the throne were four and twenty seats: and upon the seats I saw four and twenty elders sitting, clothed in white raiment; and they had on their heads crowns of gold.

"And out of the throne proceeded lightnings and thunderings and voices; and there were seven lamps of fire burning before the throne, which are the seven Spirits of God.

"And before the throne there was a sea of glass like unto crystal: and in the midst of the throne, and round about the throne were four beasts full of eyes before and behind.

"And the first beast was like a lion and the second beast like a calf and the third beast had a face as a man and the fourth beast was like a flying eagle.

"And the four beasts had each of them six wings about him; and they were full of eyes within: and they rest not day and night, saying, Holy, holy, holy, Lord God Almighty, which was, and is, and is to come." (Revelation 4:4–8)

Try to bear in mind while considering these passages that here is a man with a deep-seated Hebrew heritage, yet a strongly committed convert to the comparatively recent sect of Christianity. He is in exile on a rocky island when he is suddenly whisked away by some strange power to a place that to him defies normal description. Yet he tries. And in trying, quite naturally perhaps, he tinges the experience with all his religious awe, fervour and self-projected religious symbolism.

Take away the awe, fear and projected symbolism of the experience and you have a description of the circular control room or command deck of a gigantic spacecraft, an amazing vessel, curiously enough not unlike the Starship *Enterprise* in the American cult TV series *Star Trek*, or even perhaps the colossal, dazzling mother ship in Steven Spielberg's *Close Encounters Of The Third Kind*.

Around the commander's seat (throne) are 24 of the ship's crew and technicians (elders) in their white space coveralls (raiments), with some kind of apparatus – possibly communications devices (crowns of gold) – on their heads. Before the "throne" is a large control panel festooned with dials, lights, intercom speakers, flashing monitor screens, computer banks and other equipment, the like of which John has never seen. From this dazzling array of apparatus, flashing lights are seen, beeps, rumbles and other strange electronic noises are heard that to John are incomprehensible. Occasionally, a human-sounding voice barks out information. John cannot make any sense of it at all – until, that is, he projects his own religious ideas and interprets them as "lightnings and thunderings and voices" and "seven lamps of fire".

The "sea of glass like unto crystal" could well be a giant, master monitor screen. Again, perhaps not unlike the one aboard the *Enterprise*. And while making this comparison, why not suppose, in view of the sudden and, to John, inexplicable way that he was transported to this place, that he was "beamed up" by some kind of matter disintegrator-reintegrator apparatus?

Around the command deck are structures housing various banks of electronic equipment, bristling with flashing lights and dials. Perhaps John was aboard some orbital mother-ship, watching the departure and docking of various shuttle-craft. His description of living "beasts, full of eyes, before and behind", with characteristics that remind him of a lion, a calf, a man and an eagle, are reminiscent of Ezekiel's account of the vessel which he saw. [All of these images, incidentally, have a particular importance in Hebraic symbolism, especially in Qabbalistic philosophy and the lion, calf, man and eagle were also used later in Christian symbolism as emblems of the four gospellers, Matthew, Mark, Luke and John. In view of the great stress placed upon the significance of specific numbers that recur throughout Revelation – a feature of Qabbalistic numerology – it is almost certain that John was a student of the Qabbalah himself.]

But what of his phrase "they rest not day and night, saying, Holy, holy, holy..." etc? Again, it is a matter of projection, of an attempt at rationalisation of something ineffable. As the shuttlecraft ply to and fro, docking and leaving the orbiting mother ship, he hears the rumbles, beeps, bellows, whirs and clicks as the crafts' numerous systems tick over and interact with the command vessel's own systems. And, assuming the figure at the controls (throne) to be God, John supposes that the four "beasts" are paying continuous obeisance.

If we are to accept the idea of a Cosmic Intelligence that is omniscient, it is surely not too much to suggest that He/She/It would scarcely spend time sitting surrounded by 24 kowtowing elders and four peculiar, anthropomorphic beasts, continuously singing praises. That would not be omniscience, but acute megalomania.

Yet according to John, the "elders" do kowtow:

"The four and twenty elders fall down before him that sat on the throne and worship him that liveth for ever and ever, and cast their crowns before the throne, saying:

"Thou art worthy, O Lord, to receive glory and honour and power: for thou hast

---

created all things, and for thy pleasure they are and were created." (Revelation 4: 10–11)

It seems apparent that this is simply John's own idea of what he thought was taking place. The various crew members and shuttlecraft pilots might well have been required to report to their commander. Amid all the "thunderings" and various repetitive noises of the "beasts", it is difficult to imagine how John could have actually heard what was happening as they approached the command deck. If they were humanoid, as is indicated, perhaps it was necessary for them to remove their headgear in the area which, to John, made it seem as if they were taking off their "crowns" in respect. As to John's actual phrasing of what he thought they were saying, once again it is very difficult to conceive of a more bored Deity than one who is constantly being reminded of what He/She/It must already know. The words John ascribes to the "elders" seem more likely to be designed to impress the readers of his account that he was indeed in the presence of the Almighty.

From this point on, although John's account flits back and forth between Earth and "heaven", the remainder of the book consists of the symbols and signs he was shown that form the framework of his description of his glimpse of the Akashic Record. Here is the form that this "unveiling" takes:

He is first shown a "book, written within and on the backside, sealed with seven seals". There is some difficulty implied about the opening of these seals and the reading of the "book". John describes it like this:

"And I saw a strong angel proclaiming with a loud voice, Who is worthy to open the book, and to loose the seals thereof?

"And no man in heaven, nor in earth, neither under the earth, was able to open the book, neither to look therein.

"And I wept much, because no man was found worthy to open and to read the book, neither to look thereon." (Revelation 5:2–4)

This passage poses a lot of difficulty in theological interpretations. But let us look more closely at the circumstances. John is shown the "book" with seven seals and it is indicated to him that what it contains is most important – otherwise, if he did not realise this, he would hardly be driven to weeping at the thought of the information not being revealed. In his times, it was customary for "books" to be in the form of rolls of paper or hide, written on one side only. Papyrus scrolls were made from reeds placed side by side in a sheet and reinforced by a backing sheet of more reeds at right angles to the first. Obviously, it was easier to write on only one side – on the reeds that ran horizontally across the scroll. Besides, it would also be easier to read a scroll written on one side only. But the book in John's account was different. It was written on both sides. What can this mean?

Think of a roll of film. Film is kept in metal canisters. It would, to a person not acquainted with it, but to whom a scroll was familiar, appear to be "written" on both sides and "sealed" within its canister. It seems the reason John makes such an emotional display of his "book" is to emphasize that, even when the "film" inside was visible, no man would have been capable of interpreting it. (All of the above conditions, incidentally, could more or less be applied to a cartridge or cassette of videotape.) In any event, John is told by one of the "elders" not to despair, because, "behold, the Lion of the tribe of Juda, the Root of David, hath prevailed to open the book, and to loose the seven seals thereof."

He is then shown "a Lamb, as it had been slain, having seven horns and seven eyes, which are the seven Spirits of God sent forth into all the earth.

"And he came and took the book out of the right hand of him that sat upon the throne." (Revelation 5:6–7).

This appears to be John's way of explaining that he was told how Jesus (the Lamb, the Lion of Judah, etc) had been aware of the contents of the book (i.e. the secrets of the cosmic pattern) and was able to comprehend it, so he himself should not despair of ever being unable to understand. Obviously if, as John at first assumed, "no man was found worthy to open and to read the book" that would include himself. And yet he was allowed to see and write about what it contained.

So the first seal is broken: i.e., the first canister is opened and the first roll of film or video recording is put to use. It is not essential, of course, that this be regarded as conventional film; it could be some highly advanced method of storing recorded information that we are as yet unaware of. Since John does not mention being connected up with any piece of equipment – having a "crown" placed upon his head, as he might have put it – it may be reasonable to assume that either he was watching a film on a monitor screen throughout his time aboard the giant spacecraft, or the information was fed to him subliminally, in some advanced form of virtual reality apparatus.

The whole of what follows in John's narrative constitutes the system of prophecy. The key to this entire system is that John, as apparently was Jesus, was made aware of the cyclic nature of the Universe: eternal creation, destruction and recreation, with the patterns of events between each phase. Which is probably why Revelation appears – both philosophically and poetically – such a brilliantly conceived piece of work. It rounds off the canonical Bible perfectly. As the Old Testament begins with Creation, the emergence and "Fall" of mankind, so Revelation deals with Destruction, the End of the World... and the New Creation. As the Old Testament outlines the beginnings of humanity from clay print-outs, so Revelation deals with its ultimate destiny.

Sandwiched between the seven letters to the seven churches, the description of the giant spacecraft and the opening of the first seal, all of which form the first section of Revelation, and the blessing with which it ends, are symbolic affirmations of the cyclic, recurrent nature of the Universe that is reflected on Earth and in mankind. This is why it is possible, quite legitimately, to take sections of the Apocalypse and apply them to particular periods of the past, or even the present and future.

It should be emphasised once again, however, that woven into this prophetic system, magnificent as it is, are strong religious colourings and convictions of a man living at a time when such considerations were paramount in all aspects of his life. He was a Hebrew (a persecuted race) who had been converted to Christianity (a persecuted faith) and all the moral judgements that are set forth in the book reflect aspects of the oppressors he knows, has known and expects will be evident in the future. In fact, Revelation can be seen, as well as a prophetic book, to be an attempt to justify the "marriage" of the Hebrew traditions with the then new ideals of Christianity. The fact that the number seven plays such a prominent role – it crops up a total of 54 times throughout the book – is most significant.

For instance, the angel that brings word to John is accompanied by seven candlesticks that correspond not only to the seven churches to which he is instructed to write, but also to the seven lamps of the tabernacle built by Moses. In Moses' case, the seven lamps were all part of one lamp – the prototype of the Jewish menorah, or seven-branched candelabrum – symbolising the unity of the seven tribes of Israel at that time under his leadership. (During *Hanukkah* [Festival of Lights], Jews all over the world celebrate the re-dedication of the Temple by the lighting of an eight-branched menorah. A legend surrounding this says that the Maccabees had only enough oil to light the Temple menorah for one night, but that, miraculously, it burned for eight. Some menorahs have a ninth pilot light, called the *shammes*, or "servant".) In John's vision they are separate, standing lamps, suggesting that there is too much division and dissent and hinting that the various churches of God should be reunited under Christ.

It would be impossible here to tabulate the many hundreds, or even thousands, of possible correspondences that can be seen in a thorough study of Revelation, but a few will suffice to give an idea of how the book may be used as a "blueprint" for life on Earth. Let us, for example, look at the opening of the first four seals. As this is done, John is shown the images of the legendary Four Horsemen of the Apocalypse:

War: a rider on a white horse, wielding a bow. *Pestilence*: a rider on a red horse, carrying a sword. *Famine*: a rider on a black horse, holding a pair of scales. *Death*: a rider whose very name is Death; he has a sickly pale horse and is empowered to kill through the methods of the first three.

It is easy to associate these images with any chosen period in time in which there are wars, famines, plagues and a great many resultant deaths. It could as easily be applied to our own times by use of the following scenario:

War: already experienced in the great world conflicts, continuing in regionalised form in various parts of the Earth, and heightened in potential by the advent of the nuclear age. Famine: again, already in evidence among underprivileged Third World countries, but which could escalate to worldwide proportions through ecological disaster. Pestilence: the diseases that accompany famine or that would undoubtedly follow nuclear holocaust in the form of blight and radiation sickness, etc. Death: the ultimate plight of humanity, the end of the world and, to the religious, the judgement of men by God.

The opening of the fifth and sixth seals reveals further imagery, part moralistic and part anticipatory. The fifth, for example, describes the "souls" of those that had been slaughtered "for the word of God" – martyrs, in other words – crying out, asking when they will be vindicated. They are given white robes to wear and told to wait. Is this not the typical attitude of mankind to those who die for various "worthy" causes? Beatification, canonisation, or other posthumous glorification... and yet the ways of humanity, invidious behaviour towards one's fellow humans, do not change. Martyrs must wait.

The sixth seal anticipates a "pulsation" of the Universe, which to John appears as if "the stars of heaven fell unto the earth" and "the heaven departed as a scroll when it is rolled together". What more vivid imagery could be expected from a non-scientist of John's time, describing the collapse of the Universe? To someone on Earth, it might well appear that all the stars were falling and the heavens had been whisked away.

Before the opening of the seventh seal, there is an interlude and what appears to be a slip in chronology. Like a film, John's "visions" slip backwards and forwards in time and up and down between "heaven" and Earth. The "servants" of God upon Earth – that is, the 144,000 members of the 12 tribes of Israel – are marked with a "seal" upon their foreheads. This is a suggestion that they will not be punished in the planned Judgement of God.

This could be seen as an encouragement to the Jews; the "carrot" dangled before them of ultimate salvation – if they take notice of John's admonitory writings and in so doing, accept his word that Christ was the Messiah. Similarly, John sees a "vast throng", a countless mob of people from all nations of the Earth. John says they are standing "before the throne", but they are probably on a panoramic monitor, since at this point he obvious considers himself still in "heaven". Robed in white and waving palms, they shout:

"Salvation to our God which sitteth upon the throne and unto the Lamb."

This is probably another example of wishful thinking on the part of John, projecting the idea of an ultimate unification of all the peoples of the Earth through their acceptance of God. In fact, he is told that they have "washed their robes, and made them white in the blood of the Lamb". A clear piece of proselytising: come over to the Christian view while still accepting the Hebrew God and you could be among those who are "saved" at the Last Judgement.

After the opening of the seventh seal, there is for some reason a delay. John tells us that "there was silence in heaven about the space of half an hour". This poses a great deal of difficulty in analysis. The usual interpretation is that there is a great calm before the cataclysmic violence that erupts in the destruction of the Earth. In fact, there may be a technical reason why John cannot be shown or "fed" more information immediately. Perhaps it is to allow his conscious mind to assimilate the vivid volume of imagery he has so far witnessed on the Akashic Record: a brief period in which to collect his thoughts.

In fact, the opening of the seventh seal ultimately triggers off yet another series of dazzling events, decked with strange, surrealist imagery. First comes a relay of seven trumpets in a sequence, like the opening of the seals themselves. Those events that follow are apparently the particulars – "close-ups" or "image enhancements", if you like – of the ways in which mankind will be afflicted as the End approaches. With the first trumpet, the Earth is bombarded with hail and fire mingled with blood and one-third of the planet is burnt. The second trumpet turns a third of the seas into what seems like blood, a third of its organic life is wiped out and a third of the ships in the corresponding sectors are destroyed. On the third trumpet, a "star" falls to Earth and poisons a third of the inland waterways – rivers and springs. Here, it should be noted that "star" and "son of man" are used as alternatives to the term "angel". The fourth trumpet signals the blotting out of one-third of the light of the Sun and Moon. The fifth opens an abyss in the Earth and out of it come giant locusts – strange beasts with human faces, women's hair, golden crowns, lions' teeth, iron breastplates, stings like scorpions and their wings making the thunderous sound of horses and chariots. Even those who try to escape these creatures by committing suicide are somehow prevented. At the sixth trumpet four avenging angels are released at the head of two million cavalry. They have colourful, fiery breastplates, horses with heads like lions, belching fire and smoke and stinging with their tails. Their job is to kill a third of mankind by plagues. Still, John claims, the rest of humanity refused at this onslaught to give up their home-made gods, devils and idols of gold, silver, brass, stone and wood "which neither can see, nor hear, nor talk." Again there is an interlude before the sounding of the seventh trumpet, which indicates that these passages are indeed fragments of the overall cycle of seven. During this time John is given a scroll by an angel who stands upon "the sea and upon the earth" and told to eat it. It will, he is assured, taste sweet to his mouth but will be bitter to his stomach. It does and it is. This can be taken as a moral that the fruits of materialism are not really worthwhile, but a bitter, synthetic pill.

Next, John is given a measuring rod and told to measure God's Temple and to count the number of worshippers. He is, however, told to ignore the outer court, as the Gentiles have possession of it and will trample the Holy City underfoot for 42 months. Also, he is told, two "witnesses" symbolised by two olive trees and two lamps, will prophesy for 1260 days and have the power to inflict plagues and turn water into blood. Eventually, however, they will be defeated by the Beast from the abyss.

The sounding of the seventh trumpet signals that God has once more gained control of the world.

Now if all the foregoing symbolism is examined in detail, it will be seen that it constitutes an outline of the great battle of Light and Darkness as it affects the Earth. As Darkness gains control, the evil forces inherent in man destroy a third of the Earth, waging wars, polluting the oceans, destroying plant and animal life, decimating the human race with famine and disease. The measuring of the Temple and the counting of its worshippers indicates that there is still some doubt among the surviving sector of humanity as to the reason for the devastation. In other words, man has still not discerned the forces shaping his destiny, and made up his mind to resist the power of Darkness. Even then, prophets are ignored and cast down by the Great Beast of the abyss.

After the victory of Light on the Earth, war next breaks out in "heaven" between the hordes of the great red dragon (Darkness) with seven heads and ten horns, and the angelic forces of the archangel Michael (Light). The Forces of Darkness cannot prevail in realms of Light and the dragon and his minions are cast down to Earth again. There, Darkness fails to overcome the Jewish converts to Christianity – symbolised as a woman robed with the Sun (the Light of God) and about to give birth (Christianity). But out of the sea rises another Beast, with ten horns and seven heads. This is a different creature from the dragon and it has the appearance of a leopard, but with the feet of a bear and the mouth of a lion. For 42 months it is given power by the dragon over every nation on Earth and all except those whose names are on the "roll of the living" worship the Beast.

One of the Beast's heads, John says, appears to have been mortally wounded, yet manages to heal.

Now the imagery begins to get even more complicated. Yet another Beast, this time with two horns "like a lamb" but which speaks like a dragon, appears. This creature encourages the worship of the leopard-bear-lion Beast. Then John gives a "clue" in Chapter 13, verse 18:

"Here is wisdom. Let him that hath understanding count the number of the beast; for it is the number of a man; and his number is Six hundred threescore and six."

The leopard-bear-lion then, is the Great Beast 666. The lamb-dragon creature causes everyone to be branded with the mark of the Beast on the forehead and the hand. No one can buy or sell anything unless they have the mark of the Beast.

The symbolism of this segment of the Apocalypse is particularly interesting when trying to apply its message to our own times and future. The powerful Beast 666, given unlimited power but for a limited period of 42 months by the Dragon, could be seen as the powers of the Euro-Asian bloc; the leopard as the emergent African nations, the bear as Russia, and the Lion as Britain. If the red dragon is seen as China, the implications are awesome. What will happen when the dragon takes back the power from the Beast? The creature with horns like a lamb, but which speaks like a dragon, is identified later as the False Prophet. Under the guise of the symbol of Christ – a lamb – this false witness persuades people to fall under the influence of the Great Beast 666. It will be interesting, to say the least, to see who is the mediator if any such alliance comes about between Africa, Russia (and Europe/Britain?) in the future.

The reference to the Beast's head that appears mortally wounded but which lives has been applied by interpreters to many figures and events in history: to the Emperor Nero who, even after his suicide, was expected to return again; more recently to Germany which, seeming to suffer defeat in the First World War, rose again to become an even greater threat only 20 years later.

But let us continue with John's account. Next, upon Mount Zion, appears the Lamb (Christ), with the 144,000 who have been marked with the seal of God. Angels make various announcements, urging the worship of God and warning those who are branded with the mark of the Beast. There follows some allegorical description of an angel gathering the world's grape-harvest, and the grapes being thrown into the "great winepress of the wrath of God" from which blood flows, as deep as a horse's bridle for 200 miles. It is a preliminary to the End that is coming; a symbol of the great bloodbath that man has brought upon himself.

Seven angels bring seven last plagues as the final hours of mankind are enacted before John's eyes. The first is a plague of sores for those who worshipped the Beast. The second turns the sea to dead blood and everything in it dies. Likewise, the third turns rivers and springs to blood. An angel comments that it is fitting that man, who has caused so much bloodshed, should now only have blood to drink. The fourth plague causes the Sun to burn men fearfully (the depleted ozone layer?), yet still they do not repent and instead curse God. the fifth plague plunges the "kingdom" of the Beast – i.e. the Earth – into darkness. The sixth angel pours his bowl on the River Euphrates and "the water thereof was dried up, that the way of the kings of the east might be prepared". At this time "unclean spirits like frogs" – the spirits of devils working miracles – issue from the mouths of the dragon, the Beast and the False Prophet, a final mustering of the forces of Darkness for the battle of Armageddon. The seventh angel pours his bowl in the air and a voice out of "heaven" says: "It is done."

Next, John is shown a vision of the Judgement of the Great Whore, which gives more clues about the nature of the Great Beast. The Whore, "drunk" with the blood of those who had died in the name of God and Christ, is riding on the back of the Beast. An angel tells John:

"I will tell thee the mystery of the woman, and of the beast that carrieth her, which hath the seven heads and ten horns.

"The beast that thou sawest was, and is not; and shall ascend out of the bottomless pit, and go into perdition: and they that dwell on the earth shall wonder, whose names were not written in the book of life from the foundation of the world, when they behold the beast that was, and is not, and yet is.

"And here is the mind which hath wisdom. The seven heads are seven mountains upon which the woman sitteth.

"And there are seven kings: five are fallen, and one is, and the other is not yet come; and when he cometh he must continue a short space.

"And the beast that was, and is not, even he is the eighth, and is of the seven, and goeth into perdition.

"And ten horns which thou sawest are ten kings, which have received no kingdom as yet; but receive power as kings one hour with the beast." (Revelation 17:7–12)

Here is contained the strongest hint that the Great Beast may have been connected with the city of Rome; a city built upon seven hills, where Christians were persecuted. But the reference to the king who was "not yet come" and the ten kings who have

---

not received a kingdom but will gain power for one hour with the Beast, defies satisfactory explanation. Nero did not return, nor did any of the other Roman emperors who persecuted the Christians. The Great Beast has been associated with Popes, Napoleon, the Kaiser, Adolf Hitler and other world leaders. But the whole point of the allegory seems to be that, whether John intended a reference to Rome or not, the Great Beast represents a person on Earth who at any given time may be the driving force, the fount, the reservoir of energy for the Powers of Darkness. His number "is the number of a man". And so as the balance of influence alters throughout history, as Light and Darkness continue their struggle, particular figures become the focus of these powers, and indeed, Caligula, Nero, any number of Popes, Napoleon, the Kaiser, Hitler and any other world leaders might have been the Great Beasts of their day. The point behind the angel's advice to John is that man should be able to recognise these earthly instruments of evil as they rise to power. That would explain the reference to the Beast "that was, and is not, even he is" – the end of an era of evil tyranny does not mean that it cannot return again. It will – it is part of the Cosmic struggle. But it must be resisted, or the equilibrium of the Universe is at stake.

The fall of Babylon, which forms the next "revelation", is similarly an indication that any seemingly great state, nation or city that revels in its power and loses sight of the spiritual values of life, letting greed and materialism run away with it, will fall, not gradually, but suddenly as if "in a single hour" compared to the time it took to build such an empire. There is no shelter or security if life is based upon false values; if the gift of life is debased and abused and given over to mere synthetic "treasures".

Revelation warns that in the ultimate cosmic conflict to come the Babylonian ideal will be destroyed once and for all, never to be rebuilt.

"Thus with violence shall Babylon, the great city," says the angel, as he flings a huge stone into the sea, "be thrown down, and shall be found no more at all. And the voice of harpers, and musicians, and of pipers, and trumpeters, shall be heard no more at all in thee; and no craftsman, of whatsoever craft he be, shall be found any more in thee; and the sound of a millstone shall be heard no more at all in thee; And the light of a candle shall shine no more at all in thee; and the voice of the bridegroom and of the bride shall be heard no more at all in thee: for thy merchants were the great men of the earth; for by thy sorceries were all nations deceived." (Revelation 18:21–24)

Civilisation, as mankind has conceived it, does not work. It will be destroyed. This is not merely the cry of anarchy, however. It is a warning to mankind to reject its synthetic values, to see through the machinations of a world dominated by a system that is profitable only to a few. Those manipulators of wealth who have deceived all the rest of the people will be crushed, never to wield the power of their evil greed again.

Next in John's visions comes a rider on a white horse whose name is Faithful and True and also Word of God. The Power of Light begins to reassume the ascendancy, ruling on Earth, while casting the Beast and the False Prophet into a lake of brimstone and binding the Dragon for a thousand years in chains.

Revelation 20:3 says: "And cast him into the bottomless pit, and shut him up, and set a seal upon him, that he should deceive the nations no more, till the thousand years should be fulfilled: and after that he must be loosed a little season."

Those who died in the name of God and Christ are then revived and allowed to live and reign again for this 1,000-year period. But the rest of the dead will not be raised until the 1,000 years is up and "Satan shall be loosed".

Then the Lord judges the dead by their "works" or conduct during their lives. And those whose names were not "written in the book of life" are cast "into the lake of fire".

This section, with its binding of the Dragon for a limited period, is an affirmation that the Powers of Light cannot totally destroy the forces of Darkness. To do so would upset the first Law of the Universe. Martyrs who died in the cause of Light, meanwhile, are given special treatment, while the rest of humanity is judged to see if their lives are deemed worthy of the very name "life". Clearly, those who have lived only a shadow of what is called life, relying more upon false values and materialistic ideals, are not worth considering. The others, whose lives were meaningful and unselfish, are allowed a part in the New Creation.

"And I saw a new heaven and a new earth: for the first heaven and the first earth were passed away; and there was no more sea.

"And I John saw the holy city, new Jerusalem coming down from God out of heaven, prepared as a bride adorned for her husband.

"And I heard a great voice out of heaven saying, Behold, the tabernacle of God is with men and he will dwell with them, and they shall be his people and God himself shall be with them and be their God." (Revelation 21:1–3)

25. Countdown To Doomsday?

"Watch therefore: for ye know not what hour your Lord doth come."
Matthew 24:42.

"On a planetary level, we are faced with a scale, balanced on one side by the potential of nuclear annihilation, man's aggressiveness externalized and magnified by technology. On the other side of the scale is internal implosion, consisting of mankind's tapping the potential of the human mind and utilising it for the good (i.e., peace, justice, health, eradication of hunger and oppression on a worldwide basis."
Tom Pinkson, in *Gateway To Inner Space* (ed: Christian Ratsch, Arkana, 1983).

HAVING HAD what is perhaps a glimpse of the great cosmic design and purpose, the vital remaining question is, of course, when? When will all these prophecies that herald the imminent end of the world take place? The answer, as suggested in Jesus' words to Matthew, is an elusive matter. But there are some indications that we cannot afford to ignore; signs that it may be later than we think. For I feel compelled to remind the reader that, as I pointed out at the beginning of this work, it may be that humanity's hour will come a lot sooner than within the 80-billion-year cycle of the pulsations of the Universe. And there have been and still are, many movements that concentrate in particular on this problem. Whether or not they give a totally acceptable indication of things to come remains to be seen, but we shall do well at least to examine what they have had to say on the matter.

While among the more orthodox branches of the Church there is an increasing tendency towards a more spiritual interpretation of ideas such as the Second Coming of Christ and the Last Judgement, there are still those who adhere to a more literal expectation of the fulfilment of prophecies such as those contained in the book of Revelation and elsewhere.

The international organisation, the Jehovah's Witnesses, for example, expect the Second Advent to precede the Messiah's 1,000-year rule of peace on earth, at the millennium, that should begin in the year 2000.

Founded in 1870 by Charles Taze Russell, of Allegheny, Pittsburgh, the movement has in excess of two million members and is estimated to be growing at an average rate of about 10 percent per year. The Witnesses believe that soon, we will see the start of the apocalyptic Battle of Armageddon in which Christ, in a new incarnation, will lead the celestial Powers of Light to victory over the forces of Satan and Darkness. They anticipate that an anointed elect of their membership of 144,000 – those marked by the seal of God in Revelation – will rule with Christ, while the rest, known to Witnesses as Jonadabs, inherit eternal life on Earth. The purpose of the movement is to vindicate Jehovah as the true God. Jesus, they believe, was not God incarnate, but a man. Only in his purely spiritual resurrection did he become immortal. Immortality is what the annointed elect of 144,000 hope to attain.

Another powerful group that feels confident of its future salvation after the onset of Armageddon is that known as the Church of Jesus Christ of Latter-Day Saints, more popularly known as Mormons. They, too, feel that the Day of the Lord is imminent; that the political unrest, financial imbalance, strikes, wars and hunger that beset the world at present are indications that the hour is near. Indeed, in anticipation of pestilence and famine that will beleaguer the Earth before Christ's Second Advent, many Mormons have stocked up the basements or larders of their homes with sufficient food and water to last for a year or several years. And the church's vast mountain vaults where the names of more than 14 million Mormons past and present are stored in genealogies on something in excess of 175,000 rolls of microfilm near their mecca at Salt Lake City, Utah – the equivalent of Revelation's book of life, presumably – are seen as mass shelters where the privileged among the local citizen-faithful can take refuge from a possible nuclear holocaust.

Mormons believe that a lost tribe of Israelites fled to America in about 600BC but decimated each other in internecine wars, the only record of their existence being gold plates on which the prophet Mormon and his son Moroni engraved their history and buried them in New York State around the 2nd century AD. In 1823 Joseph Smith, the son of British immigrants, is said to have been shown the tablets in a vision by Moroni and managed to translate them.

"I had seen a light," Smith wrote, "and in the midst of that light I saw two personages, and they did in reality speak to me: and though I was hated and persecuted for saying that I had seen a vision, yet it was true; and while they were persecuting me, reviling me and speaking all manner of evil against me for so saying, I was led to say in my heart: why persecute me for telling the truth? I have actually seen a vision."

Smith and his followers were indeed persecuted, he himself being murdered by an angry mob at Carthage, Illinois, who were outraged at Smith's practise and advocation of polygamy. Fellow Mormons were attacked, their women assaulted and their homes burned to the ground.

The cause was taken up by Brigham Young in 1847. He was determined to ensure that Smith's promise to build a holy mountain city was fulfilled and led about 15,000 faithful followers to the Rocky Mountains where work began on the New Zion. Today the movement grows at an amazing pace, its magnificent temples springing up, its famous 275-voice Tabernacle Choir touring the world, its evangelist members spreading the word and its huge internal structure run like a giant business consortium. Millions more believers with their eye on the millennium.

Other, smaller groups – the Panacea Society, the Seventh Day Adventists, the Anabaptists, the Christadelphians – also look to the millennium for the triumphant return of Christ and the beginning of the end.

Whether we look at this phenomenon in a religious or secular light; whether the anticipated End of the World comes through natural, unnatural (i.e., man-made) or supernatural causes, it cannot be denied that there is at this time a remarkable, almost tangible feeling of expectancy, that the year 2000 will usher in something much more significant than a fresh century, a new number on the calendar, a fresh start to a new 1,000-year period. And whether the doctrines of the Jehovah's Witnesses, the Book of Mormon or any of the other religiously inclined millennarianist groups are accepted or not, there is something more than a purely religious drive behind all these anticipatory feelings, these presentiments of foreboding. Mankind's strange, imperfectly developed, yet highly significant intuitive powers are at work once more, as they have been spasmodically and isolatedly throughout the centuries. Now, however, there is almost a sense of common awareness – Jung's Collective

Unconscious at work, perhaps – about it. The kind of presentiments Jung wrote about when he examined the UFO phenomenon.

Since the beginnings of time, human beings have somehow sensed that this world is impermanent and yet has somehow happened before; that everything is part of a cycle; that the Universe has been created and destroyed more than once, and that humanity's chances of immortality are not a foregone conclusion. Thus, according to the Roman Stoical philosopher Seneca (4BC–65AD), the Babylonian historian Berossus expected that "the world will burn when all the planets which now move in different courses come together in the Crab, so that they all stand together in a straight line in the same sign".

In fact, at the time *The Zarkon Principle* was originally published, in 1975, such an alignment was expected seven years later, in 1982, when all the planets in our solar system lined up on the same side of the Sun, from the outermost, Pluto, to the innermost, Mercury. In 1974, the English astrophysicist and climatologist John Gribbin and an American astronomer Stephen Plagemann, produced a book, *The Jupiter Effect*, predicting that the result of this alignment would be an accumulative gravitational force that would cause enormous solar flares. These in turn might affect the Earth's rotation, causing communication disruptions, volcanic eruptions, freak meteorological effects and might even cause the long-anticipated earthquake along the Californian San Andreas Fault, bringing a major disaster to the US West Coast. Not doomsday, the authors said, but a considerable "shake-up".

Many detractors – including the English astronomer Patrick Moore – pointed out that such alignments had occurred in the past and nothing overtly catastrophic had ever been recorded at those times. As it turned out, 1982 went by relatively unmoved by global disturbances. But at least, someone had been playing watchdog, just in case...

In common with many ancient peoples, the Central American Aztecs believed in cycles of world ages in which flood, famine, hurricane, earthquakes and fire would bring about global cataclysm. Similarly, Buddhists and Hindus saw patterns in the world's evolution: four *Yugas* or ages, culminating in the Day of Brahma or *Kali Yuga*, when drought, famine and fire devastate the Earth, destroying all human life. These upheavals, prosaically envisaged as Breaths of Brahma, like the scientific theory of the Pulsating Universe, also expected that the cataclysm would affect the entire cosmos and that it merely heralded another cycle; yet another creation to begin the entire process over again.

Teutonic and Icelandic myths have similar themes. The 12th century epic poem the *Edda*, describes how, in a final battle between the gods and heroes, mythical men and fantastical beasts, such as Thor and the Midgard snake and Odin and the Fenris Wolf, the Sun grows dark, the stars fall and the Universe is destroyed. Then comes a re-creation and a new human race emerges, ruled by Balder and his brother. Greeks saw the cycle as five ages, of Gold, Silver, Bronze, Heroes and Iron, sandwiched between constant destruction and renewal.

Behind all these varying allegories is the common, universal acknowledgement of man's insight into the eternal, recurrent cycles that create, destroy and re-shape the cosmos. The real difficulty, it seems, is in recognising the true signs that herald these vast upheavals.

Which prophets should one believe? Which portents may be genuine signs that momentous events are due? It is impossible and would be foolish to be dogmatic. But at the same time, it would be equally irrational to ignore entirely the vast accumulation of evidence that (a) there are cyclical patterns in the Universe and (b) man has been influenced throughout history by some external power which we can only, in a supposedly rational age, assume to be extra-terrestrial.

I think it would be advisable to be on guard, at least, as our current century rapidly moves towards its close. It seems to me that the religious trappings often ascribed to apocryphal events have a deeper meaning than we imagine; that they are as they stand merely human projections in an attempt to piece together a colossal, finished canvas that humanity is unable fully to comprehend.

If the human race does not destroy itself in the interim, I feel that the Earth is due for a vitally significant confrontation with the external forces of the Universe; in other words, a supremely important intervention on the part of highly-advanced, other-worldly forces and powers.

The great 16th century astrologer, physician and prophet Nostradamus, in his *Centuries* prophecies, wrote:

"*L'an mil neuf cens nonate neuf sept mois,*
Du ciel viendra un grand Roy d'effrayer." (10.72)

(In the year 1999 and seven months, From the sky will come an alarmingly powerful king.)

Nostradamus, who is accredited by some with successfully predicting the rise of men like Napoleon and Hitler – in the latter's case he wrote of "Ister" and "topsy-turvy crosses" – also wrote:

"The year of the great seventh number accomplished, it will appear at the time of the games of slaughter not far from the age of the great millennium, when the dead will come out of their graves."

Unfortunately, Nostradamus gave no indication of whether the "alarmingly powerful king" would be a representative of the Powers of Light or the Forces of Darkness. Which, I think, is well worth pondering as the turn of the century speeds towards us all. Will 2000AD mark humanity's salvation – or destruction?

26. The Challenge

"Our conscious range is wide, but shallow as a piece of paper. We have no depth to our consciousness."
D.H. Lawrence (1885–1930)

"...there are things in the psyche which I do not produce, but which produce themselves and have their own life."
C.G. Jung (1875–1961)

"It is possible that there are human emanations of which we are ignorant. You remember how sceptical everyone was about electric currents and invisible waves? Science is still in its infancy."
Albert Einstein, to his biographer, Antonina Valentin.

"With mankind set on self-destruction, who needs extra-terrestrials?"
Frank Close, in a *New Scientist* review, Sept. 2, 1989.

AS SOME sectors of mankind await the millennium and the possible return of other-worldly powers, it is inadvisable simply to sit back passively and complacently and let events take their course. Indeed, if this were the stance taken – as it appears to have been so far by many – it may well be that humanity will wait in vain.

Either we will quite obviously appear of no further use – if indeed we have been of any – to such highly-advanced entities, or we will destroy ourselves before they do reappear. What good, it may be asked, is it to the human race to preoccupy itself with the possible advent of extra-terrestrial intelligences far superior to ourselves? In fact, the answer to this question could well be humanity's only salvation.

For, in addition to being able to teach humanity to improve itself, to tap its latent powers and speed up its own evolution so that it may find its true cosmic purpose and significance, the signs are that these other-worldly powers possess the greatest treasure of the Universe – the key to immortality. It is this that would appear to allow them to survive the pulsations of the Universe. It is this, perhaps, that makes them worthy of the name gods, as they have so often been considered in mankind's ancient observations.

Humanity's ultimate aim, therefore, should perhaps be to attain this godlike state itself. The old fashioned ideal of life-after-death, which still remains unproven and "heaven", in itself an archaism, are obsolete and petty.

Great visionaries that they may have been, men like Isaiah and St. John still may have misinterpreted much of what they saw and experienced of these superior powers; they became idealised as "angels" and "elders" bowing and scraping around the glorious throne of an Almighty in a tedious and pointless ritual of adoration.

For all their other-worldly experiences, the symbolic "explanations" of all the visionaries and prophets remained essentially Earthbound. How many rational men and women could, in all honesty with themselves, wish for a "heaven" that consists in this purposeless, monotonous and tedious idea? Swanning around in white robes, to the muzak of celestial harps, bowing down in perpetual awe and fear at the feet of a shining, all-powerful God, wallowing in his vanity and self-glorification.

It is this kind of "stained-glass window" imagery, this archaic, self-defacing symbolism, that has caused so many people to turn away from the various major establishment religions. Existence negates itself if it is not accompanied by purpose, by incentive. And it is no good waffling about God's "mysterious" purpose, supposedly incomprehensible to mere mortals; as science continues to erode away the foundations of religious belief by appearing to explain more and more of the true nature of the Universe, comfortable, front-parlour pseudo-mysticism such as this simply will not wash.

Just as increased leisure hours are to the idle-minded, so immortality would be pointless to the dull-witted, directionless species that a vast proportion of humanity is constantly in grave danger of becoming.

No, mankind's only hope is to reach out for these "gods", to seek their knowledge and wisdom; learning that will give the human race a greater destiny, a greater sense of purpose in the cosmos.

Is it so inconceivable that we can contact these superior intelligences on our own initiative? From the accounts of SETI members and others that I have outlined, it is clear that many believe we can. And why not? Man once appears to have been in possession of a communicative faculty beyond that of speech and writing. I suspect that what is called praying is a distorted remnant of that forgotten and long-lost faculty.

Re-establishing true contact would certainly be one way of proving our worthiness, our suitability to continue as members of the cosmic scheme of things. But where do we start? Where might these entities be found and just how are they able to transcend time and space to survive the eternal pulsations of the Universe? At this stage, I can naturally offer only theories. But they may constitute a start; a slight rending of the veil that separates us from full awareness. And if but a tiny hole can be made, perhaps others might rend it even further; make it large enough for all humanity to crawl through.

In his book, *The Roots Of Coincidence*, the scientific author Arthur Koestler wrote: "In science fiction it is taken for granted that telepathic communication and psycho-kinetic manipulation of matter will become commonplace in the not-too-distant future; and science fiction has proved to be an astonishingly reliable prophet. Another of its favourite assumptions is that intelligent beings on other planets in the universe have advanced mastery of these methods. It is equally possible, however, that in this particular field we are underprivileged species – together with our other handicaps. The grand design of evolution towards higher forms of unity-in-variety does not exclude biological freaks nor pathological developments. I do not think the universe is a charitable institution, but we have to live in it and make the best of it. The limitations of our biological equipment may condemn us to the role of Peeping Toms at the keyhole of eternity. But at least let us take the stuffing out of the keyhole, which blocks even our limited view."

While Koestler's view of mankind as an "underprivileged species" may appear true at present, it need not necessarily remain so. Indeed, there are indications that human beings have continued to evolve, even long after they and the apes parted company from a common ancestor. In 1887, the great scholar Max Muller, when he edited the monumental Sacred Books of the East, noted that only about 2,000 years ago man was virtually colour blind, or at least, had much less perception of colour than his modern counterpart.

"Xenophanes," he wrote, "knew of three colours of the rainbow only – purple, red and yellow; that even Aristotle spoke of the tricoloured rainbow; and that Democritus knew of no more than four colours – black, white, red and yellow."

Taking "the stuffing out of the keyhole", as Koestler put it, might easily be the beginning of a genuine, higher perception of the cosmos. That is exactly what I have, in an admittedly minor way, attempted to do in this book. With this in mind, let us see if we can make a sensible projection about man's latent powers and how they might ultimately prepare him as a suitable candidate for godhead.

Everything that we perceive in the physical Universe is composed of vibrations of different rates and wavelengths. Matter consists of millions of molecules, all vibrating at various rates. Light and radio waves vibrate at different frequencies; hence the colour scale of the spectrum and the tonal structure of music. The same applies to energy. As far as "solid" matter is concerned, the faster the vibrations, the more tangible to our particular receptive apparatus things appear to be. To take a single analogy, this is the reason, for example, why a television picture composed of 625 lines is sharper and more distinct than one of 425 lines. Or why a tape recording in which the magnetic tape passes the recording heads at 15 inches per second has greater clarity, fidelity or realism than one made in which the tape moves at only 7½ inches per second, or at slower speeds. Indeed, a TV picture (formed of thousands of tiny dots of light and shade in parallel lines) transmitted at too slow a frequency, would be an unintelligible mass of flashes and blobs of light unless we could slow down the receptive capabilities of our retina to piece together the seemingly meaningless code of dots and intervals. Similarly, a recording played at a much slower speed becomes a low frequency rumbling noise. Played at the correct speed, it forms a piece of music or a voice. (Speeded up infinitely, it would become an ultra high-frequency impulse that naturally passes beyond the range of human audibility.)

Since it is possible to alter the frequencies of sound and light waves, why not matter itself? The ability of yogi adepts to endure pain, or seemingly to push sharp instruments into their flesh without resultant wounds or bleeding would appear to be the result of a limited ability to alter the functioning of their own organic matter. After all, they can alter other physiological rhythms, such as their heartbeats, breathing rates and metabolism, so that they can maintain the same postures for incredibly long periods without food or drink. Why not the vibrations of the matter of which they are composed, also?

This variance of vibrations in matter – if it were possible to manipulate it – would explain a lot of seemingly "psychic" or paranormal phenomena. It could well be the very key to everything that is labelled "occult" simply because no one has been able to explain it satisfactorily. A few examples should make this point clear.

People who see "ghosts" may have more variable receptive faculties than most other people – or at least, periodic variations in those faculties – that enable them to sense latent energy in the form of images and sounds; energy given off by matter that is no longer there, but which has left faint traces of its vibrations. A genuine medium, for example, might be able to alter his "receiving" apparatus – of both vision and hearing – enabling him to perceive lingering sight and sound vibrations of people no longer alive.

The ability to alter the vibrations of matter – either of one's own mind, body or of external substances – would explain phenomena like levitation, apparent invisibility, telekinesis (the moving of objects by "will power" or some form of mental energy), poltergeists (regarded by many experts as the result of involuntary telekinesis, usually on the part of a person around the puberty stage) and astral travel. Even the involved physical and mental processes that alchemists follow to try to transmute metals – and themselves – could be a striving for the required mental and physical state necessary to alter the vibrations of external matter.

If this could be projected externally, it would explain one of the hitherto most puzzling, unexplained faculties of advanced mediumship – apportation; the ability to produce solid objects apparently out of thin air. (One contemporary exponent of this phenomenon would seem to be the Hindu mystic Sai Baba.)

It would explain the strange cures (psychosomatic or imagined illnesses and afflictions aside) of so-called faith healers or thaumaturgists.

If a man could alter the vibrations of his own molecules sufficiently at will, it should in theory enable him to fly – or to walk on water.

Telepathy, or "mind-reading", might simply be a refined form of this vibratory technique, altering the wavelengths of brain impulses at will – as in biofeedback – so that the mind is able to receive impulses from the brains of others. Something similar to this would also account for psychometry – the apparent ability to "read" the past history and ownership of objects simply by touch.

The molecules of objects are not crammed together solidly; they merely appear to be because of our limited faculties of vision and touch. If it were possible to manufacture an infinitely powerful microscope, it would then be possible to see these molecules all vibrating at a particular rate with spaces between them. Thus, theoretically, if a man could see and assimilate the vibratory patterns of, say, the molecules of a brick wall and could then cause his own molecules to vibrate "in sympathy", he should be able to pass through the wall, his own molecules passing between the gaps of the wall's component particles. On the other side, his normal vibratory rate could be resumed.

I am not suggesting, however, that all the clairvoyants, alchemists, magicians, witches, mediums, fakirs, sensitives and other "occult" practitioners were necessarily aware of how this manipulation of vibrations may work.

But I would suggest that the genuine ones somehow tapped this latent faculty unknowingly, to a greater or lesser degree, to produce the baffling phenomena for which the evidence is voluminous and often irrefutable. Buddhist mantras, or repetitious chants at certain vibratory wavelengths on particular tones, could be a preparatory method of re-attuning the body's "vibrations" so that the perceptive faculties of the mind are altered. This would account for the many verified and attested cases of Eastern mystics performing seemingly impossible feats such as levitation.

Mme Alexandra David-Neel (1868–1969), the first European woman to be admitted to a Tibetan lamasery as a monk, reported seeing adepts bounding down the sides of mountains in giant, elegant leaps, almost as if they were flying. She also materialised a *tulpa*, an entity in the form of a monk, which behaved quite autonomously in her presence for a considerable period until she "banished" it. She did this, she claimed, by intense meditation and concentration and by projecting a thought-form.

Outside a mosque in the village of Shivapur, in Western India, is a large round boulder weighing about 138 lbs. By chanting the name of an Islamic saint, Qamar Ali

Dervish, at a particular pitch, 11 men can lift the boulder above their heads, each using only one finger. When they stop chanting, they have to jump back quickly as the large rock falls to the ground with a heavy impact. Doesn't this suggest something of the order of vibration-control, or the temporary alteration of molecular structure? If one more or less person tries to join in the elevation of the rock, it will not move, which seems ridiculous as only their fingertips are used. But the key seems to be the chanting and 11 voices must be on the required level to achieve the correct pitch that makes the boulder's vibrations change and render it seemingly weightless, or at least, less heavy. The name of the saint is probably unimportant; the frequency seems to be the key factor. It may be a similar principle to that whereby a trained singer can strike and hold a note that matches the frequency of a wine glass and shatter it.

What, it may understandably be asked, has any of this to do with celestial beings from some other region of the Universe and their visits to Earth? Taking up the certainty that there is intelligent life in our Universe other than on Earth – even a conservative estimate gives 180,000 as the number of planets likely to be capable of supporting intelligent life in our galaxy alone – it is perhaps not unreasonable to assume that at least some of this life will have reached a far more advanced stage than our own. It would follow then that the most intelligent, advanced examples of this life have mastered the control of vibration of matter to a highly refined degree, way beyond our apparent accidental or ill-understood encounters with the phenomenon. They may have mastered it to such an extent that both time and space can be transcended.

Such intelligences may not only have visited our planet without any of the inherent problems of conventional space travel with all its attendant complications (power systems, travel periods greater than the average lifespan, the speed of light as the limiting factor of the Universe, etc.) but they could also escape the destruction when the Universe collapses back into a primal atom and eventually explodes again.

How? By vibrating their constituent matter at a greater rate than all other matter, they could become, to all intents and purposes, virtually free of matter. What this amounts to is a projection of their spirit or abstract being, for want of a better description, into the remaining vacuum of space when the Big Crunch occurs. Being matterless – like Mme David-Neel's *tulpa* thought-form – they would be unaffected either by the gravitational impetus of cosmic collapse or by the immense pressure of fusion into a primal egg, or even by the danger of being killed by flying fragments, radiation or shock waves, when the cosmic egg explodes into another Universe. After a suitable time lapse – time being a relatively unimportant matter to such beings – the matterless entities could then select a planet suited to their requirements and reassume form, to continue the business of maintaining the cosmic balance.

Being without matter. Absurd as it sounds, it is not impossible. In the early 1930s the pioneering Russian rocket-propulsion expert Konstantin Eduardovich Tsiolkovsky envisioned the idea of disembodied intelligence existing in space as an "island" of pure consciousness. The scientist author Arthur C. Clarke acknowledged this when he wrote:

"Since only the structure is important, cannot mind and intelligence exist and function without the hindrance of matter? Can they not, like electronic currents and radiations, exist in a relationship between pure quintessentialities of being? In this way, the mind, which has been formed through interaction with matter and has used matter as its transporting element for so long, could one day climb out of this matter as the butterfly climbs out of its cocoon. And just as the butterfly soars upwards towards the summer sky, so the mind would take flight in experiments of a scope not in any way comparable with that of its former transformations."

The transcendence of matter: that is the great secret of any powers that shape the Universe. That is the great secret that mankind must learn in order to survive indefinitely. How else explain the apparent immortality of what some call God, or the gods? How else could He/She/It or they survive the cyclic explosions and implosions of the Universe?

But, as I have indicated, before we can hope to beg or prise this information from extra-terrestrials, mankind must prove itself to be worthy of the knowledge of this great cosmic secret.

To do this, we must take the initiative.

So far, the various "skywatch" projects that have been undertaken around the world have produced no positive results. So once again, I searched the prophets for some indication of where we might look for the other-worldly intelligences.

There are works classed by scholars as part of non-canonical Biblical literature known as pseudepigraphia, meaning "false or spurious writings", not because their content may be false or spurious, but simply because their authorship is in dispute. These works form part of a whole range of religious writings belonging to the first few centuries after the start of the Christian era.

One of these is called the *Ascension Of Isaiah*, or the *Vision Of Isaiah*, and what is in doubt is that it was written or inspired by the Old Testament prophet. It was almost certainly not. But that does not mean that it is of no interest or value. Many of the Gnostic writings contained material which, whether or not one chooses to accept the authorship, demonstrate a certain amount of knowledge.

One prophet's writings may be as good as another's – particularly when they contain such fascinating information as does that of the pseudo-Isaiah.

For it actually seems to anticipate one of the effects of Einstein's Theory of Relativity, known as the Time Dilation Effect. According to Einstein's reasoning, in simplified terms, if a person flew away from the Earth in a spacecraft approaching the speed of light and returned at the same speed time would, for them, appear to be slowed down. On their arrival back from a star, say, 12 light years away, a journey taking about 28 years, they would age only about 10 years, while 28 Earth years had in fact gone by. This apparent slowing down of the ageing process has been observed, to a much lesser degree, in astronauts who have flown to the Moon and back. It is simply a demonstration that terrestrial time is purely relative. A "day" means something only to those on the planet on which they exist, in our case, Earth. Out in space, travelling at immense speeds, time has a completely different set of values, or co-ordinates. And the faster and further man goes, the more its effects would be noticed – by him – on his return. Thus a man could leave Earth for a voyage to a distant star-system only to find on his return that, while he may be only slightly older, his sons had grown old and died and his grandchildren were elderly. If he travelled far enough at such immense speeds, he might even return many generations later.

Something of this kind is implied in the account of the man who called himself Isaiah in the post-Christian text. Either that or, in writing it, he was well aware of the Time Dilation Effect.

In his account, this pseudo-Isaiah claims that he was taken to "heaven" by an angel, where he met God. It may sound familiar. After he had been there for what seemed to himself a short period, the angel informed him that it was time to return to Earth. Isaiah II protested, saying that he had been there for only two hours. But the angel told him that he had, in fact, been away from the Earth for 32 years. "Isaiah" became fearful, as he imagined that, on his return to Earth, he would swiftly age and die. What made him think that is interesting in itself. But the angel reassured him that he would not.

In view of what we know about time and space travel, it would appear that there are only two logical explanations for Isaiah's story. Either, some time in the century or so after Christ, a man was picked up, taken to a distant planet and returned to Earth, or he at least knew something of the principles of time dilation and its implications. If he was away for 32 years that to him seemed like only two hours, we can assume that he was subject to the Time Dilation Effect and that he was transported at a speed approaching that of light.

Unfortunately the account does not say whether the two hours/32-years includes both the outward and inward journeys. If it covered only the outward journey and the stay in "heaven", we must assume that wherever Isaiah went, it was about 32 light years away. If it embraced both journeys and they were made at the same speed each way, that would mean Isaiah's destination was some 16 light years away.

This is much too large a sweep of distances for us to be able to narrow it down to one particular star system with attendant planets with life-support potential. All we have are two hypothetical distances and an infinite number of directions in which to point them.

Because of the little that is known of the true nature of time itself in spatial correlations, there remains one other possibility: Isaiah may have been subjected to an effect of time aberration of which we know nothing at all.

And there is, in fact, further indication of this possibility. I believe that there are clues contained in the last section of St. John's Apocalypse. In describing what he calls the New Jerusalem, the holy city of God where selected members of the human race will dwell after the Last Judgement, John gives some highly intriguing information.

The city is a perfect cube – a hint at the Master Architect nature of the Power of Light. Its foundations are decorated with 12 precious and semi-precious stones. These stones are, in fact, the same jewels that decorate the breastplate of the high priests, as dictated by Yahweh to Moses in Exodus, when the specifications for the Tabernacle are given. The breastplate was worn over the ephod, a jewel-studded, colourful robe or vestment.

The stone of the breastplate – known as the Breastpiece of Judgement – are said to represent the 12 tribes of Israel. But in tradition, they are also inextricably associated with the 12 signs of the zodiac, as attested by the historian Josephus and the philosopher Philo. Some of the names used in Exodus are slightly different from those used by John in Revelation, but this is easily accounted for by variations in translation. The 12 stones, and their corresponding signs as the Sun passes through these constellations are:

1. Amethyst (Aries).
2. Hyacinth (Taurus).
3. Chrysoprase (Gemini).
4. Topaz (Cancer).
5. Beryl (Leo).
6. Chrysolite (Virgo).

7. Sardius (Libra).
8. Sardonyx (Scorpio).
9. Smaragdus, or Emerald (Sagittarius).
10. Chalcedon (Capricorn).
11. Sapphire (Aquarius).
12. Jasper (Pisces).

But curiously, in John's list, the precious stones are in the exact *reverse* order to this.

What can this possibly signify? I suggest that, either we are looking for a planet from which the attendant sun appears to pass through the constellations in the reverse order to that seen from Earth – i.e., on the opposite side of the galaxy – or, the other-worldly beings came from a solar system that is the exact double of ours and in which time runs backward.

Is it possible? Could there be such a parallel, invisible world, where time as we know it works in reverse – relative, that is, to our time?

I can merely refer the reader to Professor Hawking and his colleagues and their concepts of sum over histories, parallel universes, imaginary time, the nature of Black Holes, and so on. These mysterious phenomena, along with the concepts of anti-matter, are at present our only clues to this tantalising puzzle.

Bibliography

The purpose of the following list is threefold: to acknowledge and thank most gratefully those authors and publishers from whose works I have taken direct quotations; to credit works that may have provided theoretical directions or triggered off trains of thought that helped in the formulation of the underlying theories of this book; to provide the reader with further material, should he or she wish to follow up any of the areas of thought upon which the present work touches.

ADAMS, Beck L: *Life Of The Buddha* (Collins, 1959).

AHMED, Rollo: *The Black Art* (John Long, 1956).

ALBRIGHT, W. F: *Archaeology And The Religion Of Israel* (Johns Hopkins Press, Baltimore, 1953); *From The Stone Age To Christianity* (John Hopkins Press, Baltimore, 1957).

ALEXANDER, W.M: *Demonic Possession In The New Testament* (Clark, Edinburgh, 1902).

ALLEGRO, John: *The Dead Sea Scrolls* (Penguin, 1956).

ALLEN, T.C: *The Egyptian Book Of The Dead* (Chicago University Press, 1960).

ALTHEIM, F: *A History Of Roman Religion* (Methuen, 1938).

ARMSTRONG, A.H: *The Architecture Of The Intelligible Universe In The Philosophy Of Plotinus* (Cambridge University Press, 1940).

ARMSTRONG, E.A: *The Folklore Of Birds* (Collins, 1958).

ASIMOV, Isaac: *New Intelligent Man's Guide To Science* (University Of Toronto Press, 1965); *The Universe: From Flat Earth To Quasar* (Pelican, 1971).

ATTWATER, D: *The Penguin Dictionary Of Saints* (Penguin, 1965).

BAGNALL, O: *The Origin And Properties Of The Human Aura* (Kegan Paul, 1957).

BAINTON, R.H: *History Of Christianity* (Penguin, 1957).

BANDI, H & MARINGER, J: *Art In The Ice Age* (Allen & Unwin, 1953).

BARBANELL, Maurice: *This Is Spiritualism* (Herbert Jenkins, 1959).

BAROJA, J.C: *The World Of Witches* (Weidenfeld & Nicolson, 1964).

BARRETT, Francis: *The Magus* (University Books, New York, 1967).

BATEMAN, F. & SOAL, S.G: *Modern Experiments In Telepathy* (Faber, 1954).

BENDANN, E: *Death Customs* (Kegan Paul, 1930).

BESANT, Annie: *The Ancient Wisdom: An Outline Of Theosophical Teaching* (Theosophical Publishing Society, 1910); *Man: Whence, How And Wither* (Theosophical Publishing Society, 1913).

BLACK, M: *The Scrolls And Christian Origins* (Nelson, 1961).

BLAKE, William: *Complete Writings* (ed. Geoffrey Keynes; Oxford University Press, 1971).

BLAKNEY, R.B: *The Way Of Life – Tao Te Ching* (Mentor, 1955).

BLAVATSKY, H.P.B: *Isis Unveiled* (2 vols., Theosophical University Press, Calif., 1972); *The Secret Doctrine* (2 vols., Theosophical University Press, Calif., 1970); *Studies In Occultism* (Sphere Books, 1974).

BRADEN, C.S: *Christian Science Today* (Allen & Unwin, 1959).

BRANDON, S.G.F: *Man And His Destiny In The Great Religions* (Manchester University Press, 1962); *Creation Legends Of The Ancient Near East* (Hodder & Stoughton, 1963); *History, Time And Deity* (Manchester University Press, 1965); *The Judgement Of The Dead* (Weidenfeld & Nicholson, 1967); *Jesus And The Zealots* (Manchester University Press, 1967).

BRINTON, Howard: *The Mystic Will* (Allen & Unwin, 1931).

BROMAGE, Bernard: *The Occult Arts Of Ancient Egypt* (Aquarian Press, 1953).

BRONOWSKI, J: *William Blake And The Age Of Revolution* (Routledge & Kegan Paul, 1972).

BUCKE, Richard M: *Cosmic Consciousness* (University Books, New York, 1961).

BUDGE, E.A.W: *Egyptian Magic* (Kegan Paul, 1901); *The Book Of The Dead* (Routledge & Kegan Paul,

---

1950).

BULLINGER, E.W: *The Apocalypse* (Samuel Bagster, 1972).

BURLAND, C.A: *Magic Books From Mexico* (Penguin, 1955); *The Gods Of Mexico* (Eyre & Spottiswode, 1967); *The Arts Of The Alchemists* (Weidenfeld, 1967); *North American Indian Mythology* (Hamlyn, 1967).

BURRT, E.A: *The Teachings Of The Compassionate Buddha* (Mentor, 1955).

BUTLER, C: *Number Symbolism* (Routledge, 1970).

BUTLER, E.M: *Fortunes Of Faust* (Cambridge University Press, 1949); *Ritual Magic* (Noonday Press, New York, 1959); *The Myth Of The Magus* (Macmillan, 1968).

BUTLER, W.E: *Magic And The Qabalah* (Aquarian Press, 1964).

BYRNE, Patrick: *Witchcraft In Ireland* ((Mercier Press, Cork, 1967).

CAIRD, G.B: *The Revelation Of St. John The Divine* (Black, 1966).

CAMMELL, C.R: *Aleister Crowley The Black Magician* (The Richards Press, 1951).

CAMPBELL, J: *The Masks Of God, Primitive Mythology* (Secker & Warburg, 1960).

CARPENTER, Rhys: *Folk Tale, Fiction And Saga In The Homeric Epics* (Cambridge University Press, 1958).

CARRINGTON, Hereward & MULDOON, Sylvan: *The Projection Of The Astral Body* (Rider, 1958).

CAVENDISH, Richard: *The Black Arts* (Routledge & Kegan Paul, 1967); ed., *Man, Myth & Magic*, 7 vols., (Purnell).

CIRLOT, J.E: *A Dictionary Of Symbols* (Routledge & Kegan Paul, 1962).

CLARK, James M: *The Great German Mystics* (Blackwell, 1949).

CLARKE, Arthur C: *Profiles Of The Future* (Gollancz, 1962); *Voices From The Sky* (Harper & Row, New York, 1965).

COCKREN, Archibald: *Alchemy Rediscovered And Restored* (Rider, 1940).

COHEN A: *Everyman's Talmud* (Dent, 1932).

COHN, Norman: *The Pursuit Of The Millennium* (Secker & Warburg, 1957).

COLLIN, Rodney: *The Theory Of Celestial Influence* (Stuart & Watkins, 1971).

CONZE, Edward: *Buddhism, Its Essence And Development* (Cassirer, Oxford, 1953); (trans.) *Buddhist Scriptures* (Penguin, 1960); *Buddhist Thought In India* (Allen & Unwin, 1962).

COTTRELL, Leonard: *The Lost Pharaohs* (Pan, 1956); *Lost Cities* (Pan, 1959).

COULANGE, Louis: *The Life Of The Devil* (Knof, 1929).

CROOKALL, Robert: *The Study And Practice Of Astral Projection* (Aquarian Press, 1961); *The Techniques Of Astral Projection* (Aquarian Press, 1964).

CROW, W.B: *A History Of Magic, Witchcraft And Occultism* (Aquarian Press, 1961); *Precious Stones* (Aquarian Press, 1968).

CROWLEY, Aleister: *The Confessions* ed., John Symonds & Kenneth Grant, (Bantam, 1971); *Magick In Theory And Practice* ed., Symonds & Grant (Routledge, 1973).

DALE-GREEN, Patricia: *Cult Of The Cat* (Heinemann, 1963).

DALY KING, G: *The States Of Human Consciousness* (University Books, New York).

DANIEL, Glynn: *The Megalith Builders Of Western Europe* (Penguin, 1963).

DARAUL, Arkon: *Secret Societies* (Muller, 1961); *Witches And Sorcerers* (Tandem, 1965).

DAVID-NEEL, Alexandra: *Magic And Mystery In Tibet* (Souvenir Press, 1967).

DAVIDSON, D, and ALDERSMITH, H: *The Great Pyramid: Its Divine Message* (Williams & Norgate, 1924).

DAVIDSON, Gustav: *Dictionary Of Angels* (Collier-Macmillan, 1968).

DAVIES, Rupert E: *Methodism* (Pelican, 1963).

DAWOOD, N.J (trans.): *The Koran* (Penguin, 1956).

DE CAMP, L. Sprague & Catherine: *Citadels Of Mystery* (Fontana, 1972).

DE GIVRY, Emil Grillot: *Pictorial Anthology Of Witchcraft, Magic And Alchemy* (University Books, New York).

DENIS, Armamnd: *Taboo* (W.H. Allen, 1966).

DE PROROK, Byron: *Dead Men Do Tell Tales* (Harrap, 1943).

DE ROLA, Stanislas Klossowski: *Alchemy The Secret Art* (Thames & Hudson, 1973).

DEWAR, Stephen: *Witchcraft And The Evil Eye In Guernsey* (Toucan Press, 1970).

DIKSHITAR, Rmachandra: *War In Ancient India* (Macmillan, 1945).

DOBZHANSKY, Theodosius: *Evolution, Genetics And Man* (Chapman & Hall, 1955).

DRIVER, G.R: *Canaanite Myths And Legends* (Clark, Edinburghs, 1956).

DUNNE, J.W: *An Experiment With Time* (Faber, 1939).

DUTT, Romesh C: *The Ramayana And The Mahabharata* (Everyman, 1970).

ELIADE, Mircea: *Cosmos And History: The Myth Of The Eternal Return* (Harper & Row Torchbooks, 1959); *Patterns In Comparative Religion* (Sheed & Ward, 1958); *The Forge And The Crucible* (Rider, 1962).

ELIOT, Sir C: *Japanese Buddhism* (Arnold, 1935).

ELLIOTT, Ralph W.V: *Runes* (Manchester University Press, 1959).

ELLIS-DAVIDSON, H.R: *Gods And Myths Of Northern Europe* (Penguin, 1964).

EPSTEIN, Isidore: *Judaism* (Pelican, 1959).

EVANS, Sir Arthur: *The Palace Of Minos* (Macmillan, 1935).

EVANS-WENTZ, W.Y: (ed.) *The Tibetan Book Of The Dead* (Oxford University Press, 1927).

FARRER, Austin: *The Revelation Of St. John The Divine* (Clarendon Press, Oxford, 1964).

FINLEY, M.I: *The World Of Odysseus* (Penguin, 1967).

FIRSOFF, Valdemar A: *Life Beyond The Earth: A Study In Exobiology* (Hutchinson, 1963).

FLEW, A: *A New Approach To Psychical Research* (Watts, 1953).

FLYING SAUCER REVIEW: (London, 1955———).

FORDHAM, F: *An Introduction To Jung's Psychology* (Penguin, 1959).

FORTUNE, Dion: *Psychic Self-Defence* (Rider, 1930); *The Mystical Qabalah* (Williams & Norgate, 1935).

FRANGER, Wilhelm: *The Millennium Of Hieronymus Bosch* (Faber & Faber, 1952).

FRANKFORT, Henri: *Ancient Egyptian Religion* (Harper, New York, 1961).

FRAZER, J.G: *The Golden Bough* (Macmillan, 1922).

FREUD, Sigmund: *Moses And Monotheism* (Hogarth Press, 1939).

FREUND, Philip: *Myths Of Creation* (W.H.Allen, 1964).

FULCANELLI: *Le Mystère Des Cathédrales* (Neville Spearman, 1971).

GARDNER, Gerald B: *Witchcraft Today* (Rider & Co., 1954).

GARNIER, J: *The Great Pyramid* (Banks, 1905).

GHALIOUNGI, P: *Magic And Medical Science In Ancient Egypt* (Hodder, 1963).

GIFFORD, E.S.J: *The Evil Eye* (Macmillan, 1958).

GLASSON, T.F: *The Revelation Of St. John* (Cambridge University Press, 1965).

GOETZ, Delia & MORLEY, Sylvanus G: (trans.) *The Popul Vuh: The Sacred Book Of The Quiche-Maya* (William Hodge & Co. Ltd., 1951).

GOLDSTON, Robert: *Satan's Disciples* (New English Library, 1969).

GORDON, Cyrus H: *Before The Bible: The Common Background Of Greek And Hebrew Civilisations* (Collins, 1962).

GOULD, R.F: *History Of Freemasonry* (Caxton, 1951).

GRANT, M: *Myths Of The Greeks And Romans* (Weidenfeld & Nicolson, 1962).

GRAVES, Robert: *The Greek Myths* (2 vols., Penguin, 1955); *The White Goddess* (Faber & Faber, 1969); *The Crane Bag* (Faber & Faber, 1959).

GRAY, John: *The Canaanites* (Thames & Hudson, 1964).

GUENTHER, Herbert V: *Buddhist Philosophy In Theory And Practice* (Pelican, 1972).

GUILLAUME, Alfred: *Prophecy And Divination Among The Hebrews And Semites* (Hodder, 1938); *Islam* (Pelican, 1954).

GUTHRIE, W.K.C: *The Greeks And Their Gods* (Methuen, 1950).

HANSE, Chadwick: *Witchcraft At Salem* (Hutchinson, 1970).

HAPPOLD, F.C: *Mysticism: A Study And An Anthology* (Pelican, 1963).

HART, H: *The Enigma Of Survival* (Rider, 1959).

HASTINGS, James: *Dictionary Of The Bible* (revised, ed., Frederick C. Grant & H.H. Rowley; Clark, Edinburgh, 1963).

HAWKES, J: *Dawn Of The Gods* (Chatto & Windus, 1968).

HAWKING, Stephen W: *A Brief History Of Time* (Bantam Press, 1988); *Black Holes And Baby Universes* (Bantam Press, 1993).

HAWKINS, Gerald S: *Stonehenge Decoded* (Souvenir Press, 1966).

HAYS, H.R: *In The Beginning: Early Man And His Gods* ((Putnam, New York, 1965).

HENNECKE, E: *New Testament Apocrypha* (2 vols, Lutterworth Press, 1963–5).

HERFORD, Travers: *Talmud And Apocrypha* (Soncino Press, 1933).

HEYWOOD, Rosalind: *The Sixth Sense* (Chatto & Windus, 1954); *The Infinite Hive* (Chatto & Windus, 1964).

HILL, Douglas and WILLIAMS, Pat: *The Supernatural* (Aldus, 1965).

HODGES, E. Richmond (ed.): *Cory's Ancient Fragments Of The Phoenician, Carthaginian, Babylonian,*

Egyptian And Other Authors (London, 1876).

HOLE, Christina: *A Mirror Of Witchcraft* (Pedigree Books, 1957); *Encyclopaedia Of Superstitions* (Hutchinson, 1961).

HOLIDAY, F.W: *The Dragon And The Disc* (Futura, 1974).

HOLLINGDALE, R.J: (trans.) *Thus Spake Zarathustra*: Nietzsche (Penguin, 1961); *Twilight Of The Idols And The Antichrist* (Penguin, 1968).

HOLMYARD, E.J: *Alchemy* (Pelican, 1957).

HOOKE, S.H: *Babylonian And Assyrian Religion* (Hutchinson, 1953).

HOWE, Ellic: Urania: *The Strange World Of The Astrologers* (Kimber, 1967); *The Magicians Of The Golden Dawn* (Routledge & Kegan Paul, 1972).

HOYLE, Fred: *Of Men And Galaxies* (Heinemann, 1965).

HUGHES, Pennethorne: *Witchcraft* (Longmans Green, 1952).

HUMPHREYS, Christmas: *Buddhism* (Penguin, 1951).

HUNT, Douglas: *Exploring The Occult* (Pan, 1964).

HUSON, Paul: *The Devil's Picture Book: The Complete Guide To Tarot Cards: Their Origins And Their Usage* (Abacus, 1972).

HUYSMANS, J.K: *La-Bas* (Dover Publications, New York, 1972).

IAMBLICHUS of Chalcis: *Theurgia, Or The Egyptian Mysteries* (trans., Wilder: Metaphysical Publishing Co., New York, 1911).

INGALESE, Richard: *Cosmogony And Evolution* (Watkins Press, New York, 1907).

INGERSOLL, E: *Birds In Legend, Fable And Folklore* (Longmans Green, 1923).

JAMES, E.O: *Christian Myth And Ritual* (John Murray, 1933); *The Ancient Gods* (Weidenfeld & Nicolson, 1960); *The Worship Of The Sky-God* (Athlone Press, 1963).

JAMES, Joseph: *The Way Of Mysticism* (Jonathan Cape, 1950).

JAMES, M.R: (ed.) *The Apocryphal New Testament* (Oxford University Press, 1924).

JAMES, William: *The Varieties Of Religious Experience* (Collins, 1963).

JOHNS, June: *King Of The Witches* (Peter Davies Ltd., 1969); *Black Magic Today* (New English Library, 1971).

JONES, M.E: *Occult Philosophy* (McKay, Philadelphia, 1947).

JOSEPHUS: *Works* (4 vols., Loeb Classical Library, 1925–30).

JUNG, C.G: *Mysterium Coniunctionis* (trans. R.F.C. Hull, Routledge & Kegan Paul, 1953); *Psychology And Alchemy* (RKP, 1953); *Flying Saucers: A Modern Myth Of Things Seen In The Skies* (RKP, 1959); *Memories, Dreams, Reflections* (Fontana, 1967).

KASTEIN, A.M: *History And Destiny Of The Jews* (Lane, 1933).

KEEL, John A: *Jadoo* (W.H. Allen, 1958).

KELLETT, E.E: *A Short History Of Religions* (Pelican, 1962).

KEYHOE, Major Donald: *The Flying Saucer Conspiracy* (Hutchinson, 1957).

KING, Francis: *Ritual Magic In England* (Neville Spearman, 1970).

KNAPPE, A.H: *The Science Of Folklore* (Methuen, 1961).

KNIGHT, G.N., and PICK, F.L: *Pocket History Of Freemasonry* (Muller, 1959).

KOESTLER, Arthur: *The Roots Of Coincidence* (Hutchinson, 1972).

KOSAMBI, D.D: *Culture And Civilisation Of Ancient India In Outline* (Routledge & Kegan Paul, 1965).

KRAMER, Heinrich and SPRENGER, James: *Malleus Maleficarum* (trans. Montague Summers; John Rodker, 1928).

LANNING, A: *Lascaux* (Penguin, 1959).

LANTERNARI, V: *The Religions Of The Oppressed* (Macgibbon & Kee, 1963).

LENORMANT, F: *Chaldean Magic* (Bagster 1877).

LEROI-GOURHAN, A: *The Art Of Prehistoric Man In Western Europe* (Thames & Hudson, 1968).

LEVI, Eliphas: *Transcendental Magic* (Rider & Co., 1923); *The Key Of The Mysteries* (Rider & Co., 1959).

LISSNAR, Ivar: *Men, God And Magic* (Jonathan Cape, 1961).

LODS, A: *The Prophets And The Rise Of Judaism* ((Kegan Paul, 1937).

LORENZEN, Coral And Jim: *UFO The Whole Story* (Signet, 1969).

McINTOSH, C: *The Astrologers And Their Creed* (Hutchinson, 1969).

MACKENZIE, Andrew: *The Unexplained* (Arthur Barker, 1968); *Frontiers Of The Unknown* (Arthur Barker, 1968); *Apparitions And Ghosts* (Arthur Barker, 1971).

MACKENZIE, Donald A: *Teutonic Myth And Legend* (Gresham); *The Migration Of Symbols And Their Relation To Belief And Custom* (Kegan Paul, Trench, Trubner & Co., 1926).

MALINKOWSKI, Bronislaw: *Magic, Science And Religion* (Doubleday Anchor Books, 1948).

MAPLE, Eric: *The Dark World Of Witches* (Robert Hale, 1962); *The Domain Of Devils* (Robert Hale, 1966); *Magic, Medicine And Quackery* (Robert Hale, 1968); *Witchcraft* (Octopus Books, 1973).

MARAINI, Fosco: *Secret Tibet* (Hutchinson, 1952).

MASCARO, Juan: (trans.) *The Bhagavad Gita* (Penguin, 1962).

MATHERS, S.L: (ed.) *The Key Of Salomon The King* (Redway, 1888); *The Kabbalah Unveiled* (Kegan Paul, 1938).

MATTUCK, I: *The Thoughts Of The Prophets* (Allen & Unwin, 1938).

MERCER, S.A.B: *The Pyramid Texts* (4 vols, Longmans, Toronto, 1952).

MERMET, Abbe A: *Principles And Practice Of Radiesthesia* (Vincent Stuart, 1959).

MIDDLETON, J., & WINTER, E.H: *Witchcraft And Sorcery In East Africa* (Routledge, 1963).

MILLARD, A.R: *The Babylonian Story Of The Flood* (Oxford University Press, 1969).

MONCRIEFF, A.R. Hope: *Classic Myth And Legend* (Gresham).

MORRIS, Leon: *Revelation* (Tyndale Press, 1969).

MUNITZ, M.K: (ed.) *Theories Of The Universe From Babylonian Myth To Modern Science* (The Free Press, Glencoe, Illinois, 1957).

MURRAY, Margaret: *The God Of The Witches* (Faber & Faber, 1952); *The Witch-Cult In Western Europe* (Oxford Paperbacks, 1962).

OESTERREICH, T.K: *Possession* (Routledge & Kegan Paul, 1930).

OSTRANDER, Sheila and SCHROEDER, Lynn: *PSI: Psychic Discoveries Behind The Iron Curtain* (Abacus, 1973).

OUSPENSKY, P.D: *A New Model Of The Universe* (Routledge & Kegan Paul, 1931); *In Search Of The Miraculous* (RKP, 1947); *The Psychology Of Man's Possible Evolution* (RKP, 1947); *The Fourth Way* (RKP, 1957).

PAPUS (Dr. Gerard Encausse): *The Tarot Of The Bohemians* (Rider, 1929).

PARRINDER, Geoffrey: *Witchcraft* (Pelican, 1958).

PARROT, A: *The Temple Of Jerusalem* (SCM Press, 1957).

PAUWELS, Louis and BERGIER, Jacques: *The Dawn Of Magic* (Anthony Gibbs & Phillips, 1963); *Eternal Man* (Souvenir Press, 1972); *Impossible Possibilities* (Mayflower Books, 1974).

PIAZZI SMYTH, C: *Our Inheritance In The Great Pyramid* (Ibister, 1864).

PICKTHALL, Mohammed Marmaduke: *The Meaning Of The Glorious Koran* (Mentor, 1953).

PIGGOTT, Stuart: *The Druids* (Thames & Hudson, 1968).

PRATT, J.G: *Parapsychology Today: An Insider's View* (Doubleday, New York, 1964).

PROCLUS: *The Elements Of Theology* (ed. E.R. Dodds, Clarendon Press, Oxford, 1923).

RACKOCZI, Basil Ivan: *The Painted Caravan* (Brucher, 1954).

RAPHAEL, A: *The Philosopher's Stone* (Routledge, 1965).

RAVENSCROFT, Trevor: *The Spear Of Destiny* (Neville Spearman, 1974).

READ, J: *Prelude To Chemistry* (G. Bell & Sons, 1936).

REBAN, John: *Inquest On Jesus Christ* (Leslie Frewin, 1967).

REGARDIE, Israel: *The Golden Dawn* (4 vols., Llewellyn Publishing Co., Minnesota, 1969).

RHINE, J.B: *The Reach Of The Mind* (Pelican, 1954).

RHINE, Louisa E: *Mind Over Matter* (Macmillan, New York, 1970).

RHODES, H.T.F: *The Black Mass* (Rider & Co., 1954).

RIEU, E.V: (trans.) *The Odyssey*: Homer (Penguin, 1946); *The Iliad*: Homer (Penguin, 1950).

RINALDI, Peter M: *The Man In The Shroud* (Futura, 1974).

ROBBINS, R.H: *Encyclopaedia Of Witchcraft And Demonology* (Peter Nevill, 1959).

ROBERTS, Henry C: *The Complete Prophecies Of Nostradamus* (Neville Spearman, 1960).

ROSE, H.J: *A Handbook Of Greek Mythology* (Methuen, 1958).

ROSS, Anne: *Pagan Celtic Britain* (Routledge, 1967).

ROY, Protrop Chandra: *Bhisma Parva* (Bharata Press, Bombay, 1888).

SACHS, C: *World History Of The Dance* (Allen & Unwin, 1957).

SAGAN, Carl & SHKLOVSKI, Josif C: *Intelligent Life In The Universe* (Holden-Day, San Francisco, 1966).

SANDERS, N.K: (trans.) *The Epic Of Gilgamesh* (Penguin, 1960).

SARGENT, William: *Battle For The Mind* (Heinemann, 1957).

SCHOLEM, G.C: *Major Trends In Jewish Mysticism* (Thames & Hudson, 1955); *On The Kabbalah And Its Symbolism* (Routledge & Kegan Paul, 1965).

SEABROOK, W.B: *The Magic Island* (Harrap, 1929); *Witchcraft: Its Power In The World Today* (Sphere

Books, 1970).

SELTMAN, Charles: *The Twelve Olympians: Gods And Goddesses Of Greece* (Pan, 1952).

SETH, Ronald: *In The Name Of The Devil* (Jarrolds, 1969).

SHAH, Idries: *The Secret Lore Of Magic* (Muller, 1957); *Tales Of The Dervishes* (Jonathan Cape, 1967); *Way Of The Sufi* (Jonathan Cape, 1968); *The Sufis* (Jonathan Cape, 1969).

SHAPLEY, Harlow: *Of Stars And Men, The Human Response To An Expanding Universe* (Beacon Press, Boston, 1958).

SHUTTLEWOOD, Arthur: *The Warminster Mystery* (Neville Spearman, 1967).

SICULUS, Diodorus: *Biblioteca Historia* (Oxford University Press, 1956).

SIEPKSMA, F: *The Gods As We Shape Them* (Routledge, 1960).

SMITH, B: *Meditation: The Inward Art* (Allen & Unwin, 1964).

SPENCE, Lewis: *An Encyclopaedia Of Occultism* (Routledge, 1920); *Myths And Legends Of Ancient Egypt* (Harrap, 1949).

SPENCER, Sidney: *Mysticism In World Religion* (Pelican, 1963).

STACE, Walter T: *The Teachings Of The Mystics* (Mentor, 1960).

STEWART, C.N: *Bulwer Lytton As Occultist* (Theosophical Publishing House, 1927).

STRUVE, Otto: *Stellar Evolution* (Princeton University Press, 1950).

SUARES, Carlos: *The Cipher Of Genesis* (Bantam, 1973).

SULLIVAN, Walter: *We Are Not Alone* (McGraw-Hill, New York, 1964).

SUMMERS, Montague: *Witchcraft And Black Magic* (Rider & Co., 1946); *History Of Witchcraft* (University Books, New York, 1956); *Geography Of Witchcraft* (University Books, New York, 1958).

SUZUKI, D.T: *An Introduction To Zen Buddhism* (Arrow Books, 1959).

SWEDENBORG, Emmanuel: *Theological Writings* (Swedenborg Society, 1901).

SYMONDS, John: *The Magick Of Aleister Crowley* (Muller, 1958); *Madame Blavatsky: Medium And Magician* (Odhams, 1959); *The Great Beast* (Rider, 1957).

TALLANT, Robert: *Voodoo In New Orleans* (Macmillan, 1946).

THOMAS, Paul: *Flying Saucers Through The Ages* (Neville Spearman, 1965).

THOMPSON, K. Lowe: *The History Of The Devil* (Kegan Paul, Trench, Trubner & Co., 1929).

THOULESS, Robert H: *Experimental Psychical Research* (Pelican, 1963).

TINDALL, Gillian: *A Handbook On Witches* (Arthur Barker, 1965).

TOMAS, Andrew: *We Are Not The First* (Souvenir Press, 1971); *Beyond The Time Barrier* (Sphere Books, 1974).

TORRENS, R.G: *Secret Rituals Of The Golden Dawn* (Aquarian Press, 1973).

UNDERWOOD, Guy: *Pattern Of The Past* (Museum Press, 1969).

VAN OVER, Raymond: (ed.) *I Ching* (Mentor, 1971).

VERMEES, G: *The Dead Sea Scrolls In English* (Penguin, 1962).

VON HUGEL, Fr: *The Mystical Element Of Religion* (2 vols, Dent, 1908).

WAITE, A.E: *Real History Of The Rosicrucians* (Redway, 1888); *The Key To The Tarot* (Rider, 1922); *The Book Of Ceremonial Magic* (University Books, New Jersey, 1961).

WALLACE, C.H: *Witchcraft In The World Today* (Universal Tandem, 1967).

WARE, James R: *The Sayings Of Confucius* (Mentor, 1955).

WARRINGTON, John: (trans.) *Metaphysics:* Aristotle (Everyman's Library, 1956).

WATSON, James D: *The Double Helix* (Weidenfeld & Nicolson, 1969).

WATTS, Alan W: *The Way Of Zen* (Pelican, 1962).

WEST, D.J: *Psychical Research Today* (Pelican, 1962).

WEST, M.L: *Hesiod: Theogony* (Clarendon Press, Oxford, 1966).

WHITROW, J.G: *What Is Time?* (Thames & Hudson, 1972).

WILSON, Colin: *The Occult* (Hodder & Stoughton, 1971).

WILSON, Edmund: *The Dead Sea Scrolls 1947–1969* (Fontana, 1971).

WRIGHT, Harry B: *Witness To Witchcraft* (Souvenir Press, 1957).

WOOLLEY, C.L: *Ur Of The Chaldees* (Pelican, 1938).

YATES, F.A: *Giordano Bruno And The Hermetic Tradition* (Routledge & Kegan Paul, 1964).

YEATS, W.B: *Autobiographies* (Macmillan, 1955); *A Vision* (Macmillan, 1962).

ZAEHNER, R.C: *The Teachings Of The Magi* (Allen & Unwin, 1956); *Mysticism: Sacred And Profane* (Clarendon Press, 1957); *The Dawn And Twilight Of Zoroastrianism* (Weidenfeld & Nicolson, 1961).

ZOLAR: *The Encyclopaedia Of Ancient And Forbidden Knowledge* (Souvenir Press, 1971).

ALSO BY KENNETH RAYNER JOHNSON

THE IMMORTAL

Fulcanelli, Master Alchemist, & The Art Of Allegory

Kenneth Rayner Johnson's *The Fulcanelli Phenomenon* was widely acclaimed upon its publication in 1980 as the definitive interpretation of one of mankind's most ancient and mysterious disciplines – Alchemy.

Now, Johnson has completely revised and updated his earlier work, adding years of new research and evidence to provide an even more comprehensive analysis of this neglected art, once again focusing in particular of one of its most notorious exponents – Fulcanelli.

Through deciphering the story, legend and, finally, the *identity* of the man known throughout the ages as Fulcanelli, Johnson has revealed the kernel of true inner meaning oft hinted at by generations of Hermeticists, alchemists and allegorizors; and in doing so he has uncovered one of the most treasured and closely-guarded secrets of all: *the secret of immortality and eternal life.*

£9.95 • $14.95

ALSO FROM CREATION BOOKS

HAMMER OF THE GODS

Apocalyptic Texts For The Criminally Insane

FRIEDRICH NIETZSCHE

WAR • DEICIDE • NIHILISM • CHANCE • • CHAOS • ANTI-CHRIST
ÜBERMENSCH • SUICIDE • WILL TO POWER • ETERNAL RETURN

Hammer Of The Gods presents Friedrich Nietzsche's most prophetic, futuristic and apocalyptic philosophies and traces them against the upheavals of the last century and the current millennial panic. This radical reinterpretation reveals Nietzsche as the true guide to the madness in our society which he himself diagnosed a century ago; Nietzsche as a philosopher *against* society, against both the state and the herd; Nietzsche as philosopher with a hammer.

The book includes *all brand-new* translations of seminal texts by Nietzsche – including some previously unpublished – and represents an indispensable modern introduction to this master of apocalyptic philosophy, whose admonitory theories are now perilously close to becoming reality as the millennium draws to a close.

Translated, written and compiled by Stephen Metcalf.   **£9.95 • $14.95**

ALSO FROM CREATION BOOKS

BORN BAD
The Story Of Charles Starkweather
Jack Sargeant
TRUE CRIME
£7.95 • $13.95

FRAGMENTS OF FEAR
An Illustrated History Of British Horror Films
Andy Boot
CINEMA
£11.95 • $16.95

DESPERATE VISIONS 1
The Films Of John Waters And George & Mike Kuchar
Jack Stevenson
CINEMA/CULTURE
£11.95 • $16.95

KILLING FOR CULTURE
An Illustrated History Of Death Film
David Kerekes & David Slater
CINEMA/CULTURE
£12.95 • $17.95

DEATHTRIPPING
An Illustrated History Of The Cinema Of Transgression
Jack Sargeant
CINEMA/CULTURE
£11.95 • $16.95

INSIDE TERADOME
An Illustrated History Of Freak Film
Jack Hunter
CINEMA/CULTURE
£11.95 • $16.95

HOUSE OF HORROR
An Illustrated History Of Hammer Films
Jack Hunter (editor)
CINEMA
£12.95 • $19.95

ALSO FROM CREATION BOOKS

SALOME & UNDER THE HILL
Oscar Wilde & Aubrey Beardsley
DECADENCE
£7.95 • $12.95

THE GREAT GOD PAN
Arthur Machen
DECADENCE
£7.95 • $12.95

BLOOD & ROSES
The Vampire In 19th Century Literature
Havoc & Gladwell (editors)
CLASSICS
£7.95 • $15.95

IRENE'S CUNT
Louis Aragon
SURREALIST EROTICA
£7.95 • $12.95

PHILOSOPHY IN THE BOUDOIR
The Marquis de Sade
SADISM
£7.95 • $12.95

THE SHE DEVILS
Pierre Louys
EROTICA
£7.95 • $12.95

FLESH UNLIMITED
Guillaume Apollinaire
SURREALIST EROTICA
£7.95 • $12.95

DIARY OF A GENIUS
Salvador Dali
SURREALIST AUTOBIOGRAPHY
£8.95

ALSO FROM CREATION BOOKS

EDEN, EDEN, EDEN
Pierre Guyotat
MODERN CLASSICS
£7.95 • $13.95

ISIDORE
Jeremy Reed
FICTION
£7.95

KICKS
Jeremy Reed
POETRY
£8.95 • $13.95

CATAMANIA
Adèle Olivia Gladwell
POST-FEMINIST THEORY
£7.95 • $13.95

THE LAST STAR
Jeremy Reed
POP BIOGRAPHY
£9.95 • $15.95

RAPID EYE 1
Simon Dwyer (editor)
COUNTER-CULTURE
£11.95 • $17.95

RAPID EYE 2
Simon Dwyer (editor)
COUNTER-CULTURE
£11.95 • $17.95

RAPID EYE 3
Simon Dwyer (editor)
COUNTER-CULTURE
£11.95 • $17.95

you have just read
armageddon 2000
a creation book
published by:
creation books
83, clerkenwell road, london ec1r 5ar, uk
tel: 0171-430-9878 fax: 0171-242-5527
creation books is an independent publishing organisation producing
fiction and non-fiction genre books of interest to a young, literate
and informed readership.
*creation products should be available in all proper bookstores; please
ask your uk bookseller to order from:*
turnaround, 27 horsell road, london n5 1xl
tel: 0171-609-7836 fax: 0171-700-1205
non-book trade and mail order:
ak distribution, 22 lutton place, edinburgh eh8 9pe
tel: 0131-667-1507 fax: 0131-662-9594
readers in europe please order from:
turnaround distribution, 27 horsell road, london n5 1xl
tel: 0171-609-7836 fax: 0171-700-1205
readers in the usa please order from:
subterranean company, box 160, 265 south 5th street, monroe, or
97456
tel: 503 847-5274 fax: 503-847-6018
non-book trade and mail order:
ak press, po box 40682, san francisco, ca 94140-0682
tel: 415-923-1429 fax: 415-923-0607
readers in canada please order from:
marginal distribution, unit 102, 277 george street, n. peterborough,
ontario k9j 3g9
tel/fax: 705-745-2326
readers in australia and new zealand please order from:
peribo pty ltd, 58 beaumont road, mount kuring-gai, nsw 2080
tel: 02-457-0011 fax: 02-457-0022
readers in japan please order from:
charles e. tuttle company, 21-13 seki 1-chome, tama-ku, kawasaki,
kanagawa 214
tel: 044-833-1924 fax: 044-833-7559
readers in the rest of the world, or any readers having difficulty in
obtaining creation products, please order direct (+ 10% postage in
the uk, 20% postage outside uk) from our head office
a full catalogue is available on request.